Eric Beecher started his career in newspapers as a journalist on *The Age* newspaper in Melbourne. He later worked at *The Sunday Times* and *The Observer* in London and *The Washington Post* in the US. In 1984, at age thirty-three, he became the youngest-ever editor of *The Sydney Morning Herald*, and in 1987 was appointed editor-in-chief of the Herald and Weekly Times newspaper group. In 1990 he became a founder, CEO and major shareholder in The Text Media Group, a public company that produced newspapers, magazines and books, which was acquired by Fairfax Media in 2003. He is publisher of *Crikey* and a founding shareholder and Chairman of online media ventures: SmartCompany.com.au, EurekaReport.com.au and BusinessSpectator.com. He is Chair of the Centre for Books, Writing and Ideas in Victoria and in 2007 was awarded the Walkley Award for Journalistic Leadership.

The Best Australian Political Writing 2009

Edited by
Eric Beecher

MELBOURNE
UNIVERSITY
PRESS

MELBOURNE UNIVERSITY PRESS
An imprint of Melbourne University Publishing Limited
187 Grattan Street, Carlton, Victoria 3053, Australia
mup-info@unimelb.edu.au
www.mup.com.au

First published 2009
Introduction © Eric Beecher, 2009
Text © for other articles remains with individual authors
Design and typography © Melbourne University Publishing Limited, 2009

Researched by Tanya Serisier
Designed by Alice Graphics
Cover design by Phil Campbell
Typeset by J & M Typesetting
Printed by Griffin Press, SA

Contents

Introduction

To state the obvious, 2008 was a stellar year for politics and its stablemate, economics. A once-in-a-lifetime year. A year when Americans made a watershed presidential choice; when the global economic system almost collapsed; when an aspiring new Australian government, still basking in the warm inner-glow of its apology to Aborigines, watched aghast as the economy tanked and turned the entire business of government into a singular focus on managing and compromising in terrible times.

It was a year made for great political writing. The kind of news year journalists and writers and editors can only dream about. And, yes, there was enough good Australian political writing to fill a book. But only *one* book.

For despite the output generated by hundreds of professional practitioners—the journalists, columnists, academics, ex-politicians, activists and hangers-on who spend much or all of their working lives as paid political observers—the business of producing fine political writing is a problematical thing.

There is, of course, a profound difference between productivity and quality. Tens (perhaps hundreds) of millions of words of 'political writing' are produced in Australia each year. Yet most of them are meat-and-potatoes journalism, slopped up from a public relations/lobbying/propaganda commercial kitchen that is probably ten times larger than the journalism café it feeds.

This increasingly sophisticated spin industry operates from within the offices of federal and state politicians, government departments, public instrumentalities, industry organisations, NGOs, corporations and most other public and private institutions of any scale. It's a machine that spews out 'news' and 'backgrounders' and 'sound bites' and 'photo ops' on such a grand scale that it has effectively become the main source of the oil that greases the wheels of most modern journalism (also now known as 'churnalism'). And as editorial resources are being slashed by the imploding economics of the media industry, large dollops of the words and 'ideas' produced by PR and corporate affairs operatives inside the offices of politicians and governments—including a sizeable number of former journalists-turned-gatekeepers—find their way to the public almost unfiltered or unchecked by journalistic hand.

Mind you, it's not only political functionaries who devote their working lives to spinning and weaving and planting stories. The politicians do it too, federal, state, Labor, Liberal, all the time, at every opportunity. And no one does it more often or more adeptly, because they are so practised in it, than high-ranking politicians, whose seniority and perceived gravitas gives them far greater access to the media than their more junior colleagues.

> To a visitor from outer space, it would be hard to distinguish the job description of prime minister today from that of a talk show or game show host. The prime minister is a regular fixture on radio and television, where no topic is too small for him to discuss. He offers cash prizes to listeners and he sweats on the weekly ratings.
>
> The lines between celebrity and politics blurred some time ago. Our leaders are more needy because their handlers have convinced them that if they miss a single news bulletin the public will soon forget them. But voters can just as easily project wisdom on to politicians who are silent as those who blather sweet platitudes about Australian values and the noble struggle for the working family.
>
> George Megalogenis on Kevin Rudd's spin

Of course, in politics, no one ever agrees. One writer's black is another writer's white.

> The Opposition would have us believe Kevin Rudd is all spin and no substance. I think his problem is exactly the reverse.

Far from being devoid of content, I reckon the Rudd Government is running a real risk of having too much substance, too much policy fibre for the electorate to digest in just one electoral term ...

What this government needs is more so-called spin of a substantive kind. More consistent explanation about the big stuff. The really important things. The things we put them there to do. The things that, in many cases, they are doing behind the scenes.

Lenore Taylor on Kevin Rudd's spin

So was the prime minister spinning when he stood at the dispatch box in the House of Representatives in February and made one of the most moving and important speeches ever delivered in that place? His new government's apology to the Stolen Generations specifically, and to Indigenous Australians generally, was a narrative that had almost nothing in common with journalism, yet was possibly the best piece of Australian political writing of 2008.

There comes a time in the history of nations when their peoples must become fully reconciled to their past if they are to go forward with confidence to embrace their future. Our nation, Australia, has reached such a time. And that is why the parliament is today here assembled: to deal with this unfinished business of the nation, to remove a great stain from the nation's soul and, in a true spirit of reconciliation, to open a new chapter in the history of this great land, Australia ... To the Stolen Generations, I say the following: as Prime Minister of Australia, I am sorry. On behalf of the government of Australia, I am sorry. On behalf of the parliament of Australia, I am sorry. And I offer you this apology without qualification. We apologise for the hurt, the pain and suffering we, the parliament, have caused you by the laws that previous parliaments have enacted. We apologise for the indignity, the degradation and the humiliation these laws embodied. We offer this apology to the mothers, the fathers, the brothers, the sisters, the families and the communities whose lives were ripped apart by the actions of successive governments under successive parliaments ...

Kevin Rudd apologises to Australia's Indigenous people

It was a mighty speech, reportedly written by hand by the prime minister after input from a range of experts and luminaries, and it created a rare moment in the life of a nation. Millions of Australians stopped what they were doing to find a television screen in order to watch a political speech—not about war or money or crisis, but about social equity and human justice. It was a most un-Australian scene: ordinary people dropping everything in the middle of a working day to listen to a prime minister read an emotion-filled speech.

Kevin Rudd's apology speech spectacularly lifted the quality bar of Australian political speechwriting, a bar that had remained firmly fixed at near-ground levels since the days of Paul Keating's oratorial cocktail of fieriness, insults, arrogance, emotion and spontaneity. The sad truth, though, is that Rudd's apology speech was a blip on his own radar screen, a 9/10 effort delivered by someone who ordinarily scores the usual politician's 3/10 average. And as the year wore on, and the world began to marvel at the mastery of language of the man who was elected US president in November, it was obvious that whatever bar Kevin Rudd had raised in Australia, it was several notches below the new bar level created by Barack Obama. We all know that words matter in politics, but Obama's eloquence told us why.

Rudd's apology drew a large and largely predictable response: general acclaim, especially from abroad, generous support from the Opposition, non-attendance by the recently deposed Liberal prime minister, but also carping from the right and skepticism from the Aboriginal left. Yet once the euphoria passed and the political caravan moved on, the obvious question remained: did the apology make any difference to the status or living conditions of Aborigines?

> I took a 6 a.m. stroll down the Todd River in Alice Springs. It was illegal to drink along the riverbed; all Alice's public areas had been declared dry. It was a sea of green cans. The Aborigines there were playing hide-and-seek with the authorities. They were shadow drinkers. These were not people who started wondering about that gin and tonic at 5 p.m.; they were chronic alcoholics who needed to drink all the time. The town camps looked like they always had: places of wreckage.
>
> Paul Toohey on the standard of living of Aboriginal Australians

In a normal year, the debate about Indigenous Australia would have been ignited and extended by a political event as big as the apology. But it soon became obvious that this was no normal year, politically or economically. Cracks began to appear in the global sharemarkets. The Australian market dropped 1000 points—around 17 per cent—between April and June, then another 1000 points by October. The banking system shuddered, blueblood financial institutions collapsed, credit disappeared and by the end of the year most of the developed world (although technically not Australia) was in recession.

Soon, everyone became an economics professor.

> Kevin Rudd is quite wrong in his labelling of the global financial crisis ... Rudd has grown attached to his description of the crisis as a result of 'extreme capitalism'. That's akin to saying the Titanic sank because of 'extreme sailing'. The US economy and financial markets collapsed not because of the doctrine of capitalism, any more than the Titanic sank because of the practice of international shipping. The cause of the calamity was bad policy, just as the cause of the Titanic's fate was bad navigating ... Why does it matter what Rudd calls it? Because from the diagnosis comes the cure ...
>
> Peter Hartcher on the causes of the global economic collapse

The economic contagion did nothing to enhance the vocabulary of most politicians or political writers. Readers were dragged mercilessly through 'unchartered waters' from 'Main Street' to 'Wall Street' on the way to the 'edge of recession'. Meanwhile politicians were ready to 'take whatever action is necessary to maintain the stability of Australia's financial system' and not 'stand idly by while people's fears here were being fed by the stream of bad economic news from abroad'.

Which brings us to Mark Latham. The inhabitants of the parliamentary press gallery will not thank me for what I am about to write—in fact many of them will almost certainly deride me for it—but after navigating through hundreds of pieces covering a year of momentous political activity, I concluded that some of the most interesting political writing of that period was contained in the fortnightly op-ed columns tapped out by the Labor Party's former leader, a man despised by most of the people who spend their professional lives critiquing the policies and performances of politicians. George Orwell could have been referring to a Latham-like figure when he wrote, in 1946: 'In our time it is broadly true that political writing is bad writing. Where it is not true, it will generally be found that the writer is some kind of rebel, expressing his private opinions and not a "party line". Orthodoxy, of whatever colour, seems to demand a lifeless, imitative style'.

> These are demoralising times for the left. Normally it would be rejoicing at the turmoil in global markets, but with its ideology as bankrupt as Lehman Brothers, its political prospects are dismal ... This is the cruel irony facing ministers from the left, such as Julia Gillard, Lindsay Tanner, Jenny Macklin and Anthony Albanese. All began their time in politics as university radicals, tearaways determined to replace the crippling inequality of capitalism with a more compassionate and just economic system ... Now they are part of a Labor Cabinet chartered with saving capitalism from itself; a Cabinet certain to preside over rising rates of unemployment and poverty ... This is what the Australian Labor Party factional machine does to people. It is an endless series of deals and compromises which, bit by bit, drains away the idealism of mind and soul.
>
>   Mark Latham on the economic crisis and the left

How could a radical, unpredictable political loser be a more interesting political writer than most of the pros? Latham's short, blunt, elegantly argued mini-essays ventured inside the entrails of Australian politics, a place where all politics aficionados want to go. He has a raw, often cruel, honesty that he combines with an unstated but ever-present insiderness. His political experience provides an unfair natural advantage over the other hacks. He has been there, inside the ALP's smoke-filled rooms, and even allowing for his still simmering bitterness about being deserted and then hated by most people in the Labor Party, he brings to his writing a sense of gritty reality that is highly entertaining and frequently insightful. Latham discloses many of the ideas and thought processes that he, and other political leaders, can never reveal publicly while they are in office. He lifts veils and he understands—and loves discussing—the base motives and secret desires of the players. As we discovered from his *Diaries*, discretion and tact were surgically removed after he was born.

And even allowing for his cynicism and blazing flashes of sheer hypocrisy, Latham in his new career as a columnist does two things better than most experienced commentators. He challenges the orthodoxy from a position of political practice, and he provokes readers to challenge their own orthodoxies and prejudices. Latham shows how being an outsider, if harnessed intelligently, can be a distinct advantage when writing about politics. It provides distance and the kind of indifference that is useful to exploit because you're not bumping into the subjects of your writing on a daily basis.

The fact that a former politician like Latham stands out as a political writer is illustrative of the narrow institutional base of political writing in Australia, a base that is getting narrower. Very few publishers or media companies are prepared to invest heavily in quality political writing because, apart from prestige, it doesn't generate great returns and is far from commercial.

If you look through the list of the original sources of the content in this volume of *Best Australian Political Writing*, you find that apart from extracts from two books, almost 70 per cent of the stories originally appeared in just four daily newspapers (*The Sydney Morning Herald*, *The Age*, *The Australian* and *The Australian Financial Review*). But the notable statistic here is that almost half of those newspaper pieces, and nearly one-third of this entire book, appeared originally in one newspaper—*The Australian*. All the rest of the content originated in three niche media platforms (*The Monthly*, *Griffith Review* and *Crikey*, where, as publisher and the selector of the contents of this book, I must declare a considerable conflict of interest).

Those statistics confirm the unfortunate reality that there is only a handful of platforms producing thoughtful journalism in Australia, despite the exponential growth of the internet and the hype about new media vitality. The statistics also reveal the degree to which one publication, *The Australian*, dominates this country's political debate and the extent to which its op-ed and feature pages have usurped the Fairfax broadsheets as the originator of Australia's liveliest ideas and commentary. And, despite

The Australian's often strident right-leaning editorial and ownership bias, the breadth of the pieces published in this book demonstrate that, contrary to some views, it does not publish political commentary and analysis viewed exclusively through a single lens.

There is also a distinct narrowness about the kind of people who create Australia's best political writing. Barely 15 per cent was produced by members of the Canberra press gallery, the only significant institution in this country dedicated to writing about politics. In fact, based on the selections in this book, most of the best political writing is the work of columnists, feature writers, former politicians and academics—writers who have the luxury of retrospection without the responsibility of daily reportage—not by those journalists whose job it is to obsessively cover politics every day.

A conventional explanation for why the press gallery is under-represented in a book of the best writing about politics is proximity. They are too close to their subject, and their subjects, to dispassionately and forensically analyse and reflect. It is an explanation that only partly makes sense. After all, the longest serving senior journalists in the gallery should, and probably do, have the deepest corporate memories of almost anyone in Parliament House. They understand political context, history and nuance in a way that exceeds the knowledge of most of the politicians they cover, and most of the political staffers who service their needs. Yet so much of their output, while thoroughly professional, is bland and predictable (much like the politicians they write about).

The standout exception to the cult of blandness has been Alan Ramsey, who retired at the end of 2008 after thirty-two years as the oldest serving member of the press gallery. Ramsey was like a Latham of the media pack: a contradictory, obstreperous, fearsome, polarising figure whose weekly *Sydney Morning Herald* column was full of bile and bluntness, but who few readers would ever describe as being dull or boring or predictable. He accumulated more enemies than anyone in political journalism (and plenty of friends, too), but his departure removes a substantial personality with a prodigious sense of historical context from the world of political coverage.

If accelerating climate change is now Al Gore's Inconvenient Truth, John Button during those Labor years was usually the Hawke

Government's Inconvenient Voice. His candour infuriated his colleagues and delighted the journalists.

There were any number of examples.

Just before that 1990 budget, Keating's last as treasurer, a number of Treasury bureaucrats came 'in pairs, like the nuns of my childhood memory, watchful custodians of the official line', to brief Button in his office.

Button listened impatiently, and after they'd gone, he told his staff: 'We have fallen among f---wits'.

Alan Ramsey on the late John Button, who died in 2008

But if the current climate for Australian political writing seems uninspiring, the future looks even worse. That's because 2008, as well as hosting an exceptionally rich news agenda, was also a landmark year for journalism. It was the year when commercial media, and print media in particular, looked down the abyss of a faltering business model without identifying any apparent way of avoiding a catastrophe.

It was a year of despair for newspapers in most developed countries, including Australia, and that despair has raised systemic questions about the funding model for quality journalism. The combination of an economic downturn, which decimated advertising revenues, and a structural shift of advertising from traditional media to the internet, was like a perfect storm for many newspapers, especially those which are heavily dependent on classified advertising for their (now dwindling) profitability.

For marquee newspapers like *The Sydney Morning Herald* and *The Age*, covering politics used to be regarded as a measure of their stature as editorial and cultural institutions. Political coverage was a *sine qua non*; the lifeblood of their news and commentary sections; the editorial standard by which they were judged by readers and journalists.

Now that measurement seems almost irrelevant as they engage in a momentous battle to reinvent themselves as something other than a *news* paper. There are far more important issues than covering politics on the minds of their owners and editors. In the contest between investment in political coverage, because it's important, and hacking out costs, to remain viable, the commercial imperative will win.

In theory, vigorous, well-resourced political writing remains a vital cornerstone of democracy. In practice, its foundations within the mainstream media are shaky and its protectors are no longer in positions of power.

So if traditional media, especially newspapers, can no longer provide a full service to satisfy the requirements of the interested political class, who and what will fill the information vacuum? Bloggers? Amateurs? Authors? Academics? Niche websites?

All of the above. The growth of online media, combined with the erosion of mainstream media, has created platforms and opportunities for a whole range of non-professional writers and observers to stake their claim to a place in the marketplace of ideas. The challenge for such people is no longer finding an outlet for their views, or convincing gatekeepers to publish them. The challenge is lifting the quality of their work to a standard that is, frankly, worth reading. While the new models already exist to support the writing that could theoretically replace a smaller and less influential mainstream media, what's missing in Australia is a big enough stable of talented writers to fill the holes in those new business models.

In the meantime, and possibly for a long time, the gap left by the downsizing of traditional journalism is being filled primarily by political book publishing and serious magazines and journals. Increasingly, books are becoming the preferred format for long-form political writing of the kind that has always been rare in the ephemeral world of Australian journalism: narrative reconstructions, thoughtful and deeply researched analysis, the political memoir, the politician's diary, the biography and the polemic. The appeal for many good writers is the luxury of time and the prestige attached to writing serious books about politics.

In addition, there is a creative energy that seriously contributes to the political debate within publications like *The Monthly*, *Griffith Review*, *Quarterly Essay* and even *Quadrant*, and websites like *New Matilda* and (interest-declared) *Crikey*. This is the layer between the book and the blog, and even though they are mostly operating under the constraints of tight budgets and often (but not always) political partisanship, these old-fashioned printed platforms are really important and independent sources of analysis and ideas for the political class.

In 2008, this layer lost one of the great icons of Australian journalism, *The Bulletin*. Euthanasia was finally inflicted on the 129-year-old patient whose format—the newsmagazine—had become victim to an information revolution that made a weekly publication, which summarised and analysed the news, quite irrelevant for people who read daily websites, blogs and fat weekend newspapers. *The Bulletin*'s passing, while almost inevitable given its sizeable financial losses, was another clear signal that, in the world of media, all bets are off.

So the best you can say is that a flowering of serious print and online niche media as the counterweight to a dilution in the resources of Australia's op-ed pages remains a hopeful prospect. But at this stage of the media upheaval it is probably the best prospect, if only because the alternatives appear to be almost non-existent.

Eric Beecher
January 2009

1
View from the Lodge—
The Rudd Era

Prime Minister Kevin Rudd

Apology to Australia's Indigenous peoples

House of Representatives, Parliament House, Canberra,
13 February 2008

—I move:
That today we honour the Indigenous peoples of this land, the oldest continuing cultures in human history.

We reflect on their past mistreatment.

We reflect in particular on the mistreatment of those who were Stolen Generations—this blemished chapter in our nation's history.

The time has now come for the nation to turn a new page in Australia's history by righting the wrongs of the past and so moving forward with confidence to the future.

We apologise for the laws and policies of successive parliaments and governments that have inflicted profound grief, suffering and loss on these our fellow Australians.

We apologise especially for the removal of Aboriginal and Torres Strait Islander children from their families, their communities and their country.

For the pain, suffering and hurt of these Stolen Generations, their descendants and for their families left behind, we say sorry.

To the mothers and the fathers, the brothers and the sisters, for the breaking up of families and communities, we say sorry.

And for the indignity and degradation thus inflicted on a proud people and a proud culture, we say sorry.

We the parliament of Australia respectfully request that this apology be received in the spirit in which it is offered as part of the healing of the nation.

For the future we take heart; resolving that this new page in the history of our great continent can now be written.

We today take this first step by acknowledging the past and laying claim to a future that embraces all Australians.

A future where this parliament resolves that the injustices of the past must never, never happen again.

A future where we harness the determination of all Australians, Indigenous and non-Indigenous, to close the gap that lies between us in life expectancy, educational achievement and economic opportunity.

A future where we embrace the possibility of new solutions to enduring problems where old approaches have failed.

A future based on mutual respect, mutual resolve and mutual responsibility.

A future where all Australians, whatever their origins, are truly equal partners, with equal opportunities and with an equal stake in shaping the next chapter in the history of this great country, Australia.

There comes a time in the history of nations when their peoples must become fully reconciled to their past if they are to go forward with confidence to embrace their future. Our nation, Australia, has reached such a time. And that is why the parliament is today here assembled: to deal with this unfinished business of the nation, to remove a great stain from the nation's soul and, in a true spirit of reconciliation, to open a new chapter in the history of this great land, Australia.

Last year I made a commitment to the Australian people that if we formed the next government of the Commonwealth we would in parliament say sorry to the Stolen Generations. Today I honour that commitment. I said we would do so early in the life of the new parliament. Again, today I honour that commitment by doing so at the commencement of this the 42nd parliament of the Commonwealth.

Because the time has come, well and truly come, for all peoples of our great country, for all citizens of our great Commonwealth, for all Australians—those who are Indigenous and those who are not—to come together to reconcile and together build a new future for our nation.

Some have asked, 'Why apologise?' Let me begin to answer by telling the parliament just a little of one person's story—an elegant, eloquent and wonderful woman in her eighties, full of life, full of funny stories, despite what has happened in her life's journey. A woman who has travelled a long way to be with us today, a member of the Stolen Generation who shared some of her story with me when I called around to see her just a few days ago. Nungala Fejo, as she prefers to be called, was born in the late 1920s. She remembers her earliest childhood days living with her family and her community in a bush camp just outside Tennant Creek. She remembers the love and the warmth and the kinship of those days long ago, including traditional dancing around the camp fire at night. She loved the dancing. She remembers once getting into strife when, as a 4-year-old girl, she insisted on dancing with the male tribal elders rather than just sitting and watching the men, as the girls were supposed to do.

But then, sometime around 1932, when she was about four, she remembers the coming of the welfare men. Her family had feared that day and had dug holes in the creek bank where the children could run and hide. What they had not expected was that the white welfare men did not come alone. They brought a truck, they brought two white men and an Aboriginal stockman on horseback cracking his stockwhip. The kids were found; they ran for their mothers, screaming, but they could not get away. They were herded and piled onto the back of the truck. Tears flowing, her mum tried clinging to the sides of the truck as her children were taken away to the Bungalow in Alice, all in the name of protection.

A few years later, government policy changed. Now the children would be handed over to the missions to be cared for by the churches. But which church would care for them? The kids were simply told to line up in three lines. Nanna Fejo and her sister stood in the middle line, her older brother and cousin on her left. Those on the left were told that they had become Catholics, those in the middle Methodists and those on the right Church of England. That is how the complex questions of post-reformation theology were resolved in the Australian outback in the 1930s. It was as crude as that. She and her sister were sent to a Methodist mission on Goulburn Island and then Croker Island. Her Catholic brother was sent to work at a cattle station and her cousin to a Catholic mission.

Nanna Fejo's family had been broken up for a second time. She stayed at the mission until after the war, when she was allowed to leave for a pre-arranged job as a domestic in Darwin. She was sixteen. Nanna Fejo never saw her mum again. After she left the mission, her brother let her know that her mum had died years before, a broken woman fretting for the children that had literally been ripped away from her.

I asked Nanna Fejo what she would have me say today about her story. She thought for a few moments then said that what I should say today was that all mothers are important. And she added: 'Families—keeping them together is very important. It's a good thing that you are surrounded by love and that love is passed down the generations. That's what gives you happiness'. As I left, later on, Nanna Fejo took one of my staff aside, wanting to make sure that I was not too hard on the Aboriginal stockman who had hunted those kids down all those years ago. The stockman had found her again decades later, this time himself to say, 'Sorry'. And remarkably, extraordinarily, she had forgiven him.

Nanna Fejo's is just one story. There are thousands, tens of thousands of them: stories of forced separation of Aboriginal and Torres Strait Islander children from their mums and dads over the better part of a century. Some of these stories are graphically told in *Bringing Them Home*, the report commissioned in 1995 by Prime Minister Keating and received in 1997 by Prime Minister Howard. There is something terribly primal about these firsthand accounts. The pain is searing; it screams from the pages. The hurt, the humiliation, the degradation and the sheer brutality of the act of physically separating a mother from her children is a deep assault on our senses and on our most elemental humanity.

These stories cry out to be heard; they cry out for an apology. Instead, from the nation's parliament there has been a stony and stubborn and deafening silence for more than a decade. A view that somehow we, the parliament, should suspend our most basic instincts of what is right and what is wrong. A view that, instead, we should look for any pretext to push this great wrong to one side, to leave it languishing with the historians, the academics and the cultural warriors, as if the Stolen Generations are little more than an interesting sociological phenomenon. But the Stolen Generations are not intellectual curiosities. They are human beings, human beings who have been damaged deeply by the decisions of parliaments and governments. But, as of today, the time for denial, the time for delay, has at last come to an end.

The nation is demanding of its political leadership to take us forward. Decency, human decency, universal human decency, demands that the nation now steps forward to right a historical wrong. That is what we are doing in this place today. But should there still be doubts as to why we must now act. Let the parliament reflect for a moment on the following facts: that, between 1910 and 1970, between 10 and 30 per cent of Indigenous children were forcibly taken from their mothers and fathers. That, as a result, up to 50 000 children were forcibly taken from their families. That this was the product of the deliberate, calculated policies of the state as reflected in the explicit powers given to them under statute. That this policy was taken to such extremes by some in administrative authority that the forced extractions of children of so-called 'mixed lineage' were seen as part of a broader policy of dealing with 'the problem of the Aboriginal population'.

One of the most notorious examples of this approach was from the Northern Territory Protector of Natives, who stated, and I quote: Generally by the fifth and invariably by the sixth generation, all native characteristics of the Australian aborigine are eradicated. The problem of our half-castes— to quote the protector—will quickly be eliminated by the complete disappearance of the black race, and the swift submergence of their progeny in the white . . .

The Western Australian Protector of Natives expressed not dissimilar views, expounding them at length in Canberra in 1937 at the first national conference on Indigenous affairs that brought together the Commonwealth and state protectors of natives. These are uncomfortable things to be brought out into the light. They are not pleasant. They are profoundly disturbing. But we must acknowledge these facts if we are to deal once and for all with the argument that the policy of generic forced separation was somehow well motivated, justified by its historical context and, as a result, unworthy of any apology today.

Then we come to the argument of intergenerational responsibility, also used by some to argue against giving an apology today. But let us remember the fact that the forced removal of Aboriginal children was happening as late as the early 1970s. The 1970s is not exactly a point in remote antiquity. There are still serving members of this parliament who were first elected to this place in the early 1970s. It is well within the adult memory span of many of us. The uncomfortable truth for us all is that the parliaments of the nation, individually and collectively, enacted statutes and delegated authority under those statutes that made the forced removal of children on racial grounds fully lawful.

There is a further reason for an apology as well: it is that reconciliation is in fact an expression of a core value of our nation—and that value is a fair go for all. There is a deep and abiding belief in the Australian community that, for the Stolen Generations, there was no fair go at all. And there is a pretty basic Aussie belief that says it is time to put right this most outrageous of wrongs. It is for these reasons, quite apart from concerns of fundamental human decency, that the governments and parliaments of this nation must make this apology. Because, put simply, the laws that our parliaments enacted made the Stolen Generations possible. We, the parliaments of the nation, are ultimately responsible, not those who gave effect to our laws, the problem lay with the laws themselves. As has been said of settler societies elsewhere, we are the bearers of many blessings from our ancestors and therefore we must also be the bearer of their burdens as well. Therefore, for our nation, the course of action is clear. Therefore for our people, the course of action is clear. And that is, to deal now with what has become one of the darkest chapters in Australia's history. In doing so, we are doing more than contending with the facts, the evidence and the often rancorous public debate. In doing so, we are also wrestling with our own soul. This is not, as some would argue, a black-armband view of history; it is just the truth: the cold, confronting, uncomfortable truth. Facing with it, dealing with it, moving on from it. And until we fully confront that truth, there will always be a shadow hanging over us and our future as a fully united and fully reconciled people. It is time to reconcile. It is time to recognise the injustices of the past. It is time to say sorry. It is time to move forward together.

To the Stolen Generations, I say the following: as Prime Minister of Australia, I am sorry. On behalf of the government of Australia, I am sorry. On behalf of the parliament of Australia, I am sorry. And I offer you this apology without qualification. We apologise for the hurt, the pain and suffering we, the parliament, have caused you by the laws that previous parliaments have enacted. We apologise for the indignity, the degradation and the humiliation these laws embodied. We offer this apology to the mothers, the fathers, the brothers, the sisters, the families and the communities whose lives were ripped apart by the actions of successive governments under successive parliaments. In making this apology, I would also like to speak personally to the members of the Stolen Generation and their families: to those here today, so many of you; to those listening across the nation—from Yuendumu, in the central west of the Northern Territory, to Yabara, in North Queensland, and to Pitjantjatjara in South Australia.

I know that, in offering this apology on behalf of the government and the parliament, there is nothing I can say today that can take away the pain you have suffered personally. Whatever words I speak today, I cannot undo that. Words alone are not that powerful. Grief is a very personal thing. I say to non-Indigenous Australians listening today who may not fully understand why what we are doing is so important, I ask those non-Indigenous Australians to imagine for a moment if this had happened to you. I say to honourable members here present: imagine if this had happened to us. Imagine the crippling effect. Imagine how hard it would be to forgive. But my proposal is this: if the apology we extend today is accepted in the spirit of reconciliation, in which it is offered, we can today resolve together that there be a new beginning for Australia. And it is to such a new beginning that I believe the nation is now calling us.

Australians are a passionate lot. We are also a very practical lot. For us, symbolism is important but, unless the great symbolism of reconciliation is accompanied by an even greater substance, it is little more than a clanging gong. It is not sentiment that makes history; it is our actions that make history. Today's apology, however inadequate, is aimed at righting past wrongs. It is also aimed at building a bridge between Indigenous and non-Indigenous Australians—a bridge based on a real respect rather than a thinly veiled contempt. Our challenge for the future is now to cross that bridge and, in so doing, embrace a new partnership between Indigenous and non-Indigenous Australians. Embracing, as part of that partnership, expanded link-up and other critical services to help the Stolen Generations to trace their families, if at all possible, and to provide dignity to their lives. But the core of this partnership for the future is to closing the gap between Indigenous and non-Indigenous Australians on life expectancy, educational achievement and employment opportunities. This new partnership on closing the gap will set concrete targets for the future: within a decade to halve the widening gap in literacy, numeracy and employment outcomes and opportunities for Indigenous children, within a decade to halve the appalling gap in infant mortality rates between Indigenous and non-Indigenous children and, within a generation, to close the equally appalling 17-year life gap between Indigenous and non-Indigenous when it comes when it comes to overall life expectancy.

The truth is: a business as usual approach towards Indigenous Australians is not working. Most old approaches are not working. We need a new beginning. A new beginning which contains real measures of policy success or policy failure. A new beginning, a new partnership, on closing the gap with sufficient flexibility not to insist on a one-size-fits-all approach for each of the hundreds of remote and regional Indigenous communities across the country but instead allows flexible, tailored, local approaches to achieve commonly agreed national objectives that lie at the core of our proposed new partnership. And a new beginning that draws intelligently on the experiences of new policy settings across the nation. However, unless we as a parliament set a destination for the nation, we have no clear point to guide our policy, our programs or our purpose; no centralised organising principle.

So let us resolve today to begin with the little children—a fitting place to start on this day of apology for the Stolen Generations. Let us resolve over the next five years to have every Indigenous 4-year-old in a remote Aboriginal community enrolled and attending a proper early childhood education centre or opportunity and engaged in proper preliteracy and prenumeracy programs. Let us resolve to build new educational opportunities for these little ones, year by year, step by step, following the completion of their crucial preschool year. Let us resolve to use this systematic approach to building future educational opportunities for Indigenous children to provide proper primary and preventive health care for the same children, to begin the task of rolling back the obscenity that we find today in infant mortality rates in remote Indigenous communities—up to four times higher than in other communities.

None of this will be easy. Most of it will be hard—very hard. But none of it, none of it, is impossible, and all of it is achievable with clear goals, clear thinking, and by placing an absolute premium on respect, cooperation and mutual responsibility as the guiding principles of this new partnership on closing the gap. The mood of the nation is for reconciliation now, between Indigenous and non-Indigenous Australians. The mood of the nation on Indigenous policy and politics is now very simple. The nation is calling on us, the politicians, to move beyond our infantile bickering, our point-scoring and our mindlessly partisan politics and elevate at least this one core area of national responsibility to a rare position beyond the partisan divide. Surely this is the spirit, the unfulfilled spirit, of the 1967 referendum.

Surely, at least from this day forward, we should give it a go.

So let me take this one step further to take what some may see as a piece of political posturing and make a practical proposal to the Opposition on this day, the first full sitting day of the new parliament. I said before the election the nation needed a kind of war cabinet on parts of Indigenous policy, because the challenges are too great and the consequences too great to just allow it all to become a political football, as it has been so often in the past. I therefore propose a joint policy commission, to be led by the leader of the Opposition and myself and, with a mandate to develop and implement—to begin with—an effective housing strategy for remote communities over the next five years. It will be consistent with the government's policy framework, a new partnership for closing the gap.

If this commission operates well, I then propose that it work on the further task of constitutional recognition of the first Australians, consistent with the longstanding platform commitments of my party and the pre-election position of the Opposition. This would probably be desirable in any event because, unless such a proposition were absolutely bipartisan, it would fail at a referendum. As I have said before, the time has come for new approaches to enduring problems. And working constructively together on such defined projects, I believe, would meet with the support of the nation. It is time for fresh ideas to fashion the nation's future.

Today the parliament has come together to right a great wrong. We have come together to deal with the past so that we might fully embrace the future. And we have had sufficient audacity of faith to advance a pathway to that future, with arms extended rather than with fists still clenched. So let us seize the day. Let it not become a moment of mere sentimental reflection. Let us take it with both hands and allow this day, this day of national reconciliation, to become one of those rare moments in which we might just be able to transform the way in which the nation thinks about itself, whereby the injustice administered to these Stolen Generations in the name of these, our parliaments, causes all of us to reappraise, at the deepest level of our beliefs, the real possibility of reconciliation writ large.

Reconciliation across all Indigenous Australia. Reconciliation across the entire history of the often bloody encounter between those who emerged from the Dreamtime a thousand generations ago and those who, like me, came across the seas only yesterday. Reconciliation which opens up whole new possibilities for the future.

For the nation to bring the first two centuries of our settled history to a close, as we begin a new chapter and which we embrace with pride, admiration and awe these great and ancient cultures we are blessed, truly blessed, to have among us. Cultures that provide a unique, uninterrupted human thread linking our Australian continent to the most ancient prehistory of our planet. And growing from this new respect, to see our Indigenous brothers and sisters with fresh eyes, with new eyes, and with our minds wide open as to how we might tackle, together, the great practical challenges that Indigenous Australia faces in the future.

So let us turn this page together: Indigenous and non-Indigenous Australians, government and Opposition, Commonwealth and state, and write this new chapter in our nation's story together. First Australians, First Fleeters, and those who first took the Oath of Allegiance just a few weeks ago. Let's grasp this opportunity to craft a new future for this great land: Australia. I commend the motion to the House.

Christine Jackman

The future guy
The Australian, 19 July 2008

In April 2006, an energetic Geordie named Alan Milburn strode through the sandstone catacombs of Sydney's original GPO on his way to Prime, a swank steak restaurant built in what had once been the dock master's office of the former convict settlement. With its plush leather banquettes, muted lighting and power-suited clientele, the restaurant in the heart of the CBD's designer shopping precinct was a world away from the windswept mining villages and council housing estates where Milburn had grown up in north-east England almost half a century before. But New Labour is like that. With class distinctions all but dead in modern politics, there's no reason why a dedicated member of the Left can't take the fight up to the Tories and order a decent wagyu at the same time.

However, Milburn was in no mood for fripperies or small talk as he was introduced to Kim Beazley's campaign strategy group in the restaurant's cavernous private dining room. At home in the United Kingdom, Milburn had a fierce reputation for calling a spade a shovel in his political stoushes, first as a trade unionist fighting for steel and shipbuilding jobs in northern England, then as a vocal backbencher scoring hits on John Major's conservative government in the early 1990s, and finally as a rising star within the fledgling Blair Government.

Milburn had served as health secretary in the Blair cabinet—and, unofficially, as one of the prime minister's tough 'enforcers'—for four years before he shocked his colleagues by resigning the portfolio in 2003 to spend more time with his young family. Widely tipped as a likely successor to Blair, Milburn returned instead to coordinate the 2005 election campaign,

a move that exacerbated longstanding tensions between himself and rival
Gordon Brown.

ALP National Secretary Tim Gartrell and the Labor leadership team
had been introduced to the Geordie by Nick Rowley, a former staffer to
New South Wales Premier Bob Carr, who had gone on to land a position at
No. 10 Downing Street. Gartrell was impressed by Milburn's forthright
style and recognised early that he might provide a valuable outsider's perspective and the 'cold shower' that was often necessary in the heat of a
campaign.

Milburn did not disappoint. 'I was pretty blunt', he said later. 'What
they needed was a big bucket of directness. I told them I had no doubt that
if we just continued down the same path we were heading for another loss.'
John Howard's 'best days were behind him', Milburn told the group, but
they were kidding themselves if they thought that was enough to justify a
change of government when Australia's economy continued to be strong.

Instead, Milburn urged his counterparts to focus on giving voters who
had supported Howard in the past a reason to change their minds. Labor
urgently needed to find ways to demonstrate that the party had changed
and, particularly, that it could be trusted to run the economy.

In Milburn's eyes, 'it was pretty obvious there was a steam train
coming down the tracks' in the form of yet another campaign by the Liberal
Party framing Labor as economic incompetents. An engaging and incisive
speaker, Milburn received a good hearing from Beazley and his colleagues.

'It was awful at first', a frontbencher who attended the dinner con-
fessed later.

> What Milburn didn't know was that this was probably the first time
> we had talked about strategy, and it was only because Milburn, as an
> outsider, could force it. He could get away with a lot. Kim ignored it
> and ignored it but . . . the thing that eventually turned that conversa-
> tion around was that [then treasury spokesman] Wayne Swan eventu-
> ally bought into it. Until then, I think Swan had held himself out of
> strategy discussions because he thought anything he said would be
> construed as critical of Beazley, and he didn't want to risk people think-
> ing that. But Milburn kept pushing and pushing and once he [Swan]

engaged, it almost gave everyone else permission to engage and then Kim engaged and it actually became a much better calibre discussion than those we'd had in the past.

Even so, as he left the restaurant, the Englishman felt a wave of frustration with the lack of urgency shown by many of those present:

> There was too much of a sense of the Labor Party coasting out of Opposition into government, that somehow, if they just played it steady, things would be OK. It wasn't quite complacency but there was an assumption that Howard had lost the interest of the public and that would be enough, whereas I felt it would come down to Labor's fitness to govern. My sense was that we'd have to make history; it was certainly not ours for the taking.

But one member of the strategy group was not present that night. Kevin Rudd and his Channel Seven *Sunrise* sparring partner, then Human Services Minister Joe Hockey, had agreed to walk the Kokoda Track to commemorate Anzac Day, accompanied by host David Koch and Rudd's elder son, Nicholas. The trek later attracted criticism for the blatant promotion of the breakfast show during the dawn service but, for the politicians at least, the trip had been much more than a public relations exercise. Both men struggled with the arduous physical challenge, with Rudd admitting later he had doubted at times whether he would finish the journey. Labor's foreign affairs spokesman flew home nursing a severe case of footrot and was later spied hobbling through Sydney Airport in his socks.

Rudd was still walking gingerly when he greeted Milburn in the lounge bar at the Wentworth, another 5-star Sydney establishment that had been adopted by the party of the worker, a few days later. The men had never met but Rudd quickly made it clear he was utterly sick of being in Opposition and would be grateful for any advice Milburn might have about replicating British New Labour's success in Australia.

As the two talked late into the night, Milburn was impressed by Rudd's energy and 'panoramic view of what needed to be done', and couldn't help but wonder whether his absence from the earlier strategy group dinner was deliberate. Certainly, Milburn was able to talk more freely one-on-one. He confided to Rudd he thought Labor could win but that 'Kim was not the guy'. As he had done a few nights earlier, Milburn cited the strength of the economy as the biggest hurdle for Labor. The themes that had worked so effectively for Tony Blair, who adopted D:Ream's 'Things Can Only Get Better' as his campaign song in 1997, and for Bill Clinton, who adopted the mantra 'It's the Economy, Stupid' in 1992, would not have gained traction in more buoyant economic times. As such, Labor would have to find an alternative paradigm, and the only one Milburn could identify was 'the future versus the past'.

'But the self-evident problem was, no matter what his qualities were, Kim was not a future guy', Milburn said later.

> He had such a history with the party over the previous thirty or forty years. Even if he wasn't still caught up in the party's history, he looked like he was caught up in the party's history. It was not Kim's fault. It was just unfortunate that at the point at which Labor needed to become the future party, it did not have the future politician.

Throughout the conversation, Rudd kept his poker face on, steering the focus to what Beazley needed to do in order to win rather than seeking any argument for a leadership change. But when Milburn flew out of Australia a few days later, he left convinced he had met one of its future leaders. 'He had the intellect and the absolute strategic understanding', Milburn said. 'Kevin was the only person who was capable of exemplifying the level of change that Labor needed to convey to the public.'

The question was: when? Milburn thought it was possible the party could change leaders again before the election—'the very fact I'd had the conversation I did with Kevin Rudd meant that it was possible'—but time was running out for any new leader to establish a profile with the Australian public before a 2007 election.

For anyone seeking to represent generational change and a reinvigorated party, Milburn foresaw one additional problem, left like an unexploded mine after former Opposition leader Mark Latham retreated from the political battlefield. 'The danger about being seen as new was the contamination that Latham had spread', Milburn observed. 'Because he had been promoted as different, new Labor, too. And boy, was that true.'

If Milburn's instincts were correct, Kim Beazley was on a hiding to nothing; handcuffed to history, he would never be able to lead Labor to victory, regardless of the time and effort he committed to the task. But throughout 2006, what hardened the view against the leader was the perception that he wasn't putting in the time and effort.

'He was lazy, deeply lazy, and believed in political inheritance', said one former Beazley supporter, who had lost faith in the West Australian by that time. 'I began as a supporter with a belief that his essential decency would get us across the line . . . but then, he used to say to people who went to him with a problem or a challenge that he believed "if you let things lie, eventually most [problems] just disappear". And I thought, "You weak, weak man".'

Even Beazley's closest backers were growing concerned about his failure to seize the initiative and drive the political debate. 'We'd sit down and go through a whole lot of things that needed to be done but they weren't part of his era in politics', said one key ally.

> He had to be a much more proactive driver of change but I don't think in the end it was him. Unfortunately, while he could intellectually agree, he was incapable of doing it. For a while it looked like things would propel him through: IR, the polls. But he just could not maintain what was needed to remake himself as a fresh alternative to Howard.

When Tim Gartrell arrived at Kim Beazley's office at 9.45 a.m. on Friday, 1 December for his routine leader's briefing ahead of a National Executive meeting later that morning, he immediately knew something was up. A hushed staffer gave the national secretary a guarded look and shook his head. What Gartrell didn't know was that Kevin Rudd had walked in just minutes before. But, joining the National Executive in a nearby parliamentary committee room, Gartrell didn't have to wait long to have his suspicions confirmed. Within the hour, Beazley arrived and called for normal business to be suspended, before giving a brief but impassioned speech to the gathering.

'It was vintage Kim', one witness said later.

> He's always best when he's just lost or he's really under the pump. He
> gave a good little speech because he has such a great sense of history,
> and he said whatever happens this has to stop or we'll never win. He
> stood up, shook a few hands and strode purposefully out. It was one
> of the few times when the drudgery of National Executive turns to
> making history.

Back in Rudd's office, it was time for a game plan that had been years
in the making to swing into action. Rudd's senior adviser and closest confidant, Alister Jordan, had learnt a lot from his boss's previous feints at the
leadership, and also from analysing how the party's most experienced
number-crunchers had operated in the showdowns of 2002, 2003 and
2005. Jordan was determined, this time, to get it right.

'It's about making sure that from the minute it's on, we seize the
momentum', Jordan told one of Rudd's backers in Caucus.

> By the end of the first day, we need to be able to say we have a solid
> amount of caucus support. Public momentum is consumed by the
> Caucus and it will influence how some vote . . . [so] the horror scenario
> is we wake up on Saturday morning to the headline 'Rudd Challenges
> But Beazley Has Numbers'.

To seize the momentum early, the young Queenslander knew that it
was absolutely essential to generate powerful media images and for Rudd
and Julia Gillard, who was standing for the deputy's role, to execute the
perfect press conference. With as acute an eye for detail as his notoriously
fastidious boss, Jordan had noted previously how Beazley always surrounded
himself with backbench supporters during leadership contests, creating
messy, crowded images for the cameras. To contrast, he insisted that Rudd
and Gillard walk together, but otherwise unaccompanied, to their first press
conference and any subsequent media appearances over the weekend, to give
'a clean image of two fresh faces', before then greeting supporters.

After the press conference, Rudd's busy schedule was cleared almost
completely so he could devote himself to systematically calling every soft
voter. The emotional power of a would-be leader, or soon to be ex-leader,
personally appealing for one's support could not be underestimated, as

New South Wales backbencher Chris Bowen would discover when he answered his mobile phone that morning to hear Beazley's familiar tone. The parliamentary freshman, by then acting as a numbers man for Rudd, was surprised by how difficult it was to confirm he had drawn the 'reluctant conclusion' that Labor could never win with Beazley at the helm. 'We can do this now or the Australian people will do it in twelve months' time', Bowen said.

But Beazley would not be rebuffed. 'Mate, can you give me a crack of light, just some hope?' he implored. It was excruciating; Bowen told him he would have voted for him in previous leadership ballots, had he been in parliament at the time, but he could not give him 'false hope' now.

As the numbers men continued lobbying the soft votes, Alister Jordan mobilised Rudd's core supporters to contact the news agency, AAP, and go on the record with their voting intentions, to ensure the newswire had a steady stream of stories about a trend to the Queenslander.

That evening the team moved to Melbourne, where Rudd had one longstanding commitment that, after some debate within the office, had been allowed to remain on the diary. The branch member's function for backbencher Maria Vamvakinou was not expected to be an extravagant affair but, as one Rudd confidant said later, 'We had made a commitment to Maria. And she had a vote'. Rather than cancel the event to concentrate on the bid for the leadership, Team Rudd brought the bid—and the media—to the event, turning it into a rally for Rudd and Gillard. 'We had everyone up and cheering as they walked in', said an adviser. 'They were fantastic images—and right in time for *Lateline*.'

By Monday, 4 December, the opinion-makers had made up their minds. Barring a last-minute swing, most were certain Rudd would be the leader of the Labor Party by lunchtime. The Caucus duly delivered, voting 49–39 in favour of a change. When the result came through, New South Wales Secretary (now senator) Mark Arbib rang Neil Lawrence, the veteran advertising executive engaged by federal Labor in late 2005 in preparation for the 2007 election, to gauge his reaction. After all, Lawrence now had less than a year to make Australia fall in love with the Labor Party's new face. The adman was characteristically pithy: 'Mate, we just went from no chance to some chance'.

Neil Lawrence had been busy building pyramids. A former social worker with a degree in politics/psychology who had worked in Aboriginal youth welfare in the late 1970s and early 1980s, before moving on to make documentary films, Lawrence had an eclectic mind.

With the traditional left-right spectrum increasingly redundant, its one-dimensional linear model unable to capture the complexities of modern political debate, Lawrence knew the Labor Party needed to find a new way to conceptualise its position in relation to the Coalition. Scribbling on endless sheets of butcher's paper, he eventually fashioned two pyramids, based on the hierarchy of human needs first outlined in 1943 by American psychologist Abraham Maslow in his seminal paper 'A Theory of Human Motivation'.

Maslow contended that 'man is a perpetually wanting animal' who pursued fulfilment according to a hierarchy that began with the purely physiological requirements of survival—oxygen, food, water, sleep and sex—before moving up through physical safety and security to the 'higher needs' of love and belonging, esteem and finally self-actualisation. The key to the thesis was that every individual is driven by the pursuit of their most basic, or lowest, unmet need, but once that need is fulfilled, it can be forgotten 'since gratified needs are not active motivators'—only to be replaced by the next prepotent need up the ladder.

Lawrence surmised the same theory could be applied to voting behaviour. He divided his political pyramid into five corresponding segments: at the base, the most fundamental desire of any voter was to have stable government; citizens in advanced capitalist democracies had no appetite for coups or popular revolution. Next up the ladder was economic management, followed by physical safety (manifesting in a relatively peaceful country like Australia in issues of law and order, immigration and counter-terrorism). Only after a party had demonstrated it could satisfy all of the basic civic demands could it then address more esoteric needs such as an 'Australian way of life' or 'a better society'.

John Howard's Government, Lawrence concluded, owned the sturdy base of the pyramid. As Australia's second-longest serving prime minister, Howard himself personified 'stable government', and he was supported by a now-familiar team. Working up from that base, the Coalition had run hard and consistently on its economic record and ability to provide security in 'troubled times', thereby capturing the next two steps of the pyramid. In contrast, with its constant infighting and leadership changes, Labor had no firm base from which to work: how could it promote itself as ready to provide stable government when it could not even foster stability in its Caucus?

Beyond that, Labor had almost completely surrendered the 'second step'—economic management—to Howard in the 2004 election campaign, when the party and Mark Latham failed to inoculate itself against the 'who do you trust to keep interest rates low?' charge. Liberal headquarters wasn't hiding the fact that it intended to beat Rudd in exactly the same way in 2007—by utterly dominating the bottom three steps of the pyramid.

To prosecute his case, Lawrence predicted the Liberals would employ a two-pronged attack, working assiduously to portray Labor as captive to 'minority interest groups' whose interests belonged in the esoteric apex of the pyramid and, when Labor pursued more mainstream issues such as health and education, accusing it of making big-spending promises it could not afford, thereby underlining its economic ineptitude.

In the end, two simple triangles sketched on some butcher's paper had assumed nightmarish proportions. 'That's when you go: "Oh, f..k"', Lawrence said, recalling the enormity of the challenge as he presented it to the campaign team. 'There was a bit of sitting there like a rabbit in the spotlight. But I figured, I've signed up for this so what do we do about it? And you start turning the pyramids around.'

The key, in Lawrence's eyes, was for a credibly unified Labor Party to engage directly on the economy. No matter how worthy or important its other concerns were, the party would achieve nothing until it established solid economic credentials. This didn't mean it had to ignore other issues. But using the pyramids as a touchstone, the idea was to cast each through the prism of sound economics. For example, if Labor could find a way to cast education as vital to prosperity and security, it could pursue this agenda. Better yet, it could also portray the Howard Government as negligent and economically irresponsible for ignoring the issue. Lawrence would be the first to admit that the means he used to frame the debate was not particularly exceptional—'Most of the models have grapefruits or pyramids of columns'—and it was really just another way of elaborating on the truism that people who can't eat don't care about whether they can vote.

What was important, he believed, was that Labor headquarters had 'a common language' as it began developing its campaign strategy. 'I did that religiously and probably annoyingly throughout the year', he said after the election. 'I was always saying, "Let's go back to what we said we'd do".'

In February 2007, the Geordie, Alan Milburn, returned to Australia to meet Kevin Rudd and his strategy group as they formulated their election battle plan. As far as Milburn was concerned, there was only room for 'one fooking message' in a political campaign and that 'one fooking message' absolutely had to be 'The Future versus the Past'. Labor HQ eventually came to agree—even if it reserved the Australian right to poke fun mercilessly at Milburn's obsession with it. Even a commemorative video, screened at the end-of-campaign party, featured Milburn once again reminding the leader: 'You've only got one fooking message, Kevin'.

Nobody who knew Rudd well—or, indeed, understood the currents of regional Queensland—harboured any illusions that he was anything other than a social conservative.

Alan Milburn was keen to highlight this fact. By 2007, 'same old Labor' appeared to mean one of two things to Australian voters: Labor members and supporters were either union thugs or latte-sipping urban elitists. Rudd was neither but, Milburn argued, he couldn't afford to assume Liberal headquarters would not seek to paint him as either one or the other, or both, political campaigning being a game of infinite contradictions and double-talk. 'Silence is a dangerous thing', the Englishman counselled. 'If you haven't got your message out there, they'll fill the vacuum.'

Together, the group devised a detailed plan, 'Ten Steps to Victory', to direct strategy over the coming months to the election. Two Milburn ideas articulated within that plan that intriguingly never saw the light of day were directed at further differentiating Rudd from the 'same old Labor'. One was a speech, originally scheduled for late April 2007, and possibly as an Anzac Day message, in which Rudd was slated to talk about the importance of 'one society' and of 'rules' to deliver it. 'In the left, when we talk about fairness, we mean equality', Milburn would explain. 'But when the public talks about it, they mean rules. The point about rules is they are the best way of providing and ensuring fairness.' While Australians might pride themselves as a tolerant, welcoming country, most would recognise that 'you can't have a fair go without fair rules'.

Or so the argument went in a brainstorming session between Milburn, Lawrence, Gartrell and researcher Tony Mitchelmore that threw up some potentially incendiary ideas, including a proposal for an ID card. 'Anyone who is prepared to play by fair rules will not be scared of these', unattributed remarks from that session note. 'We . . . work hard, behave well . . . will tolerate difference, but not the infringement of rules to the detriment of others.'

The other idea was 'Project Rudd', a plan to elaborate on the human side of the new Labor leader. It was important, the strategy group agreed, to build on 'Sunrise Rudd', the man who was smart and competent but also openly proud of his family and capable of sharing a joke and 'taking the piss'. But Milburn wanted to take the project a step beyond the conventional positive angles; in the era of reality television and the 24-hour news cycle, voters were increasingly cynical about airbrushed portraits of high-profile people and tended instead to prefer public figures who were 'warts'n' all'.

Over a dinner and strategy sessions at Bilson's, a temple to French haute cuisine in Sydney's Radisson Plaza Hotel, attended by Rudd, Gartrell, Jordan and Wayne Swan, Milburn had pressed Rudd to expand on issues that made him hot under the collar. 'Because he was so professional, and 100 per cent disciplined, the danger was Kevin would then look a little bit plastic', Milburn would say later. 'So the idea of what gets him angry . . . was to show people he is human.'

To the surprise of some gathered around the table, the urbane Queenslander reeled off a substantial list. Some issues were predictable—discrimination against women in the workplace, violence against children and the prevalence of gambling in the community, particularly the increasing number of poker machines in public venues. But others were bound to raise eyebrows—and generate headlines—if they were raised by a Labor leader publicly. These included the failure of the school curriculum to teach the basics of literacy, numeracy and history; relativism in the drugs debate (that is, the idea that the abuse of some drugs was not as serious as others); and Muslim fundamentalism, particularly when women were required to wear the burka and children were sent to 'hardline Islamic schools'.

They were 'counter-intuitive points to centre left response', according to notes taken at the dinner. 'If you'd asked me, I'd rattle off a predictable list: social injustices, racism, inequality and 15-second Lib ads voiced over by Ted Horton', Gartrell said. 'But this was an eclectic mix and I think it reflected how Kevin thinks differently to most ALP types. I think he also avoids appearing angry and his level approach is an important part of his public persona.'

Clearly, then, there was a difference of opinion within Labor head-quarters about how 'angry' its leader should appear in public; certainly 'Project Rudd' never saw the light of day in this form.

Nicholas Gruen

The contrast could not have been greater
The Australian Financial Review, 29 February 2008

Just as Marshall McLuhan argued that, in media the medium was the message, something similar can be said about style and substance in politics. The style is the substance or at least comes to determine it. The political history of the last generation—particularly the contrast between the style of prime ministers Bob Hawke and John Howard—illustrates the point.

Their rhetoric notwithstanding, Hawke's and Howard's economic ideologies were not far apart. Each sought prosperity through a vigorous market, and each supported substantial income redistribution. But the quality of governance differed considerably—in ways that suggest lessons for the future.

In politics it's a truism that lack of resources, and timidity in the face of inevitable scare campaigns, ensures that Opposition platforms are painfully incomplete blueprints for government. But the style of government itself influences the subsequent development of that platform—for good or ill.

Three crucial and related elements of political style depend on whether:

- unity or division is emphasised;
- there is a cult of the 'strong leader' as opposed to the leader being seen as a conductor of wider forces; and
- populist themes dominate political rhetoric.

Hawke provides us with the archetype of one style. Seeing himself as the conductor in an orchestra, more than the strong man at the helm, his style was self-consciously inclusive. Of course he was happy to use populist themes, but much of his political energy was dedicated to persuasion, to arguing a principled case for economic reform.

By contrast Howard saw himself as the strong leader, and his instincts were populist and nationalist. As a result, his reign was remarkably free of policy momentum. And that robbed him of political momentum. Remarkably for a politician governing during a long boom, each federal election saw Howard come from well behind, needing to pull a rabbit from his hat.

The centrepiece of Hawke's economic strategy was tackling inflation and unemployment simultaneously by reducing real wages and doing so by agreement with the unions, rather than with an economic contraction, through the 1983 Accord. Despite widespread scepticism—such policies had failed elsewhere—things fell into place with great felicity.

Like all successful prime ministers, Hawke had his luck. But his consensus was the template on which a rich new style of politics developed. A highly productive relationship grew around the framework of the Accord. The unions delivered lower disputation and wage restraint. Treasury and the central agencies sold the new government a backlog of economic reform at which the previous government had baulked.

Though not formally part of the structure, business leaders were also involved in the process. These new nodes of ideas and influence existed in a productive and dynamic tension with one another so that within a few years the Treasury, the ACTU, some business peak bodies and the government—each under the sway of competent and pragmatic leaders—were working very productively together.

Within just five years of Hawke's election, the process of microeconomic reform had been articulated in a wide-ranging and mature form and it continued to unfold as governments committed and then implemented new policies over the next decade. And on the back of the revenue from rapid growth, the government bought continuing wage restraint, economic reform and major increases in transfers to poorer households.

By contrast, Howard's accession to power was much less constructive. Sacking six departmental heads at the outset, his government's relationship with the bureaucracy was serviceable but not particularly creative or productive. And while its relationship with business was close and sympathetic, business wasn't a particularly useful partner in developing and implementing a political agenda.

Where Hawke enjoyed an extended honeymoon, lasting beyond his 1985 re-election, Howard was in trouble within his first year. Introducing gun control and slashing expenditure showed political courage, but policy was a series of episodes rather than the progressive unfolding of an evolving vision.

Within twelve months of Howard's taking office, there was increasing alarm at his directionlessness. In this circumstance, Howard took his economic policy vision, 'off the shelf' as it were, promising the goods and services tax that Hawke and Prime Minister Malcolm Fraser had shied away from. Though his subsequent re-election was inevitably regarded as a vindication, it was a difficult election to lose. And Howard actually lost it on votes, though he held sufficient marginal seats to retain government.

A leader with greater policy vision wouldn't normally have needed this grand gesture, and had he done so, might have tried one that toyed less ardently with political suicide. To use the ungainly terminology of our time, Hawke's strategy was 'triangulation', Howard's, wedge politics. Coined by Bill Clinton's adviser Dick Morris, triangulation involves a leader presenting themselves as someone 'above and between'—above partisan politics, finding a creative but commonsense course between left and right. As political scientist Katherine West used to observe, for quite some time Hawke appeared 'above' the ruckus and 'between' left and right.

Wedge politics, as the expression suggests, focuses on dividing one's opponents—or their constituency. Where it's been most devastating, wedge politics has appealed to populist sentiment. It appeals to the idea of a nation or a national culture besieged—either from without, as in the case of terrorism and asylum seekers, or from within as in the case of the culture wars against effete elites who are seen to court relativism and cultural disintegration.

These sentiments can make a good speech. In the right circumstances, they can win an election. But they are expressive not deliberative—'we decide who comes here and the circumstances under which they come'—and ill-suited to the unfolding of a coherent policy platform.

Of course all democratic politicians juggle tensions between popular sentiments and policies that must be more carefully considered. Yet, not surprisingly, political strategy-making dominates the mind of most professional politicians. And where wedging is at best a distraction from the policy substance of governing, triangulation is a political strategy that is about policy rather than value-laden gestures. It facilitates a constructive integration of political strategy and rhetoric, and policy development.

Further, though a government practising triangulation frequently steals its opponent's policies, its focus remains itself. To the extent possible in the chancy game of politics, it remains the author of its destiny. By contrast, wedge politics is reactive both to evolving events and to its opponents. Thus, although one can think of some exceptions to this generalisation, while Hawke's broad strategy was to marginalise his opponents as irrelevant, Howard's approach was to exploit opposition weaknesses, so much so that his own conduct seemed often shaped by little more than the desire to draw his opponents into political dilemmas.

If Howard's first year in office left onlookers wondering what he was trying to achieve, his last year in office was an apotheosis in which the style of sledging and wedging his opponents had become the substance. What policy direction there ever was had leached away, overtaken by the clearing of the policy decks (numerous policies being hurriedly reversed to neutralise the Opposition's policy advantage) and a symphony of improvised attacks on its opponents.

Howard launched one political feint after another. It's hard to remember a time when one had less knowledge of what alarms and excursions might turn up in the next day's papers—except during the chaos that was the Whitlam Government. The Brian Burke saga was surely the nadir.

With the recent AWB scandal having just refreshed the electorate's memory of the Government's distain for the principles of Westminster Government, with the Government in high dudgeon about Kevin Rudd having met persona non grata Brian Burke, it turned out that the Environment Minister had done the same—quite appropriately in his ministerial duties. At this point the principle of ministerial responsibility appeared, like a digitised folkloric creature in a Harry Potter movie, its uncanny weightlessness betraying its essential unreality.

The environment minister resigned. His prime minister said he'd done nothing morally wrong. Others in his party said that in resigning he'd done the right thing. The ex-minister emerged transformed from his travails, smiling and magnanimous, and transparent about what motivated his resignation—which was to clear the decks for intensified attacks on the Opposition leader. And so the once grave principle of ministerial responsibility reasserted itself for one last time under Howard, this time transformed into an ironic simulacrum of its former self—a walk-on walk-off cameo—the tactical *feint du jour* in the news cycle.

Then, apparently seeking to expose divisions in the Labor Party over nuclear power, Howard managed to wedge his own party by embracing the nuclear option. He then downplayed the conversion—as its electoral unpopularity became evident.

One might call it the rudderless in pursuit of Rudd.

Though Hawke never gained control of the Senate, the style and institutions of consensus politics helped insulate him from this kind of political overreach. The search for consensus often identified politically viable means of making policy progress while addressing the concerns of major interest groups. And once policies had been broadly agreed, the partners to the process then helped sell the sometimes difficult messages that emerged—like the need to reduce real expenditure, wage costs and protection.

WorkChoices (now living in ruin) provides another example. As right-leaning labour economist Mark Wooden observed, WorkChoices itself was far from clean or coherent as labour market liberalisation. In addition to introducing new red tape and arbitrarily restricting what could be negotiated, it maintained minimum wages that were both relatively and absolutely among the highest in the world. And it was not integrated with other arms of policy, particularly welfare.

WorkChoices eroded wages and conditions for lower paid workers, though perhaps less dramatically than many feared. But Howard never clearly acknowledged the obvious political problem—responding to the inevitable scare campaign with an Orwellian mix of advertising and spin seeking to highlight the positives. Even WorkChoices' regulatory impact statement (RIS) read like a marketing brochure and was duly rejected as an inadequate appraisal of costs and benefits by the independent red tape watchdog. (As an aside, this happened while the Howard Government-appointed Banks

Committee was devising a red tape-busting agenda. In 2007, the hastily cobbled together 'fairness test' itself fronted with an inadequate RIS).

More importantly for the fate of the Howard Government, in eliding the policy problem (the costs imposed on some) it ignored the cognate political problem.

It needn't have been that way. Hawke's approach to engineering lower real wages was straightforwardly negotiated with stakeholders and so addressed these issues as an integral aspect of its design. Wage restraint was sold as equality of sacrifice for the greater good of the economy and community, and other arms of policy were mobilised to compensate workers through the social wage (for example, Medicare) and through a wage tax trade-off.

Ironically, in 1999 the Business Council outlined something in this mould. It proposed and met with the ACTU to seek support for a wage tax trade-off, which would have seen the minimum wage frozen in return for tax credits to compensate low-income working families. But the government showed little interest.

Cost might have been the problem or the fact that the compensation packages were highly targeted and so created some losers in childless households. But these constraints evaporated as the mining boom drove soaring company tax receipts. Remarkably, during the embarrassment of riches that followed, the government seemed endlessly caught short, cutting taxes in different ways in four successive years (without ever trying to 'buy reform' through such measures) and improvising any number of different giveaways—invariably in multiples of $100—to specific groups. Beneficiaries included pensioners, self-funded retirees, parents. One-year apprentices got $800 for their 'tool kit'.

Had the government acknowledged the losers from WorkChoices, explained its rationale and explicitly compensated them for it, history could well have been different.

Triangulation has been the political style of left-of-centre parties, while wedging has characterised the right. Yet there's no logical necessity for this. It would be perfectly possible for right-leaning parties to triangulate and so dominate the centre as to render their opponents irrelevant, but both in Australia and in other countries—particularly the United States—conservatives have practised divisive and populist wedge politics.

In fact in Australia we've had three right-leaning political leaders who have had powerful policy visions. They've not embraced wedge politics. Yet in presenting themselves as strong leaders, each has forsworn the resources—the inclusion—of triangulation. And each of those leaders—John Hewson, Jeff Kennett and Nick Greiner—was less politically successful than Howard the wedger, while enjoying no worse circumstances. We've also had a left-leaning political leader—Paul Keating—mix the economic policy of triangulation with a new, more divisive style focused on his own strong leadership. Like the three Coalition politicians mentioned above, Keating's style had more than a little of the crazy–brave about it and, like Kennett and Greiner, his time in office was surprisingly short given his talents. The most memorable passage in Kevin Rudd's election victory speech was classic triangulation:

> Australia's long-term challenges demand a new consensus across our country. I want to put aside the old battles of the past ... between business and unions ... between growth and the environment ... between federal and state, between public and private.

Of course in politics there can be a wide gulf between words and deeds. Hawke's success was built not just on his own style, but on what that style brought forth—particularly the consensus-driven Accord.

Critics could say—did say—that Hawke's corporatism was essentially undemocratic—that the right avenue for such deal making was not behind closed doors, but within parliament under public scrutiny. But surely agenda setting, both within and outside parliament is what all governments do and should do. In any event, parliament retains its role in forming governments and passing laws.

With hindsight, at a time when the executive so dominates parliament and when political debate is degraded by the relentless infotainment values of the mainstream media, Hawke's centrist corporatism offered possibilities for deepening debate and for enriching deliberative democracy. Although invitations to the Hawke table were at the grace and favour of the government, the conversation at the table became a genuine search for solutions, something that's increasingly rare within the stage-managed public theatre of parliament.

The Accord was a vehicle for the Hawke Government's early and mid-term success. But the government had lost much of its vibrancy by the end of his term. Its role in wage setting was always going to wane, and perhaps rightly so. But as its period in power lengthened, the group with the greatest access to government—the bureaucracy—gradually grew in its influence at the cost of the other social partners.

Australia has a high-quality bureaucracy with a first-class Treasury and central agencies, but its bureaucracy was at its best when operating in dynamic tension with the social partners. And bureaucracies can shield their masters from emerging changes in society. By the end of the Labor Party's reign, economic reform had become formulaic. And those promoting the formula had become sufficiently preoccupied with fighting off those who were proposing alternatives that they also fought off those who offered the prospect of renewing the vision.

Amazingly, while we debate across the trenches between left and right, using examples of policies from the United States, England and New Zealand, there's one other country to which we pay surprisingly little attention. It's a country in which an Accord not unlike Australia's of the mid 1980s grew to being substantially more. And if Australia congratulates itself as being among the best economic performers of recent times, it doesn't come close to this country. Since it introduced its accord in 1987 and has subsequently developed it, Ireland has roughly doubled Australia's per capita income growth—no that's not a misprint—taking itself from being a poor man of Europe to among the wealthiest countries in the world.

The idea that innovation in practical affairs might be central to Australia's destiny has deep roots in our history. In the late 1930s Australian economic statistician Colin Clark expressed his own ambitions in response to John Maynard Keynes' entreaties to Clark to return to England.

> I am reaching the conclusion I want to stay in Australia. People have minds which are not closed to new truths, as the minds of so many Englishmen are: and with all the mistakes Australia has made in the past, I still think she may show the world, in economics ...

By the mid 1990s Australia was the world's pre-eminent economic reformer. Dubbed a 'miracle economy' during the Asian crisis, the world watched and imitated our best innovations like HECS, the Child Support Agency, Rural Research and Development Corporations, welfare targeting and the list goes on. But the atrophying of the Accord, and the loss of political confidence and momentum engendered by the early 1990s recession (and Keating's more divisive style) meant the country lacked the imagination to build confidently on that remarkable achievement. We can only hope the Rudd Government will take that as its central challenge, and that exploratory initiatives such as the 2020 summit help it find the political style and institutions to achieve it.

Margaret Simons

Why I won't be going to the 2020 summit
Crikey, 3 March 2008

On Friday of last week an organisation of which I have been a member for many years asked me to be their nominee to go to the 2020 summit. My heart leapt—as though I had been waiting to be asked.

I said yes without too much thought, and in between appointments in a crowded day began to dream of all the fine things I would say and do were I in Canberra on that April weekend as one of the chosen few.

Yet by the end of Friday I had decided—with many pangs and some anguish—to refuse the nomination.

Flattery is such a dangerous thing, and for a journalist it is particularly risky.

I don't want to make too much of this. There are several country miles between being nominated and invited. Most likely I would never have made it to the summit in any case, but I think my reasons for ruling out the possibility are important enough to justify this piece. The lesson of history is that the journalist with something to lose—the one who has been embraced by the powerful, whose career and sense of self depends on being well regarded—will be safe for those in power. Such journalists won't take risks. They will be proper and acceptable, with an eye for their own reputation affecting what they write and how they write it.

Journalists these days are everywhere co-opted—most of all by flattery, by being fed tidbits of information, and by the seductive sense of being insiders.

It is not that I don't think the summit is a good thing. I take it as a given that it is three-quarters public relations and symbolism, but that is not a criticism. Public relations and symbolism are important political tools and I approve of them being used to build an event that gets the nation's attention focussed on the medium-term future, and on big ideas. I think the summit may be broadening and strengthening, not only or even chiefly in itself but in the debates it will spark in schools, streets and homes. I hope it succeeds.

Criticisms could be made. Once upon a time the political process combined with parliamentary debate was the accepted method for working out national directions and big ideas. The idea of having a chosen few perform this task could be seen as counter democratic.

But I don't really buy that argument. We live in the real world, and our political and parliamentary processes are debased. It is fanciful to imagine that all the ideas worth discussing can emerge through the political process.

That this is so is, of course, largely the fault of the media, and the silly way in which politics is reported—as a highly managed spectator sport, rather than as though it actually mattered. Doubtless the Rudd summit is a politically smart response to these facts, and the impossibility of getting big ideas reported in any other way.

Yet politics-as-spectator-sport has emerged because journalists are co-opted and made safe—literally and metaphorically herded on to busses to cover events designed for their consumption. Is it any wonder that they become cynical about big ideas?

I am all for scepticism, but I regard habitual cynicism as a personal and professional failing.

These days although much lip service is given to the notion of journalistic independence and media freedom, the practice is everywhere eroded.

The most powerful media executive in the country, News Limited's John Hartigan, is helping to run the summit, and I gather Fairfax editors have either been invited or are touting for invitations—itself an unedifying spectacle.

This is against a background of our major media organisations being sponsors of almost everything that moves in cultural Australia. Alliance, rather than independence, is the media marketing model of our times.

The media executives involved in the summit are the same as those who have recently been campaigning for more media freedom—yet their co-option in this summit suggests a constrained idea of what might be done with such freedom.

Certainly, their outlets will run criticism of the summit—but from within a framework that accepts the broad thrust of what Rudd is trying to do. They will be inside the tent, rather than pissing in from outside.

There will be drinks parties. There will be—must already be—behind the scenes consultation. There will be backslapping and mutual congratulation.

The historian Mitchell Stephens has concluded that once journalists have investments, good wardrobes and networks of friendship with the powerful, then they will probably be satisfied with an occasional exposé.

Prosperity and the business of media mean it can no longer be a revolutionary force. At most it may be a force for reform and often it is not even that.

Now I am no revolutionary, but nor do I want to be neutered. I was trained and gained my experience in the belief that journalistic independence was very important indeed, and I still believe these things. The new media world makes them more important, not less. We should be focussed on carrying the good things of past journalistic practice into the future, rather than giving up the ghost.

I have spent a good part of the weekend regretting my decision to refuse nomination. I am not silly enough to think this stand will make a jot of difference when the most powerful media figures in the country are already inside the tent. It may well be a pointless act of sanctimony—a choice of impotence, rather than power.

But in the end the only reason I might conceivably be invited is because of what I have written as a journalist and author. And if journalists are any use at all, it is because of the potential for them to provide disinterested reporting and analysis.

Journalistic independence either matters, or it doesn't.

I think it matters a lot.

Sigh.

Michael Costello

Distant goals out of focus
The Australian, 25 April 2008

The 2020 summit is over, the marker pens and butcher's paper have been put aside, a touch of post-summit disappointment has set in here and there. What's to be learnt from what was, after Sorry Day, the Rudd Government's most successful official event in its six months in office?

These two things: symbolism matters, and don't let the immediate push aside the important. On a symbolic level, the summit fulfilled a useful national function, an opening of the windows and clearing of the fusty, tired air of Howardism from parliament.

Australians from many walks of life came in good spirit and good faith to make a contribution where they could.

In glowing blanket media coverage, their spirit and willingness were amplified throughout Australia in a way that could draw others into that same positive ethos.

The summit showcased Rudd's particular political strength: brilliance at the media moment, and the ability to look friendly, humble and sincere.

Canberra insiders tend to look at this gimlet-eyed. They know the driven, ruthlessly focused behind-the-scenes Rudd, the one who cultivated colleagues, eliminated rivals and climbed over dead political bodies to make it to the top. Rudd's assiduous attention to ensuring no slight, real or imagined, goes unpunished is in stark contrast to his friendly, relaxed, easygoing public persona. The contrast is too much for some to bear. These people should stop gritting their teeth and get over it.

While it lasts, Rudd's media-friendly public persona is a big plus for the Australian Labor Party. It has restored to a considerable extent Labor's glow as a political brand, and that can only be good for the achievement of progressive long-term goals.

Which brings me to the second lesson from the summit: not to let the immediate push aside the important.

The summit outcomes were surprising in some obvious ways that many have commented on in the past few days: generally speaking, their smallness and oldness.

But that's not the most important defect in their complexion. The defect, for me, is their short-term nature.

The ideas that garnered most of the attention and prominence were overwhelmingly directed at 2010 or, at most, 2012. This is a pity because, heaven knows, we desperately need some serious long-term planning in this country. Had 2020 been the real focus, there would have been different issues front and centre.

Two that have to be at the heart of any serious forward plan for Australia, but which barely got a guernsey at the summit, are higher education and security policy. This leaves two serious gaps.

It's true that much government policy effort has to be directed at the short and medium term. The prime example of this is the budget in a few weeks, which will be the government's first significant policy and political test. An incredibly complex and contradictory set of domestic and international pressures and uncertainties have been swirling around in Treasurer Wayne Swan's first months in office. If the government doesn't get the economic and political settings right, little else will matter politically.

But while managing the macroeconomics of the budget successfully is essential, it's not enough for a government thinking of the future.

Our higher education system, so important as an export earner and even more important to the future competitiveness of our economy, faces exploding competition in the region. It is falling behind, starved of resources and focus. A real goal for the summit would have been that by 2020 Australia should have at least one university in the world's top 10, at least two more in the top 20, and at least another two in the top 30. That's the sort of big ambition we need.

It's a similar story on the security front. We're dropping behind rapidly. By 2020, it will be clear that India, Indonesia, China, Malaysia and others in our region are leaping ahead in population, technological and economic capability, and in advanced weaponry, totally changing the regional security balance and confronting us with extremely formidable security challenges. Yet this was not mentioned in coverage of the summit. Let's hope the forthcoming strategic white paper is forthright and radical, and that we act on it.

Rudd was never more convincing as Opposition leader than when he spoke of the equity and economic imperatives of the education revolution, in the tradition of Hawke's Clever Country and Beazley's Knowledge Nation. It's essential over the next few years that significant resources be put into this.

Competent management and political adroitness in dealing with day-to-day affairs, especially media management, are essential tools in the political armoury of any leader and government. But Australia has never needed thinking and investment for the long term more than it does now. In the absence of that, our 2020 will be much grimmer than most of us imagine.

John Hewson

Rudderless PM needs focus

The Australian Financial Review, 11 April 2008

While his workload and commitment have been impressive, Kevin Rudd is acting like a mosquito in a nudist colony, so much work to be done, so many fleshy opportunities to bite into, it seems he doesn't quite know where to start, short of biting into everything.

Rudd is in danger of taking on too much, doing a little on a lot of issues, but doing none of them really well and, in the end, standing for little and achieving very little. He needs a clear strategy and clear focus.

After all, Rudd was elected without a clear strategy, and without detailed policy positions on most issues. Some key promises are already proving difficult, if not impossible, to deliver. For example, the popular commitment to provide a laptop for every high-school student as a fundamental element of his 'education revolution'.

While the necessary laptops may have been affordable and deliverable, few schools have the power supply capacity to carry them, and even fewer have trained teachers to supervise their use.

The commitment is already being watered down to something like a laptop for every one-in-two students, in just years nine to twelve and, despite Rudd's commitment to end the 'blame game' and promise of a new federalism, his government is now involved in a public stoush with the states as to the funding and division of responsibilities in relation to the laptop commitment.

Similarly, this overseas trip has all the earmarks of a cheap and nasty, exhaustive, package tour. Today is Tuesday, it must be Brussels, and we need to get up early to make sure we catch the Manneken Pis in the best light! No strategy, no focus, no priorities, but worrying, costly gaps, for example the exclusion of Japan.

Rudd is further compounding his difficulties in at least two respects. First, by being a 'control freak', wanting to run and control virtually all aspects of the government and all its portfolios. Hence, when issues break, as with the carer issue while Rudd was overseas, nobody was game or authorised to step up to the plate and deal with it.

Government ministers are already openly critical of having to clear virtually everything through some green apparatchik in Rudd's office, who seems to have been trained to mostly say 'no'.

By contrast, Bob Hawke was a very successful prime minister, at least until he fell out with Paul Keating, in large measure because he focused his role on being a very effective chairman of the board—he gave his ministers scope to do their jobs, but clearly held them fully accountable, stepping in when they were seen to have failed.

Second, Rudd failed to take the opportunity, available immediately on his appointment as prime minister, to stamp his mark on the public service—to move those he did not really want or need, and to appoint his own.

Much of Rudd's criticism of the previous government in the run-up to, and since, the past election could just as easily have been directed at those who controlled the public service. For example, the Rudd/Swan focus on inflation as public enemy No. 1, which they claim is essentially due to the failings of the previous government, was undoubtedly 'sold' to them by the authorities who were at least equally responsible. Sir Humphrey is never wrong. He never makes mistakes!

Rudd and his team have now had long enough to formulate the detail of a strategy, in both domestic and foreign policies. There is an urgent need for this to now be set out in some detail in a series of key policy statements, particularly given the significance of present and prospective domestic and global uncertainties.

Specifically, we need a clear sense of direction, and a clear statement of priorities. Nevertheless, Rudd is assured a long honeymoon by an essentially 'embedded', if not sycophantic, media. Indeed, I have noticed that in recent interviews among themselves, some journalists refer to Rudd as 'Kevin', rather than as prime minister, or even Mr Rudd.

In these circumstances, where the Opposition is not being taken seriously and where Rudd has a relatively small direct support base in his party, Rudd's greatest threat is from those behind him, many of whom dislike him or his style and have at least as much ambition. Rudd really can't afford to stumble. His lack of focus increases the risk that he will.

George Megalogenis

Politics of style over substance
The Australian, 21 June 2008

Kevin Rudd and Brendan Nelson have a couple of things in common. Each leader gives the impression that he sees the other as a phony. They could both be right, of course, because it takes a stunt man to know one.

But what really binds the combatants is that they learned their craft under John Howard, when politics eclipsed policy and the media changed the way leaders talked to the public.

To a visitor from outer space, it would be hard to distinguish the job description of prime minister today from that of a talk show or game show host. The prime minister is a regular fixture on radio and television, where no topic is too small for him to discuss. He offers cash prizes to listeners and he sweats on the weekly ratings.

The lines between celebrity and politics blurred some time ago. Our leaders are more needy because their handlers have convinced them that if they miss a single news bulletin the public will soon forget them. But voters can just as easily project wisdom on to politicians who are silent as those who blather sweet platitudes about Australian values and the noble struggle of the working family.

Peter Costello joked this week that he has become more popular since he closed his mouth after the election last year.

'The poll rating is much higher now than when I was talking', the former treasurer told a business meeting in Melbourne on Monday.

Obviously the incumbent Opposition leader can't afford to hit the personal mute button. Nelson is damned either way because, so far, he stands for nothing. But what would happen if Rudd scaled back his media appearances and retreated to his desk, where the real work of government lies?

We may never know because Rudd, like Nelson, knows only one way to present: as a political celebrity. Rudd no doubt lifted the idea of continuous campaigning from Labor premiers. He doesn't let a week go by without an announcement or three.

Although it is tempting to see Rudd as merely the sum of his past lives as a Queensland bureaucrat and diplomat to China, his approach to federal office is, in a way, no different from Howard's.

'The moment you start campaigning for the next election is today', Howard told his partyroom at the first meeting after the Coalition's 2004 election win.

'I'm a great believer in perpetual campaigning.'

This happens to be a worldwide trend. Tony Blair noted last June, just after leaving office, that a large part of his time as a British prime minister was spent 'coping with the media, its sheer scale, weight and constant hyperactivity'. Blair measured the compression of the news cycle by the number of topics he ran a day: 'When I fought the 1997 election we took an issue a day. In 2005, we had to have one for the morning, another for the afternoon and by the evening that agenda had already moved on'.

Thankfully, the Australian market is still small enough to keep Rudd to three issues a week rather than three a day.

It was not always thus. Remember when sit-down press conferences took precedence over the door stop and parliament was the place to announce big policies? The last government to practise politics the old-fashioned way was the Hawke–Keating regime between 1983 and 1996. To be fair, Howard's administration began as Paul Keating's ended, with a sense that the public was intelligent enough to handle a detailed policy debate over months and years, not hours and days.

The GST was Australia's last old-school reform. Howard needed four years, from 1997 to 2001, to discuss, draft, amend and bed down the new tax system.

But something switched in Howard after the GST. He decided less information was more than enough for the electorate.

The change coincided with the acceleration of the news cycle as the internet fragmented the media market which, in turn, dumbed down politics another notch. Add to the mix the September 11 2001 terror attacks on the United States, which also played a part in shrinking the public attention span here and abroad.

Howard thrived between 2001 and 2004 because he projected strength as a warrior and as a real estate agent, against suicide bombers and against the gravity of the business cycle. But his approach didn't survive a second term, which should be the clue that it isn't viable in the long run. Yet Rudd and Nelson seem to be suffering a collective hangover from the Howard era.

Rudd has taken the Howard model to its logical conclusion by adding morning television and FM radio to the media pit stops, extending the theatre of trivial announcements to overseas tours and by stepping up the micro-managing being done out of the prime minister's office.

As Howard's former press secretary David Luff has observed this month, Rudd shares the former prime minister's passion for generating paper out of the public service.

'Last year, (the Department of Prime Minister and Cabinet) provided about 7500 detailed documents or briefings for the PM', Luff revealed in his column in *The Sunday Telegraph*. 'Twenty a day. Every day. John Howard is to blame. Centralisation expanded under his watch. To cope with his hands-on approach, PM&C evolved to give competing, complementary advice, independent of others.'

All this control, and still Howard lost office at the top of the boom.

And herein lies the problem. There is precious little corporate memory in the Rudd Government and Nelson Opposition for the way politics used to operate before Howard thought he could run the lot, government and the media.

Nelson, notwithstanding this week's abysmal Newspoll, still kids himself that Rudd will be a one-termer, and that the Coalition will be returned to office once the public sees through Labor's flim-flam man.

Kim Beazley made the same mistake when he thought Howard would fall at the first re-election attempt in 1998. When that prophecy did not come to pass, Beazley simply readjusted the cruise control and assumed victory would be his in 2001.

He even told his partyroom at the end of 2000 that Labor would surf back to office on the wave of an anti-GST backlash.

With Nelson, there is no sense that the Coalition has grasped the lesson of Beazley Labor's lost years.

Oppositions that refuse to engage in serious internal soul searching on policy only make it easier for bad governments to prevail at the ballot box. It is absurd, in this context, that Nelson panicked Rudd on petrol prices immediately after the budget. The voters noticed and didn't like this side of Rudd, just as they didn't approve whenever Howard followed Beazley down the populist road.

The latest Newspoll shows Rudd's personal satisfaction rating has been on a mini roller-coaster. Before the May budget, the prime minister had 68 per cent of voters happy with the job he was doing. By the end of May, that figure had been pared back to 56 per cent.

Now Newspoll has Rudd up again at 59 per cent, coincidentally after he stopped agonising over his FuelWatch scheme and went to Japan to promote world peace and green cars.

The danger here is that Rudd doesn't see the wobble for the recovery. Voters revealed an interesting side to themselves in the petrol price debate. They clearly weren't impressed with Rudd following Nelson into an argument over loose change. But they didn't transfer that gut reaction into support for Nelson.

Perhaps Australians really do understand the difference between spin and substance.

The price of petrol cannot be controlled by politicians. Rudd's mistake was to pretend that he had a better gimmick than Nelson when voters wanted to hear a different conversation altogether: namely, what could be done to protect the national interest in a world with permanently elevated petrol prices.

The media may have altered the way politics is practised, but it hasn't changed the basic role of leadership. Rudd would recall one of the reasons he beat Howard at the election last year was that voters craved a long-term agenda. Which raises the question, again, why Rudd governs as Howard did, by rapid response.

Under Rudd, Labor operates on the delusion that the electorate can absorb two or three earth-shattering announcements a week. Darting from topic to topic, like a shock jock or newspaper columnist, is why Howard lost the plot in his final year in office.

Has Rudd forgotten Howard's increasingly hysterical public conversation of 2007: the Murray–Darling takeover, tax cuts, the Northern Territory intervention, a federal rescue of one hospital in a marginal seat in Tasmania and more tax cuts?

What really binds Nelson and Rudd is their mistaken belief in the 24/7 media cycle as an end in itself.

The reason Blair and Bill Clinton have such dismal legacies in the deeper ponds of British and US politics is that they wasted too much time thinking of the next line instead of honing policy.

This is not a curse of either the left or the right. US Republican President George W. Bush followed the Democrat Clinton by devoting more time to crafting the headline for invading Iraq—weapons of mass destruction—than worrying about securing the peace afterwards.

The media has reduced politicians into thinking by the minute.

Howard didn't get the mail through in his final term because he assumed that after thirty years in politics he no longer needed to explain himself. He thought that simply presenting each day was enough to convince the electorate that he was there for them.

Coalition frontbenchers still bemoan Howard's failure to sell WorkChoices. Funny word, sell. It implies that a better marketing strategy would have seen the Coalition re-elected. The real blunder was in the time Howard took to argue the case for reform.

The ACTU and Labor were in the field for three years making the case for abolishing WorkChoices. Howard, by contrast, drifted in and out of the WorkChoices debate. He delivered 1000 pages of legislation and explanatory memoranda on a take-it-or-leave-it basis, then changed the topic to things such as the citizenship test. No attempt was made before the package was released to explain what was wrong with the old system, as had been the case with the GST.

When the electorate revolted, the government responded with ads, as if a slick 30-second slot on television was all that was required to restore the public's faith in the brand.

Think about the issues on which Rudd hopes to build a new reform consensus, from climate change to the Federation to the tax, welfare and retirement incomes systems. Rudd can't win any of these debates by press release alone. He has to patiently explain himself again and again, one big idea at a time.

To date, Rudd has shown a Howard-like inability to stay on any one topic long enough to be sure he really has taken the people with him.

Lenore Taylor

Cut the spin and tell us what you're doing
The Australian, 5 July 2008

The Opposition would have us believe Kevin Rudd is all spin and no substance. I think his problem is exactly the reverse.

Far from being devoid of content, I reckon the Rudd Government is running a real risk of having too much substance, too much policy fibre for the electorate to digest in just one electoral term.

The emissions trading regime, with its price ramifications for households, drivers, businesses, farmers, exporters and, well, pretty much everybody in the country really, would probably be enough new policy to be getting on with all on its own.

But then there's a complete review of the tax system and all the payments people get from government.

Oh, and an industry policy review, which takes in everything they pay to business.

And through the Council of Australian Governments they are reworking all the payments they make to the states as well.

No, the problem is not a lack of substance. It's just that the substance is not the stuff they are talking to us about.

Which brings us to the allegation that they have a surfeit of spin.

If by spin the critics mean bowling up a news story with an accompanying prime ministerial picture opportunity every day to feed the hungry maw of the 24-hour news cycle, then they certainly practise too much of it. Of course governments do things and have to be seen to be doing things. But Rudd does a different thing every day. He has about as much continuity of message as a bot fly.

On Thursday he was talking about business regulation and the Murray–Darling Basin at a COAG meeting with the premiers. On Wednesday he was talking about organ donation. On Tuesday he was talking about the car industry with the global president of Toyota; and before that he was talking about how great it was to be at a community cabinet in Mackay.

Important things, all of them.

But that kind of message-a-day spin doctoring is more suited to election campaigns or the permanent campaign mode of late-term Opposition.

What this government needs is more so-called spin of a substantive kind. More consistent explanation about the big stuff. The really important things. The things we put them there to do. The things that, in many cases, they are doing behind the scenes.

Take emissions trading. Cabinet and the nine-person Cabinet sub-committee on climate change have been meeting late into the night discussing this fundamental economic change. They've not made final decisions yet. They're not ready to make announcements. Fair enough.

But surely the government could be responding to Opposition politicking on the issue by reminding us in a straight-talking, no-nonsense kind of way exactly why we need an emissions-trading regime.

Kind of like the New Zealand Minister for Energy and Climate Change David Parker, who was interviewed on the ABC on Thursday morning.

After weeks of utterly pointless posturing over petrol policy and days of debate about how emissions trading was going to mean we'd all be ruined in all manner of different ways, Parker managed, in just a couple of sentences, to bring it all back to the basics.

Emissions trading, he reminded us, was just a means to an end. Once you sign the Kyoto Protocol, once you accept that you will play a part in the international effort to stall climate change—which we just did, remember, with considerable national enthusiasm—then establishing a carbon market is simply the cheapest and most efficient available way to make good that aim.

It was like he was clearing away a rhetorical fog, between our mouthfuls of morning Weet-Bix. And according to one of the country's most experienced mood-takers, that's exactly the kind of policy leadership we want and need. Researcher Hugh Mackay's latest mind and mood survey, based on focus group surveys across the country, found that people were hankering after a statesmanlike prime minister with big ideas and the courage to back them. Like the one they thought they had voted for last year.

People were willing to take some personal pain as part of the response to climate change, he says, but they want a prime minister who will lead the way.

Two weeks ago in this column, in the context of the populist debate about petrol prices, I ventured the view that voters might be smarter than politicians were crediting them with.

More in hope than on the basis of the evidence available at the time, I suggested voters might understand full well that neither party could hold down petrol prices, and in the end it was a bad idea for either of them to pretend that they could.

The Ipsos Mackay poll this week provides some evidence that this might indeed be true: it suggests, for instance, that 56 per cent of voters are prepared to pay more for petrol under an emissions-trading regime.

Interesting. As was an old news clip I came across quoting Alastair Campbell, Tony Blair's spin doctor, on mistakes made during the first term of the Blair Government. The British Labour administration, he said, had been more worried about daily perceptions of the government than the long-term effectiveness of its policies.

'When we came into government, if I were honest about the whole thing, we hung on to some of the techniques and ways of Opposition for too long', he said.

A view backed by the conclusions of Polly Toynbee and David Walker's book *Did Things Get Better?*, which evaluates the successes and failures of the Blair Government's first term.

The two *Guardian* journalists conclude that for all its famous preoccupation with spin, much of what the Blair Government had done had gone unnoticed. It had been a busy, fidgety government, but had been unable to register its big policies in the minds of the public, even though it was implementing them.

For all the reviews and initiatives and glossy brochures and daily announcements, much of the farthest-reaching policy changes had, in terms of public perception, vanished into thin air.

Six months in, the Rudd Government appears in danger of making the same mistake. It's time it started spinning us the real stuff.

Imre Salusinszky

Pollies caught in tale spin
The Australian, 4 October 2008

For a discipline whose reputation is barely above that of economics, literary criticism has contributed a surprising number of terms to contemporary political and social discourse, including 'discourse'.

There's also 'deconstruction', whose dissemination (which is another one, by the way) was demonstrated a few weeks ago when ABC football commentator and former Hawthorn coach David Parkin wondered aloud who would be able to 'deconstruct Geelong's game'.

And what do our children spend all day and night doing? Why, texting, of course: the ubiquity of 'text' is another spin-off from my former profession.

But none of these can compare with the present popularity, in political discussion, of the term 'narrative'. A quick electronic survey of the main Australian newspapers reveals the word has been used in connection with Kevin Rudd on more than 300 occasions during the past twelve months.

For literary critics, narrative simply means a story. Narrative is closely related to plot, except that with plot the emphasis tends to be on the shape of the story, while with narrative the emphasis is thrown on to the manner of getting the story told.

The rudiments of a theory of plot were laid out by Aristotle in *Poetics* a couple of thousand years ago and not much has changed. Aristotle deemed a good plot should have a beginning, middle and end; it should have unity of action, that is, a certain necessity in the relation of its parts; and it should be serious rather than trivial.

Modern critics who follow Aristotle—pre-eminently, the Canadian scholar Northrop Frye (1912-1991)—have added depth and complexity to his account of plot. Frye distinguishes four basic plot structures—romance, comedy, tragedy and satire—and relates them to ancient ritual and myth.

Aristotle's precepts were built around drama, the highest form of verbal art for the ancient Greeks, and do not fit particularly well to the novel, which has been the pre-eminent Western genre since the nineteenth century.

This is where narrative—from the Latin for 'to recount'—comes into its own. Compared with drama, where there is no unmediated access to the characters' minds, the novel opens up virtually infinite ways of telling a story, including via the so-called omniscient narrator who has full access to what everybody in the story is thinking. Frye's contemporary Wayne C Booth (1921–2005) did more than anyone to advance the understanding of the modes of narrative available in modern fiction (including the use of an unreliable narrator) and to distinguish the voice that tells the story from the physical author whose name adorns the cover of the book.

Much has also been written recently on the point of narrative: on why we seem to find it inherently pleasing, from a very early age, to be told stories that have a beginning, middle and end. Most of this discussion has taken place under the influence of Freudian psychoanalysis. While Freud thought stories were simply wish-fulfilments, like dreams and free associations, Freudian critics such as Peter Brooks have a more nuanced view of the point of plots. Brooks argues that the pleasures of narrative capture the twin Freudian drives: the drive for sex, as the story moves penetratingly forwards; and the drive for death, as it achieves closure ('closure' being another term that has migrated from English 101 into the wider culture).

So, back to politics: '"Narrative"… is simply a pretentious way of saying "message"', my colleague Christian Kerr observed in *The Australian* recently. And in the context in which he was writing—a highly anticipated attempt by the prime minister to redefine his government's bearings in a speech to the National Press Club—it probably is.

Or perhaps, rather than a message, a narrative is a fancy way of saying a political party needs a rationale or policy framework, rather than simply a list of disconnected proposals.

These would be harmless applications of narrative to politics, even if they had little to do with the word's literary uses. I'd certainly caution against expecting more elaborate forms of storytelling from our political leaders. It is a sub-category of the misunderstanding exhibited by those who demand high-flown oratory or 'the vision thing' from politicians. They want the nation to feature as the hero in a romance or comic plot in which a series of trials and obstacles are overcome and some sort of permanent state of utopia achieved (utopia being universal acceptance of their values).

But those are narratives that liberal democracy is ill-suited to provide. I prefer the more moderate view of what politics can offer, such as was recently put forward by former New South Wales Treasurer Michael Costa: imperfect, transitory compromises that keep the place ticking over. (This would seem to suggest that, of Frye's four plot types, irony and satire are closer to political reality than comedy and romance.)

If Costa is right about what politics offers a liberal society, what would explain the desire to hear it all couched in some kind of 'overarching narrative' (to quote Paul Keating on what the Rudd Government suppos- edly lacks)? Nostalgia, I would suggest.

Aside from liberal democracy, the two competing forms of political organisation in the previous century were communism and fascism, both narratives of operatic dimension. They were, precisely, romance or comic plots, culminating in the triumph of the favoured class or race as everybody lives happily ever after (apart from those not in the favoured class or race). They both envisaged a closure to history and illustrated, all too well, Brooks's point about the death drive.

The collapse of these grand narratives, and the yearning for what they once delivered, is surely the background to some of the calls for the art of storytelling to be given greater sway in our political discourse. I'd say the same thing about some of the bizarre claims we've encountered—particu- larly among the gibberers who populate the opinion page of *The Age*—that somehow the nation's collective soul or identity (a dangerous idea in its own right) is caught up in selecting governments. Related to these claims were the complaints in the life of the previous federal government that somehow John Howard's rhetoric did not measure up to the standards of soul improvement. (Anyone who actually listened to Howard speak on a complex policy issue, without notes, would have realised he was easily the most articulate Australian politician in living memory.)

While suggestions our politicians should fashion their remarks into a national epic usually proceed from the left, they do have fascist antecedents, and represent a mistaken attempt to discover in politics satisfactions liberal politics cannot offer. Australians have a very limited tolerance for this sort of blarney and will not be disturbed if Rudd, like Howard before him, leaves the Homeric mantle to the creative writers who, at least theoretically, know how to wear it.

Robert Manne

What is Rudd's agenda?
The Monthly, November 2008

Before he became the Labor leader in late 2006, I held in my mind three wildly contradictory images of Kevin Rudd. In the first—derived from the memorably scurrilous portrait in *The Latham Diaries*—Rudd was a media-obsessed, vaultingly ambitious, duplicitous opportunist. In the second—based mainly on my observation of his near-successful attempt to prove that the Foreign Minister, Alexander Downer, was lying when he claimed he knew nothing about the bribes paid by the Australian Wheat Board to Saddam Hussein—Rudd was an outstanding parliamentary performer: focused, diligent, courteous but remorseless, quick-witted and intelligent. In the third—which was based on the Dietrich Bonhoeffer article published in this magazine, and which, as we can now see, he used as the launching pad for his bid to lead Labor—Rudd was a true believer in Christian social justice, a politician who identified not with power but with the powerless, who believed that the impending catastrophe of climate change was the overwhelming challenge of our age, who had given his life to politics to try to make the world a better place. The hope that he might actually have meant at least some of what he said in the Bonhoeffer essay was the reason why, even before he was elected Labor's leader, I had become a Ruddite.

In 2007, I was involuntarily drawn into an argument about the likely performance of the Rudd Government. Before the election, many people on the left in Australia were beginning to express misgivings about what was called Kevin Rudd's 'me-tooism': his support for the Howard Government's Northern Territory intervention; his timidity during the Dr Haneef affair; his basic fiscal conservatism. In this magazine, I argued that the left should stick with Rudd. His government would, I hoped, restore the tradition of a more independent Australian foreign policy; soften and humanise industrial-relations law; help bring the culture wars to an end; strengthen universities; and create a less poisonous atmosphere between the government and the left-liberal intelligentsia. *The Australian* responded to these modest hopes with a characteristic editorial, 'Daydreaming Left is in for a Surprise'. It was theoretically possible, it argued, that Rudd 'may turn out to be the most convincing actor ever to walk the Australian political stage and once in office might reveal his true identity as a starry-eyed activist waiting to unleash a Whitlamesque program of social reform'. It was far more likely, however, that 'the agenda of a Rudd government' would be 'much closer to the position advocated in the editorial columns of this newspaper than the outdated, soft-left manifesto supported by our broadsheet rivals'. For years *The Australian* had been the most aggressive apologist for the Howard Government's neo-conservative foreign policy—support for the Bush doctrine of preventive war and the invasion of Iraq—and for its anti-Kyoto foot-dragging and climate-change denialism. The newspaper had also been the most enthusiastic promoter of the Howard Government's version of free-market capitalism and of the culture war it had waged against the left-wing 'elites'. In the view I expressed in these pages last year, the Rudd Government was likely to change Australia's political direction in a variety of ways. In the view of the editorial writers at *The Australian*, the Rudd Government was likely to continue the fundamental neo-liberal, neo-conservative cultural, economic and foreign-policy trajectory of the Howard years, for which their newspaper had barracked for the past decade.

The Rudd Government is approaching its first anniversary. It is not too early to consider its relation to the philosophic and policy disposition of its predecessor, and whether or not, since the last election, under Rudd, the country has begun significantly to change.

Since Gough Whitlam, no prime minister has arrived in office with a greater interest in foreign affairs than Kevin Rudd. Whenever he speaks about his government's international policy he refers to the three pillars: close relations with the United States; strong support for the United Nations; active engagement in the Asia-Pacific region. Although Rudd frequently speaks about strengthening the American alliance—it is one of the most important elements of his government's continuity with the Howard years; another is his praise for the Australian military tradition—it is not at all clear how he thinks this can be achieved. Short of petitioning to join the United States, it is hard to imagine how the alliance could become closer than it was under Howard. Under Bush, Australia was forced to choose between the United States and the United Nations. We all know the choice that Howard made. No doubt, Rudd hopes this will not be a choice he will have to face. Rudd has always been highly critical of the Bush doctrine of preventive war. He is a strong supporter of multilateralism in international affairs. Implicitly at least, he has no sympathy for American unilateralism. Since assuming office, Rudd has quietly withdrawn Australian troops from combat duties in Iraq. Even more significantly, he has signalled a determination for an independent Australian voice in shaping the allied military strategy in Afghanistan. Rudd presumably knows that the United States is now poised between two foreign-policy eras. Perhaps he has been waiting for Obama, whose foreign policy will be much closer in both content and style to his own than was the Bush policy John Howard so enthusiastically and uncritically embraced.

Deeper engagement with the Asia-Pacific is by far the most concrete of Rudd's foreign-policy goals. Rudd hopes to make Australia the most 'Asia-literate' and 'China-literate' country in 'the collective West'. This is more easily said than done. My own experience suggests that while during the Howard years universities became increasingly financially dependent on attracting Asian students, in the areas of both culture and language interest in Asia faded. Rudd believes that we are entering the century of the Asia-Pacific, in the way the nineteenth and the twentieth were centuries dominated by the countries of the Anglosphere. Sometimes he even speaks as if he believes China and India will replace the United Kingdom and the United States as the world's new hegemons. More usually, he suggests that the United States will inexorably move its focus from the Atlantic Ocean to the Pacific. In the coming century, Rudd believes, the Asia-Pacific region will become increasingly militarily unsettled—by the rise of China and India, by old disputes (the two Koreas; China and Taiwan; China and India; India and Pakistan), by an accelerating arms race and by new disputes over resources in a region of steeply rising population and accelerating climate change. This sense of growing Asia-Pacific instability drives Rudd's defence and foreign-policy plans.

Rudd is committed in the international sphere to the Labor ideal, stretching back to Dr Evatt, of Australia as an independent foreign-policy player on the world stage through the deployment of what he invariably calls, in language borrowed from the standard Australian foreign-policy textbooks, 'creative middle-power diplomacy'. Here Rudd is at his most ambitious or, as some might think, grandiose. It was no accident that Rudd was very keen to address the United Nations General Assembly at the first opportunity; that he is keen to make Australia a player in the diplomacy leading up to the Copenhagen conference on climate change; that he has signalled for the first time an Australian interest in the international struggle to combat extreme poverty within a generation, the United Nations Millennium Development Goals; and that he has tried to inject Australia into the current international negotiations over the financial markets' meltdown. Rudd aspires to be the architect of a new Asia-Pacific Community—not a trade bloc nor a political or customs union but a somewhat amorphous regional entity comprising all the major Asia-Pacific powers, from the United States through China to Russia, where the habits of peaceful co-operation, conversation and good-neighbourliness will somehow be learnt. He also aspires to establish a process for reviving global disarmament and nuclear non-proliferation. Rarely in the history of Australian diplomacy has the distance between ambition and action been quite so great. To build a new Asia-Pacific Community and to revive the momentum of the nuclear non-proliferation movement, Rudd appears to have done little more than to bring the former departmental secretary, Dick Woolcott, out of his well-deserved retirement and to employ part-time the busy former Australian Foreign Minister, Gareth Evans.

Howard's foreign policy was dominated by loyal and automatic participation in international causes alongside the United States. His government supported American unilateralism, American hostility to the United Nations and the dangerous post-September-11 international doctrine of American-initiated preventive war. Among the leaders of the G7, Howard's most natural ally was President Bush. In its interest in the Asia-Pacific, his government focused overwhelmingly on considerations of trade. Rudd's foreign-policy orientation is significantly different. He has sought to strike a balance between close relations with the United States, and support for the idea of multilateralism and the humanitarian purposes of the United Nations and the international community. He has sought to refashion Australia's international reputation—from that of an invariably loyal ally of the United States to a pro-American but still independent middle power and an active player in the international sphere. Among the leaders of the G7, Rudd's most natural ally is the dour Christian internationalist Gordon Brown, the British prime minister. His interests in Australia's relations with the countries of the Asia-Pacific are dominated as much by questions of culture and strategic architecture as they are by trade. In spirit and in substance, Rudd has already taken Australian foreign policy in a decidedly new direction.

Where does Rudd place his government in fundamental philosophical terms? In two of the more important speeches he delivered since taking office—one delivered to the neo-liberal Centre for Independent Studies, and the other a lecture which, revealingly enough, honoured the 'great prime minister' Gough Whitlam—Rudd associated his government with a position on the political spectrum that he called 'the reforming centre'. What did he mean?

In essence, Rudd's reforming centre represents a position distanced from both the socialist left and the neo-liberal right. Unlike the traditional left, the reforming centre understands and embraces the significance and power of market forces. Unlike the contemporary right, it understands the limitations of markets and the problem of market failure. The reforming centre understands that there is no need to choose, on the one hand, between the kind of 'heavy-handed regulation' associated with Brezhnev and the communist centrally planned economies and, on the other, the belief in 'unrestrained market forces' hostile to almost all forms of government intervention, associated in Rudd's mind with the theoretical writings of Friedrich Hayek. According to Rudd, the most interesting and challenging questions of contemporary public policy are found at precisely those points where the need for both government action and market forces intersect. On occasions, Rudd calls the reforming centre 'social democracy'. Frequently, he calls its contemporary conservative alternative 'neo-liberalism'.

Rudd's rejection of the 'heavy-handed regulation' of the traditional left is of no real-world importance. There is no party or tendency of any significance in Australian politics that still defends either central economic planning or national ownership of the means of production, distribution and exchange. In contemporary Australia, socialism, as traditionally understood, is dead. Rudd's rejection of 'unrestrained market forces', by contrast, matters a great deal. Neo-liberalism in contemporary Australia is very much alive. It is the position advocated, in whole or in part, either consciously or unconsciously, by think-tanks like the Centre for Independent Studies and the Institute of Public Affairs; by right-wing columnists and some business lobbyists; by the editorial team at *The Australian*; and, most importantly, by many leading members of the contemporary Liberal Party. Sometimes Rudd identifies the position where he stands on the political spectrum as 'beyond Left and Right'. (He has clearly been influenced not only by the title of the David McKnight book.) But in practice, the position he has adopted can most accurately be described as 'beyond neo-liberalism'.

There are three main reasons why Rudd has moved beyond neo-liberalism. Rudd is still a defender, both in theory and in practice, of the postwar enterprise called the welfare state. In his lecture to the Centre for Independent Studies, he told his audience that members of the Labor Party 'explicitly reject Hayek's view that society has no obligation to others who are unknown to us' and that it is Labor's purpose and unbending commitment 'in this country, in our own Australian way, to discover the ancient wisdom of St Francis, that in giving you receive'. For Kevin Rudd, the Christian social-justice tradition trumps Hayek and the Chicago school. But there is more to Rudd's rejection of neo-liberal fundamentalism than that. Industrialisation has conjured the deepest crisis human beings now face: catastrophic climate change. In the famous words of Sir Nicholas Stern—which Kevin Rudd fully accepts—global warming represents the greatest case of 'market failure' in the history of humankind. Neo-liberalism, for Rudd, systematically underestimates the place of market failure in public life. With its innate suspicion of government action, and its superstitions about the capacity of the invisible hand of the market to solve our problems for us, neo-liberalism acts as a powerful inhibitor of the kind of decisive state intervention which is now needed to combat climate change at the national and international levels, without which we are doomed.

In very recent times, Rudd has also drawn a direct causal connection between the dominance of neo-liberalism and the arrival of the current financial-market disaster that the world must now confront.

> We've seen the triumph of greed over integrity . . . This culture was never challenged by a political and economic ideology of extreme capitalism. And this crisis bears the fingerprints of the extreme free-market ideologues who influence much of the neo-liberal economic elite. Free-market ideologues who have a naive belief that unrestrained markets are always self-correcting and that markets if left to themselves will achieve optimum outcomes . . . Ideologues who believe that government is always the problem, never the solution. Except of course when there is a crash—then the self-same ideologues argue, having privatised their profits, we should socialise their losses . . . There is an alternative political and policy narrative to the one that has tended to prevail in recent times.

This was the most savage and revealing speech the prime minister has delivered since assuming office. As a Christian social democrat, Rudd has offered an analysis of the financial crisis that is simultaneously economic, ideological and moral. In his first year, Howard openly condemned what he called the oppression of 'political correctness'. It was a matter of major significance for the cultural politics of the next ten years. In his first year, Rudd has condemned what he calls the ideology of 'extreme capitalism' or 'neo-liberalism'. This may matter no less.

Harold Macmillan once spoke of politics as being about 'events, dear boy, events'. For this version of the life of politics Rudd has nothing but contempt. Unlike the Liberal Party, Labor believes in action and reform. There is simply no point in holding power if it does not lead to a commitment to change. Liberal governments, most recently the Howard Government, are characterised by 'policy inertia'. They do not understand that there is no point in simply 'being there'. Labor is historically the party of reform in

Australia. To achieve its purpose it knows it needs 'a plan'. The only alternative is 'drift'. In its emphasis on fulfilment of a coherent and comprehensive program of reform, the Rudd Government is curiously reminiscent of the Whitlam Government, whose transformative achievement the prime minister hopes to emulate. Rudd is also acutely conscious of the danger of chaos, which eventually overwhelmed Whitlam. Earlier this year he told the Victorian branch of the Australian Labor Party that a reforming government needed 'iron discipline'.

What, then, is Rudd's plan? It begins with the economy. In macroeconomic matters, the government is "conservative" and "responsible". Until the current crisis, it had hoped to achieve a $22-billion surplus in this financial year. In its fiscal conservatism, the trajectory of the Rudd Government is consciously continuous with the Howard years. In microeconomic matters it is, however, different: creative and activist. The Howard Government, Rudd argues, was responsible for Eleven Wasted Years, where the mining boom was squandered in consumption. In the mid 1990s, under Labor, Australia was experiencing an annual productivity growth of 3.3 per cent. By the time Howard left office, such growth, the key to rising living standards, had declined to 1.1 per cent. To restore productivity growth will require a return to what Rudd calls, in traditional Australian and Labor language, 'nation building'—of the kind once seen in the 1940s in the Snowy Mountains Scheme and, less grandly, with Whitlam in the 1970s, in the laying down of the outer-suburban sewers and streets. There are five pillars to strengthen in Rudd's project of nation building: roads; transport, energy, water; national broadband; health and hospitals; education. To fulfil the vision, the government needs money. While maintaining budget surpluses, Rudd will find it by diverting some of the Costello Future Fund. Some $76 billion has already been committed. Unlike previous Labor nation builders, much of this work will be undertaken in the form of public-private partnerships, the preferred model of the Labor states in recent years.

Since the time of Chifley, no Australian prime minister has been as enthusiastic about the government project of nation building as is Rudd. There is even in Rudd an instinctive Keynesianism reminiscent of these earlier times. As the financial crisis deepened, the capital markets froze and recession threatened, last month Rudd decided to pump-prime the economy with $10 billion of his surplus and to bring forward his plans for large infrastructure projects, so that significant public spending could begin earlier than had been anticipated.

Under the influence of neo-liberalism and the market fundamentalists, 'nation building' was not the only descriptor of state action in the economy that was banished from the respectable political lexicon during the Howard years. Also banished was the idea of 'industry policy'. Governments, we were told, could not 'pick winners'. All forms of assistance to industry would be exploited by 'rent seekers'. Industry policy was nothing but a euphemism for protectionism. The market was the only rational allocator of resources.

The Rudd Government has broken with this way of thinking with a cleanness and a clarity that has surprised. When he was in Japan, negotiating the deal to bring Toyota to Australia to produce a new hybrid car, Rudd declared: 'We believe in innovation policy; we believe in industry policy'. For Rudd, industry policy is neither backward-looking nor a form of disguised protectionism. 'The government', he has argued time and again, 'is building a twenty-first century innovation-driven industry policy—not the old industry policy based on protection and resisting change'. Rudd has given his energetic Minister for Innovation and Industry, Senator Kim Carr, very strong support. Since taking office, Carr has initiated major reviews of Co-operative Research Centres (led by Mary O'Kane), innovation (Terry Cutler), automobiles (Steve Bracks) and textiles, clothing and footwear (Roy Green). He has already promised considerable resources to what is called Enterprise Connect ($250 million), whose purpose is the dissemination of cutting-edge information to Australian industry, and to the Green Car Innovation Fund ($500 million), although whether the Rudd Government will be able to revive the fortunes of the automobile industry, which is already suffering very badly, only time will tell. Carr is an industry-policy enthusiast. He argued on one occasion that the periods of 'darkness' in the history of the Australian political economy (Fraser and Howard) could be distinguished from the period of 'light' (Hawke-Keating) by the presence at the centre of the state of 'two words—industry policy'. Carr's mentor and political hero is John Button, the Hawke and Keating governments' industry minister. He looks to Germany as a model of what our clothing and textile industry might become if it focused exclusively on the high end of the market, and to Israel, which devotes over 4 per cent of its national wealth to research and development, as a reminder of the failure of policy during the Howard years when, despite the vast minerals wealth, the proportion of income devoted to industrial R&D went backwards. Although during the Howard years Carr bore the insults of the neo-liberals (for example, Richard Alston's oft-repeated joke about Kim Il Carr) with exemplary calmness, it is hardly surprising that he is acutely aware of the power and ideological nature of the resistance to all forms of industry policy posed by the group he calls the 'economics club'. 'It's time', he argued on one occasion, 'we got some balance back into the policy-development process, which has been distorted by neo-liberal orthodoxy for too long'. Although he supports all sectors of industry, it is clear from his speeches that he has a special eye to the future of manufacturing. 'When Kevin Rudd said he wanted Australia to remain "a country that actually makes things"', Carr told a group of manufacturers who met in Geelong earlier this year, 'I cheered'.

During the period of his prime ministership, John Howard famously declared the problem of finding the balance between the demands of work and family 'a barbecue stopper'. Until the end of the Howard years, however, barbecues continued to be stopped. Australia was the only country in the OECD other than the United States without some scheme of state-paid maternity or parental leave for those with newborn babies.

In coming to office, promisingly, the Rudd Government established an inquiry into maternity leave. Less promisingly, it chose one of the redoubts of narrow neo-liberal orthodoxy, the Productivity Commission, to conduct the investigation. Recently the commission offered some interim conclusions: eighteen weeks of paid maternal leave at minimum-wage levels; two weeks of paid paternal leave; continuation of the Howard baby bonus for 'stay at home' mothers, although with a means test added; a required employer contribution of guaranteed positions and continued superannuation payments. Both Kevin Rudd and Maxine McKew pledged in-principle support for something of this kind. The proposals were better than many had anticipated. They could, though, only be construed as generous if measured against Australian historical standards or the miserable example of the United States: three months of unpaid leave. In the United

Kingdom, new parents are offered nine months of paid leave. The government hopes to lift this in 2010 to one year, something Canada already has achieved. In Sweden, Norway and Finland, parents of babies are offered much more: two or even three years of paid leave.

In the advanced-capitalist democracies there are now two ideal types of welfare state: the minimalist neo-liberal model, as seen in the United States, and the maximalist social-democratic model, as seen in the countries of north-west Europe. Parental leave is one of the areas where the differences between these ideal types are most stark. For the Rudd Government, maternity or parental leave will prove an interesting test case, one where its instincts are likely to be torn. My guess is that in the short term, especially as the implications of the global recession become clear, its fiscal conservatism and the continuing influence of old-style feminists, who are still fighting battles of an earlier era about women's right to work, will combine to determine a choice of fewer than six months of maternity leave. In the longer term, the Rudd Government's belief in evidence-based policy, and the influence of the new coalition that has formed between the New South Wales trade-union movement, the expert group National Investment for the Early Years and the New South Wales Commission for Children and Young People, which argues the need for a longer time with children before mothers or fathers are compelled to return to work, may push it along the same parental-leave trajectory as the one previously travelled by Tony Blair, from neo-liberalism to social democracy.

Education is, of course, at the heart of the Rudd agenda—its twin concern for economic productivity and for social equity. Although its influence has yet to be felt—universities are still bleeding—Rudd's program for university-research expansion is ambitious. At its centre is a plan to double both the number of positions available to mid-level researchers and the number of postgraduate scholarships. These reforms will have an enormous and, if properly overseen and funded, entirely beneficial effect. One of the most pleasing features of the university reform is the government's guarantee that it will never interfere in the allocation of research funding on political grounds, in the way the previous government threatened seriously to do. Even more pleasing—to me, at least—were the words spoken by the minister in charge of research, Kim Carr, at the National Press Club in September this year.

I believe the creative arts—and the humanities and the social sciences—
make a terrible mistake when they claim support on the basis of their
commercial value. Whatever they may be worth in the marketplace, it
is their intrinsic worth we should treasure them for. We should support
these disciplines because they give us pleasure, knowledge, meaning
and inspiration. No other pay-off is required.

Perhaps I have not been concentrating. But I cannot recall a minister
of higher education since the era of John Dawkins speaking in this
timbre.

Even more important than the expansion of university research are
the school reforms outlined by the prime minister in late August. Rudd's
emphasis is now precisely where it ought to be—on the quality of teaching.
His aim is to do what has not been done for a generation or longer—
attracting the brightest university graduates back to schools. This will be
done through improving the salary prospects of outstanding teachers,
through rational promotions procedures but also, less tangibly but no less
importantly, through restoring to the vocation of teacher the social esteem
it once possessed then lost during a time when teachers came increasingly
to be looked down upon. Rudd knows that there is no greater gift that
can be offered to a bright and inquisitive young mind than the presence of
an inspiring teacher. He also knows that improvements in the quality of
teaching will not be easy. Principals must be given greater autonomy.
Mediocre principals must be replaced. Performance at schools must be
measured, not against some general abstract measure, but against the
standards of schools of similar socio-economic status. Results must be published. Schools that are performing poorly will receive special funding. If
their performance does not improve, they may be merged or even closed.
By this means, resources will be gradually and seamlessly directed away
from relatively wealthy private schools and back to government and impoverished Catholic schools, where they have always needed to go. To achieve
all this, Rudd will use a constitutional mechanism previously pioneered by
Menzies for universities and then systematised by Whitlam: the assertion of
Commonwealth control over the states in areas beyond its constitutional
authority, through the use of conditional grants.

These are radical, practical and admirable reforms. They will be costly.
They will most likely meet with fierce resistance from vested interests

and from state governments. But they deserve, in my opinion, very strong support.

On the fiftieth anniversary of *Quadrant* magazine, John Howard proclaimed formal victory in the culture war he had waged on the side of the 'common sense' of the 'ordinary people' against the 'political correctness' of the 'elites'. Among the leading members of the Beazley shadow Cabinet, only Kevin Rudd thought it necessary to reply. What, then, since the election of the Rudd Government, has happened on the fields of battle in the culture war?

If the Howard Government is eventually judged harshly, one of the reasons will be the astonishment future generations will come to feel about the brutal ways in which it treated those asylum seekers fleeing from Saddam Hussein, the Taliban and the Iranian theocracy. In his Bonhoeffer essay, Kevin Rudd expressed moral objection to the Howard Government's asylum-seeker policy. In general, policy has followed what the sentiments in this article might have led people to hope. Since Labor arrived in power, a great deal of the former government's policy has been quietly dismantled. The Pacific Solution has been abandoned. There are no more temporary-protection visas. All new asylum seekers will at first be detained only for a brief period. Adults will be detained for prolonged periods only if the government can prove to an independent authority that, in the public interest, it is necessary. The only major part of the old system that will be kept is the excision of large parts of northern Australia from the operation of the Migration Act. If any asylum seekers arrive on the Australian coastline, they will be detained not on Nauru but on Christmas Island and will be allowed access to legal advice.

In truth, this new policy is logically nonsensical. If asylum seekers reach Christmas Island and are found to be refugees, Australia will have no alternative but to settle them. It is inconceivable that other countries will offer homes to refugees already on Australian territory. The hope of the government is, however, that because of the success of the Howard Government's brutal deterrence policy, people smugglers will continue to give Australia a wide berth. The new humanitarianism of the Rudd Government's asylum-seeker policy is free-riding on the 'success' of the

Howard Government's inhumanity. The Rudd Government is gambling on the fact that the shaky logical and moral foundations of its asylum-seeker policy will not be tested. Last month two boats arrived.

Concerning reconciliation, the picture is more straightforward. The Indigenous policy of the Howard Government was based on an astonishingly empty supposed choice: either practical action to attend to the dreadful problems of existence haunting the lives of Indigenous Australians, or symbolic action, at whose heart there would be a national apology delivered by the prime minister in which the non-Indigenous part of the nation would express its acceptance of the profound injustice that attended the nation's foundation, and the Indigenous part of the nation would be asked to find it in its heart to forgive. It was always clear that the reason supplied by the government for its unwillingness to apologise was bogus. The prime minister told us repeatedly that contemporaries could not apologise for the deeds of earlier generations. No one believed that he really thought the present German government was unable to apologise for the Holocaust.

By more or less universal agreement, the finest moment in the short history of the Rudd Government was the apology delivered to the Stolen Generations at the opening of the parliament earlier this year, where Kevin Rudd delivered the only memorable speech of his prime ministership so far. If there was a false note in the speech it was in the suggestion that we could all now 'move on'. The depth of the Dispossession necessarily resists this facile hope. But what is true is this. Far from imperilling practical action, the apology created a moral basis that government programs like the Northern Territory intervention, which the Rudd Government has essentially continued, had always needed. That the apology will not ensure the success of the practical tasks is obvious. Nothing can do that. That it has somehow imperilled their likely success, one of the premises of the former prime minister's refusal to apologise, has come to be seen for what it always was—absolutely daft.

One of the most difficult social issues that arose during the second half of the Howard years was the rise of anti-Muslim sentiment. The success story of Australian post-war migration is usually told in the following way. When a new group of migrants arrives it confronts some hostility and suspicion. Through acquaintance, the hostility and suspicion for this group fades. When the next new group arrives the pattern is repeated. And so on.

With Muslim migration, the story lacks the normal happy ending. Mass Muslim migration from Turkey, Lebanon and elsewhere began in the 1970s. Empirical studies suggest that the suspicions and hostilities surrounding Muslim Australians have been rather resistant to change. Even more, these underlying patterns of feeling have risen to the surface during the 'war on terror'.

It is obvious that the vast majority of Australia's Muslims bear no responsibility whatever for the rise in tensions. It is also obvious that no matter what any Australian government might have done following September 11, some increased tension between Muslims and non-Muslims was inevitable. From such tension no Western society has been altogether immune. However, it also seems plain that by its post-September-11 words and actions the previous government made things worse. Several ministers, especially after the London bombings, lectured Muslims on the question of their loyalty to Australia. Blatant racism in speech and writing by government supporters went unresisted and even undiscussed. Twice before the last election—in the detention of Dr Haneef and the attack on Sudanese refugees—the desperate government even sought to gain some electoral advantage by exciting anti-Muslim feelings.

On all these matters Rudd Labor conspicuously failed to oppose. I once believed that its silences were tactical and even justified, as part of a fierce determination to avoid another pre-election Tampa. Unfortunately, since it took power nothing much on this front seems to have changed. While there is no reason to believe that the Rudd Government would be tempted to exploit Muslims for electoral advantage in the ways its predecessor did, I cannot recall an occasion when the prime minister has used his authority and moral suasion to help build trust between Muslim and non-Muslim Australians. The new government has followed the previous one in abandoning the language of multiculturalism as an official descriptor of desired interethnic equality, and as an aspiration for Australian society in the long term. Commitment to the ideal of multiculturalism was most powerful when it seemed scarcely needed. At the time of probably the most serious ethnic tension experienced on the ground in Australia in the past thirty years, the Rudd Government has allowed the language of multiculturalism to lapse. Following the policy eras of assimilation, integration and multiculturalism, for the first time since the beginning of the post-war non-Anglomorph mass migration both settlement and ethnic policy are being pursued without the guidance of any philosophy or abstract noun.

Kevin Rudd's relations with the left-leaning intelligentsia began famously at the 2020 Summit, where he was treated as hero and national saviour. This atmosphere did not last long. When he first became acquainted with Bill Henson's beautiful photograph of a naked, nubile girl, he described it as 'revolting'. The left was appalled. No issue could reveal more precisely the gulf in values that divides this group from ordinary people. (It is precisely because the gulf is real and not a construct that Howard was so easily able to exploit it over Aborigines, asylum seekers and Muslims.) For the left, the attempt to prosecute Henson was a sickening outrage, both an attack on art, the only sacred in a secular world, and a sign that the philistinism of the recent puritanical past was making a return. For ordinary people, in the age of sexual freedom and the internet, the Henson affair sounded a warning that the final sexual taboo, directed against paedophilia—the taboo that protected their children—might prove less solid than supposed. In this cultural controversy, neither side was wrong. It was rather that the values the different sides were willing to defend to the death, as it were, were basic but also incommensurable and irreconcilable. There is no reason to believe that Rudd adopted his position on the Henson photograph for populist reasons. In a conflict between the claims of artistic freedom and the protection of children, for him the choice was not in doubt. The prime minister is a Christian and a social democrat. He is not an aesthete or a libertarian.

There is one issue where the performance of the Rudd Government has disappointed me deeply, although the disappointment has been no surprise.

Several decades ago a scientific consensus began to form, which made it clear that the carbon dioxide released into the atmosphere by the burning of fossil fuels, which had taken hundreds of millions of years to produce, in combination with the release of other greenhouse gases, was causing the temperature of the Earth to rise. Since the industrial revolution, average temperatures have risen by 0.7 degrees Celsius. Already another 0.6 degrees is inevitable. The CO_2eq measure in the atmosphere is already higher than it has been in 650000 years. Unless it is stabilised soon, average temperatures will rise by 2 or 3 or 4 degrees. Models suggest that on a business-as-usual scenario, by the end of this century a rise of 6 degrees is possible. Long before this, we will have passed the point of no return for the kind of Earth human beings have always known. Nonetheless, in the past three decades, despite the near-unanimous scientific consensus, especially as the industrialisation of China and India has gathered pace, CO_2 levels have continued to rise steeply. The ice in the Arctic Ocean is retreating in summer at a pace no one even a few years ago imagined possible. For the first time in several thousand years there is now a North-West Passage. About what is happening what we lack is not knowledge or understanding but the courage to face what we know, and the energy and capacity to act.

Concerning global warming the performance of the Howard Government was a complete disgrace. The Rudd Government came into office supposedly to repair the damage. In the speeches he has delivered this year, the prime minister has returned time and again to two lines. With regard to climate change his government inherited 'a decade of denial and neglect'. And: 'Climate change is the greatest moral, economic and social challenge of our time'.

What, then, has the government done to reverse the decade of denial and to meet the greatest challenge of the age? It ratified the Kyoto Protocol. This was costless. It began work on a modest emissions-trading scheme. As it began its work, it suggested that the scheme would compensate the worst emitters: the trade-exposed emissions-intensive industries and even the coal-fired electricity plants. Ross Garnaut was last year given the task of reporting to the government. Even though he understands fully the implications of climate science, even though he believes future generations will deplore 'until the end of time' our incapacity to take decisive action, Garnaut has advocated a paltry target of 10 per cent emission cuts by 2020 if the Copenhagen negotiation is successful and of 5 per cent if it is not, although he would accept a 25 per cent cut if at Copenhagen a presently inconceivable global agreement to a reduction of this size was agreed. It is almost certain that the Rudd Government's target will resemble Garnaut's, or be even more modest. Those who think this irresponsible will be written out of the national conversation, in the language of the new official orthodoxy, as 'deep greens'.

Recently, the American climate scientist James Hansen, of NASA, wrote to Kevin Rudd suggesting that we close down our coal industry. Coal is by far the most important source of atmospheric CO_2. We are the world's largest exporter of coal. Our per-capita CO_2 emissions are close to the highest in the world because of our near-exclusive reliance on coal for the production of electricity. Hansen's suggestion was not, of course, taken seriously. Rudd has told us that he is 'a big believer in coal'. The response of the Rudd Government to our national coal addiction is to promise miserly amounts of money for the conduct of research into 'clean coal' technologies, especially geosequestration. The search for clean coal is Australia's new Lasseter's Reef. The mirage, however, has a purpose. It operates as a permanent alibi, as an excuse for not changing our ways.

Humanity's main chance now for avoiding catastrophe is for individual nations to take unilateral action on carbon-dioxide and other greenhouse-gas emissions, in the hope that their actions will have what I have called a benign domino effect on other nations and help lead towards a successful international agreement. It would actually be too optimistic to say that this hope is very slim. Climate change demands more of politics and international relations than I think they can deliver: the end of politics as the art of the possible and of compromise between interest groups; the negotiation of an international agreement of an unprecedentedly altruistic kind; the creation of an atmosphere of wartime emergency in the absence of an enemy. Despite the prime minister rightly regarding climate change as the greatest moral and political challenge of our era, on present indications Australia's contribution to the struggle to meet the challenge will be negligible. Kevin Rudd has failed as much and as little as would every imaginable Australian prime minister. Even more than Rudd would find it comfortable to acknowledge, it is the crystal spirit and the wisdom and the courage of Dietrich Bonhoeffer that we now need.

In its first year, the Rudd Government has begun upon an impressive, far-reaching and practical program of reform. It has been widely criticised for preferring investigations to actions. But that is rather unfair. For reforming governments, inquiries are not alternatives to deeds but their mode of preparation. Whitlam led the most active reforming government in Australian history. He also established close to a hundred commissions of inquiry to report on almost every aspect of national life. Rudd has set out on a similar path. Already, in one area after another, his government has broken with the neo-liberal and neo-conservative trajectory of its predecessor. For me, the Howard years already seem like ancient history, leaving little but the memory of a strangely unsettling dream.

History has often been unkind to the Australian Labor Party. After 13 years in the wilderness, James Scullin was elected in the month of the great 1929 Wall Street crash. After two years of permanent political crisis—during which Joseph Lyons defected to the conservatives and the New South Wales Langites staged a mutiny on the left—Labor collapsed, first losing its majority in the parliament and then suffering an unprecedented electoral catastrophe. After twenty-three years in the wilderness, Whitlam—at the midpoint of his prime ministership, with the unanticipated arrival of general stagflation—faced the worst global recession since World War II. After eighteen months of economic turmoil and political comedy, the Labor government was dismissed by the governor-general and then rejected overwhelmingly by the people. And now, within its first year, after almost twelve years of Howard, Rudd Labor confronts the second great Wall Street crash. Although the circumstance is eerily familiar, no one can know what will be the government's fate.

So far, Kevin Rudd's response to the financial meltdown and the impending global recession has been extremely impressive: decisive, good-humoured and calm. He has been blessed by an entirely disciplined party, something neither Scullin nor Whitlam had, and also, after the brief episode of Nelsonian populist tomfoolery, by the arrival of an Opposition leader at once responsible, intelligent and mature. We cannot yet know whether the Rudd Government will be able to weather the coming storm and continue with its ambitious plans; or whether it will become preoccupied in its second and third years by little more than crisis management; or even whether, like the governments of Scullin and Whitlam, it will be overwhelmed and then destroyed by economic turmoil.

Machiavelli knew that in the end the Prince relied on Fortune. If he is lucky, Rudd may turn out to be one of Australia's more impressive leaders. If he is unlucky, he may come to be seen as a great prime minister we never really had.

2
After the Apology

Noel Pearson

When words aren't enough
The Australian, 12 February 2008

There is no one simple angle to take on tomorrow's apology by Prime Minister Kevin Rudd to members of the stolen generations and their descendants and families on behalf of the parliament of Australia.

There are different angles, some of which are at odds with each other. On the eve of its delivery, I remain convulsed by these contradictions. But the majority of Australians—black and white, progressive and conservative, Labor and Coalition, young and old—believe the apology is the right thing to do.

Before I yield to this overwhelming view, I will discuss the various fraught angles from which the apology might be assessed.

First, one can analyse the apology through the prism of cultural war. The imperative to apologise is a product of Australia's culture wars of the past decade. The political and cultural right's motivations for making Aboriginal history and policy the killing floor for the culture wars predated the conservative ascendancy of the past eleven years.

The right's culture wars were an accumulated reaction to the left's own vociferous cultural crusades of the 1960s and 1970s. The right launched a relentless blitz on an intellectually hapless left, vulnerably bloated by the excesses of political correctness. The right returned the contumely to which it had been subjected, with interest.

John Howard's refusal to apologise to the stolen generations was used by opponents as a bludgeon to morally and politically beat him. The chief motivation was not policy or spirit or moral philosophy, it was cultural war. The progressives wished for Howard to either humiliate himself by saying sorry, or he had to show what a heartless bastard he was.

Howard refused to prostrate himself in the way his cultural opponents demanded, and in retrospect they can say Howard was out of step with the feeling of decent Australians. But this was not the case for four consecutive parliamentary terms.

Howard was equally engaged in cultural war. He understood the excesses of leftist political correctness yielded the right huge cultural advantage, which meant his refusal to apologise was an electoral plus.

As with so many cultural battles of that decade, progressive contempt for Howard in respect of Aboriginal history and policy only increased Howard's standing. The Teflon with which Howard for so long was coated was made from the spit of his opponents. The more spit, the more Teflon.

So let's not get too caught up with the 'this is an act of decency whose time has come' line. The imperative for the apology was a product of cultural war. If that was not its original intention, then it immediately became a weapon in this war.

A second way the apology might be considered is from a philosophical angle, and my argument here has been pre-empted by Keith Windschuttle, writing in *The Weekend Australian*. Which is more sincere: to say 'we will not apologise to the stolen generations and we won't pay compensation', or 'we will apologise but we won't pay compensation'?

If this issue is of such importance to the majority of Australians, then surely an appropriate fraction of the $30 billion tax cuts could be committed to compensation.

It is not possible to say there are no legal grounds for compensation, because the Trevorrow case established that the wrongs done against stolen generations member Bruce Trevorrow gave rise to a legal entitlement to compensation. It may be argued that the liability falls on the states rather than the Commonwealth, but if the Commonwealth is tomorrow assuming moral responsibility on behalf of the country, why not assume the responsibility for redress?

It is not possible to say those entitled to legal redress can chase their claims through the courts. What if this position were taken with James Hardie asbestosis victims? Those likely to be entitled to similar claims as Trevorrow are soon going to die. The greater number already have. There are thousands of Bernie Bantons involved here. How sincere is it to say sorry and then leave them to the pain, cost, inconvenience and uncertainty of interminable court proceedings?

A third way is to look at the psychological angle. There is no doubt a majority among the political leadership and ordinary white Australians hope the country will be able to, to use the prime minister's words, move on. There are two ways to take this hope. The first is ominous: that it represents a hope to dispose of the apology in as decent (and politically and financially cost-free) way as possible, and to put the subject into the 'box ticked' compartment. The second is optimistic: it represents a necessary start for a genuinely hopeful era in Indigenous affairs.

But who will be able to move on after tomorrow's apology? Most white Australians will be able to move on (with the warm inner glow that will come from having said sorry), but I doubt Indigenous Australians will. Those people stolen from their families who feel entitled to compensation will never be able to move on.

Too many will be condemned to harbour a sense of injustice for the rest of their lives. Far from moving on, these people—whose lives have been much consumed by this issue—will die with a sense of unresolved justice.

One of my misgivings about the apology has been my belief that nothing good will come from viewing ourselves, and making our case on the basis of our status, as victims.

We have been—and the people who lost their families certainly were— victimised in history, but we must stop the politics of victimhood. We lose power when we adopt this psychology. Whatever moral power we might gain over white Australia from presenting ourselves as victims, we lose in ourselves.

My worry is this apology will sanction a view of history that cements a detrimental psychology of victimhood, rather than a stronger one of defiance, survival and agency.

Then there is the historical angle on the apology. The 1997 report by Ronald Wilson and Mick Dodson is not a rigorous history of the removal of Aboriginal children and the breaking up of families. It is a report advocating justice. But it does not represent a defensible history. And, given its shortcomings as a work of history, the report was open to the conservative critique that followed. Indigenous activists' decision to adopt historian Peter Read's nomenclature, the stolen generations, inspired *Quadrant* magazine's riposte: the rescued generations.

The truth is the removal of Aboriginal children and the breaking up of Aboriginal families is a history of complexity and great variety. People were stolen, people were rescued; people were brought in chains, people were brought by their parents; mixed-blood children were in danger from their tribal stepfathers, while others were loved and treated as their own; people were in danger from whites, and people were protected by whites. The motivations and actions of those whites involved in this history—governments and missions—ranged from cruel to caring, malign to loving, well-intentioned to evil.

The 19-year-old Bavarian missionary who came to the year-old Lutheran mission at Cape Bedford in Cape York Peninsula in 1887, and who would spend more than fifty years of his life underwriting the future of the Guugu Yimithirr people, cannot but be a hero to me and to my people. We owe an unrepayable debt to Georg Heinrich Schwarz and the white people who supported my grandparents and others to rebuild their lives after they arrived at the mission as young children in 1910. My grandfather Ngulunhthul came in from the local bush to the Aboriginal reserve that was created to facilitate the mission. My great-grandfather, Arrimi, would remain in the bush in the Cooktown district, constantly evading police attempts to incarcerate him at Palm Island but remaining in contact with his son and later his grandson, my father. My grandmother was torn away from her family near Chillagoe, to the west of Cairns, and she would lose her language and culture in favour of the local Guugu Yimithirr language and culture of her new home. Indeed it was the creation of reserves and the establishment of missions that enabled Aboriginal cultures and languages to survive throughout Cape York Peninsula.

Schwarz embodied all of the strengths, weaknesses and contradictions that one would expect in a man who placed himself in the crucible of history. Would that we were judged by history in the way we might be tempted to judge Schwarz: we are not a bootlace on the courage and achievement of such people.

The past is a complex place, and no amount of what Robert Hughes called 'anachronistic moralising' can assist us in its appreciation or understanding. My own view is that Aboriginal people's lives were stolen by history. It wasn't just that children were stolen in a literal sense, it was more the case that the prospects of Aboriginal people being able to pursue any form of sustainable and decent life were stolen.

Yes, there was grog, there was prostitution, there was untold misery in Aboriginal camps. And if an Aboriginal mother brought her child to the gates of the mission for their protection, were not these lives stolen from them?

Even where Aboriginal people carved out a life in an unforgiving and unrelenting white society, they were still vulnerable to the state's arbitrary removal powers.

This history cannot be understood simply through the specific policy intentions of the governments and the missions. It must be understood by reference to the severe life options available to Aboriginal people in the wake of European occupation and Indigenous dispossession. The life options of the Guugu Yimithirr on the frontiers of Cooktown in the 1880s had near collapsed. Without the Cape Bedford Mission, the Guugu Yimithirr had no good survival options. Yes, like missions throughout colonial history, the Cape Bedford Mission provided a haven from the hell of life on the Australian frontier while at the same time facilitating colonisation.

It was Schwarz's possible role in bringing about the end of the traditional life at Barrow Point, north of Cape Bedford, through his influence on government policy, that troubled my old friend Urwunjin Roger Hart—the last native speaker of the Barrow Point language—to his dying day. On many counts this old man had reasons to respect and thank Schwarz, but history is never simple.

There is a political angle to this week's apology. For the Rudd Government, the apology will work politically provided there is no issue of compensation.

If compensation had been part of the deal, electoral support for the gesture would have unravelled. For this reason there is no conceivable way Rudd will revisit the issue of compensation, no matter what the hopes of Indigenous leaders.

The tide of support in the Australian community no doubt influenced the Coalition to change its opposition. But this bipartisan support makes it even more certain the issue of compensation will never be revisited. Which brings me to the main political point about the strategy of Aboriginal leaders. Dodson said recently: 'I think this is monumental. It is something people have waited for, for a very long time. It's hugely important to us as a nation and to members of the stolen generations'. Dodson says the case for compensation would be pursued in the future. Lowitja O'Donoghue said last December that an apology without a compensation fund 'won't settle anything', but it appears she is prepared to take the apology now and defer compensation until a later campaign.

National Aboriginal Alliance spokesman Les Malezer last weekend said the apology was 'not enough'. But even the alliance is prepared to defer compensation.

From a strategic angle, these Indigenous leaders are fooling themselves or their constituents. If they were serious about compensation, the time to address it is at the same time as the apology. Blackfellas will get the words, the whitefellas will keep the money. And by Thursday the stolen generations and their apology will be over as a political issue.

Then there is the emotional angle. There is a more advanced discussion in Canada about what history teachers call historical empathy. However, this discussion has drawn an important distinction between historical empathy, which is said to be legitimate history, and emotional empathy, which can be shallow and simplistic. Hollywood films present history through emotional empathy. One of the most basic mistakes in this context is to assume we can understand past epochs and events by simply imagining ourselves situated in that past. Without first having a thorough understanding of the political economy of that past, any act of imagination based on contemporary feelings, values and moral convictions will be teleologically silly and misleading. This is the problem when history as a discipline meets history as popular culture.

The final angle is spiritual. There is a remote place of striking magnificence on the lands of the Guugu Yimithirr which I visit about a half dozen times a year. From the top of a massive parabolic dune that changes shape with the winds, you can see south across the distant bay the two mountains of Cape Bedford, where Schwarz dedicated his life's work. Down near the water is an ancient Aboriginal camp site with evidence of occupation going back hundreds, possibly thousands, of years. The fresh water, clean sand and shelter, and a clear view to approaching strangers, made it a good place to camp.

People could hunt and fish along the river and in the surrounding swamps and rainforests during the day and return to this camp in the afternoon. The last time camps such as this were occupied by Aboriginal people who still lived traditional lives outside the mission was in the years leading up to World War II.

This place in particular was a good place to hide from the police; not just children but adults and old people were also removed to Palm Island. My constant thought when I return to this place is the history of this camp when children laughed and played.

But then I think of the camps when there were increasingly only the last of the old people living in the bush. People like my great-grandfather Arrimi. Depleted of their children and young people, these camps must have become increasingly sad and lonely. The old people who escaped being removed to Palm Island ended their days in loneliness.

Every time I visit this place I have cause to think about these old people. And the mission. And their children gone.

Phillip Adams

Only the ignorant oppose an apology

The Australian, 12 February 2008

Tomorrow's Sorry Day has been a long time coming.

How many people in the community or in parliament opposed to saying sorry have bothered to read *Bringing Them Home*, the 1997 report of the national inquiry into the separation of Aboriginal and Torres Strait Islander children from their families?

Had John Howard had his way, nobody would have read that report. The document was damned and denigrated before it was reluctantly and belatedly released, following a shameful campaign to ridicule the chairman of the inquiry, the thoroughly decent Ronald Wilson. Little wonder Howard won't show his face in parliament.

I've met scores of Indigenous people whose lives were mutilated by that brutal policy. I've heard the stories from weeping men and women, including accounts of mothers driven insane after children were torn from their arms. To hear fools and bigots still arguing about the appropriateness of the word sorry—or, worse, insisting the children were rescued or saved— sickens me and shames this country.

Wilson's co-chairman Mick Dodson joined me to discuss the apology on Radio National's *Late Night Live* along with Phil Fontaine, the national chief of Canada's Assembly of First Nations. And the parallels between the treatment of indigenous families in our two countries are, to say the least, instructive.

The kidnapping of children from Aboriginal families and communities played a big role in the social wreckage we see today. Many of the children were mixed race and the policy was about eugenics: the breeding of aboriginality out of our population. Ditto in Canada. Fontaine, a member of Canada's stolen generations, quoted a leading politician's justification for the policy: 'If we can't kill the Indian, we can kill the Indian in the child.'

Between 1870 and 1996, vast numbers of children were removed from their families and placed in so-called Indian residential schools for the purpose of cultural genocide, euphemistically described as civilising. As in Australia, a great many of these rescued kids were appallingly treated.

Canada's federal government committed to formally apologise to these victims of racism. In May 2007, members of parliament agreed unanimously to apologise to the former residents of these wretched schools for 'the sad legacy of emotional, physical and sexual abuse'. But the process has been stalled by conservatives who parrot the same bigoted bilge we're hearing here this week.

As well as characterising cruelty as compassion, Australian critics of an apology are fearful that it will open the gates to demands for compensation. In Canada, compensation is preceding the formal apology. On behalf of the tribes and the families the Assembly of First Nations represents, Fontaine negotiated a nearly C\$2billion reparation scheme and since last September almost 80 000 survivors (that's Fontaine's word) have received their payouts. Canada is to establish a Truth and Reconciliation Commission along South African lines, which Fontaine says 'will ensure that all Canadians understand the serious harm done to our people and send the message around the world that "never again"'.

I doubt we need a commission here. The work of Indigenous leaders such as Dodson, who was also counsel assisting the Royal Commission into Aboriginal Deaths in Custody, ensures we already know the truth. If we want to know it. Now, after years of stalling by the Howard Government, the reconciliation process can be resumed.

In *Bringing Them Home*, Wilson and Dodson sought more than an apology from MPs. They wanted our parliaments to 'officially acknowledge the responsibility of their predecessors for the laws, policies and practices of forcible removal . . . that state and territory police forces, having played a prominent role in implementation of the laws and policies of forcible removal, acknowledge that role' and apologise, along with churches and other non-governmental agencies.

That process began years ago in state parliaments, with the churches joining in. The Rudd Government has, at long last, ended the Howard veto.

Never again. That's perhaps the most important part of the apology. To have that undertaking formalised. On the record. In Hansard.

This historic occasion recalls another great day in Canberra when the Mabo legislation passed through both houses. 'Australia has achieved this without blood on the wattle', I wrote at the time. That's not to say it wasn't bitterly fought, particularly on shock-jock radio. And never forget the abhorrent role played by mining companies that ran repulsive television commercials designed to panic the public, particularly in Western Australia. The miners have long since learned their lesson. These days they negotiate with more cultural sensitivity and decency. It's fair to say some of the biggest companies are now leaders in the reconciliation process.

Long overdue and still bitterly opposed, mainly by those ignorant of its purpose, the apology should be equally helpful. Sorry and reconciliation aren't dirty words. Let's sign up and move on.

Raimond Gaita

Sorry, but it's no time for minds to slam shut
The Australian Literary Review, May 2008

Even if Kevin Rudd believes (as clearly he doesn't) that some of the Stolen Generations were victims of genocide, it would have been foolish for him to have said so on the day when he offered them a prime ministerial apology. It would have been unnecessarily offensive to many Australians who would understandably have been hurt as much as they would have been scandalised.

Paul Kelly said of the *Bringing Them Home* report that its 'verdict of genocide [was] so extreme that it provided no resolution to the injustice it identified' (*The Australian*, 16 May 2001). Rudd would agree, I suspect. Adapt what I quoted so that it no longer expresses Kelly's judgement on the report but instead is a statement about how many people perceived it, and you have the reason why it would have been foolish for anyone to want Rudd to mention genocide on the day of the apology.

But that does not mean it is foolish or offensive for academics, journalists, lawyers and others to argue that genocide was committed against the Stolen Generations at certain times in some parts of Australia.

Writing in 2003 in the *ALR*'s predecessor, *The Australian*'s *Review of Books*, Inga Clendinnen said that in Australia the minds of many good people tend to 'slam shut' when they hear such claims. She was right.

It is not always bad for minds to be shut. It is not a moral or intellectual virtue to have an open mind about whether we should publicly castrate male pedophiles, to believe a case might be made for that proposition and that one should be open to being persuaded by it. Or that the injustices committed by Israel against the Palestinians proves that Hitler

got at least one thing right. Some things are morally terrible even to contemplate and others betray gullibility or other failures of judgement in
those who contemplate them. Some forms of open-mindedness make one
vulnerable to the joke about a person whose mind was so open that their
brain fell through. Sobriety in moral and political judgement requires that
there are some things we do not even consider.

And it is precisely sobriety—moral, intellectual and political—that
people who argue that the Stolen Generations were or might have been the
victim of genocide are alleged to lack. Those arguments, Clendinnen said
in the 2003 article, constituted 'a moral, intellectual and . . . political disaster'.

When *Bringing Them Home* was released, and for some years after,
the dispute over genocide was not, for the most part, about the facts. It was
about whether the concept of genocide could be applied to crimes that
did not involve mass murder. 'To take the murder out of genocide',
Clendinnen wrote, 'is to render it vacuous, and I agree with Orwell that it
is essential to keep such words mirror bright because . . . we will surely
continue to need them'. Last month, Gerard Henderson wrote in the *Sydney
Morning Herald* (8 April 2008) that 'in general parlance, the term genocide
denotes murder or attempted murder' and general parlance, he added,
expresses its 'real meaning'.

Given the kind of disagreement that exists about the word genocide,
and that people who have different views about it are at least united in
lamenting that it is badly and persistently misused, I doubt that anything
counts as its ordinary or common meaning. Certainly the concept has never
been mirror bright.

Henderson was commenting on the fact that genocide is again under
discussion in Australia in connection with the Stolen Generations. Paul
Bartrop (*The Dictionary of Genocide*), Ben Kiernan (*Blood and Soil: A
World History of Extermination from Sparta to Darfur*), Robert Manne
(*The Monthly*, March 2008) and Inga Clendinnen (*ALR*, February 2008)
have written recently about it. Henderson believes that some people (among
them, Manne and probably me), who argue that the Stolen Generations
were the victims of genocide, are retreating from their arguments. He
appears to believe that one cannot consistently claim that *Bringing Them
Home* was wrong in the way it arrived at its conclusion and also that it

provided evidence to support a *prima facie* case for that conclusion, or even that it provided compelling evidence to support the judgement, more limited than it makes, that genocide was committed against the Stolen Generations for a limited period in some parts of Australia.

Nonetheless, I readily admit that although there is nothing on offer that could justifiably claim to be the 'real' meaning of genocide, it is probably true that many Australians associate the word with mass murder. But anyone impressed by that should note that the term refers not only to deeds that are morally terrible but also to a crime. The United Nations Convention on the Prevention and the Punishment of the Crime of Genocide (1948) is the legal instrument that for 60 years told us what kind of crime it is. The International Criminal Court has adopted it and it defined genocide for International Criminal Tribunals trying suspects from the former Yugoslavia and Rwanda. According to the Convention (and, it should be noted, to Raphael Lemkin who coined the word in 1943) genocide can occur without a single killing in the service of a genocidal intent.

The Convention states that 'forcibly transferring children of the group to another group' when that is done 'with the intent to destroy in whole or in part an ethnical (or) racial group as such' counts as genocide. Given that Australia is a signatory to the convention and therefore bound to consider its definition as law, it is hard to see how the authors of *Bringing Them Home* could responsibly have failed to consider whether the forcible removal of mixed-blood children from their Aboriginal parents was genocide. One can argue that having considered it they were mistaken to conclude that it was, or that even if they were right, their reasoning was shoddy. How, though, can one rationally be indignant or intellectually incredulous that they raised the question? Or rationally believe that having raised it, they should instantly have dismissed it as a conclusion 'too extreme'?

Five years after she asserted that without murder the concept of genocide was vacuous, Clendinnen, commenting on Kiernan's reminder that among the acts that the convention prohibits is 'the non-violent destruction of a protected group', wrote in her *ALR* essay: 'Nonetheless (here we feel the force of history) for the rest of his introduction and nearly all of his book, we are back with explicit violence'. If she intends reference to the 'force of history' to register scepticism that a serious concept of genocide need not require violence, then I assume she can only mean that the examples that have most persistently informed our thought about the concept have all involved mass murder.

Nobody disputes that. But what does history give us? Lemkin's definition of genocide, which includes cultural genocide; the Holocaust and Rwanda presented as paradigms; other mass murders, such as in Cambodia, the former Yugoslavia and Guatemala, that some people call genocide and others decline to; the convention that has defined genocide in law; and of course arguments over the Stolen Generations and similar cases. Taking note of all that, it is not for lack of sobriety or historical sensitivity that many people do not feel the force of history pressing them to the conclusion that genocide must involve murder.

Perhaps only the concept of a crime against humanity is as obscure and contested as to its proper application as the concept of genocide. That, I think, is because both are responses to morally charged political experiences that humanity is still trying to understand. It is therefore reasonable to ask whether the convention is badly mistaken in not requiring murder to be necessary to its definition of genocide.

Important though it is to acknowledge that for sixty years the convention has legally defined the nature of genocide, appeal to it can no more prove that Clendinnen was wrong when she said that without murder the concept is vacuous than appeal to 'general parlance' can prove her right. How the concept should be understood and to what it applies requires jurisprudential, philosophical and historical thinking informed, I believe, by a literary sensibility responsive to the experience that has so far proved resistant to our efforts fully to understand it.

Although what is necessary to the concept of genocide is radically contested, there is almost universal agreement that genocide requires a genocidal intention. As Michael Ignatieff put it in a December 2000 lecture delivered in honour of Lemkin at the Holocaust Museum in Washington, 'genocide has no clear meaning whatever unless the word can be connected to a clear intention to exterminate a human group, in whole or in part'. It is therefore puzzling that Clendinnen should ask, 'Why isn't the use of a weapon of mass destruction against the civilian population of an enemy race an act of genocide?' She was thinking of Hiroshima. Having asked the question, she does not, as far as I can see, explain why she resists what appears to be obvious: the bombing of Hiroshima was not in the service of a genocidal intention.

To probe this more fully and to take more seriously what may have been behind Clendinnen's question, it is important to distinguish motives from intentions and both from other psychological conditions that enable people to plan, and others to commit, mass murder. When racism is the motive that issues in intentions to murder people of a denigrated race, those intentions may or may not be genocidal. Racism was the motive that issued in, for example, the murderous intentions that were realised in the pogroms against the Jews in parts of eastern Europe and Russia but (rightly in my judgement) those pogroms have not generally been regarded as instances of genocide. That is because actions that are motivated by transient, if frequent, outbursts of murderous racial hatred do not of themselves express the intention to 'destroy in whole or in part' the group that is the victim of the hatred, even if thousands of people are murdered. That would remain true even if many of the people who committed the murders did so thinking that they were ridding the world of vermin.

Racism may have been the condition that psychologically enabled the atomic bomb to be dropped on Hiroshima (differently as an enabling condition in those who planned and authorised the bombing and those who dropped the bomb). Were it not for racial hatred of the Japanese, the bombing may have been unthinkable. Suppose, for the sake of argument, that is true. Even so, the intention of the US government that ordered the bombing was not to destroy in whole or in part an enemy race 'as such', though of course it did in fact destroy part of an enemy race.

That is why, to go back to my previous example, even if some of the authorities who initiated the pogroms swore to wipe out every Jew in this or that village, that does not mean they had an intention, in the sense required for their murderous acts to be called genocide, to 'destroy in whole or in part a racial group as such'.

Clendinnen wrote in the *ALR* that 'the Nazi example is too extreme, too sustained and the ideology too explicit to help identify the attitudes adequate to sustain genocidal action. Of more general use, in my view, is Jan Gross's *Neighbours: The Destruction of the Jewish Community in Jedwabne* (2002), a study of how the Poles of Jedwabne set out about the business of killing their Jewish neighbours when the newly arrived German soldiery refused to supply them with guns.'

Distinguishing genocidal intentions from the motives from which they can issue, and both from the enabling conditions of mass murder, enables me to explain why that strikes me as partly right and partly wrong. If one is interested in psychological explanations of the various events that collectively constitute what we now call the Holocaust, then reference to Nazi ideology will sometimes shed a lot of light, sometimes a little and sometimes none at all on 'the attitudes adequate to sustain genocidal action'.

But it is also important to see that the attitudes that sustain genocidal actions need not themselves express a genocidal intent. The murder of the Jews of Jedwabne was a genocidal act because of the part it played in the Nazi genocide. But the motives, intentions and other psychological factors that sustained the attitudes of the villagers, that made those horrific deeds possible, may have been no different from those that sustained earlier pogroms.

The facts here are controversial. But if I am wrong about Jedwabne, I am sure that an account of the kind I outlined must be given of the complicity of many villagers in the murder of their Jews during the genocide in the east. If one asks how it was morally and psychologically possible for those villagers to have murdered their Jewish neighbours with such vicious alacrity during the Holocaust, then the concept of genocide need not enter into an explanation, though of course it might.

Why do people's minds slam shut when they hear claims that the Stolen Generations were victims of genocide? Because, I think, they take the Holocaust and Rwanda to be paradigms for our understanding of genocide. Their minds do not slam shut merely because they think it is a massive intellectual blunder to believe that what was done to the Aborigines during even the worst periods of the absorption programs in the 1930s should be brought under the same legal category as the Holocaust. Their minds slam shut because they think—and rightly—that anything that counts as genocide must be morally commensurable with what makes the Holocaust our paradigm. They believe that anything less is morally offensive to the victims of 'real' genocide and also to those who are denigrated when they are

unjustly accused of having committed it. In all this they are, I think, basically right. And they are right to think (insofar as they do) that the
Convention and even Lemkin are answerable to the moral imperative that
informs their indignation.

The trouble, however, is that although the Holocaust is rightly a, if not
the, paradigm of genocide, it is a misleading one. The Holocaust is a paradigm of genocide because it expressed, as nothing before or after it, the
relentless determination to rid a people from the face of the earth because
they were regarded as vermin that polluted it. It would have remained our
paradigm if the Jews had been sterilised rather than murdered.

The belief that Jews were vermin made their murder the psychologically inevitable means to Nazi genocide, but the fact that they were murdered is not what made the Holocaust a paradigm for understanding of the
concept of genocide. That is one reason why the Holocaust can mislead us
when we think of genocide.

Improbable though it is that sterilisation should be a means chosen to
commit genocide, considering the possibility is a useful thought experiment
that helps go clarify the concept. If one believes sterilisation of a people
with the intention to destroy them as a people should count as genocide,
then one will be open to the idea that there are other forms of genocide that
do not involve mass murder. The forcible, often brutal and relentless abduc-
tion of a people's children, intending that to lead to the extinction of the
people, looks to me to occupy the same conceptual and moral space.
Whether the Stolen Generations were treated that way is disputable. From
the time we first engaged with that dispute, Manne and I believed that if
they were victims of genocide, then it was only in the 1930s in Western
Australia and the Northern Territory. We were particularly struck by a
1937 speech by AO Neville, commissioner of native affairs in Western
Australia, in which he asked: 'Are we going to have a population of [one
million] blacks in the Commonwealth, or are we going to merge them into
our white community and eventually forget that there were any Aborigines
in Australia?'

On the face of it, Neville's rhetorical question suggests that he implemented the absorption policy with the intention that they would ensure
that the Aborigines would disappear as a race, assuming that full-bloods
would naturally die off. That too is, of course, disputable. The reason

Manne writes of 'genocidal thoughts' rather than genocidal intentions is because he doubts the facts will support anything as strong as the latter, even during the period when Neville administered the absorption program in Western Australia.

The fact that the program could realise an intention to ensure that non-Aboriginal Australians would 'eventually forget that there were any Aborigines in Australia' only if the assumption that the full-bloods would die off were also realised, does not of itself show that Neville administered the program with something less than a genocidal intent. Whether or not he had such an intention will depend, in part, on what he would have done—or even what attitude he would have taken—if he came to believe that he was mistaken in his assumption about full-bloods.

Whichever way one goes on this, if one believes there is even *prima facie* reason to believe that Neville had a genocidal intention, one must conclude that genocide is not, as is so often claimed, always the gravest of the crimes against humanity. There are many crimes worse than genocide. The Aborigines suffered some of them. Some people will, understandably, find that conclusion too paradoxical to accept and will therefore take that as a compelling reason to reject the arguments that led to it. In my book *A Common Humanity* (to which Henderson referred) I tried to address such concerns.

Many people of different political outlooks now believe, I suspect, that after the apology, discussion of genocide in connection with the Stolen Generations and, perhaps, in connection with crimes against the Aborigines more generally, often distracts from and sometimes obstructs the urgent work belatedly undertaken to alleviate the terrible miseries that many Aborigines suffer. It is, however, inconceivable that Aborigines and their fellow Australians will stop thinking for long about which concepts are necessary to describe their past truthfully. Discussion of genocide will then be unavoidable. It would be a 'moral, intellectual and political disaster' if academics and others were to censor themselves because minds slam shut or to refuse to discuss outside academe whether the Aborigines were the victims of genocide.

Whether they were victims of genocide is a matter of concern not only to Australians, or to Australians only because they are Australians. Because the matter is controversial as much for conceptual as for factual reasons, the crimes against the Stolen Generations are an important example with which to probe the limits of the concept of genocide. Whether Australians like it or not, those and similar crimes will be discussed by anyone who wants to understand genocide.

To a heartbreaking degree humanity has come to understand itself because of the crimes it has committed. It is therefore important fully to understand the nature of those crimes and to give them their right names. Genocide, as defined by the Convention, is universally acknowledged to be a crime against humanity. Just as it is a mistake to think that genocide is one of the gravest of the crimes against humanity, so it is a mistake to think that crimes against humanity are always crimes so horrible that, as Geoffrey Robertson put it, they are unforgettable and unforgivable (*Crimes Against Humanity: The Struggle for Global Justice*, 1999). The conceptual core of crimes against humanity, I suggest, is that they are crimes that should concern the citizens of all nations insofar as they belong to a community of nations, constituted as such by their answerability to international law, insofar as that is informed by a sense of the common humanity of all the peoples of the earth. Crimes, initiated by states, that are informed by the belief that some people are not fit to inhabit the earth are crimes of concern to all human beings for whom it matters that their political identity is partly formed by the fact that they belong to such a community of nations.

It is understandable that people should become impatient and even feel moral disgust at the many distinctions that need to be drawn to understand what it means for a crime to count as genocide and as a crime against humanity. When that happens it is worth reflecting on an aphorism by GK Chesterton.

'Civilisation', he said, 'is suspended from a spider's web of fine distinctions'.

Paul Toohey

Life and death of a crisis
The Australian, 7 June 2008

All of us wanted our parents to be gentle. Some of us got it, some didn't. Mostly we needed our parents to protect us. A home may have had an open gate and an unlocked front door, but it needed to be a sanctuary, watched over by protective eyes, a place where children were permitted to grow without being subject to interference from groping hands. But what if the greatest threat to a home came not from outside its walls but from within?

Such was the charge levelled against Aborigines on 21 June 2007, the day the federal intervention was announced: of forming a parental fifth column that molested and raped children while ignoring their more mundane rights to be fed, washed and educated. The initial effect of the emergency response on the grounds of child sex abuse was to accuse remote-area Aborigines en masse of failing to provide their children with these fundamental protections and human rights. These were no less than charges of crimes against humanity, their own humanity.

It is hard to find another example, recent or past, of one race being so singled out for failing to nurture its children or charged with turning so inwardly against its most intimate relatives. Even in nature, animals have their reasons for abandoning or devouring their young. Being stuck on the piss or stuck on the gambling blanket is no reason.

We were asked to accept that Aborigines, after 60 000 years of survival in some of the most hellishly harsh country known to humans, had, in the past forty years, forgotten how to rear children; that the part of the

Aboriginal DNA allotted to parenthood had been cast adrift from the genome or, perhaps, was never really there.

When the intervention arrived, the bush was unprepared to meet the allegation that Aboriginal men were by and large child-rapists or that women in their silence were co-conspirators. There was no one to speak for the bush. Since the departure of Galarrwuy Yunupingu from the chairmanship of the Northern Land Council, and the death of Gatjil Djerrkura, the inaugural chairman of the former Aboriginal and Torres Strait Islander Commission, there had been no stand-out Aboriginal leader operating in the Northern Territory, whether man or woman, firebrand or considerate, urban or bush-based, from within politics or from its outskirts.

And the intervention did something remarkable. All that fighting talk we were so used to from politicised Aborigines, of '200 years of white invasion' and its ugly offspring, genocide, had been ripped from Aboriginal mouths and thrown right back in their faces.

Now it was they who stood accused of slow-burn genocide, of conducting a systemic sexual invasion against their own young.

But was it a fair cop? Would you, as a remote-area Aboriginal parent who had managed to rear and house and feed children despite the great obstacles—the most basic of which might be having no access to a fridge and washing machine—have had a right to feel just a little wounded, a little angry, that you had been branded as the most failed kind of human being on the planet?

Might you not wonder how it all came to this? All those missionaries and teachers and cops and nurses and government-types and land-council staff and anthropologists, all of them in their acronym-marked white Troop Carriers, bush hats and sturdy shoes, who through the years had come to your secluded communities in effect to ridicule the notion of self-determination, and who would secretly drink their red wine and cold beer and smoke joints behind locked cyclone fences as the sun set on another hard day's pointless hand-wringing in paradise: hell, didn't they have some explaining to do?

Perhaps, but such people were the mere tiny creatures of policy. Policy itself wore no recognisable face in the bush, unless it was miserable underspending.

Yet it was not in the bush that Aborigines were harming each other. It was in the main towns of the territory, up and down the highway, in full public view, where women and children were suffering most.

Reporting last year on the case of an Aboriginal stab victim, Northern Territory coroner Greg Cavanagh said: 'Alice Springs has the highest reported incidence of stab wounds in the world. There were 1440 cases there in a seven-year period'. The territory's real sickness was routine urban adult slaughter, not remote child sex abuse.

The federal intervention caught everyone off-guard. The enforcer was then Indigenous Affairs Minister Mal Brough. In his drill-sergeant way, he really did care. Passion and outrage were his weapons. And he used them most decisively on the Northern Territory government. The national press, led by *The Australian* and *The Bulletin*, had been hammering territory Labor, hard, for years. By 2006, the ABC's *Lateline* had joined in, citing the frustration of Alice Springs crown prosecutor Nanette Rogers at ongoing brutality against women and children.

Things may not have been worse than they ever were, but neither were they better. The homicide rates were unceasing, the sexual assaults were horrific and imprisonment rates of Aboriginal men higher than ever. On this last point, territory Labor brandished the statistics with pride: it showed white voters that it was tough on crime. But Indigenous life was not improving under its watch. Women, and therefore children, were as vulnerable as ever. So was territory Labor.

Clare Martin, having unexpectedly won power for Labor in 2001 and become chief minister, showed little interest in the torment of her Aboriginal constituents. Her only stated purpose appeared to be building more boat ramps to get more white people with dinghies into the water and cheering on the V8 Supercars on their annual Darwin circuit. Indeed, history showed she was attending a Supercar function on the day Brough announced the federal intervention. She had her head down in a high-octane donk and didn't see it coming.

Martin had five Aboriginal Labor parliamentarians, the most ever, anywhere, in the nation's history. They wanted action but Martin wasn't listening to them or to her senior policy staff, who were anxious for her to reveal a plan to tackle overcrowding in Aboriginal housing, to address bad kidneys and rheumatic hearts and the sniffer kids and chronic alcoholism and, most of all, education and domestic violence.

There was a strong sense that Martin needed to outline a vision that showed she wanted to take the Aboriginal population with her. She declined.

Brough, meanwhile, seemed certain he'd find a pedophile under every outback rock. He talked recklessly of rings, implying there was a degree of organised, ritualistic sophistication in the bush. It did not exist. But Aboriginal child-sex offenders did, same as anywhere, and they were hard to get at. As men, they held the political power in their communities and shared with other men cultural networks across the lands that were privileged and secret and excluded women. Women and children were silent and powerless, rarely able to call on the wider, collective support of Aboriginal men when serious individual offenders were operating in their midst.

Most Australians had never been to an Aboriginal community in the Northern Territory. Why would they? The signposts on entry into Aboriginal land pointed to the dire consequences of having a bottle of wine in your car (you could lose the vehicle) or for being there without a permit. And there was nowhere to stay once you arrived. They might never encounter the slow-lighting fuse of Aboriginal warmth and humour, or discover that Aborigines did not represent the last vestiges of a doomed society but a living culture with some intriguing modern modifications.

In Arnhem Land towns and outstations, people buried their loved ones in their back yards and covered the dirt graves with plastic flowers. Death was supposedly a touchy subject among Aborigines. Yet there was Grandma, just inside the fence, six feet under, right in everyone's face. Delegations of representatives from communities near and far flew in on light planes to assist relatives in the burying of the dead or to participate in the beautiful boys-to-men ceremonies; the teenage girls swayed through the night in neat lines to the beat-box music. Family groups lit fires on the sunset beach.

And women were brained with tree branches and tomahawks. Out of sight of most Australians, too, were the red-eyed kava drinkers with 'crocodile' skin who didn't talk but gibbered; or the petrol-sniffer boys flitting about in the woodlands, publicly wanking themselves, having lost that part of the brain that governed inhibition.

Yet, when seeing such things in communities, you had to measure them against what was happening in your own neighbourhood. I lived on a main road in Darwin, in one of the supposedly better suburbs. It had an open-door loony bin (mostly white residents) and a single man's hostel (all white residents) near the primary school.

There were clusters of housing commission flats just off the main road, with many Aboriginal residents. The public drunkenness on nearby inner-suburban Parap Road, right outside Martin's electorate office, was borderline anarchy. Women were prostituting themselves for liquor.

The brutality visited on Aboriginal wives and mothers was the emergency; it always had been. With mothers dead and fathers jailed, children were farmed out to reluctant relatives who had their own problems or into foster families. This was when children became most exposed to risk.

Any inquiry, if it was genuine, needed to go straight to the heart of the violence Aboriginal adults committed against each other. It should have been public, not secret. The inquiry chaired by Pat Anderson and Rex Wild visited forty-five towns and communities, taking evidence in-camera. The result was the *Little Children Are Sacred* report.

On its release, we learnt child sexual abuse was happening in 'almost every' community. But in all the places where evidence was taken, the inquiry was sufficiently disturbed to relay to police only six allegations of what they regarded as reportable instances of child sexual abuse. How, then, was it happening in every community? Where was the evidence?

The authors knew what the real picture was and even wrote about it, saying in their introductory overview: 'The parents of Aboriginal children in many communities are failing to accept and exercise their responsibilities. The literature convinces us that neglect leads to physical and emotional abuse and then, as we have said, in worst-case scenarios, to sexual abuse'. That passage nailed the heart of the problem, though it was the only criticism the *Little Children* report dared level at Aborigines.

I half-expected Northern Territory Aborigines would react badly to *Little Children*. The 'almost every' remark did not correspond with anything in the report and represented the first set of unfounded allegations in the case against Aborigines. But it seemed no one had really read it; people took in only the general thrust, which was: 'Send in the counsellors'. So when, immediately after its release, Brough said, 'Send in the army', *Little Children* naturally became the preferred model.

Brough couldn't quite believe *Little Children*. The babysitting tone of the report was best exemplified by the weak position it took on child brides, some of whom had become the subject of national news reports after they'd been raped. The report said Aborigines were confused about the age of consent.

And Brough had expected at least some of the ideas he was tossing around the nation would get a look-in, such as ending welfare, ending the permit system and 99-year leases for townships. None had cracked a mention in *Little Children*. There was not even an attempt to offer a counter-argument.

There was only one recommendation in which Brough was interested and it was No.1: 'That child sexual abuse in the Northern Territory be designated as an issue of urgent national significance by both Australian and Northern Territory governments'.

What Brough did, first, was to cripple Martin as chief minister. He would seize control of all of the Northern Territory's Aboriginal towns by forcibly acquiring them for 5-year periods, and announced a mass influx of officers seconded from the Australian Federal Police and state police forces to stand guard over communities. He would remove the requirement for outsiders to have permits to enter Aboriginal townships (while maintaining the permit system for all Aboriginal land surrounding them). He would introduce legislation quarantining 50 per cent of all welfare payments and link parents' welfare payments to their children's school attendance.

(Brough also said money earned on Community Development Employment Projects would be quarantined, but he soon found it was unlawful to do so; while many labelled CDEP 'work for the dole', it was in fact real wages and he had no power to touch the money. He eventually abolished CDEP altogether in the Northern Territory.)

Further, he would eradicate X-rated porn from communities, enforce compulsory sexual health checks for Aboriginal children (overturned because it was unlawful) and force people on income support work to keep towns clean. Alcohol would be banned except at community wet canteens and there would be no more takeaway sales from such clubs. Alcohol was already generally prohibited on Aboriginal land, but Brough seemed to be saying the bans would be rigidly enforced.

Called away from her Supercars function to briefings and a press conference, Martin bravely claimed she would work with the federal government. But she wasn't being asked to work with the federal government; it had just removed her governance of half of the Northern Territory.

The residents of four small central Australian communities were the first to have their incomes managed. There were initially mixed messages and anger as some welfare recipients missed out on money during the changeover. Yet some of those living under the first effects of the intervention—voluntary health checks for children, increased police presence and income management—were reporting benefits. A group of Aboriginal women from Hermannsburg said intervention critics had no understanding of what it was like to live in the upheaval of a community. No anti-intervention politician or alleged Aboriginal spokesperson had an answer to that.

The federal election came and with it went Brough and Howard. Martin went two days later after a party push. She admitted the intervention had cost her.

There was still no sign of Brough's pedophile rings. In early 2008, Northern Territory Police Commissioner Paul White said that Operation Themis, which operated separately but in conjunction with the emergency taskforce, had received thirty-six reports of abuse since the intervention had been announced. But abuse had many variables. 'A lot of the cases are child abuse, physical, mental, children in need of care and so on', White said. 'So it's a bit tricky when you are trying to split hairs and say just how many.'

Major-General Dave Chalmers, who led the practical implementation of the intervention, early on realised there was a broader picture than sex abuse. 'This is about targeting what it is that creates an environment that allows sex abuse to occur at a rate that is much larger than the rest of the community', he said. 'So it is looking at making (sure that) issues of employment, housing, health and education are all addressed so that the next generation of Aboriginal children have some chance of growing up safe, happy and healthy.'

The emergency had turned out to be less invasive than many feared. The Northern Territory government, initially shocked and humiliated, could see benefits: it knew the intervention's five-year life would bring a big injection of Commonwealth funding to the bush.

Brough's replacement, Indigenous Affairs Minister Jenny Macklin, had said pre-election that she would remove two key tenets of the intervention by reinstating the CDEP program and keeping townships closed to outsiders by reinstating the permit system. She kept her word. So when intervention funding took a heavy hammering in federal Labor's first budget, the whole thing was looking shaky. Federal Labor maintained it supported the intervention but quietly began dismantling it.

What had been achieved? The Northern Territory and federal governments, having long neglected the bush, seemed finally to accept they had a responsibility to improve Aboriginal towns. There was better policing and broad, non-invasive health examinations of 15 000 children that uncovered, at the softer end, thousands of minor but hindering ear, nose and throat problems. The interventionists identified hundreds of remote-area children who had never spent a day at school (as distinct from the thousands who rarely attended). The real question was what Aborigines had learnt from it. Would they send their kids to school?

In early April, I took a 6 a.m. stroll down the Todd River in Alice Springs. It was illegal to drink along the riverbed; all Alice's public areas had been declared dry. It was a sea of green cans. The Aborigines there were playing hide-and-seek with the authorities. They were shadow drinkers. These were not people who started wondering about that gin and tonic at 5 p.m.; they were chronic alcoholics who needed to drink all the time.

The town camps looked like they always had: places of wreckage. Income management meant half of the welfare money went into a bank account and the other half came in the form of a voucher to be swiped for food or essentials at accredited stores. Liquor and cigarettes could not be bought. Locals I spoke to said the cards—not linked to anyone's name—had become highly tradeable. If you had $200 credit on a card, you could sell it for $150 in cash and head to the bottle shop.

There were reports of people shifting away in numbers, to Mount Isa and Port Augusta. Thirsty liquor refugees were arriving in Darwin in unprecedented numbers to make their homes in the long grass, where they could be left alone to drink.

It became possible to consider the intervention in the terms of a spectacular but short-lived life. It was more or less over, ten months after it had begun. Brough's departure had been fatal. If one definition of conservative was someone who liked things how they were yesterday, not tomorrow, it was clear now who the real conservatives were.

Marcia Langton

Indigenous affairs
Dear Mr Rudd, March 2008

This chapter is being finalised in a hotel room in Hong Kong, a wondrous megalopolis on the edge of the most populous, fastest-growing, fastest-changing nation on earth. For a China expert like Kevin Rudd, the depressing Aboriginal fate and the dynamic Chinese destiny would no doubt make for a strange contrast. But it is a very apt place to revise these ideas, while reading newspaper articles about a Japanese denialist of the Rape of Nanking and thinking about one of the many challenges Rudd faces as the new prime minister of a nation that exports much of its natural wealth to China to feed its voracious industrial appetite.

By the time this book is published, Kevin Rudd will have delivered the apology to the victims of the child-removal policies of earlier Australian governments. What prospect does it offer of assisting them to heal after the years of abuse and humiliation they have suffered, first as a result of being taken from their families, and second as the targets of Howard's cheer-squad for White Australia?

Apologising to the victims of the historical policies of Aboriginal child removal achieves at least two important goals: first, it will help to restore the sense of dignity and legitimacy that the victims ought to feel but were denied, and second, it is a national acknowledgement of the wrong and harm done by previous governments to an entire class of people on the grounds of race-hate, an acknowledgement which should state explicitly that this should never occur again. The victims' inheritance has been denied by their removal. The denial of that inheritance is the key to their suffering and the correct grounds for compensating them: they were denied their family lines and their link to a family past and legacy, their material inheritance, their culture and history, and most importantly, a sense of self shaped by the people who brought them into the world.

The primary significance of an apology must be for the victims of the policies of removing Aboriginal children from their families. But nearly as significant is the effect of a formal apology on the citizens on whose behalf the apology would be made.

The denialists will not stop terrorising the victims, nor perverting the nation's history, but Rudd's leadership has the potential to relegate their falsehoods to the margins of the debate about our past. There will be tears of relief and words of praise as well as harsh, cynical and just plain evil verdicts; but whatever the assessment, the political impact will be irreversible. By removing this canker from the national dermis—by simply apologising—a brave new future opens up.

The *Bringing them home* report of the Human Rights and Equal Opportunity Commission Inquiry by the late Sir Ronald Wilson QC and Professor Michael Dodson was made public ten years ago, and a national debate has wrung every teardrop and every cynical impulse from the nation. The commissioners found that the race-based child-removal policies were a special instance of genocide under the definition in the convention. This is crystal clear, for instance, in Western Australia, where the instructions and justification were aimed at eliminating the entire 'race'.

Whatever scurrilous nonsense is bandied about by the unsavoury characters who inhabit the murky purgatory between amateur history and fascism that is Australia's own denialist history school, there can be no doubt that some Australian governments deliberately and knowingly set out to eliminate the 'Aboriginal race'. Informed by proto-Nazi eugenicist thought, or, put more simply, fruitcake ideas about racial purity and the duty of the white man to destroy the lesser races for the good of the nation, some governments set up breeding programs to ensure that no so-called 'full bloods' ever 'mated' with 'half' or 'quarter' castes, and that 'part Aboriginal' people 'mated' only with lesser 'castes'.

Throughout the last decade, Andrew Bolt, Christopher Pearson and their ilk have engaged in abominable, highly personal baiting of Lowitja O'Donoghue and Professor Michael Dodson, among others, polluting Australian political debate with a vicious account of the nation's history. I have heard the life stories of many of the victims and read the documentary evidence. There can be no doubt that the policy, officially adopted as an eugenicist assault on the Aboriginal 'race' at the meeting of the Commonwealth ministers with their state counterparts in 1937, was wrong. The files show the evil disregard of the officials for their subjects in many of the individual cases. Read the Malcolm Smith case report by Commissioner Hal Wootten for the Royal Commission into Aboriginal Deaths in Custody. Some state governments have formally apologised and so too has the Northern Territory government for its part in this sinister history.

In May 1997, the Australian Reconciliation Convention, under the chairmanship of former Catholic priest and Aboriginal leader Pat Dodson, was attended by thousands of Australians and international visitors. It was at this convention that John Howard expressed his views on the Stolen Generations in a furious performance. He slammed the lectern and hectored the audience with a barely comprehensible account of his beliefs: Australians should not be held accountable for events that took place in the past. Privately, he and his advisers, his supporters writing in *Quadrant,* and the now ageing adoptive parents and bureaucrats involved in the policy, labelled them 'the rescued generations'.

The revelations that unknown numbers, perhaps tens of thousands, of children were removed, and the direct evidence of the survivors, who number about 13 000, of the sometimes extreme physical and sexual abuse at the hands of adoptive and foster families and employers (to whom some were indentured or enslaved), led to several court cases, including the unsuccessful Cubillo and Gunner case and the successful case in 2007 brought by Bruce Trevorrow in Victoria. Trevorrow was awarded $775 000. The survivors have argued that the federal government should establish a compensation fund and apologise to them. It is a great shame that the advocates for the Stolen Generations have not spelt out the justification for this. There is a case for compensation, and especially for a government fund rather than a case-by-case consideration by the courts.

From 1996 until it lost government in 2007, the Howard Government refused to apologise on the grounds that it would establish the grounds for financial compensation. Unfortunately, Kevin Rudd's Government has also ruled out setting up a fund for the victims. There can be no good reason for denying the right to compensation to these people. The usual suspects, such as the incompetents in the Queensland government involved in the Aurukun race case, will argue on shoddy logical, and even worse moral, grounds that it will not be possible to remove Aboriginal children at risk from dangerous family situations if an apology to the stolen children is made. This argument is a peculiar form of racism: somehow it manages to convey the racist message that it's OK to remove children from their Aboriginal families when they are not at risk, in order to racially purify the great White Australia, but it is not okay to remove children at risk in Aboriginal families. Refusing, in this perverse way, to remove children at risk is a cowardly attack on Aboriginal people because they have objected successfully to the former policy of destroying us as a people through enforced removals. It is an attack on the Aboriginal leadership who argued the case, but, like well-known methods of torture, the attack is directed at the innocent—in this case children at risk—to 'teach' the Aboriginal leadership a lesson for bringing White Australia into disrepute over the issue of the Stolen Generations. That this was found to be genocide is regarded widely, for instance among the followers of Howard and Abbott, as a disgraceful misrepresentation of the nation, and it is this issue—more than any other—that inspired Howard's vengeful 12-year reign of terror against us. In this way, the culture wars are as responsible for the terrible fate of so many Aboriginal children as are racism or neglect.

The courts have a role to play in the compensation question, although the courts are not always successful at assessing Aboriginal evidence. I remain, years after the decision in the Cubillo and Gunner case, disgusted that a judge could reason that a young, frightened, illiterate Aboriginal mother's thumbprint taken by a government officer could necessarily be voluntary. What is the point of years of heartache when the government could admit, and there is more than enough evidence for such an admission, that the inheritance of the victims was denied by their removal? The denial of that inheritance is the key to their suffering and the correct grounds for compensating them. Some people say that it would be better to have been killed than to lose a sense of self and suffer alienation and anomie for the rest of one's life. As well as this, they were denied their material inheritance. Jews whose possessions were confiscated by the Third Reich have had property, including bank accounts, land, houses and art works returned, but the records were available in this case. Without records, the problem for Australian victims of the race-based child removal could be tricky for the courts, and for those contemplating this course of action.

I contend that the apology and the establishment of a compensation fund are necessary to enable us to move to the next task, that of economic reform and building social capital. There cannot be an Aboriginal person alive today who was not tragically touched in some way, directly or indirectly, by these policies. Without an apology to the Stolen Generations, the co-operation of thousands of Aboriginal people will not be forthcoming. This is because of the impact of the policy of removing Aboriginal children on several generations. The evidence is the lateral violence that is now endemic in Aboriginal communities, to which I will return.

Inevitably, Kevin Rudd's words on Aboriginal matters will be compared with Paul Keating's Redfern speech, a rare act of leadership in interpreting our history.

At Redfern Park in Sydney on 10 December 1992, one of the most famous speeches in Australian history was delivered by the then Prime Minister of Australia, Paul Keating. Keating is credited with bringing the dispossession and marginalisation of Aboriginal people to the forefront of the Australian imagination with the powerful message he delivered at the launch of Australia's celebration of the 1993 United Nations International Year of the World's Indigenous People. He traversed the terrible history of Australia's treatment of Aboriginal people, the need for reconciliation, the Aboriginal deaths in custody, the then very recent High Court decision recognising Aboriginal native title that had survived the British declaration of sovereignty. The venue—Redfern—was significant because of the high proportion of Aboriginal people in the suburb's population and their troubled history as an impoverished and despised minority in the city of Sydney. Keating asked Australians 'to try to imagine the Aboriginal view'. He said,

> There is one thing today we cannot imagine. We cannot imagine that the descendants of people whose genius and resilience maintained a culture here through 50,000 years or more, through cataclysmic changes to the climate and environment, and who then survived two

centuries of dispossession and abuse, will be denied their place in the modern Australian nation.

He argued that the test of Australia's nationhood—'a first-rate social democracy, that we are what we should be—truly the land of the fair go and the better chance'—would be whether or not 'we have . . . managed to extend opportunity and care, dignity and hope to the indigenous people of Australia—the Aboriginal and Torres Strait Island people'.

Most Australians recognise these lines from that speech:

> We took the traditional lands and smashed the traditional way of life. We brought the disasters. The alcohol. We committed the murders. We took the children from their mothers. We practised discrimination and exclusion.
>
> It was our ignorance and our prejudice. And our failure to imagine these things being done to us. With some noble exceptions, we failed to make the most basic human response and enter into their hearts and minds. We failed to ask—how would I feel if this were done to me?

Can Kevin Rudd imagine these things done to us, and still being done to us?

Prime Minister Rudd will also remember that I was a senior member of the Queensland Public Service seconded to his inter-departmental committee in Cabinet on Aboriginal land rights, and that Noel Pearson was a consultant on this issue. Frank Brennan has written a fairly clinical account of the Machiavellian campaign to minimise the recognition of Aboriginal land rights in Queensland, and although Father Brennan was not privy to the nasty games as Noel and I were, and unaware of much of the treachery involved, he gives some hints as to how the Queensland government set out to hinder the success of the impending High Court decision in the Mabo case, which was expected within the year. Wayne Goss set out to deliver 'land rights as minimalist as a dot painting'.

My memories of that experience are seared into my being: they are not pleasant, but I am prepared to give Rudd the benefit of doubt, and hope that he has the courage to depart from the ways of the Howard regime with honour and forthrightness.

How would he fix a few of the fundamentals in Indigenous affairs and make settler Australians comfortable with an explicit approach to Aboriginal poverty and misery in the midst of smugness and wealth? How does he intend to pull this off—appearing to be a good Christian reaching out to *les misérables*, free of the race-hate wielded with callous deliberation and deviousness by Howard's regime, demonstrating his social-democratic credentials by achieving some actual results for the betterment of Aboriginal Australians? His Christian discipline will be a handy part of his strategy in finding the right mix of practical and symbolic policy initiatives that acknowledge our situation as a burden of history while also confronting the self-inflicted aspects of poverty and social dysfunction that have transformed poverty and racial exclusion into violent self destruction.

Rudd will remember the culture wars, perhaps not as keenly as I do, but there is a lesson for both of us in reviewing the debates as they pertain to the present conditions of Aboriginal people. First, Rudd's advisers will be incapable of sharing one important fact with him about the present state of affairs. A growing number of highly educated and cynical Aboriginal people will not tolerate being managed into silence and fear. The left, and the apparatchiks of his party, like to believe that Howard's regime cornered us and reduced us to passivity. They are wrong. Howard's regime debilitated our social and economic capital and the political structures that might have enabled us to participate more effectively, but we were not silenced and we were not passive. Indeed, the lessons of the Howard years have served to make us very keenly aware of how we have been economically and politically marginalised throughout Australian history. The most painful lesson was the complicity of state and territory Labor governments in the crippling of our families, communities, businesses and institutions.

Many Aboriginal people, especially those without a special sinecure in government circles, have developed a fine analytical sense with regard to the Orwellian double-speak from both the left and the right, and this too is one of the features of the new Aboriginal intellectual and professional ranks which Rudd's advisers and ministry would know little about. The special place to which Aboriginal people are relegated in the Australian imagination—as a class of political mendicants, as Noel Pearson has hinted—is greatly resented by those Aboriginal people with a larger sense of what we deserve and what we are capable of.

Some want a special representative body, while others want to be free—socially, politically, and legally—to carve out that special place we could hold as the inheritors of the ancient legacy of being Aboriginal, but playing a role in a modern society as entrepreneurs, professionals, tradespeople, artists and hunters and gatherers.

Having that freedom means that some ideas about us must change radically, and Rudd's most difficult challenge will be, just as it was for former Prime Minister Paul Keating, to contend with the most difficult ideas from history, the hatred and self-serving racism, and to hold out the idea of Aboriginal people as full citizens of this young nation, different and distinctive, but as entitled to equality, the freedoms and opportunities, as any other Australians.

Paul Keating had a glimpse of that dream and he was able to articulate it. He also worked hard to see its realisation. He failed in some respects, and we failed too, unable ourselves to see the dream and to transform our own lives to its shape. Rudd has the opportunity to pick up Keating's baton and run with us in the next relay. Who will run with him? He will find extraordinary Aboriginal people on his team if he is able to overcome the habits of racial abuse, cynicism and managing the Aborigines as if we were social-work cases—such habits as currently constitute the arsenal of political tactics among both the right and the left.

The prime minister has expressed his horror at one of the most shocking cases of child abuse reported in the media—the Aurukun tragedy—and he is presumably well aware of the warning from Noel Pearson, myself and a few others that this case is the tip of the iceberg. One of the intellectual muddles that we inherit from the culture wars concerns the responsibility to protect children from danger: should child-protection officers remove children from families where they face the risk of abuse? The argument has been touted by child-protection officers involved in the Aurukun case that Aboriginal children should not be removed from their communities because, first, they have a responsibility to avoid creating another Stolen Generation, and second, if removed, the children will be denied their 'cultural and spiritual' legacy. As a practising Christian, Kevin Rudd will have his own view of what should be classified as 'spiritual' and what should not. Unfortunately, the social workers who allowed the victim in the Aurukun case to be returned to the place of the crimes against her, and the officers who fail to remove children from dangerous situations on the grounds of another Stolen Generation, do not have the same clarity of mind.

If we focus on the needs of these children, and secondly on the needs of their abusers, we begin to see the difficulty of the challenge: how to transform the present Aboriginal society, so full of potential and yet so degraded by poverty, alcohol and anomie, into the habitus of happy, healthy, active, educated people who should partake of both their Aboriginal traditions and the material and social wealth of the modern nation.

To focus on the needs of children means, necessarily, to look again at the Aboriginal family, not through the lens of race-hatred that led to the policies of removing children to bring about the demise of the 'race', but through the lens of social opportunity. The literature on development, and indeed some recent publications in Australia, noticeably Noel Pearson's work and that of Michael Dillon and Neil Westbury in *Beyond Humbug*, shows that the same institutional environments that exist in the poorest and most underdeveloped places in the world exist in Australia. Dillon and Westbury use the term 'failed state' in their examination of state, territory and federal incompetence in developing and managing political and administrative responses to the peculiar conditions in the poorest Aboriginal communities.

Developing institutions and opportunities for Aboriginal citizens will mean the end of the old protectionist and assimilationist thinking, much of which had little to do with human development and everything to do with incarceration and humiliation. Land titles, permit systems, Aboriginal non-government organisations, all will require rethinking and rebuilding in order to allow Aboriginal social and economic development. Just as the Howard regime refused to apologise to the Stolen Generations, it also refused to come to terms with the special dilemma of Aboriginal difference arising from our ancient links to this continent and need to find a place in modern Australia. Hence the bully-boy tactics, the tearing down of institutions and legal rights, and the failure to replace them with anything workable.

It is crucially important for the future of the children to cast a cold, objective eye over Aboriginal society. With Howard and his class of haters on the sidelines, it will be possible to do so. It need not be the case that every aspect of Aboriginal tradition is defended as worth retaining, in a Manichean struggle with racist ideology. Rather, we should be able to rationally and calmly consider the potential benefits that might flow from shortening the funeral 'sorry camp' periods of confinement, or limiting the impact of traditions such as 'house-cursing'. There are those who cling to a view of what Aboriginal society ought to be, argued generally and vaguely with respect to cultural values, and who are completely oblivious to what it is happening now, most particularly how Aboriginal culture and society have changed, are changing and what the implications of those changes are. Such people ignore the much-weakened hold of cultural values and, subsequently, norms of social behaviour, and the descent into anarchy and lawlessness. Appeals to Aboriginal culture are unable to prevent this. Without denying that there are many aspects of Aboriginal culture that are crucial to the maintenance of healthy norms, such as the kinship system and the bonds it creates, the fundamental problem with the appeal to recognise Aboriginal culture—when this is used to deflect attention away from lawlessness and criminality or, sadly, as a kind of displacement activity that serves to uphold a fragile identity—is that the evidence has been mounting for three decades that even the most stalwart upholders of Aboriginal laws feel powerless to deal with new plagues of alcohol and drug abuse.

Moreover, even senior Aboriginal people who cling to a largely imaginary past find some solace in the belief that Aboriginal society was peaceful. Common sense should tell us that this was not the case. How could Aboriginal tribes hold out for so long against the marauding settler enemies if not with extreme violence? The sexual abuse and assaults in Aboriginal communities, and the general violence, are the result not simply of the traditions of violence in Aboriginal society, but, more to the point, of the terrible violence inflicted on Aboriginal people by colonial officers, police, missionaries and the general citizenry in the long orgy of race-hatred. The result is not an uprising of angry Aboriginal people against their oppressors, but lateral violence, violence committed against our own. This is why children suffer so much: they cannot escape the bursts of fury and rage that erupt on a nightly basis. They cannot escape the sexual violence and sexualisation of their world. This is the most insidious aspect of this lateral violence.

Let's look at some of the evidence that the sexualisation of Aboriginal children, associated with acts of sexual assault and abuse by adults and other children, begins at a very early age. The Northern Territory health department found about 91 per cent of gonorrhoea notifications between January and June 2007 were among Aboriginal people—forty times the non-Aboriginal rate. Between January and June 2007, forty-one cases each of gonorrhoea and chlamydia in children under fifteen, including one case of each in children under five, was reported by the department. The figures rise significantly for young adults, with 498 recorded cases of gonorrhoea between the ages of fifteen and twenty-four. There were also 347 cases of chlamydia and thirty-eight cases of syphilis between the ages of fifteen and nineteen.

The Queensland health department is more reticent to share health data with the public, but I warrant that the results, if they were released, would be much worse in that jurisdiction.

Sending incompetent social workers and lazy legal officers into this situation is worse than pointless; it exacerbates these dreadful circumstances because the *laissez-faire* tolerance of lawlessness in the name of political correctness permits grossly illegal acts to meet with a blind eye. The mental anguish caused by lateral violence is trans-generational and must be confronted by its victims. There is a role for police, and even for competent social workers, but the hard work must be done by the neglectful parents, the addicted gamblers and drug users, the drunk and indigent, whose sense of self and responsibility towards others has been degraded by their own actions. This is not to say that all Aboriginal people live in these circumstances or even accept such conditions; on the contrary, there are hundreds of Aboriginal business people and professionals, as I have said earlier, who want to be successful. There are many more working as teachers, nurses, carers and volunteers, tackling these problems but always talking about the never-ending 'band-aid' industry. Most Aboriginal people who have left behind the poverty, segregation and harsh confines of administered settlements and missions understand the freedom and opportunity that education, employment and enterprise offer. Economic reform, diversification of land titles, microfinance models, enterprise hubs and hot-housing, employment programs, rapid training: all are essential to release the choke-hold of the politically correct who want the Dreamtime preserved in political formaldehyde.

The transition from the marginalised postcolonial Aboriginal special administered settlements, epitomised by Aurukun or Wadeye, to the inter-connected nodes of modern globalism that Aboriginal communities, businesses and institutions could become, is occurring at a furious pace, just as economic change in China has. It cannot be stopped, and it can barely be shaped and directed. The need for clear rational intellectual and policy effort has never been greater. This is more important than Australian Labor Party managerialism, which will produce resentment and resistance. This is more important than the social-worker approach, which relegates us to a case-file and denies our agency and responsibility. This is the heart of Kevin Rudd's responsibility as leader of the nation—to support and encourage clear, empirical thinking and to demand change.

This piece was first published in Dear Mr Rudd: Ideas for a Better Australia, *edited by Robert Manne, Black Inc Agenda.*

Nicolas Rothwell

Indigenous insiders chart an end to victimhood
The Australian Literary Review, September 2008

Gradually, persistently, over the past decade a revolution has been pushed through in our understanding of remote Aboriginal Australia and its many difficulties. It is a revolution that came from deep roots and had many participants. It was based on engaged, heartfelt observation and clear, precise analysis. Above all, it broke the colonial flow of ideas: it was the first shift in our picture of the traditional Aboriginal domain achieved and disseminated by Indigenous intellectuals.

This revolution placed alcohol fair and square at the heart of the present-day Indigenous crisis, as cause, not mere attendant symptom. It identified the controlling vice of passive welfare as the poison rotting away Aboriginal communities. Paradoxically, with these two bleak conclusions, which have been derided and resisted by many critics, black and white, it restored a degree of power and potential to Indigenous people and gave an explanation of their failure, under the conditions of seeming freedom they now enjoy, to thrive.

Marcia Langton and Noel Pearson, the originators of these ideas, were viewed, throughout their early, tumultuous years on the political stage as radical activists, if ones of a particularly able, driven kind, burning with a desire to win land rights and obtain recognition for Aboriginal native title. They were campaigners, possessed of fierce devotion to their cause. But there was always a broader, more questioning aspect to their immersion in the thought-codes used by mainstream Australians to describe and administer the protean, elusive, unruly Aboriginal world.

Langton and Pearson were highly suspicious of the welfare paradigm, the broad set of remedial prescriptions endorsed and pursued by politicians and academics, by engaged, reconciliation-minded idealists and community workers. The belief in welfare as a panacea for Indigenous ills stemmed, as a matter of logic, from the plain truth that remote communities were plunged in poverty and so needed assistance if they were to aspire to Western standards of life. Large, creative programs to direct and encourage this brand of social engineering spread across Indigenous Australia. Money, and the commodities it buys and appetites it feeds, swept in but economic advancement stubbornly failed to materialise. It was only a short while into the welfare era that an urgent quest for a revised model began: work-for-the-dole programs, more purposive, culturally fitting forms of occupation were trialled, and all required their administrative teams.

Welfare had been conceived as a form of balancing aid to make up for pain, displacement and social trauma. It went hard against the grain to imagine that this seemingly benign force could itself be a destructive poison in the lifeblood of remote Aboriginal communities, or that it could be linked to the tide of alcoholism and drug abuse that has been swamping the Indigenous domain for years. But Langton and Pearson, in their separate ways, found themselves forced to sift the evidence: they made deductions, developed their ideas and then launched a protracted campaign of persuasion. It was one that played out against the wreckage of the traditional Aboriginal world and against a prolonged, carefully preserved discretion among the mainstream intelligentsia about this plight—a problematic discretion, for if we are unable to describe the circumstances of our Aboriginal fellow citizens with a degree of accuracy and candour, there is scant hope of helping them escape their present difficulties.

That pervasive culture of silence has been broken, in significant part through the words of Langton and Pearson, and through their key texts, among the most resonant, accusatory pamphlets and public broadsides of our time. Step by step, their campaign, which has evolved and taken new forms to suit new circumstances, has succeeded in building a coalition of supporters across conventional party lines, and in creating the climate for radical change in the management of that strangely designated field, Indigenous affairs. They have not only highlighted the appalling conditions in remote communities, they have succeeded in providing a new understanding of the causes of the crisis, and from that diagnosis flows a new set of prescriptions for action. The most obvious signal that this new thinking had hit home came, of course, in an abrupt stroke, just before midday on 21 June 2007, when the then Prime Minister, John Howard, and his Minister for Indigenous Affairs, Mal Brough, launched their 'emergency response': the intervention into remote Aboriginal communities across the Northern Territory.

But even before the intervention, the fresh portrait of the Aboriginal landscape sketched by Langton and Pearson had begun to exert a strong influence on public policy: shared responsibility agreements and regional partnerships were among its early, unripe fruits. The detailed provisions of the Howard intervention are now under review by the Rudd Government: but it is clear the underlying shifts in thinking will remain.

The deep background to this crusade is illustrative. In its beginnings and its inputs, its spread and slow success, it shines a light on the landscape of ideas in this country, on the field of interracial understanding and on the fraught arena in which Aboriginal and non-Aboriginal Australians play out symbolic roles for each other. It is also a tale of almost intuitive breakthroughs in our comprehension of how disadvantaged societies work—and it is an intriguing detail that those breakthroughs were made not by the cluster of outside scrutineers, but by figures implicated directly in the realm under threat.

Reconstructing the thought-world of the decades before one's own is always a tricky task, and in Australia, where the achievements of the previous generation are routinely consigned to the flames, it becomes doubly difficult. It was in the 1960s, a time of grand designs, when Aboriginal affairs were rather less central to the nation and less coated in despondency that were sown the seeds of the present social landscape in the bush. The passage of the 1967 referendum, which embraced Aboriginal people as equals under the Constitution, coincided with a period of vast disruption in remote central and northern Australia. The equal wages ruling in the cattle industry in 1965 had the paradoxical result of ending, almost overnight, the large-scale employment of Aboriginal stockmen. Those stockmen, most of them skilled, proud men in the prime of their working lives, moved to little settlements and newly established communities with their wives, children and other dependants: there was no alternative wage-based economy for them to fall back on. Reliance on a system of welfare payments became entrenched. Soon the land rights age dawned in the Northern Territory; many Indigenous groups thus found themselves land-rich and job-poor, with fledgling representative councils set above them staffed by politically committed experts and campaigners from urban backgrounds. Much about today's institution-choked Aboriginal landscape stems from those days, when Indigenous people became of interest to academe, when Aboriginal protest movements gained a critical mass and the left took up and identified strongly with their fight. A generation of young, idealistic Australians gave themselves to the Aboriginal movement and many of them have since spent their working lives in the remote world, engaged in a twisting, continually metamorphosing journey of struggle, making up a kind of informal, self-perpetuating civil service cadre dedicated to the cause of Aboriginality.

Several competing templates for conceiving the Indigenous future were circulating in those foundation years. The dominant minister with responsibility for Aboriginal affairs in the 1960s conservative government, WC Wentworth, much admired the economic ideas of Peter Bauer, an expert on development aid projects in West Africa. Bauer had made the terrifying discovery that foreign aid, in the post-colonial context, tended to breed corruption and dictatorial politics, and that intentions, in the field of development, were no guarantee of results. This led him to a broad and principled scepticism about welfare: he went on to become one of Margaret Thatcher's intellectual gurus.

By contrast, Labor politicians were receptive to the ideas of another economist, HC 'Nugget' Coombs, whose guidance in the Whitlam era helped determine the land-rights regime in the north. Coombs believed that communal tenure was essential for the preservation of Aboriginal life-ways—and who knows, perhaps his core instinct was right and it was only through this land-based retention of group identity that the tides of modern assimilation have been resisted. It is certainly a policy that has formed the landscape, and collective title remains at the heart of remote Indigenous society today.

In her days as a young researcher, Marcia Langton was much influenced by Coombs, as she was by two other prominent mid-century Australian intellectuals: anthropologist WEH Stanner and archaeologist John Mulvaney. These figures had a strong sense of their duty as thinkers articulating ideas for the broad public and there was a pronounced moral component to their engagement with the world of policy and debate. By the late 1980s, Langton, for all her fervent activism, had absorbed a wide range of idea streams from different traditions and perspectives regarding her people and their place in Australian life. She had worked for the Central Land Council as a land claims anthropologist and she knew the structures of government bureaucracy. Above all, she knew the grassroots: she had been raised in south-central Queensland, in the wide, haunting brigalow country, which still brings thoughts about the vanished Aboriginal past to mind.

Langton took a post with one of the endless succession of landmark inquiry commissions that seem to measure out the record of our progress in Indigenous affairs. This was the 1989 royal commission into Aboriginal deaths in custody, headed by Elliott Johnston, QC. Its report did much to convey to the broader nation the depth of the grief and chaos hanging over the remote reaches of the continent. Langton and her assistants in the grandly named Northern Territory Aboriginal Issues Unit wrote a special annex for the commission: it appeared as Appendix D(I): 'Too much sorry business'. At its heart were strictures about alcohol. It was written in words of fire that, almost two decades on, ring with the disturbing tone of fulfilled prophecy. In perfect 20-20 vision, it predicted the future of remote Aboriginal Australia. Had the recommendations of that appendix been implemented by the Country Liberal Party government of the Northern Territory at the time, we almost certainly would not be quite where we are today, with a civilisational crisis on our hands so grave the survival of remote Aboriginal society is in doubt.

Langton conceded that the standard factors routinely adduced by Western experts did form part of the picture in leading to custodial deaths: poverty, dispossession, lack of education and so on. She then wrote that 'from an Aboriginal perspective and from the Aboriginal experience alcohol plays a primary role in both the reasons for detention and for the subsequent chances of deaths occurring', and she went on to argue that alcohol was, in the Indigenous realm, a drug of dependency. It was the alcohol that needed to be controlled, in order to set drinkers free. But this idea ran counter to the universalist claim that everyone had basic rights and should be treated equally, and those rights included the right to drink, a right that had been denied Aboriginal people in the bush for much of the mid-twentieth century. Langton's argument, which provoked a storm of hostility from health and social-affairs experts, was based on bitter, plentiful remote-community experience: she knew it not just because she had seen it, but because it was affecting her own people. She felt bolstered, too, in her diagnosis by an odd, fluent submission, sent to the inquiry by a senior traditional man from Cape York, who has since died. Langton asked about this submission: it had been written, it turned out, with the help of Noel Pearson from Hope Vale, then a very young trainee lawyer, whom Langton had met, briefly, once. This was the start of a close intellectual alliance, with influences running both ways.

Soon after the release of 'Too much sorry business' Langton moved to Cairns, where Pearson was setting up the Cape York Land Council. A certain insight into this meeting of minds that has done so much to reshape Aboriginal policy was given by Langton in a pivotal lecture, delivered for the radical literary journal *Overland* in autumn 2002. She looked back a decade, and more; she sketched her impressions of the young Pearson; she gave a rather memorable cameo of her subject listening to hard-core black rap in his student quarters at the University of Sydney, before she moved to her main theme: an excoriation of the Australian left for its failure to speak out on the true conditions of Aboriginal life and its preference for airy, symbolic issues. This was not a turn to the right, or anything remotely so crude: Langton remains in many respects a pure Aboriginal rights campaigner, with a strong sense that race and racialised thinking are key features of the Australian landscape. No, she had decided to articulate a distinctly Aboriginal, rather than ideological, set of priorities. She had reached the view that being used, and owned, by the left as a moral weapon was a kind of trap. She was aware, as only an urban-based bush Aborigine can be, of the way Indigenous causes serve the psychological needs of the progressive class. (This was very much a distinguishing trait of the Howard era, when the cause of reconciliation and the desire for a Stolen Generations apology became markers of enlightened social outlook.)

At the time of this lecture, Langton had recently accepted a professorial post at the University of Melbourne: it was a period when she was spreading her wings and taking her distance from the bruising, male-dominated world of Aboriginal politics. She also began publishing a series of majestic essays on Indigenous art, explored through her particular perspective as an intellectual sunk in the field of aesthetic studies, and as an Aboriginal woman conscious of all the order and tradition that she felt shimmering in her blood. Her style, in those years, underwent an intriguing evolution: it took on a rich, almost Augustan roll and confidence and yet it was bush-accented and brisk, and there was another register lurking inside her words as well, a kind of reverential involvement in the intricacies of desert and Arnhem Land traditions, a tone so grand it seemed to match the sweeps of ceremonial belief it described and conjured up.

These shifts in Langton's life and thought and writing were matched by developments on Cape York: Pearson was moving fast to establish a network of social reform projects. Even as he commanded the national headlines, negotiating with Canberra to determine the new native title regime, on the local scale he was recasting the traditional role of the land council, exploring co-operative schemes with the private sector, attempting to find a new pattern for his people and for the whole region. He had become the master of his own traditional languages, his sense of place was strong. Pearson is a private figure, with a firm conviction of his own worth and a desire to be the author not just of his fate, but of his own image, and so the crucial influences operating on him remain opaque. But the strong Lutheran strain in his background at Hope Vale is clear, as is his fascination with English common law, a coded system he deploys with a fluid grace. He loves the essay form, and the testing and pursuit of logical arguments in written words and, unusually among Indigenous intellectuals, he takes all human experience, rather than his own ethnic subset of it, as his legitimate subject and as a model for his work. Thus he is an enthusiast of Indian economist-philosopher Amartya Sen, whose notion of layered identities appeals to him; like another of his overseas heroes, Barack Obama, he knows well how to exploit his position and prominence on the political stage. But above all Pearson deals in pure ideas, he believes in their power, and their power to convince, he lives the life of the mind—and this makes him, in the context of Aboriginal far north Queensland, one of the loneliest, most self-sustaining intellectuals on the surface of the earth. His remoteness from fad and fashion has its benefits, as well as its costs.

Once he had based himself definitively in his home country, Pearson began reflecting on the drinking culture he saw around him; he ranged widely in his research, but his core insights were personal. He remembered the old Hope Vale, and could see what had happened to it; he knew the Cape's various communities and the bizarre drinking canteen system operated in them with the approval of the Queensland government. They were the grim laboratories in which patterns of alcohol dependency could be watched: theory became clothed in human flesh. Pearson assembled his thoughts: word of his work began to spread.

At which point, for a moment, the focus should widen: for this story, even though it traces a set of Indigenous breakthroughs, involves the wider world. There is a further cast of characters, who were themselves moving towards the analysis Langton and Pearson had reached, men and women who worked with them, anthropologists and land council researchers, social scientists, even politicians and priests.

At about this time, in the late 1990s, the spring time of the Howard era, I had become caught up in the landscapes and the writing of north Australia. I was travelling extensively across that region and turning my thoughts to the life ways of remote communities. In the course of these journeys, I would often cross the path of John Herron, the newly appointed federal minister for Indigenous affairs. Herron was already in his late sixties when he accepted this contentious post. He was a distinguished surgeon; he had done volunteer work in Rwanda during the aftermath of the genocide. He proved to be one of the most appealing men I have encountered in politics.

Herron actually liked bush Aboriginal people and spent much of his term in the ministry fighting to have the Aboriginal and Torres Strait Islander Council budget redirected towards remote communities. He had ten children, itself an impressive credential in the Aboriginal domain. His biography was intriguingly dark: he came from a hard-scrabble Irish background in far north Queensland and went through a roving phase in his teenage years, jumping the rattlers, scouring the silent western corners of the state, until an impulse brought him to walk conventional paths.

But not that conventional: he read, and was much influenced by Luke Rhinehart's 1970s cult novel, *The Dice Man*, and lived his life, for some while, under the guidance of its alarming precepts. When he was a successful young doctor, he came home from work one day and saw his home spontaneously ignite in front of his eyes. This episode left him permanently opposed to possessions or ownership of any kind: when we travelled together, I could not help noticing that he only ever carried one spare shirt and a single pair of socks, and he washed them himself each night. Herron was in no doubt about the factor that lay behind the travails of remote Indigenous communities—it was drink.

His essentially medical understanding of the crisis in the bush and his insistent presentation of that view to his ministerial colleagues and to the higher reaches of the bureaucracy did much to pave the way for new policy thinking in the last years of the Howard Government. Dry, confiding, languishingly witty, he would regale those travelling with him with wild tales from the world of Indigenous politics, and one of those anecdotes in particular stayed in my mind: it concerned his vague attempt, at the outset of his term, to interest Pearson in the chairmanship of ATSIC—a conjuncture that would have sent shock waves through the political scene in those days, when Pearson seemed a Labor-flavoured man and was even spoken of as a possible ALP Senate candidate.

'Absolutely', said Herron, 'You should catch up with David Byrne, and talk to him about all that: he knows the story'.

There was a pause. The ministerial plane's engines droned on high above the red dunes of the western desert.

'You mean the singer from the Talking Heads?'

'Well, I like the Talking Heads', Herron said, 'very much. But actually I was thinking of David Byrne from the Cape York Land Council'.

Two weeks later, after a drive down rough dirt roads on through the back blocks of the Atherton Tableland, I pulled up near the ghost town of Topaz. Before me was a wide green paddock. Mt Bartle Frere, cloud-flecked, loomed close by. A house, or rather an exiguous shack with a tiny veranda, stood in the distance. Inside it I found a tall, solemn man, with a slightly lugubrious expression, clutching a farming journal in one hand. Byrne, by that stage in his eventful life, had already been an Augustinian monk and the youngest Liberal member of the Queensland parliament; he had lived in the scenic community of Bamaga at the very tip of Cape York; he had been a vital backroom figure in the land council and had served as Pearson's intellectual sparring partner. Now, though, he was devoting himself to his extensive herd of cattle, brahmans, each one of which he knew personally. He controlled their movements, as if by magic, through the simple expedient of stretching out his arm and creating an imaginary fenceline, which the cows extended in their thoughts and took as real.

After much discussion—cows, and their temperament, which was preferable to that of humans, the availability of attractive dairy farming land, nearby—he got around to Indigenous affairs, sketched the drastic new thinking being done by Pearson, and produced a dog-eared document. I leafed through: it was a faint photocopy: maybe eighty pages in total, densely argued. It was an early version of Our Right to Take Responsibility, a soaring, intense text that set out Pearson's first conclusions on drink, dependency, the welfare culture and their many connections. I pocketed it, or tried to.

'Hang on', Byrne said. 'I didn't say you could have it. You can read it, though, here, and make notes, if you like.'

For a couple of hours, I sat there, transcribing the document in shorthand, and perhaps it was because of that unusually concentrated immersion in Pearson's thought-world that the thrust of his interweaving arguments, their originality and the sparks of genius in them seemed so immediately clear. Pearson's subsequent speeches and lectures, columns and addresses have explored and publicised those notions with such effect that the ideas he was then developing have come to seem almost commonplace: at the time, both they and their concatenation were quite new. Not only did he see the link between the large-scale provision of passive welfare and the erosion of social capital in remote communities, he understood that drinking and drug-taking were best conceptualised as syndromes, or self-perpetuating diseases, rather than symptoms of overarching social ills.

With the subtlest empathy, Pearson had penetrated the mindsets of the drinkers and drug-takers around him. He had not turned away from them, or scorned them, or seen them as helpless victims of their circumstances. He knew them as if from within. His theory of drink and its effects in the Cape York Aboriginal setting had much in common with the 12-step program of Alcoholics Anonymous: it sees alcoholism as a condition that relies on enablers, those who allow or encourage the drinker to drink, and those who simply fail to understand the impossibility of social drinking for an alcoholic. Pearson had expanded that insight to the world of Aboriginal remote communities. State policies that condoned or even encouraged drinking were enabling policies. More than that, the passive welfare system had much in common with enabling. Pearson had here reached one of his core insights: not only passive welfare schemes, but the agencies committed to delivering them, were among the key problems that his people, and all across Indigenous Australia, now faced.

This quick X-ray simplifies Pearson's thought flow to the point of near caricature: he includes, as if in multiple overlay, historical, geographic and traditional patterns in his analysis. But at its heart there is a tense, urgent causal chain being identified, one that has proved deeply unwelcome to the bureaucracy, which fitfully resists its conclusions to this day. It is no longer an isolated view: historian John Hirst, a clear, disturbing voice on Indigenous affairs during the past fifteen years, has moved, step by step, towards the same position: 'Every aspect of Aboriginal society (taken to be) dysfunctional has been supported, encouraged and protected', he concluded recently, 'by those Europeans who deal with Aborigines in some official capacity'. This can be distilled further, almost to a syllogism: for if one foregrounds the thought that autonomy is critical, it follows that social programs cannot produce what a healthy community needs: self-control, order and good morale. 'The longer the list of programs, the more it presages failure': Hirst's formula is so accusing and terrifying it seems to hunt one down.

Almost at the same time Pearson began presenting his ideas in speeches and small seminars, a startling paper by one of the country's most brilliant anthropologists was doing the rounds. The Politics of Suffering: Indigenous Policy in Australia Since the 1970s, was a detailed, impassioned lecture-text, delivered before the Australian Anthropological Society by Peter Sutton in September 2000. News of its content filtered out slowly: Sutton, one heard, had gone over the top, his personal grief at the deaths of his

Aboriginal friends had spilled into his work, he had been close to tears while delivering his *mea culpa* on stage. I had known of Sutton for a while: my dear friend Warren Osmond, former foreign editor of the *Sydney Morning Herald*, now dead, but still present in my thoughts, had been in the same year at a small Christian Science school with Sutton and it must have been a rather elevated classroom, with these young prodigies, dragooned by the austere code of their cerebral faith, duelling for attention and pre-eminence.

Sutton went on to specialise in the ethnography of Cape York, and the Wik people of Aurukun: he collaborated in writing the catalogue for 'Dreamings', the first international exhibition of modern Aboriginal art. He became known not just for his finesse of mind but for his unstinting commitment to the cause of Aboriginal rights. I tracked down *'The Politics of Suffering'* only after long search, months later, in a land council library: it had been filed in the closed area, where confidential materials, sacred songs and images were kept. 'Please, take it away', the librarian said: 'That thing! You can have it!' It was a preprint, slated for some academic journal: it had been covered with reproving comments in red ink. Sutton's paper was indeed emotional: it was a sharp, demolishing attack on the pieties of anthropology and the 'helper' professions. His arguments, subtly spun out, meticulously marshalled, formed a kind of complement to Pearson's views: but they were directed rather at the intellectual group, and the generation, that had conceived the passive welfare trap for remote communities.

Sutton left little intact: he took aim at the 'exhausted 1970s paradigm', the flawed beliefs of Nugget Coombs, the tendency of well-known Aboriginal spokesmen to live their lives far from communities, the underacknowledged plague of domestic violence, the pitfalls and incoherencies of the reconciliation dream. Obfuscations in language, reluctance to hear bad news, the tendency to blame colonial history—he ran through them all. At the Stygian core of Sutton's paper was the idea, which he has since elaborated, that certain patterns within traditional Aboriginal societies may not actually be well designed for the promotion of cultural survival in the modern Australian context. Sutton's thoughts reached, and branched, repeatedly: the paper contained in embryonic form pointers to many of the most critical dilemmas emerging to confront remote Australia today, almost a decade on. Intervention was a word he used often in his text, with a medical sense.

For newspaper reporters then out in the field, attempting to frame what they were routinely seeing—petrol sniffing, family violence, copycat suicide—this document was a key aid: it provided at least the beginnings of a framework, and a liberal intellectual context, and it was, eventually, given a slight quantum of media coverage, in a broadly indifferent environment. It is hard to imagine any anthropologist or administrator reading Sutton's words, or seeing him at the brink of tears on stage at the University of Western Australia when he was delivering them and not being troubled at heart.

Yet 'The Politics of Suffering', a vastly sophisticated document and also a call to arms, was soon pushed from sight. It resonated in the shadows, quietly, while the old guard pursued their researches and complex new kinds of welfare-to-work projects were conceived, and the patterns of chaos in the bush intensified. Herron had left his ministerial post by then, and was busy representing Australia as ambassador to Dublin and the Holy See, and dictating his memoirs—tantalisingly, they have yet to be published. It was the era of Philip Ruddock and Amanda Vanstone, and late Howardism, when ATSIC was being closely scrutinised, and was failing fast. After Mark Latham, in the run-up to the 2004 federal election campaign, declared Labor's opposition to ATSIC's continued existence, it was promptly dismantled. Potent Canberra bureaucrats, who had heard and absorbed the headline components of the Pearson position, began implementing cosmetic reforms to bush social services: a pre-revolutionary atmosphere, tense, like a build-up season sky, mantled the Indigenous policy realm.

By this stage, a new Labor government had come to power in Darwin, after more than a quarter-century of conservative control, and high hopes were invested in its reform program. Prominent bureaucrats came north to help direct the change in course; among them were Mike Dillon and Neil Westbury, who, some years later, after their disillusioned retreat south, co-authored a succinct manifesto on Aboriginal policy. *Beyond Humbug* contained a brisk summation of the state of play in the world of the communities: it concluded that remote Indigenous Australia was a 'failed state' within the greater nation. The view, from high-flyers at the airy apex of the public service, was plain: massive investment and engagement had become necessary. Indeed, structural change was already quietly under way. By the early months of last year, Pearson was deeply involved in preparing a local agenda for the Cape. His ambitious welfare reform project had received federal backing, the first steps were going ahead—it at last began full-scale operation on 1 July in four communities, including Hope Vale.

Pressure had been building for similar steps in the Northern Territory, the Kimberley and desert South Australia. In the Anangu Pitjantjatjara lands, report after report had indicated devastating social meltdown and a rampant drug culture. In the far north Kimberley communities of Kalumburu and Forrest River, sexual abuse and youth suicide were the salient features of the human landscape. But it was the centre, rather than these more inaccessible redoubts, that gained national attention. In Alice Springs, crown prosecutor Nanette Rogers went on television in May 2006 to detail the tide of child sexual abuse cases she had dealt with in the communities and camps around the town.

In all these areas of Aboriginal Australia, the interlock identified by Pearson and Langton was to the fore. Alcohol and drugs were invariably a factor in violence and abuse: passive welfare money paid for the intoxicating substances; the dependency culture, with its slow, empty rhythm, created the anomie that was damped down by the drink and drugs. Faced with the intensely public broadside from Rogers, the Northern Territory government naturally commissioned an inquiry. As is well known, the ensuing document, 'Little Children Are Sacred', confirmed the impression of widespread child abuse. The Northern Territory government under chief minister Clare Martin unconscionably delayed releasing and reacting to the report. Howard and Brough seized the moment, and launched the intervention, which has been so much reported on and analysed in the year since. Troops and medical teams fanned out across the centre and the north to restore a degree of order. A line, deep, and definite, had been drawn.

Perhaps the most striking feature of the federal intervention was the hostility it engendered among broad sections of the intelligentsia, among many Indigenous leaders and even among territory politicians faced with the prospect of an extra billion dollars being spent on their neediest constituents. The negative reaction was sharp, and instinctual: many reasons were given; many others were plain beneath the surface. The money committed, so the critics said, was to be spent haphazardly, and new layers of control were being brought in. Compulsory acquisition of township leases was an outrage; income management an insult; the alcohol bans iniquitous. These new measures were restricting the basic rights of bush Indigenous communities, and, by highlighting a shocking pattern of behaviour, they served to stigmatise all Aboriginal people.

There was much in this vein: Howard and his government had always been disliked by the urban Indigenous world and by the progressive classes for whom reconciliation and an apology were key questions of national life. And much of the critique was quite justified: for the intervention was a rush job, it was broadbrush and uncalibrated, it applied collective sanctions to very varied individuals and communities. But with all its shortcomings, it did have one important consequence: like a thunderclap, it marked the end of the passive welfare age—and this was well understood by many of its most perceptive and determined critics.

Just ninety days after the 'emergency response', the chief intellectual forces arrayed against it released their denunciatory reply. *Coercive Reconciliation*, like most campaign volumes, seems somewhat dated now, with the Howard Government swept away, Labor in control in Canberra and Kevin Rudd and Jenny Macklin clearly disposed to preserve several aspects of the initial intervention. The book, however, tells much about the deep landscape of Aboriginal affairs. It collects a range of essays, by mainstream and Indigenous academics, bureaucrats, lawyers and columnists; and many of its themes were to the fore in the city protest rallies held in the wake of 21 June. A progressive, sharply politicised interpretation of the recent history of Indigenous Australia formed the *basso continuo* of these arguments, which were often covertly targeted against Pearson. I attended a seminar in Darwin at this time, filled with the academic gratin of the Charles Darwin University and the public service class. There were various windy speeches, before a mid-level adviser to the Northern Territory government, Kim Hill, today the director of the Northern Land Council, took the stage: 'I am not Noel Pearson', he began—and the auditorium burst into thunderous applause.

Such was the mindset in those heady days, so short a time ago. But *Coercive Reconciliation* is most intriguing now for the tone that emerges from it in retrospect: it exudes not just anger but a kind of grief, and it is the grief of mourning for the lost paradigm. At the heart of the progressive academy's worldview for the past generation has been an attractive, almost Edenic dream: the idea of the Aboriginal outstation, or homeland—and the future of the homeland movement was very much at the centre of the first intervention diatribes.

Perhaps Jon Altman, the supple, combative director of the Canberra-based Centre for Aboriginal Economic Policy Research, and the co-editor of *Coercive Reconciliation*, best illustrates the depth and appeal of these ideas. Altman works as an economic development expert, but his temperament is artistic: in fact his ideal job might be as an upscale newspaper editor, for he clearly spends a great deal of time reading newspapers and writing tart little letters to them, correcting errors in the reportage of Indigenous affairs. He came to Darwin some years ago; we met on campus, in a frigid research office; he sat very close to me, locked eyes and, for an hour, breathed over me his sweet breath, exuding friendship. So it was something of a surprise, some months later, when I received a rebuking email about a story of mine on a promising new trend in Indigenous job-creation. Wasn't he in favour of Aboriginal economic advancement? I decided to investigate, and what I found was intriguing. I take Altman not to make light of him or falsify him, but because he both marshals and incarnates an important trend in thinking about the Aboriginal domain. He did his doctoral work in the hinterland of Maningrida, a large, troubled coastal community in north Arnhem Land. He remains close to some of the best-known traditional Indigenous artists of the region, chief among them John Mawurndjul. Altman is a proponent of the idea that a 'hybrid economy' can be nurtured in remote Australia, or at least parts of it, based on land use and management, art production, maybe even remedial control of the effects of climate change. Such a life-path would be consistent with the intense ceremonial calendar of Aboriginal people living in the homelands, and there are little pockets of the Top End where something vaguely akin to this model is, at times, lived out.

But this dream relies on vast external inputs and on layers of control and help and management, and at present the broad educational and social landscape of remote communities and their satellite settlements across the face of north and central Australia is decidedly unpromising. The nodal centre of Maningrida, a large multi-tribal township, is often regarded as a showpiece, and its outstations as state of the art. It is in fact a place with grave social problems, which was in the news last year because of an awful gang sexual abuse case. Set against this kind of metropolis, the local homelands shine—but they depend on subsidy, are rain-isolated for much of the year and are less than popular with many young people. Nor is the case clear-cut that Indigenous health is better in such remote outposts, though the claim is often confidently advanced. Whether plausible or implausible in the long-term perspective, the homeland dream, with its weird mix of tribal separatism and zoo-like dependency, has failed, for now, to convince the official echelon of policy. In the late Howard era, plans were afoot to rationalise services to satellite communities and to develop a spoke-and-hub model for the delivery of services into the deep bush—and that preference is still ingrained in the Canberra departments that hold the funding for these settlements in their hands.

Altman and his fellow travellers on the road to the new Eden may have Indigenous backers and allies, but they are the campaigning spokes-people—and here we reach the nub of things.

There's a lot of ventriloquist-like 'speaking for' in Indigenous affairs. Western intellectuals, who know what 'their' traditional subjects think; urban Aboriginal political leaders, who see the Indigenous struggle as a contest for rights and acknowledgement, politicians of all stripes, who wish to 'solve' a problem, to 'close the gap', and whose default settings tend towards a dream of ultimate integration in a harmonious, smoothly levelled world.

Pearson and Langton, by contrast, seek no one's authority: they seek to speak to what they see on the ground, and they believe conditions have to change. In her phosphorescent essay early this year in the *Griffith Review*, Langton bluntly advised opponents of the intervention that 'those who did not see it coming were deluding themselves', and that the time had arrived for dismantling 'the shibboleths of the old Left, who need perpetual victims for their analysis to work'. Hence her focus on fostering direct agreements between mining groups and Indigenous landowners, mediated by grassroots native title representative bodies. Hence Pearson's low-key concentration on the new Family Responsibilities Commission, a Queensland statutory body charged with overseeing the new conditional welfare system he helped create. Hence, too, the support by Langton and Pearson for a plan to provide, with federal government blessing, 50000 Indigenous apprenticeships.

Behind them they leave a transformed landscape and several disturbing questions. During the political and ideological struggles of recent years in this domain, almost the entire Australian intelligentsia, mainstream and Indigenous, tended to highlight complex, near-theological issues such as treaties and reconciliation, native title and representation. But the all-dominating plague of alcohol dependency and the sapping curse of welfarism were constantly swept to the margins of public discussion.

There are obvious reasons for this record: progressive thinkers often accepted the idea that alcohol was the result of disadvantage, a pleasing, almost consoling idea, because disadvantage can be remedied, of course, by such tools as welfare, and if past oppression is the present, hidden cause of trouble, that trouble can be tactfully excused and subtly, constructively, addressed. The enlightened class wished to give no help to their grim conservative adversaries, while the majority of Indigenous intellectuals found themselves unable to 'let down their own side' and talk plainly about the alcoholic syndromes that had trapped their cousins in the bush. And so silence reigned. The spokesmen would not speak. It was left to a pair of Indigenous thinkers to take back power and responsibility.

Naturally there is a tragic aspect to this saga: a generation of well-intentioned figures, whether intellectuals or activists, hands-on community workers or discriminating scholars of Indigenous life-ways, found it their fate to preside over a grinding social crisis that their best efforts failed to solve. Indeed, the Aboriginal societies they wished to help fared worse and worse. This was a spectacular failure of understanding, one that which will stand out clearly in the record of Australian history.

But there is a darker twist. Indigenous societies across Australia today are intensely studied, watched and surveyed. How minutely detailed our surface knowledge of them has become: we operate, in truth, a kind of collective Truman Show. Yet changing the fundamental behaviours of those societies has long seemed an elusive, distant goal—and this may well be precisely because of the mainstream presence there. In today's Australia, there are very few purely Aboriginal spaces left: the frontier is closed, and closed forever. All through the remote Indigenous world there are outside helpers, the enabling army, delivering services, building capacity, looking on through engaged, compassionate, post-colonial eyes. With their art, and their troubles, their spirituality and their mesmerising difference, Aboriginal people in the bush have become ever more necessary to the mainstream. It is a strange dance: as we waltz into the future, a relationship of co-dependency, marked out by the bright ring of racial thinking, controls our fate.

Don Watson

The lives sent down the drain
The Age, 5 July 2008

Until forty or fifty years ago, thousands of Australian children were educated in schools consisting of one room and one teacher. Classes of less than a dozen were common. That the schools were in remote areas did not matter. Australian children had a right to education regardless of where they lived. It was an all but universal principle: education bestowed benefits on individuals and society that easily outweighed the cost of providing it. Among other things, it was the means by which children might escape the poverty of their parents and raise healthier and more adept offspring of their own.

To this end, Australian governments made education free and compulsory, and as the logical proof of their good faith, built and maintained these little rural schools and trained, paid and housed the teachers.

Students did not leave these schools with much command of physics or the classics, but they were numerate and literate. They were not qualified for university. But they could read a newspaper or a book or a summons or a form from the government. They could write a letter or read one from their mothers, prepare an invoice, measure distances, add, subtract, multiply and divide and point to Sydney on a map.

And having these abilities, should they wish, they could further educate themselves, and inevitably they did.

These things are proverbial and we are well past needing to mention them in any conversation about education or 'education revolutions'. But among Aboriginal communities in the Northern Territory, they are for all practical purposes unknown.

Children on Aboriginal homelands grow up unable to do any of the things that eight years in a remote school fifty years ago taught kids to do. At a homeland 250 kilometres west of Gove, the teacher comes three days a week sometimes, and sometimes only two. On the other days, educating the children falls to the Aboriginal assistant teacher who lives with her family next to the school. She is bright and dedicated, but very young and untrained and cannot exercise the authority of a qualified and experienced teacher.

So for half of most school weeks the kids muck about in the grass and dust outside the new school. You can feel their future ebbing away—like the community tank, which has been leaking for two-and-a-half years and empties itself every night. The children have spoken English vocabularies of perhaps fifty words. As each day the rest of Australia's children learn something new and build on what they learnt the hour, the day, the week, the year before, these children learn nothing and have nothing to build on. They play and laugh, and the gap grows wider and hope fades by the minute.

It's not for want of a school. The old school, built with funds from Rotary, is still in good condition, and the new school finished just last year is cool and well-equipped. There's a new house for the teacher, a telephone, television, shower and flushing toilet.

It's not that the parents don't want the kids to go to school, or that the kids don't want to go. The new school was built by the Northern Territory government and opened by the then minister for education because for a while two years ago thirty-seven kids were attending the old one. At the same time, a dozen teenagers and young men were learning trade skills and English in a new workshop funded by Melbourne charities and built by volunteers and the homeland people. Education is what everyone wants on this homeland, and English—they are, they say, 'trapped by the language'.

It's not for want of a teacher. They have a first-rate teacher who receives a full-time salary to teach full-time at the community. And this, she says, is what she wants to do. But, by all reports, the college on Elcho Island responsible for the homeland is primarily concerned with national benchmarks and university entrance standards. No one on the homeland has any chance of doing that. The college has decreed that homeland teachers will spend only five or six days a fortnight in the classroom, and the other days in classroom 'preparation'. We were told that the school principal believes doing more would 'set a precedent'.

While the schoolteacher comes barely half time, the trade teacher no longer comes at all. He was taken away because the college insists that the workshop is not a bona fide educational facility. The young men who were learning skills and English have drifted away to join the wayward, lost and hopeless in the larger centres.

The homeland parents could move to one of these places. The nearest to this homeland is one-and-a-half hours away. There's a school there with teachers present five days a week. Perhaps the federal intervention will force them there eventually. But the parents do not want to go. The homeland is safer and measurably healthier, and in all ways save education, better for children. So much better, parents in the bigger centres send their children to relatives in the homelands.

We might wonder why, if it does not intend to provide teachers, the Northern Territory government builds schools and ministers of education fly out to open them. The answer is, they're not schools. It's a sort of trick, you see. They're community learning centres. And CLCs don't get teachers in the way that schools do.

With two school buildings and playground equipment and kids running around, education is not the first thing to register when you get there. The leaking tank, the overflowing long-drop lavatory that serves two families and the pool of parasite-infested sewage and water between their houses have a more immediate effect on the mind than the absence of any activity in the schoolroom. These things, despite repeated requests, have never been fixed: not by the Northern Territory government departments whose officials were led to them three years ago, not by the Homeland Resource Centre and, so far, not by the federal intervention.

What registers is the almost incomprehensible neglect and incompetence of government, its bizarre bureaucracies and its corrupt contractors. Looking at the putrefaction, hearing the stories and meeting the bureaucrats, it is not education that comes to mind, but cannonballs landing on that grotesque parliament in Darwin.

Without warning, an official from the Homeland Resource Centre drops in from the sky in a plane. Ignoring such futile proprieties as introducing herself to the owners of the land, with her two Yolngu assistants she strides to the schoolroom, there to enrol eligible people for the Community Development Employment Projects. They emerge in the early afternoon, having enrolled eight people. A ninth who, like the others, did not know they were coming, is 120 kilometres away. After the officials have gone, we hear he is walking back in the hope of catching them.

The Homeland Resource Centre official reads to us from a list that purports to show how often the centre has sent tradesmen to repair and maintain the basic services and how often the people of the homeland have wrecked the services. She is determined to add reproof to deprivation: they can't be trusted with tractors or mowers or toilets or machinery of any kind. But very little of her story tallies with voluminous records kept by the community's volunteer organiser or with the memory of the people.

Nor does it tally with the long-drop, the broken septic system or the tank. The truth is that in three years all the resources of the Northern Territory and the Commonwealth and all the employees housed in sleek offices have not been able to dig a hole—to take an auger and dig a hole, or take it and let the local people dig the hole.

The homeland resources person boards her plane. It's not her fault. She is just another cog, one of hundreds, with good will and bad, fecklessly turning in the worthless Northern Territory machine.

This is the machine the federal intervention ought to fix. It has brought to the district a new general manager with energy, goodwill and openness. These communities would not face even half the problems they do if half-a-dozen bureaucrats made up their minds one Monday morning to fix them before the end of the week.

That remains the promise of the intervention—but only just. In the first ten months its officers visited the homeland four times. Once to deliver a summons to a young man charged with driving an unroadworthy car and failing to wear a seatbelt in a town 300 kilometres away that he was— demonstrably—not in at the time. Once to investigate a rumour that the same young man was having sexual relations with a minor—who, as it happens, was at least twenty-three years old. A third time to deliver the summons again. And the fourth, despite the protestations and humiliation of the homeland elders for whom such things are unimaginable, to investigate malicious rumours of child sexual abuse—a crime that no one associated with the homeland in its forty-year history has ever seen a sign of.

Knowing the community well, the visiting nurse did not believe the rumours, but decided to conduct her own examinations and tests. She found no evidence of child abuse or sexually transmitted diseases.

The intervention has conducted 7433 health checks on children in remote Aboriginal communities and has reported 39 at risk of abuse or neglect. Nationally, last year, protection agencies received 310 000 notifications: 58 000 were substantiated.

Thirty-nine is about the same number of children needing to be saved from illiteracy on this one homeland. As one volunteer said, if only the residents had some beer cans (and rum bottles) to throw around, if only the settlement had looked more like bedlam, perhaps the intervention would have stayed to fix the water tank, the septic system and the long-drop. And then, who knows, they might have noticed the kids were not in school and the young men who remained after the trade teacher left had nothing to do.

There's a lot of debate about education in the Northern Territory. In some places they can't get the kids to go to school, so politicians—including the federal minister—talk about forcing the issue by making money or food or work dependent on attendance. Everywhere ideologues and educationists argue about whether they should be taught in their traditional languages or in conjunction with English or in advance of it, or not at all.

Bureaucrats argue about who is responsible for education. A person from a federal body called the Indigenous Co-ordination Centre told us in the boardroom of an elegant new building in Gove that, while the aim of the centre was to see that money got to the 'grassroots', her organisation was not responsible for education. Nor was it responsible for any failings of the Homeland Resource Centre, which means it's not responsible for roads, sanitation, machinery, fuel or food. Nor, although it boasts a health solutions broker, does it give any sign of being responsible for health. So what are you responsible for, we asked? What do you co-ordinate? The 'different buckets of money', we were told. They co-ordinate the buckets and the movement of people between them, it seems, and the impressive thing is that they do it from the new building with the internal security doors and the plasma televisions. Like the health solutions broker we met six months earlier, the ICC person had never seen the grassroots of a homeland.

It seems simple. The Northern Territory government ought to educate these people. Since it is not, the federal government should do it. And if it can't do it, it should outsource it to New Zealand, which seems to hold more strongly to its founding beliefs.

At Gove airport, a bevy of teenage schoolkids and teachers, all of them white, were on their way to walk the Kokoda Trail in Papua New Guinea. Among them was a man who looked very like the former minister for education who less than two years ago opened the new homeland school. He was wearing the same blue T-shirt as all the others with the words 'courage, endurance, mateship'—all the great Australian values—written across the back.

3
The Leadership Question

Paul Kelly

The artless dodger

The Australian, 13 September 2008

It is the politics of the absurd: when Peter Costello wanted the leadership, he found the Liberal Party denied him. But when the party was keen to anoint him, Costello chose his own form of denial. The Liberal Party declined Costello and now Costello has declined the Liberal Party. This saga is a bizarre end to the leadership ambitions of the man widely hailed from the time of his 1990 entry into national politics as a certain future Liberal prime minister.

Costello fooled everybody and, perhaps in the end, he fooled himself. He was the perfect candidate for the highest office, possessing stature, brains, wit and projection.

Yet Costello's political character fell short of the requirements for the prime ministership in a conundrum that will be debated for many years.

The golden path that Costello travelled towards the Lodge was too golden and his progress seemed too perfect. Elected to parliament at thirty-two, deputy leader at age thirty-six, treasurer when he was thirty-eight years old to John Howard, a generation older, a leadership transition seemed inevitable. It is scarcely a surprise that Costello, the Liberal Party and the media felt his ultimate appointment was in the Lodge.

But politics is a morality play on life. It never delivers the easy path. It conspires instead to obstruct and plague those whose ambitions are highest. Consider the two most successful Liberal prime ministers.

Robert Menzies was a first-time failure compelled to stand down as prime minister in 1941 during World War II and, in his second incarnation, he struggled for six long years as Opposition leader, losing the 1946 election and prevailing only in 1949 at his final chance, when defeat would have cast him as one of the great failures in Australia's political history. People have forgotten that Menzies' post-1949 success was built on a series of brutal rejections and long years on the Opposition benches.

Howard's story is well known because it is more recent. Like Menzies, Howard had two incarnations as leader, and like Menzies, he served six years as Opposition leader, initially 1985–89 and then 1995–96, before becoming the second longest serving prime minister after Menzies.

The idea of Menzies or Howard rebuffing the Liberal Party when it desperately needed their leadership would have been inconceivable. Howard would have walked over broken glass to accept the Liberal leadership on any day the party extended that privilege. Not Costello.

Costello's decision to put his leader's cue in the rack is understandable. Those who know the crippling pressures of politics would not deny such consideration. It means, however, that Costello is different. Costello does not possess the same commitment or stamina in adversity as Menzies and Howard in their trench struggles to become successful prime ministers.

The idea that Gough Whitlam, Malcolm Fraser, Bob Hawke or Paul Keating would have walked away from a chance to become leader of their party is also inconceivable. Such politicians had a will to power in its elemental and honourable dimensions. In politics they strove relentlessly to marshal support, develop plans for Australia's future and plan an assault on their party's leadership. They went to political war in these struggles not because they were power crazy but because they were consumed by a self-belief that is the lifeblood of political victory and achievement.

Costello is made from different mettle. The signs were always there. 'I am not going to retire in politics', he told me during an interview in August 1998. He was adamant. His mind had settled that question, and it was still in Howard's first term. Costello was ever aware of the limits of political existence.

'I have always decided that, in my life, politics won't take its totality', he said. 'I have a limited view of politics. There is an awful lot that politics can't fix. I think politicians have let themselves down by claiming to be able to do too much.'

Costello can be either admired or damned for this perspective.

Such remarks reveal sharp differences between Howard and Costello. Howard was a lifelong political warrior who never planned a career after politics.

For Howard, politics was enough. Howard, more than Costello, was a Liberal Party tribalist. It was not unusual to hear Howard declare that he loved the Liberal Party. It wasn't just a vehicle he supported but fundamental to his way of life. Howard had a deep sense of responsibility and obligation to the Liberal Party.

Costello, of course, was loyal and deeply attached to the Liberal Party. My argument is that his attachment to politics as a vocation and to the Liberals as a party was of a different dimension to that of Howard. This is partly a function of generations.

It was tied, however, to Costello's singular belief there was only one path for him to the Lodge: in a smooth transition gifted by Howard's retirement.

For Costello, this path had an irrefutable rationale: it was in the interests of the Liberal Party, of Howard and of himself as successor. It was a 'best of times' transition. It was neat, it avoided political bloodshed and it renewed the government.

'I think the party realises that I have deposited a lot of loyalty with the party in the bank', Costello told me in 1998. It was a loyalty strategy that finally became too frayed at the edges.

The evidence is that Costello could never bring himself to seriously contemplate an alternative: marshalling numbers against Howard, resignation to the backbench or a challenge. He wasn't going to gamble. He shunned brinkmanship or any hint of 'crash through or crash'. For Costello, there was no other path to the prize.

As time advanced, Costello's position became fatalistic. He didn't believe Howard would resign yet, and unable to adopt another strategy, he clung to a doomed option. In the end, he let Howard decide his fate. Denied the prime ministership by Howard, Costello was left after the 2007 election loss unwilling to create a new narrative for himself. That remains the position. The shadow of Howard overhangs Costello still.

He has no future as an Opposition backbencher. Any such ongoing status is a farce. Leadership or the exit door are the only viable options and Costello, this week, seemed to rule out the leadership.

There is no gainsaying what the Liberal Party needs: it is crying out for a sustained period of strong and credible leadership on policy, presentation and organisation. The re-establishment of the party's credentials will take time and effort. There is no easy, overnight or public relations answer.

Costello is the outstanding candidate and his removal from the field is a serious setback for the Liberals. If Costello is ever to become leader, now is the hour.

His rejection of that call must only provoke more speculation. If Costello thinks there is a real chance of defeating the Rudd Government, would he not accept the responsibility of leadership? If he stays on the backbench, does he not recognise that his mere presence undermines the leader?

Tony Abbott predicted this week that Costello's decision means 'he will live forever with this haunting sense of what might have been'. Abbott's argument is correct. Yet it underestimates Costello, who has had many years to decide what he is prepared to live with.

Paul Sheehan

Costello is standing by his voters
The Sydney Morning Herald, 15 September 2008

Are we, the voters, so irrelevant? Were the hundreds of thousands of people who stood and waited to cast their votes at council elections on Saturday really wasting their time? These are logical questions to ask given the collective reaction of the political press pack to both *The Costello Memoirs* and its author.

Not once in the welter of fabricated outrage about Costello's decision to stay on as a backbencher have the Canberra media courtiers mentioned his obligation to the people who voted for him last November, the people of South Yarra, Glen Iris, Toorak and Malvern, who, like voters everywhere, are entitled to expect their member of parliament to regard their vote as a sacred trust.

Instead, the media want Costello to either challenge for the leadership or leave parliament, so that the candidate for whom they are relentlessly lobbying, Malcolm Turnbull, can be installed as the Liberal leader as soon as possible. This idea appals Costello. *The Costello Memoirs* does not paint a pretty picture of the Point Piper plutocrat who wants to be king. While the portrait of Turnbull has been created with light brush-strokes, the implicit suggestion is that he is a self-absorbed opportunist.

Costello's decision to retire to the backbench and serve out his full term was, and remains, not only the understandable course to take, but the right course to take. What the Liberal Party needs to do now is wait for this latest confected media storm to pass. It needs to see that all the media's polling, its constant speculation, constant agitation, and constant anonymous sourcing, is designed to feed a beast that has been a significant driver of the bloody attrition of Liberal and Labor party leaders in state and federal politics.

The past decade has seen the arrival and/or departure of fifteen Liberal and Labor leaders in Canberra and Sydney: Kim Beazley (twice), John Brogden, Bob Carr, Kerry Chikarovski, Peter Collins, Simon Crean, Peter Debnam, John Howard, Morris Iemma, Mark Latham, Brendan Nelson, Barry O'Farrell, Nathan Rees and Kevin Rudd.

Fifteen leadership changes in ten years. One every eight months. The Liberals should ignore the media's insatiable appetite for fresh kill and start creating good policies. Costello's presence provides desperately needed intellectual ballast for a party that is short on ideas. It also serves as political ballast against the Turnbull leadership campaign, which is being run by the media because in the federal parliamentary party the main Turnbull activists are: Steven Ciobo, from the Gold Coast, Senator Michael Ronaldson, from Melbourne, and another Victorian, Chris Pearce, after he was left out of the shadow ministry.

Peter Costello's decision to stay contrasts starkly with the behaviour of another former minister over the weekend, New South Wales Labor's Reba Meagher, who announced: 'I have decided to retire, as of today . . . It has been a source of great honour and pride to represent such a dynamic and rich multicultural centre of Sydney'.

Such a source of honour and pride that she lived in Coogee, far from her electorate of Cabramatta. Such a source of honour and pride that she couldn't be bothered to serve out her term, preferring a tax-funded dummy spit after being dumped from the ministry. It is a graceless end to an often graceless career marked by this unedifying parliamentary exchange on June 3, 1998:

Peter Collins [then leader of the Opposition]: 'Let me draw the attention of the House to the honourable member for Cabramatta, whose Canley Vale branch includes Phuong Ngo and two others who face serious criminal charges, which I will not go into in this place. The Cabramatta branch, the largest ALP in New South Wales, is comprehensively stacked. The honourable member for Cabramatta lives in fear of that branch, and rightly so.'

Reba Meagher: 'Are you saying that all Asians are criminals? You're a racist.'

It was straight out of the Paul Keating handbook—not surprising given that Meagher began her career like Keating and ended her career like Keating, who represented the people of Bankstown, Cabramatta, Canley Vale and Greenacre, before moving to the eastern suburbs. So proud to represent them that in 1996, after they had just re-elected him, he resigned and never spent another day in parliament. Contrast this with Costello, who was betrayed by his own party.

In this space on 26 March last year I wrote a column that began:

> The people have spoken. John Howard should go. Now. The era of Howard's political ascendancy is over . . . He should do the right thing, the honourable thing, and step aside in favour of his deputy, Peter Costello, who is almost 20 years younger . . . a highly successful treasurer for 11 years, and the most brilliant performer in the Parliament. He deserves his moment in the sun.

It was self-evident to me then that the Liberals were doomed if they clung to the past, just as it is self-evident to me now that the party will be equally gutless and deluded if they seek to depose their leader this year. *The Costello Memoirs* is irrelevant to this need for stability. What the memoir does is offer further evidence that Costello was the right man to lead the Coalition into the last election, and he was right to refuse the poisoned chalice of his party's belated leadership offer. More importantly, it asks the big policy questions that his party has failed to acknowledge, let alone answer.

Peter Hartcher

The conflict business
The Monthly, November 2008

One of the standout episodes illustrating the tomfoolery of federal parlia-mentarians is the time that Peter Costello flung a sheaf of paper across the table into Paul Keating's face. It ranks with the occasion when Gough Whitlam tossed a glass of water into Paul Hasluck's face, but because it happened in the era of parliamentary cameras Costello's effrontery will prove more enduring.

And he isn't too proud to revisit the moment in his memoir. If any-thing, he seems a touch pleased with himself in looking back on his antics.

Keating, seven months from oblivion, was defending one of his min-isters, Carmen Lawrence, over a scandal that had followed her to Canberra from her previous job, as premier of Western Australia. Under Lawrence's leadership, a Labor member in the state parliament tabled a petition claim-ing that a Perth woman, Penny Easton, had perjured herself in the Family Court. Four days later, Easton killed herself. Lawrence said she had no foreknowledge of the parliamentary claim. But a royal commission found otherwise, and she now stood accused of lying to parliament.

In Canberra, the Opposition was in hot pursuit. Its leader, John Howard, asked the prime minister in question time whether he accepted that Lawrence had told the truth about the matter in a speech before the National Press Club some months earlier. Keating began by doing Howard the favour of giving him a character assessment: 'You are a joke, you are a fraud'. He said he had not read the speech. 'Why should I?'

Costello takes up the tale:

I then sought leave to table Lawrence's Press Club speech. When leave was refused, Keating invited me to table it. I tossed a copy across the table. Unfortunately it was held together by a large bulldog clip. The clip went up in the air and landed on Keating. I was very surprised. I was not aiming at him. Keating immediately jumped up as if to take a swing at me.

The Speaker decided that the parliament could do without the services of Costello for an hour. If Australia's longest serving treasurer has any regrets over the 1995 incident, they are not in evidence:

> When I was returning home from Canberra at the end of that week, a taxi driver at the airport walked across to me and said in broken English, 'Mr Costello, you throw papers in Mr Keating's face. Next time you throw brick.' Ron Walker, then treasurer of the Liberal Party [now chairman of Fairfax Media] asked for a copy of the papers. He thought they would go for a fortune at a fundraiser. I gave them to Tony Smith [now shadow assistant treasurer] for safekeeping. He still has them.

Some political diaries are dashed in the reader's face. *The Latham Diaries* is the case in point. The former Labor leader complained bitterly about 'Parliament House's culture of small talk and smear', then proceeded to write a 400-page book full of small talk and smear.

Mark Latham made no entry for the two great events of his time. He wrote nothing about September 11 because, he said, he had nothing to add. And he wrote of the Southern Asian tsunami of Boxing Day, with societies destroyed and hundreds of thousands dead and suffering, only as a media-driven 'nuisance' to spoil his holiday.

But there was no end of smear. Latham criticised at least seventeen of the Labor Party's key figures, including the former leaders Gough Whitlam and Paul Keating, as well as the leader at the time the book was published, Kim Beazley, and the future leader, Kevin Rudd. Indeed, Rudd was one of his principal targets. He was 'treacherous, a nasty piece of work, addicted to the media and leaking', and 'a junior minister in government, at best'. Worse, Latham accused Rudd of exploiting sympathy over his mother's death in an effort to get promoted in the shadow ministry.

In common with many political memoirs, including Peter Costello's, Latham's diary devoted most of its time and energy to a critique of his own side of politics, rather than an assault on the putative enemy. For example, Latham mentioned Rudd, then the shadow foreign minister, thirty-seven times in his memoir, but Alexander Downer, the actual foreign minister, only nine. Similarly, Costello gives his opposite number for half his time as treasurer, Wayne Swan, a mere three glancing mentions in his 337 pages (374 if you count his old speeches reproduced in the back of the book).

Yet Malcolm Turnbull, though he spent a scant ten months in the Howard cabinet, appears ten times in the Costello narrative. And he doesn't look his dashing best in a number of these appearances. Costello fits him up for leaking a cabinet discussion, and for undermining the success of the Howard Government in campaigning on its record of cutting income tax. He also implies that Turnbull was either a bit slow on tax policy or a bit hypocritical:

> I explained to Turnbull that the best way to cut tax further was to restrain expenditure . . . He understood this point and accepted it as a backbencher. Later in that term, when he became a minister in charge of expenditure programs, he produced an array of them.

To Latham and to Costello, political Opposition is a backdrop to the real action: the internal intrigues of their own parties. Winning power over the opposing side is, apparently, incidental to the true business of winning power over colleagues.

Both diaries are the work of frustrated men, wannabe prime ministers who were but a single step from the job. And both were frustrated by the same man: John Howard. Nevertheless, Costello's memoir is a very different proposition to the former Labor leader's. It is put before the reader with good humour and considerable restraint. It is not flung into the reader's face but presented for inspection.

Latham's diary was promoted as offering 'an insult on every page', and it boasted at least as many profanities. In politics, which Keating likes to call 'the conflict business', public figures have to expect the odd insult. The unforgivable injury that Latham committed, and committed repeatedly, was to claw at the wholly innocent bystanders: the spouses and families of his former colleagues. It is an extended horror story of gratuitous insult and hurt.

His writing utterly lacked self-awareness. This led to some very revealing anecdotes. He couldn't bring himself to go to the 1999 Labor dinner to farewell Gareth Evans from politics, so instead he and his wife, Janine Lacy, and his mate Joel Fitzgibbon, now the defence minister, went to dinner by themselves and made prank phone calls to the Evans function. 'In my best deep African accent I convinced the hotel reception that I was Kofi Annan and needed to speak to Gareth Evans urgently', Latham wrote. When the staff informed him that Evans was on his feet speaking, Latham left a message: 'Please call Kofi Annan urgently in New York. He has good news about the African votes for the UNESCO job'. Next, he phoned the Labor frontbencher Bob McMullan and left him a voicemail 'asking a few questions about his comb-over. He never got back to me—totally humourless'.

Costello's is a much more measured, thoughtful and, needless to say, grown-up piece of work. That doesn't make it dull. He has an eye for an anecdote. He recalls, for instance, the comprehensive final briefing he gave the Howard Cabinet in 1998 on the tax-reform package that included the GST. His briefing ran for seven hours. The treasurer used a PowerPoint presentation, the first time one had been used in the cabinet room. As the meeting broke up, Costello asked a fellow minister what he thought of the briefing. 'I didn't understand much of it', came the reply, 'but I thought the coloured diagrams looked great!'

Latham's book was written in a bitter fury; Costello's is written more in sorrow than anger. Latham flung himself about in a froth-mouthed frenzy for someone to blame; Costello knows exactly who to blame. Latham blamed everyone—including the Australian people, for daring to elect someone other than him. 'Maybe my mindset is not suited to the consumerism of middle Australia', he pouted. Costello's book carefully, deliberately, leads the reader to the man he blames: 'Leadership is not only about winning: it is also about departing', he writes. 'Unlike Menzies, Howard never managed a transition. He did not accomplish generational change . . . We lost because we failed to renew.' Costello accepts no responsibility.

These diaries, like all diaries, are firmly about the past. Certainly, both men offer a glimpse of their views of the future. Latham's was dismal and despairing of politics as a way of achieving anything useful. Costello sees a country with its best years ahead, but with a policy agenda whose top items—fixing federalism and addressing Aboriginal disadvantage—are already on the Rudd agenda.

No, these diaries are not about the future. These are men with more behind them than in front. The purpose of each diary is for the author to give an account of himself. At the exit points of their political careers, Latham and Costello each wanted to try to tell his own version of what he did and, most importantly, why he failed. George Orwell wrote in *1984* that 'who controls the past, controls the future'. Latham and Costello no longer pursue power over the country's future, but they crave power over the future of how the country regards their past.

Costello's version will not go uncontested. Howard plans to write his account next year. As for Latham's diaries, there was no need for anyone to respond. What sane person would take such ranting seriously?

One prominent federal politician is writing a book about the future, though. Tony Abbott is writing not a memoir but a manifesto, under the working title 'Conservatism After Howard'. One of the strengths of the Howard Government was that Howard, John Hewson and others had done a good deal of thinking in the Liberals' thirteen years in Opposition, and this had equipped them intellectually for government, Abbott argues. 'I think it's important we don't wait seven or eight years to start thinking— I think this is potentially our point of political recovery.'

His book, due in April, will set out broad philosophical directions as well as specific policy ideas. 'In the end, the best policy ideas don't necessarily emerge from a committee.' One radical concept: Abbott will detail a plan for a constitutional referendum to give the federal government the power to override the states whenever it so wishes. 'When it comes to the crunch, the federal government is in charge', he proposes.

Abbott agrees that the book is, in part, a job application for the leadership: 'I accept that I'm unlikely to be leader any time soon but I think I have reasonable credentials to be considered for the leadership at some point and I hope I can burnish my credentials', he said in July. It will be much more than a personal statement, however. Abbott represents the conservative wing of the Liberal Party; Malcolm Turnbull is the leading figure in its liberal wing. Abbott's work is likely to be a piece of competitive philosophical and intellectual direction-finding for the Coalition.

It's routine for federal Labor politicians to write books setting out their ideas: Wayne Swan's *Postcode: The Splintering of a Nation*, Lindsay Tanner's *Crowded Lives*, Craig Emerson's *Vital Signs, Vibrant Society: Securing Australia's Economic and Social Wellbeing*. Kevin Rudd did not write a book but he did pen a pair of substantial articles for this magazine—one on religion and politics, the other on the limits of the marketplace in public policy—as part of his campaign for the Labor leadership. Abbott's book, though, is startling in its rarity. It will be the first of its kind by a conservative in sixty-five years.

The closest thing to a precedent came in 1943. It was *The Forgotten People and Other Studies in Democracy*, by the Liberal Party's founder, Robert Menzies. The book, based on a series of radio broadcasts, sought to set out the philosophical basis for the party. Menzies, at this point, had already served two years and four months as prime minister and leader of the United Australia Party. Now, in Opposition, he was trying to craft the platform for a new political party.

Abbott's publication promises to make the manifesto-style book as important for conservative politics as it is for the progressive side. This would be no big deal in the United States, where John McCain has five books to his name and Barack Obama two. But in Australia, it would be a serious intensification of the intellectual effort that goes into political campaigning. This is a happy development. For the key figures on both sides of politics to canvass ideas for our political future, rather than just settle scores from their political pasts, offers the prospect of a leadership class that is better prepared and a voting public that is better informed.

Tony Smith, custodian of the Carmen Lawrence speech, may think that he has an important historical artefact on his hands. But sometimes old papers are just old papers.

Jennifer Hewett

The opportunist

The Australian, 25 October 2008

Malcolm Turnbull is waiting to be entranced.

His media minders hover in the background, burrowed into their phones. Around the country the political debate is focused on the global financial crisis. The next appointment for the leader of the Opposition is a 30-minute drive away. But at the Bellevue retirement village in suburban Brisbane, Turnbull is determined that resident Ruth must get her violin from her room and play for him. Soon the strains of 'Danny Boy' waft over the egg and lettuce sandwiches on offer for morning tea. Turnbull is delighted.

'Magic', he tells Ruth cheerily. 'I won't ever forget it.' And the truth is, he probably won't.

'I love the diversity of humanity', he says later.

> I love the idea you sit down in a retirement village and chat to an older lady and you discover that she was born in Dublin, worked for years in the Royal Opera House in Covent Garden, and then moved to Townsville to set up a tennis centre with a colleague. And she comes out with the violin she played in the Royal Opera House and does a few numbers for us. It's so rich, it's so beautiful, it's so human. How could you not be touched by that?

Hold the scepticism. This willingness to be seduced and ability to seduce is an important part of Malcolm Turnbull's success as a politician. Underneath the aggressive political rhetoric, alongside the relentless struggle for supremacy, behind the journalist turned lawyer turned banker turned politician turned would-be prime minister is a man who really enjoys that human interaction, however brief, with the many, many ordinary people he encounters. Turnbull connects. That's not so unusual, of course—despite the frequent public scorn for politicians' motives. The surprise is how quickly Malcolm Turnbull has been able to pull his energy, intellect and charm into a far more appealing political package than his predecessor, Brendan Nelson. Turnbull looks and sounds the part of a leader, and a rather likeable one at that.

Labor remains well in front but the government is increasingly watchful. Suddenly, the next election doesn't seem quite so much of a sure thing—particularly not given a treacherous economic outlook. And as Turnbull manoeuvres through a once-unforgiving political landscape his nervous colleagues are hanging on tight. Malcolm difficult? Malcolm a risk? Malcolm unpredictable? Whatever gave you that idea?

Political audacity is part of the Turnbull style. He presents a constantly moving target even as Labor tries to keep him in a confined frame. Instead his tactic is just to keep circling, always looking to take advantage of any government vulnerability. Political opportunist? Absolutely. Policy lightweight? Definitely not. Too smart for his own good? We'll see.

In a startlingly brief four years in parliament, Turnbull leapt over his more experienced colleagues to become the obvious choice for a despairing party. All those who said he was too arrogant, too rich and too ill tempered for politics have repeatedly been proven wrong. These days, when crossed, he tends to use humour to make his point rather than anger. He is blunt but usually determinedly courteous, at least in public. He does amusing lines in self-deprecation well. In some media interviews there is still an aggressive tone, threatening to spill over the smoothed patina. There's always the Turnbull edge. Now, however, it's controlled. He also laughs a lot, if only to deflect criticism or difficult questions.

He showed his sense of comedic timing when he went on ABC TV's *Q&A* show with Tony Jones last month. 'He's always got a good word for me', he joked of Peter Costello. 'He started it', he dead-panned about his spectacular fallout with Kerry Packer. Even in private he's learning to finesse his opponents rather than bending them to his considerable will.

But at fifty-four (his birthday was yesterday), he is not into self-analysis. He refuses to enter the constant debate about his super-sized personality. 'Have I ever been angry?' he says. 'Yes. Who hasn't? I try, like everybody, to approach things in a measured way. How successful I am is for others to judge.'

He has also—belatedly—learnt to take his father's advice and 'lighten up'.

> My father was an incredibly funny guy. He was very charismatic and he had quite a bit of magic about him and he always used to say to me when I was young, 'Oh come on, Malcolm, lighten up, you're so serious.' So maybe in my older years I'm recognising that you can't be heavy all the time. Even the bleaker situations can have an amusing side to them.

Does he ever get depressed? 'Look, honestly, only at being asked questions like this', he groans. 'You know, everyone gets a bit gloomy at times but I'm generally a pretty happy fellow.'

So has Turnbull really changed? Or is it that the times have changed around him so that the Malcolm Turnbull who once seemed so dangerously different to John Howard is now the Liberal hero who might, just might, lead the party to victory?

Turnbull dismisses any sense of inevitability in politics but there was no doubting his absolute certainty that he should and would be leader. Now that he is, the reign of John Howard truly does seem an age and generation away. It's not only a matter of a lost election; Turnbull is no conservative cultural warrior, no fierce Liberal tribalist. Even while Howard's environment minister he fought to modernise the party on the more obvious social issues such as the apology for the Stolen Generations, signing the Kyoto Protocol and rights for same-sex couples. As leader, he has retreated on opposing changes to WorkChoices in the Senate. But he's deliberately vague on specifics.

'I think the really big difference between our side of politics and Labor is that we have a much more optimistic view of human nature', he says. 'We celebrate the ability of people to make the best choices for themselves and see the role of the state above all as enabling people to do their best.'

It's all part of the Turnbull mantra. Flexibility in all things. He hates labels, he says. He has always read widely on political philosophy—his favourite is Edmund Burke—but insists that the key to understanding the Liberal Party is to see it as a very practical party. 'I certainly live in the here and now', he says. And that means, more than ever, the main game is the economy. He is not about to be diverted by the lure of his once so passionately pushed republican ideals. Instead, he is content to play mainstream gesture politics every bit as hard as Labor did in Opposition.

A few days after the Brisbane encounter, Malcolm Turnbull and his wife, Lucy, are in Sydney's Centennial Park. There are no dogs today, even though the couple spend hours every weekend walking Mellie and JoJo around the park and the eastern suburbs of Sydney where they both grew up. They are often photographed in dogwalker mode for the local paper, *The Wentworth Courier*. But today is a working day, the day when the Reserve Bank is announcing a rate cut, and Turnbull—former investment banker, very rich man—is on the job on behalf of the mums and dads.

He has been insisting that the banks pass on in full any cuts by the Reserve Bank, refusing to be persuaded by the paralysis in the global credit markets, the real fears of systemic financial collapse and the banks' rising cost of funding. When the RBA cuts rates by 1 per cent, he promptly claims victory after the banks pass on a cut of 0.8 per cent. It generates an immediate swipe from Treasurer Wayne Swan: 'I know Mr Turnbull thinks the whole world revolves around his ego, but there are some events in the world that are much bigger than his ego'.

Neither has Turnbull's approach gained him any new friends in banking or corporate circles, many still deeply suspicious of him from his time as a bombastic merchant banker. Now they are aghast at what they see as his populist irresponsibility in such a fragile environment: Turnbull, of all politicians, should know better, they mutter. Yet that's the point, of course. Turnbull deliberately confounds stereotypes.

It helps that Turnbull has a direct style of speaking—very different to the style of bureaucratic jargon now associated with prime ministerial speeches. The former journalist knows the value of a cut-through line.

Malcolm 'always speaks in short sentences', Lucy Turnbull says. 'Not short enough sometimes', retorts her husband with a laugh. It's a reference to his habit of speaking a little too freely for his colleagues occasionally. That includes an expansive radio interview straight after the election that put a handful of colleagues off voting for him and paved the way for Brendan Nelson's brief ascension.

But he still describes himself—with a broad grin—as a 'plain blunt man'. 'I have observed that by and large when people speak in a way that cannot be easily understood, it is because they haven't cleared up their own thoughts', he says. 'Often, obscurity of language conceals confusion in the mind of the speaker.' (Take that, Kevin. It's a jab, a sharp one. And being received. It's been obvious of late that Rudd is attempting to speak more directly.)

Still, the financial crisis has also short-circuited Turnbull's potent criticism that the government is too busy with rhetoric and reviews and committees to do anything much. The dramatic government moves on shoring up the banks and stimulating the economy with a $10 billion spending package now even up that particular battleground. It will be up to Turnbull to manoeuvre around the largesse and gravitas available to governments rather than oppositions in times of crisis. He is walking a perilous line between appeals to bipartisanship and attempts at finding political advantage.

Yet Turnbull's political instinct is broader and deeper than most people realise. Even though he quickly rejects the sensitive notion that he has a better understanding of Labor than most Liberals, he has certainly enjoyed intimate personal dealings with his political opponents over decades. This is a man who, after all, spent years of his business banking life in partnership with one of the icons of the Labor Party, Neville Wran, and—much less happily—Nick Whitlam, the son of another. Turnbull also cooperated extremely closely with Paul Keating in the Australian Republican Movement. 'The relationship was like a mutual seduction', says one of those involved.

Nor were Labor connections restricted to the professional context. A young Malcolm met 19-year-old Lucy Hughes when he interviewed her famous barrister father, Tom Hughes, a former Liberal attorney-general. Lucy was spending her law school university holidays working in his chambers. For their first date, Turnbull asked a young married couple along for company—his good friends Helena and Bob Carr, then a fellow journalist but later to become long-serving Labor Premier of NSW. 'I am not sure why Malcolm wanted a foursome for dinner but it was sweet and charming', laughs Lucy Turnbull. She was more taken, she says, by his mischievous smile and his lively personality—and how handsome he was. Marriage followed in 1980, the year he began practising law.

The two still have a very tight partnership, evident in their joking camaraderie and close family. They have two children, Alex, 26, who works for a hedge fund in Hong Kong, and Daisy, 23, who works for an online advertising agency in Sydney. Turnbull has often said he regretted not having more children. (Lucy recently revealed she had two miscarriages when in her 30s.) Alex and Daisy are in constant contact, despite having moved out of the family home that cascades down the Sydney waterfront at Point Piper. Malcolm and Lucy bought the house, built in the 1920s, for $5.4 million in 1994, then added the neighbouring property for $7.1 million five years later. The interior is stunning but reasonably casual and comfortable in style. There are two Bill Henson photos on the wall—definitely not nude children. The large living room spills out on to an open deck where the couple loves to entertain in the warmer weather. Down below, they often push out from their boatshed to paddle around in their double kayak.

His beloved seat of Wentworth covers the eastern suburbs of Sydney, which have long been Turnbull's stamping ground. The electorate, he insisted in his maiden speech, is egalitarian and far from homogenous, contrary to popular myth. But it is still home to some of the most concentrated wealth in Australia. Turnbull takes pride in being an assiduous MP and is highly visible, particularly given he almost always catches public transport. He has sentimental dog blogs on his parliamentary website and is a regular at local functions, however obscure. And he always loves a chat.

Not that Lucy Turnbull is any stranger to the voters, either. She shares Malcolm's restless energy and passion for participating in public life. Just like Therese Rein, Lucy Turnbull has had a successful and independent career. As well as being closely involved in the Turnbulls' many investment companies she ran as an independent councillor for the city of Sydney and ended up becoming Lord Mayor. In 2004 the New South Wales Labor Government, led by that same old mate, Bob Carr, decided that Malcolm's new career in federal politics required a withdrawal of Labor support for his wife. In retaliation, Lucy threw her support to another independent candidate, Clover Moore, who won. The episode has clearly frozen hard a relationship Lucy now coolly calls 'civil'. 'My suitability was deeply impacted by my husband's emerging political career, which I didn't think was a very profeminist position to take', she says in irritation. 'It was very disappointing.'

She was not about to let it slow her down. She may have a famously articulate father, uncle (art historian Robert Hughes) and husband, but she maintains her sense of self without apparent difficulty. The Turnbulls are big philanthropists. These days, Lucy spends more time in the not-for-profit sector as chairman of the Salvation Army Red Shield appeal and working closely with—and helping fund—the Redfern Foundation to encourage Indigenous community self-help organisations. Busy, busy, busy.

While Brendan Nelson was plotting to bring on his ultimately disastrous leadership spill and Peter Costello was teasing the Liberals with would-he-or wouldn't-he games ahead of his book launch, the Turnbulls were in Venice. But it was Malcolm who was there as the handbag while Lucy was commissioner of the Australian pavilion at the Venice Architecture Biennale. The day they returned, Nelson called the surprise leadership vote for the next morning, 16 September. Turnbull had not been actively lobbying his colleagues, so confident was he that political reality would erode any remaining resistance. Just not quite that soon. He spent much of the night on the phone talking to the undecided. Next morning, it was done. Malcolm Turnbull was leader.

It has been a circuitous route. Half a lifetime ago, at just twenty-seven, he had tried for Liberal preselection in Wentworth. 'I threw my hat into the ring really with no expectation of winning', he says of that first attempt. 'I thought "this will be good experience, and I will meet a lot of people and it will be interesting". Then some momentum developed and I very nearly won it. I think Lucy would have been horrified if I had won, actually. I would have been astonished.'

More than two decades later, in 2003, any hesitancy had evaporated. The Turnbulls decided Malcolm must defeat the sitting Liberal member,

Peter King, in the preselection. Those who had become frustrated by Turnbull's domineering style during the republic campaign didn't believe he could constrain his personality sufficiently to manage localised democracy in action. Instead, it was another Turnbull gamble that paid off. He may have fallen out dramatically with John Howard over the republic, famously denouncing him as the prime minister who broke the nation's heart, yet he was able once again to repair his personal relationship as needed. When he puts his mind to it, the Turnbull charm and persuasiveness are hard to resist.

That doesn't mean he plays it safe. Few backbenchers would have immediately challenged the treasurer on the core of his economic policy, tax. To Peter Costello's lasting fury Turnbull did precisely that, using research he had personally commissioned and paid for to argue the case for lower rates. He was promptly promoted by Howard.

Not that Malcolm's eventual triumph in politics surprised those who had watched him over the years. Trevor Kennedy, former *Bulletin* editor, joked at Turnbull's 30th birthday party that they were all there to 'celebrate Malcolm's ambition to become prime minister of the world'.

'Firmly tongue in cheek', Turnbull recalls now. He's adamant there was never any certainty about anything. 'If I hadn't won the preselection in 2003, I wouldn't have felt that my life was somehow or other empty or unfulfilled', he says. 'Quite the contrary. I am very committed to what I am doing in politics but I am there, I am in politics, genuinely to serve others. It is not a question of fulfilling a personal ambition. It is a means of public service.'

Of course, public service and personal ambition are not so easily disentangled in Malcolm Turnbull's life. What is clear is that Turnbull keeps aiming high, then ever higher, often at a radically different target. Success in one career is no reason to stay there. Confidence is one thing, he says, complacency is quite another. And he has always worked double time to avoid any sense of that. 'I like to be busy', he says. 'I have always sought to do things that are exciting and interesting and worthwhile and so forth. I would have got bored if I hadn't been doing what I was doing I guess.'

In his twenties he was the hardworking journalist studying to be a lawyer and then a Rhodes scholar taking a first at Oxford and later becoming Packer's lawyer. As a new barrister he took on the Spycatcher case, successfully defending a former British spy turned author against a British government that wanted to block the book's revelations. That alone would have guaranteed him a long and lucrative career in the law—except he decided to go into investment banking in 1987. 'I had done that big Spycatcher case and I just felt I could spend another twenty years as an advocate, barrister or solicitor, doing cases, and I would never do anything as exciting as that again', he says. 'So I thought, well, let's have a go at something new. That was a big part of it.'

It reflects a personality in permanent search mode. He's always happiest, he says, when he is learning something new. He loves history, especially classical, medieval and Byzantine. He cites with enthusiasm a book he read on Roman aqueducts when he was water minister.

Nor is his relentless curiosity limited to matters of policy. He was baptised a Catholic—Lucy's religion—about a decade ago, although he's not keen to expand on his reasons. 'It's a question of faith', he says.

> It is important to me but I'd prefer not to talk about it. I genuinely believe that politicians demonstrate their values by their conduct and by their actions and by the way they lead their lives. I believe people have a healthy scepticism about people in public life who go on at great length telling everyone how virtuous or religious or whatever they may be. I have always taken that view.

Just as he has always taken the view that people are there to be charmed, to engage and to be engaged by. Turnbull has a seemingly effortless habit of forming a vast range of relationships, often with very important people. It's a world in which everyone and everything eventually seems to connect. His has been a remarkable climb through the top levels of law, business and politics, framed by an intricate web of connections stretching back decades. At his private school, Sydney Grammar, for example, one of the boys in his debating team was David Gonski, now chairman of the ASX, lawyer, investment banker and long-term confidant of the Lowy and Packer families. As a teenager, Malcolm often ended up at the Gonski family home for dinner. Gonski recalls his mother's lamb stew was a particular Malcolm favourite.

At that stage Malcolm was a boarder, the only child of a single parent, Bruce Turnbull, a hotel sales broker who travelled a lot. His mother, Coral Lansbury, had effectively abandoned them both for New Zealand then the

United States when Malcolm was nine. She stayed in regular contact but died of cancer in 1991 in Philadelphia. At that stage she was dean of the graduate school of English at Rutgers University.

Turnbull recalls that his father, who died in a plane crash in 1982, had never said a word against Coral when Malcolm was a boy, always trying to protect his son's feelings and his relationship with his mother. 'My impression is that Coral was a very powerful personality, very intelligent and very focused on Malcolm's success', Lucy says. 'She was very involved in his early education and development. She taught him to read by the time he was three. They had a very close bond when he was a young boy—which made her sudden departure all the more painful.'

Many Malcolm-watchers are convinced that his driving desire to succeed—and to seek affirmation—have their origins in the sense of loss felt by a bright little boy. Turnbull rejects that sort of pop psychology. But he is happy to use his family history to persuade the public of his 'humble' beginnings, living in rented flats with only one parent.

From his first press conference as leader, he wanted to avoid the attempt by Labor to paint him as a rich and out-of-touch investment banker who lived a life of harbourside luxury and couldn't relate to ordinary people. He has been effective—and not only because these days even our Labor Prime Minister is wealthy thanks to the business success of his wife, Therese Rein. It's also because Turnbull plays the politics so well. His emotional praise of his father's selfless devotion to him is both genuine and politically resonant. It reminds people that there's humanity behind the Turnbull image, a person who has succeeded due to his own efforts but who will not forget his roots.

Still, he is undeniably a very wealthy man as well as a well-connected man: acting for years for Kerry Packer—and then so spectacularly against him in the fight over Fairfax—was only part of it. Turnbull had two massive breaks financially. In 1999, he sold a $450 000 stake in one of Australia's early internet companies, OzEmail, for $59.3 million. He also sold his investment house, Turnbull & Partners, to Goldman Sachs in 1997. In a wonderful example of timing it meant he became a partner in the global investment bank just before it went public in mid 1999. By the time he left in 2001, the association is believed to have been worth about another $50 million to him. It's classic Turnbull: risk-taking, good timing and successful opportunism.

For a while it looked as if he would be haunted by his role in advising Rodney Adler's FAI Insurance. The takeover of the financially compromised FAI by HIH contributed to the subsequent collapse of HIH insurance group, leading to a royal commission. Until recently, Liberal and Labor politicians would talk in ominous tones about the impact on Turnbull's reputation of an impending court case by the liquidator. But the case has just been settled.

And while he may have made some enemies along the way in business, Turnbull's experience also left him with plenty of significant relationships for later life. He got to know Hank Paulson, now US treasury secretary and back then senior partner of Goldman Sachs. Turnbull visited him in Washington last April, before Paulson became a household name around the globe courtesy of the Wall Street crisis. 'Being in business teaches you so many things', Turnbull says.

> Working with other people, the importance of collaboration, the value of careful analysis. I think it also teaches you a lot about the need to be able to make decisions in a timely fashion. Politics is competitive, too, but in a different way. If you are in a business, and you've got a bunch of others doing the same thing, you have got to act and react to changes quickly.

Business, especially investment banking, also tends to reward an aggressive personality even if Turnbull points out rather indignantly that he has always worked as part of a team. Others remember him quite differently. 'No one has ever accused me of being bureaucratic', he laughs. Just autocratic.

So here he is. A social conservative long regarded as too progressive for his party. A man devoted to family, in part because of his broken one. A former investment banker from Australia's wealthiest suburb determined to court Rudd's working families. A staunch republican who says there's no point in thinking about it until the Queen dies. A convert to Catholicism in middle life. A politician who came late to Canberra but has already gone far and fast.

Malcolm Bligh Turnbull—in constant motion.

Tom Dusevic

The great Gillard experiment
The Australian Financial Review, 23 December 2008

After only ten weeks in government, some of Julia Gillard's colleagues were wondering whether the deputy prime minister would be able to handle her workload. After all, she had bundled together under a bird cage-sized marquee a fair slice of Labor's to-do list. There was the 'education revolution', from cradle to spanner, from blackboard to mortar board; in workplace relations, Gillard would be interring John Howard's WorkChoices and giving birth to a new wage-bargaining system; a fresh portfolio of social inclusion would put fairness and prosperity at the heart of government.

'Gillard put her foot down and wanted a big job', a senior minister said privately at the time. 'Well, she's got one now.'

Others in Cabinet felt the same way as a new parliament opened. Why overreach? If Gillard failed, the *schadenfreude* would seep out, as it had in 2007 when her industrial relations policy caught some snags. By February, she was accustomed to being acting prime minister, a member of key Cabinet groups (such as the expenditure review committee), and the main strategy teams. Gillard was at the centre of Ruddland.

That mix of scepticism, blokey chauvinism and professional jealousy has long evaporated in the ministerial wing. Maybe not the jealousy, for Canberra is nothing if not an arena for ambition and opportunism.

'She has been the government's stand-out performer. By a country mile', the original doubter says now. Gillard, forty-seven, is Labor's next in line. If Kevin Rudd disappeared under his paperwork, Australia would have its first female prime minister.

That this has come to pass will not surprise Gillard's intimates, who have never doubted her talents. In Rudd's meritocracy, where truth is work and beauty is competence, Gillard is the fairest of them all. That she has travelled from Victoria's socialist left, the unions and radical politics, changing trams at Swanston Street, is becoming a mere historical curiosity. She is the co-producer of *Australia*, the pragmatic epic. The personal makeover is still interesting, but not as good a story as how the rise and rise of Gillard opens up the chance for a new style of politics and national leadership.

On the day she was sworn in last December, Gillard sought to make sense of her super-sized portfolio, what she described as 'an awesome responsibility'. 'In today's world', she told a gathering of the Australian Industry Group, 'the areas covered by my portfolios—early childhood education and child care, schooling, training, universities, social inclusion, employment participation and workplace co-operation—are all ultimately about the same thing: productivity'.

She may not have used her seniority to take a traditional, central portfolio like Treasury, but she was determined to put a bit of steel into areas perceived as 'soft' by linking them to Labor's long-term economic mission. 'I'm going to be ignoring the old battles between unions and employers, public and private schools, the trades and universities and welfare and work', she said quite regally at the time, signalling a centrist sales pitch that has become the government's default setting. 'Instead, I'm going to be measuring policies against the all-important criteria of how effectively they increase national productivity.'

An economy in slowdown is not the place to be talking about raising productivity—doing more with less. It is one part of the project that will stay dormant until political and economic circumstances allow the public language to escape the shackles of austerity.

Within the government, and among those groups that form her vast constituency, there is a strongly held view that Gillard is on top of her responsibilities. She is diligent and, like her busy-beaver colleagues Rudd and Treasurer Wayne Swan, she has the mental and physical constitution for playing at the highest level. Gillard's ministerial colleagues say that her office functions well: the paper trail flows, meetings happen, work is delegated, the boss is generous and of good humour. Gillard is forensic in seeking and absorbing detail; unlike Rudd, she is not exasperatingly so. Says one minister: 'Julia progresses an issue. Kevin generates more meetings, more work'.

On top of her day jobs, says another minister, Gillard has an additional role, one she has made her own: deputy prime minister. 'It's an entire portfolio in itself and it emboldens her in all the key committees of the government.' In the recent past, that title has been marked as a factional gift or taken by the leader of the junior party in a coalition: Labor's Brian Howe under Paul Keating or the Nationals' John Anderson and Mark Vaile to Howard. Gillard has, through engineering and circumstance, transcended the deputy's gig. Some of the scoffers around the Cabinet table will not like to hear it, but she is in new political terrain.

Since being sworn in, Rudd has been a frequent overseas traveller. Diplomacy warrants the visits, it is the prime minister's passion, our troops are in several theatres and the global economic troubles have called for that sort of international leadership and co-operation. It has meant that since last December, due to Rudd's absences and leave, Gillard has been acting prime minister for eighty-four days; this Christmas she will be running the country from her cottage in Altona, in Melbourne's working-class western suburbs.

It was a huge deal when Gillard first sat in the big chair when Rudd went to the Bali climate-change conference, a breakthrough for women.

'I love the job I do day to day', she told ABC TV's Barrie Cassidy on the eve of the first anniversary of winning government. 'I love being deputy prime minister and that gives me a set of responsibilities and I'm happy to mind the store when the prime minister is away.'

Invariably, this leads to the question of Gillard chasing the top job, sometimes couched in the broader question of when Australia will get its first female prime minister. Her stock answer is that if she lives a long and happy life, then she'll witness that landmark.

'A lot has changed for women in politics very quickly', she told ABC2's *News Breakfast* program the following morning:

> I'm hoping I will see the day where women are so routine in all of the
> jobs that politics provides that no one even bothers to remark on it any
> more; no one bothers to do the count of how many men and how

many women because they just expect it to be basically equal and it's all very ordinary and normal, and I'm sure we'll get there.

And her own ambitions? At this stage, it would be crazy–brave for Gillard to stray from the shield she uses, whether facing the Canberra press gallery or Kerri-Anne. It goes like this: politics is unpredictable. She is focused on her job and is happy being deputy. One day Australia will have a female prime minister. If she finished her political career before getting to the summit, it would not mean she had failed.

Gillard was born in Wales, the second daughter of John and Moira, who came to Australia as assisted-passage migrants in 1966. Studying law at the University of Adelaide in the early 1980s, Gillard became involved in student politics. She rose to be president of the National Union of Students and moved to Melbourne, where she and her 'comrades' became motivated to work with and for unions. 'It inspired me to spend eight years as an industrial lawyer defending trade unions and working people', she said in her first speech to parliament, on Remembrance Day 1998. 'Our youthful anger may now be tempered by experience, but the same beliefs in fairness and the same fire remain.'

Melbourne brought her into contact with the socialist left of politics and unions, people with extreme and radical views. Gillard, however, was not of that ilk. She was chief of staff to John Brumby before Steve Bracks replaced him as Victoria's Opposition leader. Her social, industrial, economic and national security positions have evolved as the member for Lalor, towards the pragmatic centre of modern Labor. She's been a critic of the party's 'winner-takes-all' factionalism and, like Rudd, does not attend meetings. 'The factional structures of left and right are now ossified and devoid of meaning', she argued in a 2006 essay.

'I'm not sure that she was ever of the hard left', says a close friend of Gillard's beliefs. 'She's certainly never been a hardline, left-wing ideologue.' Anyway, says the friend, who is also a federal Labor MP, it is not as if the deputy prime minister is now compromising her values. 'It's really distinguishing between means and ends. We are not so fussed about the operating procedures, we just want to get the best results. So there's less focus on means and more on ends.'

In government, Gillard has put distance between herself and organised labour, particularly the education unions. From several accounts,

Gillard has grown more comfortable in the company of business people and the private-school crowd. As one of Labor's economics team, she identifies with the badge-slogan of 'economic conservative'. More frequently, you will hear her speak about choice and market-based solutions for a wider range of policy issues—from child care to housing.

One area that Gillard has come to only recently has been foreign policy and statecraft. In June, she attended the Australian–American Leadership Dialogue in Washington, met Vice-President Dick Cheney and made a nuanced, albeit short, speech about the alliance to DC's diplotragics and Canberra's 'fo-po' scribblers. It was described as Gillard's 'international coming out'.

Some in those circles had associated her with the anti-United States rantings of former Labor leader Mark Latham, rather than the tradition of prime ministers John Curtin, Bob Hawke and Rudd. 'In the world we try to help to build—in the civilisation we want to persist and prevail—the United States has a unique role', she told a State Department dinner.

'Our alliance is bigger than any person, bigger than any party, bigger than any government, bigger than any period in our history together. That alliance is enduring and indispensable.'

Gillard would be aghast, but like Rudd in so many ways she has a little bit of John Howard in her personal style. As the years wore on, and on, the former prime minister was often observed regarding his younger colleagues with approval as they stood at the dispatch box in the House of Representatives. Howard's gaze slipped from proud to wistful as the years passed. Still, he bathed his team in a fatherly beam when they were performing well.

Rudd, particularly during question time, is self-absorbed in his doodles and paper piles. Gillard, when she is acting prime minister, sits in the chamber with an expression that suggests, for that instant, that the person with the call—be it the minister for health or infrastructure or environment, or anyone for that matter—is the most captivating person on the planet. It's the opposite of smug (she saves that for attack mode).

In those moments, you see the nurturing side of Gillard's personality. Which is in tune with what you hear about her generosity from staff and those who worked with Gillard on the way up. It also gels with the views of those close watchers of all our MPs: drivers and security. They are used to being treated as wallpaper or robots, especially by the top man; when someone with Gillard's authority shows normal human warmth and respect, these judges tend to reach for nines and tens.

Another parliamentary role that Gillard has assumed is enforcer. She is doing the bayoneting in the skirmishes—buoying her own side, scornfully touching up the Opposition—that was done with aplomb in their time by former Treasurer Peter Costello and Keating, grand master of barbs. Where the younger man was lawyerly, rehearsed and well-briefed, the elder was a visceral street fighter. Gillard is very much the former. 'Whenever the government was under pressure this year, Gillard would bring the issue back to industrial relations', says a senior Labor strategist. 'Then we would get back on top of them. Her performances were very important.'

Gillard works the chamber with props, and she prefers to know the destination before she sets out on an answer. During the year, she favoured the computer mousepads the Howard Government ordered to promote WorkChoices. She made merriment with statistics, usually to claim some folly on the part of her predecessors. But from nine years of sitting on the other side of the House, Gillard knows that these set-pieces are largely about show rather than substance. 'We've got two hands tied behind our backs in terms of making progress', Gillard said of question time in 2006 and Labor's hunt on the wheat-for-weapons scandal. 'I mean, we ask questions, ministers don't have to answer them, there is nothing that makes them be relevant to the question and they can basically get up and say whatever they like.'

A different, harsher side of Gillard was on display during the closing days of the parliamentary year as she vigorously pursued deputy Opposition leader Julie Bishop. In contrast to governing, Bishop has lacked authority and poise in Opposition. In response to a Gillard insult, Bishop made a feline-style gesture in the heat of the moment. Absolving his deputy of bad form, Malcolm Turnbull told an interviewer that Gillard 'is very vicious and insulting'. 'I reckon if she spent less time rehearsing nasty lines about Julie Bishop in front of the mirror and more time focusing on her job, we'd get some better outcomes in terms of the government.'

More time for focus on work is probably not possible (or even desirable) for Gillard. But better policy outcomes sure are. She has made false steps in politics and policy, although none of them seems to have slowed her momentum. At the 2004 election, in the shadow health portfolio, Gillard had carriage of Medicare Gold, a policy targeted at the aged that combined the worst excesses of the lax Gough Whitlam in the 1970s, and his latter-day, spendthrift bastard son John Howard.

In 2007, charged with Labor's pre-election industrial relations policy, Forward With Fairness, Gillard botched the job; it swung the power balance back too far to unions, and Labor had to recalibrate its approach to appease business. More recently, Gillard's partner Tim Mathieson, a part-time hairdresser and purveyor of hair creams and gels, was appointed by Health Minister Nicola Roxon to a role promoting men's health. The move invited claims of nepotism, scrutiny of Gillard's personal life and questions about her political judgement.

In the first year of a new government, Rudd, Swan and Gillard have been the mainstays. The prime minister is omnipresent, above and below deck; the treasurer has been covered in oil and grease in the engine room as the economy was knocked off course by the global financial troubles. Gillard, however, has been doing a different sort of job. She has had responsibility for guiding two of Labor's key policies: the 'revolutions' in workplace relations and education are core election promises, long-term reforms and messy works-in-progress. In both areas, Gillard has deployed fiddly consultations and reviews.

In March, she began the phase-out of Australian workplace agreements. For reporters, Gillard even did a stand-up death notice for WorkChoices at Kirribilli House, the prime minister's Sydney residence. Last month, after a convoluted journey with unions and employer representatives in a variety of forums, she introduced to parliament the Fair Work Bill, which will reshape the nation's workplace relations system. 'It's a good bill for employees, for employers, for families and for the economy', Gillard claimed in her second-reading speech. 'Only a Labor government could have introduced this bill because only Labor believes that the ideal of fairness should lie at the centre of our national life.'

The legislation, which is now the subject of a Senate inquiry, was welcomed by interest groups with faint praise ('workable', said industry, 'a good start', said unions) and the relief that comes from tortuous negotiation and compromise. Gillard built a review structure that reined in the critics and anticipated the practical difficulties of the new regime. All the while, she seemed to be listening to most of the voices in the room.

Labor insiders, who have worked in the union movement and government, believe Gillard has done a remarkable political sales job. Expectations within organised labour were high, given the role in Rudd's victory that industrial relations played. Many new Labor MPs and vulnerable backbenchers owe their places to the ACTU's emphatic Your Rights at Work assault on WorkChoices in 2006 and 2007. 'An outcome that had the unions outraged would have been really hard for the government internally', says one well-connected source. 'To get the bill through in its current form the way Gillard did, so it is externally and internally palatable, was an extraordinary effort.'

The battle is far from over, of course, as the lobbying effort directed at Greens and independent senators gathers pace. The bogy of so-called 'pattern bargaining' remains, where wage deals struck at enterprise-level spread to other parts of the economy. Employers are also worried about the access unions will get to employment records of non-members. Many business people argue unions will now have the upper hand in bargaining, and that the suppleness in the labour market that has evolved over fifteen years will be lost—at precisely the time when economic conditions require flexibility.

Education, a career-long obsession for Gillard, will be a more difficult challenge, especially given how high community expectations have been raised by Labor. In some popular respects, the 'revolution' means computers in high schools. The first piece of business considered, and approved, by Rudd's Cabinet was funding for computers, information tools and internet services for schools. But there was no allocation for the costly maintenance for state governments (who run schools) that comes with the mass rollout of hardware. Last month, Gillard announced an extra $800 million for states and territories to meet these on-costs.

Beyond arguments about the 'tools' of education has been the minister's pursuit of teacher quality, national standards and the publishing of school achievement reports. In this, Gillard has followed the previous government and run foul of the education unions; she has also retained Howard's funding model for private schools so far. Along the way, Gillard has discovered an education guru beloved by conservative think tanks: Joel

Klein, the man who runs schools in New York, visited Australia in November. Klein talks and acts tough; closing schools, firing teachers, it is claimed he has lifted standards and provided resources to the most disadvantaged students.

Higher education is another area of great expectations. The other day, on behalf of the expert panel she led, Denise Bradley handed her exhaustive review into universities to Gillard. Among many recommendations, including $6 billion worth of new funding, the report called for a voucher system for students. Yet another conservative ideal. The Rudd Government will respond in the early part of 2009.

So this demonstrates Gillard's new ideological flexibility? Well, yes. So flexible that she is also implementing a heartland Labor equity policy: Gillard will be phasing out full-fee paying university places from 1 January. If Gillard and Rudd are serious about matching their education rhetoric with action, it will be a policy world without end.

Then there are all the other major roads they are on—climate change, broadband, health, welfare, 'nation building'. Revolution may be a political slogan, but also runs the risk of turning into a heavy burden indeed. Are they up to it? Gillard, you sense, is just beginning the hard work of administration in all her portfolios and at the same time seems intent on doing it her way. Her consultative skills are so far proving effective. They will become essential as she travels a path that may be less predictable than even some of her closest supporters anticipated. Every now and then she takes off the safety belt. She is prepared to experiment. This is called leadership.

4

The Politics of Coming Clean

Annabel Crabb

St Kevin smites global sinners
The Sydney Morning Herald, 12 July 2008

Repent ye, for the Kingdom of Kevin is at hand. Impending apocalypse does funny things to people, doesn't it? As the climate change debate runs to new heights of biblical frenzy, all the signs of an imminent catastrophic event are visible to the naked eye right here in Sydney.

Flights of nuns in sturdy sneakers roam the streets.

A plague of iguanas is reported with much fear and wonderment.

In the churches, worshippers gather fervently around the long-dead bones of saints.

(In Perth, the rare public appearance of the Liberal Party's own holy relic, John Howard, causes the party faithful to ululate and part spontaneously with wads of cash; they are rewarded by hearing their former leader promise not to engage in a running commentary on the present government, especially not the fact that Kevin Rudd is a total fraud.)

In the streets, the godless masses queue in their thousands outside phone shops, keen to acquire their own personal false iDols; these trinkets are manufactured, with breathtaking biblical literalism, by Apple—a company named for a fruit whose role in the inauguration of human sin is so famous as to need no further explanation.

Naturally, the advance of environmental Armageddon has flushed out a vocal array of prophets. King among them is St Kevin, whose spotless zeal is the gold standard in environmental crusading, and whose warnings of famine and pestilence are already legend: it is harder for the proprietor of a coal-fired power station to enter the kingdom of Kevin than it is for a camel to pass through the eye of a needle.

St Kevin took himself to Japan this week, where he mingled with world leaders agonising over the end of the world.

They cannot yet agree, and St Kevin does not have the power to compel them to agree, but in the event that they one day do reach agreement, St Kevin needs to be able to demonstrate that he was around for the negotiations.

Like a rooster who crows every morning just before sunrise, he hopes to acquire a reputation for causing the dawn.

At home, Doubting Brendan piped up with something of a contemporary heresy, insisting that there is no use being pure of heart when the rest of the world is still yet to repent.

Why rush to install an emissions trading scheme, he argued on the steps of the temple, before other nations have done the same?

Doubting Brendan's disciples were quick to claim that he had meant nothing of the kind.

Several people—Malcolm the Inevitable, Greg the Usurped and Julie the Long-Suffering—lined up to explain that Brendan had actually been massively misreported, and was now resting quietly in his tent.

But Doubting Brendan could not be silenced; he kept sneaking out to do press conferences and to confer with his Senate leader, Nick Minchin, the Desert State Denialist.

Minchin is a pale-eyed David Koresh type, a rogue prophet who lives and preaches amid the parched rubble that used to be known as South Australia.

He is not the official environment spokesman for the Coalition—a fact of which we were reedily reminded on Wednesday by Greg the Usurped, who is.

But Minchin bought Doubting Brendan for a fair price late last year—three crucial votes—and he is determined to make his investment work.

This relationship may account for the circularity and tortuousness for which the teachings of Doubting Brendan have quickly become known. To the goat-herders, he says one thing, to the money-changers another.

Journalists venturing into a Nelson transcript are best advised to lash themselves to something large and heavy first, so as not to disappear permanently into the maelstrom.

But how the orthodoxy has changed in less than a year.

It used to be that anybody advocating unilateral Australian action on climate change, unmatched by corresponding efforts in the developing world, was immediately set upon, denounced, beaten, and cast out into the wilderness.

Just ask the Environment Minister, Peter the Exile, who was nearly stoned to death during last year's election campaign when he said that a Rudd Government would sign up to emissions reductions with or without the rest of the world.

Sources close to the Exile's mountain cave this week would not comment on the irony of this, but took the opportunity to reiterate that the above occasion was the only time the Environment Minister has ever been stoned in his life.

These days, the sceptics have the lower hand, and precious few survive; Michael Costa aboard the flaming wreck of HMAS Iemma, the Desert State Denialist himself, and Tony 'People Skills' Abbott.

What comforts them? Perhaps it's the words that so nearly appear in the Gospel of Matthew: Blessed are they which are persecuted for righteousness' sake, for theirs is the Kingdom of Kevin.

Tim Flannery

The time for action is now
The Sydney Morning Herald, 19 March 2008

There are moments when the beauty of our great cities of Melbourne and Sydney is so sublime that it almost tricks me into losing hope that we can achieve a better future.

Crossing the harbour at night, or looking westwards across the Yarra, with the great buildings, the roads and houses blazing so that their reflections dance on the water, I can't help but ponder that this beauty is produced by the digging and burning of mountains of coal. As we enjoy our cities' wonders, we seem to suffer Saint Augustine's curse: so many of us want to change, but not yet. If you doubt me, fly over either city and try to spot a solar panel or solar hot water system amid the sea of unadorned roofs. And this despite the most generous rebates (both state and federal) offered to those wishing to green their lifestyles.

The science on what we need to do is very clear. If we wish to give ourselves a reasonable chance of avoiding dangerous climate change, our fossil-fuel caused pollution must be curtailed swiftly and dramatically. Projections made by the Intergovernmental Panel on Climate Change last year indicate that to have the best chance of a stable future, global emissions need to peak within seven years and we must create economies all but free of fossil fuels within the next four decades. That means no conventional coal-fired power plants, no petrol and little gas being used by us by 2050. If we do not achieve this the atmospheric burden of greenhouse gas will have exceeded a key threshold, beyond which dramatic changes in climate become increasingly inevitable. Forty years may seem a long time.

But just think back. Elvis was fading forty years ago and many people recall Elvis as if he lived just yesterday.

What might the outcome be if Saint Augustine's curse continues to blight our state governments, unions, industry and populace? No one can know the future, but some consequences are already clear. I attended the United Nations climate meetings in Bali last year and they were a revelation. Enthusiasm for change was infectious among the normally sombre delegates. Even the traditionally reluctant Chinese were expressing a willingness to cut emissions, leaving the Bush administration out of arguments and isolated in its reluctance to engage. A great shift to clean energy is under way and any nation that does not carve out its share of the action will be left behind.

Here in Australia there has been much talk, by government and industry alike, about a shift to clean-coal technologies. The federal government has pledged half a billion dollars to foster it, yet no one seems to possess any urgency about actually building a commercial-scale clean coal power plant. Indeed, in New South Wales all the talk is about building a new dirty (conventional) coal-fired power station. The time has come for both industry and the state government to put up or shut up, for if work is not commenced on commercial-scale clean coal soon, the opportunity will be lost to competing technologies such as solar thermal, geothermal and wind. And that will mean that our advantage in possessing coal reserves will be lost forever. We have forty years to make the transition, which means that much new infrastructure must be built and old infrastructure decommissioned in this coming decade.

What are the state governments doing about public transport? Rail tunnels are about three times cheaper than road tunnels to build (because they're smaller and often don't need exhaust systems because the trains push the air through). Yet those few rail tunnels that are being built in New South Wales are on a virtual go-slow program. Engineers tell me that they could have been completed well ahead of schedule, yet because the state Treasury sees every rail traveller as a burden on its finances, the state government has no interest in their early completion.

Toll roads, in comparison, return money directly to the government, meaning that the state gives priority to them. I sense that things are a little better in Victoria. But if New South Wales is to play its part in the transition to a clean economy, all of this must change, and very soon.

The worst outcome of a state government terminally afflicted by St Augustine's curse would be dire. Our precious biodiversity is already under threat from a shifting climate, as is our water security. And of course we sit beside a rising sea. The medium-term projections for Earth's climate indicate that we have a few years of relatively slow climatic change ahead of us before things accelerate again around 2010–2013. That's about the time of the next New South Wales state election and any government that has been sitting on its hands that long will surely be hounded out of office.

In my darkest moments I fear that the New South Wales state government is dead on its feet, that even if the premier rose indignantly from his chair and demanded action on all of this, a swamp of incompetence, ignorance and self-interest would swallow his resolve without a ripple being seen. Small things, from the thousands who continue volunteering to pay a little extra for clean electricity, and the new, energy efficient buildings going up as a result of past good legislation and the determination of a few good developers and clients, are all we have to cling to at present.

Last year, Earth Hour demonstrated just how many of us really do care about our common future. I hope that the initiative can be expanded until one day the people of big cities such as Sydney and Melbourne can once again enjoy the light of the heavens on many days each year, unobscured by a wasteful blaze fuelled by a black, polluting rock.

Paul Kelly

Make or break

The Australian, 19 July 2008

This is the moment Kevin Rudd could not avoid, when his government had to take a stand based upon conviction. Now the entire future of the Labor Party and the new Rudd Government rests upon its response to climate change, a situation without precedent in Australian politics.

Having come to power pledging to limit cost-of-living pressures, Rudd is now imposing new costs across all households and businesses in the cause of cutting carbon pollution. It is an ironic fate that has befallen Labor: the party formed to improve the lot of Australian workers has become a century later the party pledged to change the nation to redeem its new faith in a lower carbon economy.

While Australia believes in a hotter globe caused by greenhouse gases, a majority of the world outside Europe, Japan, New Zealand and parts of North America rejects the imperative for such action. Despite periodic optimism from our government, the odds are against the United States—with its economy reeling—adopting a national scheme any time soon. China and India reject emission targets.

When the Keating Government lost office in 1996, nobody could have imagined climate change would become the make-or-break issue for the next Labor government. It is a gift and a curse for Rudd.

A gift because it terminates the creepy caution of Rudd's opening months. It invests his government with a meaning that it so conspicuously lacked. The recurring question—what does Rudd believe?—surrenders to an agenda that is complex, idealistic and high-risk. Just as John Howard saved his government by embracing the GST reform, so Rudd now has a cause that will define him. It reminds us that political power is enhanced through use and erodes through disuse.

It is a curse because, as Ross Garnaut argues, climate change is a 'diabolical policy problem' that he brands as 'harder than any other issue of high importance that has come before our polity in living memory'.

Harder than solving unemployment, cutting tariffs or tackling inequality. Harder because, contrary to the mantra that it is about belief, this issue is plagued by uncertainty and imprecision.

As Garnaut argues, Australia must act now to deliver results in future decades. Yet Australia cannot solve this problem—the solution is global and lies beyond our national domain. Finally, Rudd can only guess about what penalty Australians are prepared to accept now in the possible or probable hope that their children and grandchildren may live in a world less hot than it would be otherwise.

This week's government green paper discussing emissions containment enshrines three core decisions in Australia's response. First, that Australia has decided to act now rather than await more definitive global progress. Second, that our response is built around a cap and trade scheme, rebadged as a carbon pollution-reduction scheme, as opposed to a simpler carbon tax. The difference is that cap and trade involves an emission-reduction delivery target. Rudd pledges a 60 per cent cut by 2050 with the nearer targets yet to be decided. Third, the green paper shuns a purist approach and involves a series of interventions designed to cushion the impact on households and to reduce the adjustment pain for industry.

This has provoked the ire of the Greens. But it is entirely predictable. The message is that no Australian government will commit electoral suicide over climate-change mitigation nor undermine in one stroke much of Australia's globally competitive industry. The absence of anything remotely resembling a global emissions reduction deal post-2012 after Kyoto must compel any Australian government to a path of caution.

Indeed, the 'shocking' truth is that Rudd's scheme is not too different from the model Howard would have adopted given the former government's commitment to the Shergold report. Howard would have been softer than Rudd, but not too much softer.

Rudd's political strategy is apparent: he wants to occupy the middle ground. This message permeates the 516-page green paper. The government declares its approach will be 'methodical, careful and consultative'. This is Labor's mindset. Climate Change Minister Penny Wong is dedicated to this philosophy. For Rudd, it is essential.

Early impressions are that the government is well placed to deliver household compensation for a price impact less than the GST. The real problem lies with industry, where any shift to a low-carbon economy ultimately means a major shake-out. The alarm signals have been raised by Woodside chief Don Voelte arguing that liquefied natural gas is disadvantaged. This is just the start, and it comes from a company enjoying price rises of more than 100 per cent. Pricing carbon will alter the profitability of firms, industries and regions. But separating genuine concerns from special corporate pleading will be essential.

It means further talks with business on the scheme's design and maybe more concessions by Rudd. Above all, it points towards modest targets in the near term, leading to the 2020 cap. This is the critical decision that will define Rudd's scheme. Consider the flexibility the government gives itself for its scheme starting in 2010.

The white paper later this year on policy will provide an indicative trajectory for 2010–11 to 2012–13. Then in 2010 the government will announce the finalised caps out to 2014–15. The design envisages caps set five years in advance, extended each year but operating within a future 'gateway' that extends ten years ahead, offering long-run market guidance.

Australia's Kyoto target is emissions at 108 per cent of 1990 levels. It is impossible to predict our commitment under any post-Kyoto arrangement but Australia would be looking at a 2020 target at about 100 per cent of 1990 levels—a ballpark that would enrage the Greens and be depicted widely as a sell-out.

The concessions in Rudd's scheme point to the future politics: Labor will be attacked by Greens and true believers for rewarding polluters and for having a model that does not sufficiently cut greenhouse emissions, just as Howard was attacked for being a sceptic. Such attacks will play perfectly into Rudd's hands, helping him look responsible.

The Coalition is in a weak position. It cannot afford to oppose Rudd too much, otherwise he will brand it as locked into another bout of Howard climate-change denialism. That would be politically fatal.

Despite its useless noise and confusion, the Coalition has no choice but to ride with Rudd most of the way. After all, this is where Howard was finally located anyway. For these reasons, Coalition Treasury spokesman Malcolm Turnbull said yesterday the issue was not about which side was more pledged to climate-change action, but rather about competence and management.

It is a sound stance since, in truth, the scheme is an administrative nightmare. This week launches a massive lobbying campaign in Canberra to save jobs, profits, win free permits and obtain financial relief. Special interest politics will be licensed on a frightening scale, the result of a huge government intervention in the economy sanctioned by climate change on policy grounds yet to be exactly defined.

For households, electricity prices would rise about 16 per cent in 2010 based on a carbon price of $20 a tonne for an overall consumer price index effect of 0.9 per cent.

By declaring the scheme revenue neutral, Rudd ensures that 'every cent' raised by permit sales will be redistributed to households and business to help with the adjustment.

Rudd's interventionist concessions are significant. Forewarned by Liberal leader, Brendan Nelson, Rudd took the sensible political decision on petrol—offsetting fuel increases by cutting fuel taxes until 2013, the life of the next parliament. It is a straight political fix. The impact on petrol from pricing carbon will begin only post-2013. What else was Rudd expected to do? Hand Nelson on a plate an election agenda for cheaper petrol? Nelson's furious campaign on petrol prices during the past eight weeks has alerted Rudd to closing off this option, and constitutes a Coalition tactical win for a bigger strategic loss.

To assist business, the government offers three provisions. First, it will cap the price for permits out to 2014–15 to limit the cost any company has to pay for the privilege to pollute and to limit the overall cost of the scheme. The purpose is to guarantee a 'measured' start and guard against a sudden lift in the carbon price.

Second, it offers special assistance to trade-exposed industries. This was a firm Howard commitment. The aim is to dissuade industry locating offshore with no global emission gain: the dreaded carbon leakage. It is a delicate trade-off, since the more the competitive position of such industry is protected the more the rest of the economy has to bear a greater adjustment burden.

The government proposes to allocate about 30 per cent of carbon pollution permits to such activities on the basis of industry average emission intensities. There will be a scramble for such concessions. The political dilemma is acute—after all, the purpose of the scheme is to phase out such industry that is non-viable in Australia in a carbon-constrained world. And sound economic practice is that the market, not government intervention, should determine issues of viability.

The justification, as the green paper says, is to 'smooth the transition of the economy' to a carbon price. Such free permits would be granted at the start of each compliance period.

Third, the government has heeded the campaign from the coal-fired electricity generators and the New South Wales government. The Rudd Government is worried about the investment risk in this sector, the flow-on from sharp cuts in asset values and the need to encourage the sector to invest in carbon capture and storage technology. Such aid will be delivered through a new Electricity Sector Adjustment Scheme. The aim is to retain confidence in the electricity-generation sector and smooth structural adjustments for workers, firms and regions as they enter decline.

The Rudd Government has moved a fair distance from the Garnaut model in offering concessions and carve-outs. The problem is that once the door is opened, the demand for special assistance escalates. Voelte's memorable line this week was that he had 'booked a plane ticket to Canberra'. Rudd is operating in completely uncharted waters.

Shaun Carney

Lethal emissions
The Age, 5 July 2008

Sometimes in politics, the public can get lucky. With the demise of the Australian Democrats in national political life this week, there's been an orgy of retrospective finger-pointing about who was to blame, which has made it all too easy to forget or ignore the country's good fortune in having Don Chipp as a parliamentarian for twenty-six years. The Democrats were, more than anything else, an expression of Chipp's charisma, political imagination, force of will and skill as an organiser, and they existed in the Senate for thirty years—quite a feat.

Chipp, who died in August 2006, was an engaging and courageous man who left the nation's body politic in a better condition than he found it. In 1977, when Sir John Kerr's dismissal of the Whitlam Government was still an open wound on the society, Chipp put himself and the original members of his party forward as a healing force. It is not excessive to describe the party in its early years as a social and political movement. The essential idea of the Democrats was to save the major parties from themselves—to use goodwill and common sense as a brake on the unbridled pursuit of power. Unfortunately for the Democrats, that's one of the things that ultimately brought the party undone. The longer it existed as a broker on legislation, the more it accumulated responsibility for the results.

Nowhere was this more potent—and damaging—than when John Howard played Meg Lees like a violin in 1999 and made her a 50–50 partner in the GST. A stronger, less egotistical leader than Lees might have been able to keep her party together post-1999 but, highly impressed by her newfound importance, she had none of those capacities and, more than anyone or anything, set the Democrats on a course for destruction. But the Democrats were conceived as a party that carried policy arguments as well. As a party that contained a decent proportion of small business operators in its membership, it stood for moderate deregulation of labour markets and responsible environmentalism. When political parties die, it's always with a series of whimpers rather than a bang and this was the case with the Democrats, who suffered the ignominy of two successive federal elections, in 2004 and last year, in which they failed to win a seat.

In the next few years, Australian politics is likely to suffer for the lack of a party such as the Democrats. With the release of the Garnaut report yesterday, the tenor and policy territory for the remainder of this electoral term is set. The political debate will be very nasty and highly desperate. The Rudd Government is going to find itself running against every grievance that can be articulated and a few that cannot.

There remain many Australians who do not believe that climate change exists; Rudd cannot expect to win them over. As for those who do subscribe to the presence of climate change, Rudd can also expect to run up against quite a few of them as well.

The Greens, who have replaced the Democrats as the third force in national politics, have learnt the lessons inherent in the death of Don Chipp's party. They are unlikely to stay on board with Labor and go down with the ship, should Rudd's emissions trading scheme prove to be an unwieldy electoral monster. The Greens are a combination of two elements: unyielding environmentalist ideology, and protest at the inadequacies and self-interest of modern capitalism and the major parties, especially the ALP. The contradiction of the second of those two elements is implicit in the Greens' preferencing strategy, which overwhelmingly favours the ALP, except in safe Labor seats with high concentrations of white-collar and young voters, in which case Labor becomes the enemy that must be defeated. Whether this can continue in the future political environment, where an emissions trading scheme will dominate public and economic debate, is an interesting question.

The essential shift that's taken place during this decade is the move of the third political force from the centre (Democrat preferences generally ran 55–45 to Labor) to the left (Green preferences mostly favour Labor 80–20). Given the nature of the climate change debate, this isn't especially good news for the Rudd Government. The Greens leadership and the party's constituency, which is 7 to 10 per cent of the electorate, is unlikely to be fully satisfied with whatever Rudd produces. If, for example, Greens leader Bob Brown locks in behind a Rudd carbon trading scheme, what then is the compelling point of difference between his party and the ALP?

The potential for the emissions trading regime to mess Labor up is substantial. The Coalition's course on the issue now seems clear. Having originally disputed climate change and then in its final few years accepted it and finally, as the 2007 election approached, sent out some hard-to-ignore signals that it wanted to be seen to be doing things on water and solar power, it is now in retreat. The position being formulated by leader Brendan Nelson and environment spokesman Greg Hunt will look comforting to many Australians.

Politically, the Coalition's key objective on emissions trading is to inflict the maximum amount of damage on the government. Hunt's job is to fashion an intellectual and policy package that conforms to that objective, while simultaneously giving the impression that the Coalition subscribes to the reality of climate change and the need for action. In the short term, this should be relatively easy. With petrol prices wreaking havoc in the lives of many voters and sending shudders through the global economy, it will not be difficult to argue that a 2010 start date for an emissions trading scheme is hasty and economically reckless, especially when China and India can be held up as recalcitrants undoing our good but ineffective contribution.

Rudd will find himself caught between a climate change adaptation of the Augustinian request for 'chastity but not just yet' on the right and, on the left, purists who can always be relied upon to demand more. In the new political order where extreme positions are increasingly common, it could well be that old standby, money, that has the final word. Providing sufficient compensation measures for those disadvantaged by any scheme is Rudd's best—perhaps his only—hope.

Lenore Taylor

River will flow when the blather breaks
The Australian, 12 July 2008

Nineteen years ago as a young reporter, I travelled to the banks of the Murray River to hear then Prime Minister Bob Hawke deliver what he modestly called 'the world's greatest environment statement'.

It involved $500 million over ten years to plant one billion trees. (Actually it started out as 500 000 trees but then a young prime ministerial adviser called Craig Emerson bounded on to the press bus to say the figure had been bumped up to one billion by factoring in self-seeding.)

Hyperbole aside, that day was the start of political and popular public recognition that something was terribly wrong with our most important river system.

Unfortunately it didn't make much of a start on solving the problem.

Over the ensuing two decades there were numerous further attempts: the 1992 Murray–Darling Basin agreement; the 1994 Council of Australian Governments agreement to put a cap on surface water diversions; the 2004 Living Murray agreement to spend $1 billion to return 500 gigalitres of water to the river; John Howard's hastily cobbled together Australia Day 2007 effort to spend $10 billion to solve the problem; and the Rudd Government's subsequent attempts to recast that plan (with an additional $2.8 billion) through its version of not-so-co-operative federalism. And the result? As the amounts of money promised rose, the amounts of water in the river kept getting less.

This week, Kerry Muller, an ecologist specialising in the internationally recognised South Australian Lower Lakes and the Coorong, said that without 400 gigalitres of water (almost as much water as is in Sydney

Harbour) coming down the river this year, those lakes would acidify, their fish and marine life would die and the damage would take decades to reverse, if it ever could be.

It's not solely the politicians' fault, of course. Well, not solely our politicians' fault, anyway. The cumulative effects of drought and global warming have reduced available water alarmingly, and total inflows to the Murray–Darling in June were only 95 gigalitres, the lowest on record. Water allocations to irrigators this season are either zero or negligible.

As politicians of all persuasions repeatedly say, they may have a lot of power, but they can't make it rain. But what they are less fond of admitting is that they have not done all they have the power to do, which is to overcome state bickering and vested interests and reduce the over-allocation of water being extracted from the rivers.

Just last week, despite the false protestations of historic breakthroughs at COAG, the prime minister and the premiers squibbed it again, with Victoria blocking a deal to remove the limitation on how much water the federal government can buy back for environmental flows from any single irrigation district in a given year.

Victorian Premier John Brumby is right to say that lifting the cap now would not mean immediate flows of water down the river, because at the moment there is no water. But it sure would have helped the government to use some of its $12 billion to buy back water licences so that water will start flowing down the river the very second it rains.

Now Climate Change and Water Minister Penny Wong, apparently the minister responsible for all the country's 'diabolical problems', has to find other ways to return water to the river, when there is some.

Conservationists believe that since governments have now slowed down the rate at which they can acquire water voluntarily—right at the time they should be speeding it up—they will need to consider some other difficult options.

'Since they keep limiting the extent to which they can purchase water from willing sellers, they now need to look at buying entire properties with the water rights attached to them, at acquiring entire irrigation areas and even at compulsorily acquiring water rights', says Arlene Buchan of the Australian Conservation Foundation.

No one in government has been prepared to countenance compulsory acquisition—that phrase is like a red rag to farmers—but the government is looking at buying entire properties, and then, as the owner of the associated water licences, returning that water each year to the river.

And this idea has particular attractions for the $350 million it allocated to Queensland at COAG for 'irrigation planning . . . and water purchasing from willing sellers', since the Darling River system still has some actual water that could be bought.

But there's a big few hitches in the apparently neat solution of buying, say, some of the Sydney Harbour-worth of water that can be stored on the notorious Cubbie Station, a cotton irrigation property, and returning it to river flows.

First, as was reported in *The Australian* this week, the Queensland government is only now considering issuing Cubbie with tradeable licences (worth up to $100 million) for most of the water the station has been diverting for years.

So our governments would effectively be giving Cubbie a property right and then using our money to buy it back. According to Liberal Senator Bill Heffernan, who has been raging about Cubbie Station for years, this would amount to a 'fraud on the public purse'.

Second, given that much of the water diverted by Cubbie and other stations in southern Queensland is from so-called 'overland flows', there are significant difficulties in returning it to the river rather than allowing it to flow on overland until it hits the next properties' diversion.

And, as Murray–Darling Basin chief executive Wendy Craik cautioned this week, water bought in the upper parts of the system would not be much help to the lower lakes because of evaporation, and all the other irrigators' diversions it would have to negotiate along the way.

But if water bought in Queensland can be returned to help other parts of the river it still seems like a worthwhile exercise.

Because at the moment what we have is an intergovernmental agreement to set up an authority to produce new water-allocation plans between now and 2019.

I'll sit up and take notice when somewhere, among all the myriad plans and all the verbiage, and all the billions of dollars and squillions of trees (with almost twenty years of self-seeding they must surely be running into the squillions by now), someone does something that actually returns significant amounts of water to the rivers.

Michael Duffy

Carbon warrior Rudd has found his version of Howard's way

The Sydney Morning Herald, 12 July 2008

Both the following speakers are Australian politicians. One is announcing an increase in the war effort in World War II. The other is talking about climate change. Spot who's who.

'No longer can this nation rest upon the basis of the ordinary way of life, of conducting business in the way we did, of working the way to which we have been accustomed. The [current crisis] has put an end to that period in our history.'

'The penalty clause for us not acting is almost unthinkable . . . This country is on the verge of cataclysmic times, such as the human collective experience has never known.'

You can probably tell the difference because of the hysteria in the second quotation. Prime Minister John Curtin and his generation did not do hysteria, at least not in public. Senator Bob Brown (in the second quotation, from his address to the National Press Club this week) and many of his colleagues don't only use hysteria, they get elected on its back.

The rhetoric surrounding global warming is drawing increasingly on notions of religion and war. As has been often noted, environmentalism in its more extreme forms is deeply appealing to those of us with a need to believe in something, but who have decided that science has killed off Christianity.

Brown, with his apocalyptic talk of cataclysm, exemplifies this. Ross Garnaut's use of the term 'diabolical' when presenting his report pressed the same button. The Four Horsemen of the Apocalypse certainly get a good gallop in the report, with predictions of war (geopolitical instability), famine (collapse of agricultural productivity), pestilence (dengue fever) and death (all the above, plus heat-related fatalities).

ABC TV's political editor, Chris Uhlmann, picked up on the religious element in the carbon crusade on *Insiders* last Sunday. Speaking, he said, as a former seminarian,

> one of the things that strikes me most strongly about this debate is its theological nature—and that's essentially that we have sinned against the environment, that we are now being punished and the only way we can escape that punishment is to wear a hair shirt for the rest of our lives.

Uhlmann said that while he was willing to 'sign up' to climate change, 'I do not believe every proposition that's been put. When the weather department can tell me what the weather is going to be like next Friday with any certainty and Treasury can get within a million dollars of what the surplus is going to be next year, I'll believe an economic model that marries those two things and casts them out over 100 years. I'll make one prediction—that whatever number Garnaut puts on where we'll be in 2100, it will be at least a trillion dollars either way wrong.'

Turning from religion to war, it's not hard to see why politicians might be attracted to the military connotations of a carbon crusade. Wars, after all, are usually good for democratic governments, who see their support go up in the early stages of the conflict because in the public mind the ruling party's interests have become the same (at least temporarily) as the nation's. This phenomenon has been widely noted, and forms the basis for the rather splendid novel *American Hero* by Larry Beinhart, and the 1997 film version, *Wag the Dog*.

Wars have proved so useful in attracting or maintaining voter support that the war model has been extended into non-military zones by politicians around the world, with inventions such as the 'war on drugs' and the 'war on obesity'. But the war approach, whether military or not, presents dangers.

John Howard in his 'war on terror' took Australia into Iraq in search of weapons of mass destruction that proved to be non-existent. Time will tell whether Kevin Rudd, in his 'war on carbon', ends up harming another nation (in this case our own, by damaging the economy) in pursuit of another illusory danger.

Still, there will be lots of press releases and photo stops along the way, and Rudd will get the opportunity to talk at plenty of televised gatherings of international leaders, something he seems to enjoy very much. Already you can see the heads of powerful nations giving Rudd that nervous look Howard attracted at these gatherings. He, too, would approach them with one hand ready to pat them on the back, the other grasping theirs in a remorseless handshake for as long as the cameras were pointing the right way.

While it might be argued that Iraq got Howard in the end, it provided him with a lot of benefits along the way, and not just photo sessions with the American president. It made Australian politics and the thousands who earn their living from it (yes, including journalists and commentators) feel important.

Another useful result was that many on the right felt it was inappropriate to criticise the government for other things (such as its betrayal of much of the liberal policy agenda) in a time of crisis. And the left became so excited they became obsessed by minor issues such as David Hicks, instead of domestic matters of substance.

The benefits of the Iraq war couldn't last for ever, of course. But they helped John Howard have one of the longest runs of any Australia prime minister. If carefully managed, the war on carbon could do the same for Kevin Rudd.

Clive Hamilton

Politics trumps science in Garnaut Report
Crikey, 30 September 2008

Ross Garnaut's interim report in February was a remarkable document; unlike all previous official reports on climate change, it recognised the true implications of what the scientists are trying to tell us.

For the first time, the analysis of emission reduction targets and the international structures required to achieve them were linked closely to the climate science.

The unusual directness of this link meant that the interim report's analysis was less clouded by implicit political judgements about 'what is feasible' and less attenuated by undue emphasis on scientific uncertainties.

The dismay felt by many people on the release in early September of the Garnaut draft supplementary report *Targets and Trajectories* stemmed from the decision to sever the close link between the science and the policy recommendations and allow political judgements to intercede. In the intervening months Ross Garnaut had redefined his job: his task was no longer to tell the Rudd Government what it needs to do to avert climate chaos but to strategise politically on its behalf.

Garnaut concedes it is no longer the science that governs his recommendations. Instead of aiming to stabilise global emissions at 450 ppm CO_2e or below, as the science demands, he has recommended to the government, albeit reluctantly, that Australia take a target of stabilising global emissions at 550 ppm to the Copenhagen conference in late 2009.

Garnaut summarised his strategy in his 5 September Press Club address:

The path to 450 parts per million lies through early progress on 550 parts per million. The path to 400 parts per million, lies through early progress on 450 parts per million.

The rationale he gives is that the world is not ready to accept the economic impacts of a 450 ppm target. It requires more economic sacrifice and political resistance than some governments are willing to absorb. Garnaut believes that if we aim initially for 550 ppm it will become apparent that the pain is less than anticipated, a realisation that will allow Australia to argue to the world that we should pursue a 450 ppm target and then a 400 ppm target.

Apart from several serious flaws set out below, the argument is wholly contradicted by the report's economic modelling. The results show that pursuing the 550 ppm target will shave a little more than 0.1 per cent from GNP growth through to 2050. This means that instead of growing annually at, say, 2.5 per cent if we do nothing, GNP would grow at 'only' 2.4 per cent if we aim at 550 ppm. What does this mean?

At an annual real growth rate of 2.5 per cent, then with no emissions target, Australia's GNP will double in 2040. We will be twice as well off. If the Rudd Government adopts policies aimed at the 550 ppm target our GNP will not double until 2042. In other words, we will have to wait an additional two years before we are twice as rich.

What about the extra cost of aiming for the 450 ppm target that Garnaut says is not feasible? According to the modelling, if we aim for 450 ppm we will have to wait an additional six months before our income doubles. Instead of two years we will have to wait for two-and-a-half years.

History matters

A better understanding of the history of international climate change negotiations and how they have framed notions of fairness would have signalled to Professor Garnaut that his proposed strategy is dangerously misguided. Any one of the serious flaws in the approach renders it self-defeating. Together they risk turning Australia from a potential global leader into a laggard once again, reducing the momentum to reach a bold agreement. I explain each of these flaws.

1. Reduces expectations. A negotiating strategy based on the assumption that the Copenhagen conference will fail to reflect the science is self-fulfilling. Adopting a strategy with a soft interim ambition pre-empts the outcome and contributes to it. Garnaut puts forward no real evidence that aiming for 450 ppm at Copenhagen is infeasible, and his own economic modelling indicates that the difference in cost between a 550 and a 450 target is disappearingly small.

Garnaut may turn out to be right that a more stringent global target will prove too difficult; but that does not mean we should not try. The strongest agreement at Copenhagen will emerge if all parties push for the strongest outcome. This seems blindingly obvious, yet Garnaut is saying that the strongest outcome in the long-term is to accept a weaker outcome in the short term. Even if this is true, to flag that this is what Australia expects reduces the chances of getting something better than 550.

Professor Garnaut is reported today as saying that we should not be too ambitious because we do not want another Kyoto. This reflects a mistaken understanding: the Kyoto Protocol was not too ambitious. Its failures were due to the intransigence of governments in Washington and Canberra dominated by sceptics and captives of industry. Climate science and public opinion have hardened a great deal since then.

2. Naively flags intentions. Flagging one's negotiating strategy in advance of the Copenhagen conference is naive. Other nations and blocs may well go to Copenhagen with 550-type scenarios as fall-back positions, but it is unlikely that any other government would signal its reserve position before the negotiations have even begun. Garnaut is able to describe game theory well but his report suggests he needs practice playing the game.

In attempting to base an approach on subtle political assessment, Garnaut has already spiked his own strategy. Its success depends on the Rudd Government having the authority to persuade the world that it is a credible one, yet recommending Australia adopt cuts of 10 per cent by 2020 when the science calls for 25 to 40 per cent and Europe is willing to agree to 30 per cent, destroys our credibility. This is the contradiction embedded in Garnaut's position.

The Garnaut Report is hobbled by delusions of grandeur, as if an Australian Government, advised by Garnaut, can cut through all of the complex difficulties and solve the problem with a strategy no one else had thought of.

3. Alienates key players. It is not clear whether Garnaut believes the obstacle that makes the 450 target infeasible is the Australian public or major players in the international community.

If it is the Australian public then he is saying to them: 'Here are the facts on climate science and economic cost. The science is much worse than you think and the abatement costs are much lower than you think. However, I don't believe you are able to appreciate these facts so I am recommending a soft option I think you will accept. Then later, when you have accepted it, I am going to spring tougher action on you'. In my view, he should treat the community as adults.

If his target is developing countries then he is saying to them: 'Here are the facts on climate science and economic cost. Although it's strongly in your interests to aim for a 400 ppm target I don't think you are ready to accept that so I am recommending a soft target that I think you might be willing to accept. Then after you have become used to the idea you might be willing to face up to what we really need to do'. This is arrogant and condescending and will not be well received by the cadre of experienced, sophisticated and well-informed negotiators around the world.

4. Misjudges time frames. The report's strategy assumes that agreeing initially to 550 ppm will buy enough time to persuade the world we should in fact be aiming for a much lower target. A 550 ppm agreement would allow emissions to increase through to 2021. Any sort of agreement at Copenhagen will lock the world in until 2020 before an opportunity arises for a tougher set of targets.

Yet the scientists tell us we do not have that much time, that global emissions must peak in 2020 at the latest, so the path mapped out by Garnaut leaves a very high probability of irreversible, catastrophic changes.

5. Ignores how fairness is conditioned by history. Because he came to the climate change issue late and does not have a good understanding of the history, Garnaut does not seem to appreciate the political meaning of his recommendations. He argues that a 10 per cent target for Australia is much tougher than it looks when set against the European position of 20 per cent without an agreement and 30 per cent with one, and against the

25 to 40 per cent Bali number that the scientists say rich countries need to pursue.

Some of his arguments about relative economic burdens are persuasive (and some, such as the population growth one are not—more on this below). But the headline rate has enormous political significance. We must remember that the huge ovation for Prime Minister Rudd at Bali reflected the profound relief after years of enormous hostility towards Australia for the role we played at Kyoto where we almost destroyed the treaty at the last moment and extracted a deal seen almost universally as outrageous. The chief EU negotiator said Australia had misled everyone and had 'got away with it'. Another senior negotiator said the Australian increase was 'wrong and immoral'. The subsequent repudiation of the Protocol and sustained attempts, with the United States, to sabotage it, dug a deep well of bitterness.

Unlike trade negotiations where the public and the media have no real concept of the meaning of various proposals, in climate change negotiations the optics are everything. The optics are set out in the table below, which puts together the 2020 emission reductions for developed countries proposed by Garnaut and those agreed at Kyoto in 1997.

	Kyoto emission targets from 1990 to 2008–12	Garnaut emission targets from 2001 to 2020 with 550 ppm concentration
Australia	+8%	–10%
Canada	–6%	–33%
EU25	–8%	–14%
Japan	–6%	–27%
USA	–7%	–12%

Looking at these headline numbers leads to an obvious question: After Australia extracted the most lenient target at Kyoto (even without allowing for the land-clearing loophole), why would Australia be allowed the most lenient target again?

The rest of the world is fully aware that Australia was required to do nothing to meet its Kyoto target, while some other countries—Japan, United Kingdom, Germany—have made substantial efforts to meet theirs. Why would Japan, which started from a more difficult position after picking the low-hanging fruit in response to the oil shocks of the 1970s, agree to a 27 per cent cut after all it has done when Australia, which has done nothing, is allocated a 10 per cent cut?

This must seem like some sort of joke. If Australia goes to Copenhagen saying the best we can do is 10 per cent this will be seen as Australia reverting to the role of laggard and spoiler once again, reducing global expectations about what can be achieved, eating away at the willingness of other nations to act boldly and forfeiting any leadership ambitions the Rudd Government may have.

6. Failure to think about reception of the plan. Blind Freddie could have predicted the immediate reaction to the lamentable optics of the draft report. Yet, innocent of history, neither Garnaut nor the Rudd Government seems to understand the critical role of the environmental NGOs in setting expectations about an acceptable benchmark. Both here and abroad, the media judge outcomes against what the NGOs say is necessary to avoid dangerous climate change. In the past the NGOs have gone as far as the climate science allows, but over the last two to three years their demands have fallen well short of what the science indicates is needed.

Garnaut has developed a roundabout approach to getting to the science-based target of 400 ppm, yet he evinced surprise when environmental organisations and climate scientists criticised his recommendations for being soft.

So for all of the strategising, the Garnaut Review forgot to account for the immediate reception the report would receive and how that reception would undermine, perhaps fatally, perceptions of the plan.

As this suggests, no matter how cogent the counter arguments are, the Garnaut recommendations look like a special deal for Australia. There are an additional three ways in which the scheme proposed does in fact represent special pleading for the country putting it forward.

7. Australian special deal 1—Unfair model of per capita. For many years, most environmentalists who have been involved in the international debate have agreed that in the long term the international sharing of the emission reduction burden should be based on per capita allocations. There is thus widespread support for the contraction and convergence model as the only principle that can include developing countries in a fair way. It is gratifying to see this principle adopted by Professor Garnaut.

However, he has interpreted and applied it in a way that makes Australia look self-serving, and therefore not truly interested in fairness. Garnaut has assumed that convergence should occur in a linear manner. The model of contraction and linear convergence to equal per capita emissions in 2050 gives rise to the proposed 2020 emission cuts reproduced in my table. As I have said, anyone with even a vague sense of the history of this debate will immediately see that the burden-sharing scheme Garnaut proposes just happens to allocate the most lenient headline target to Australia among all Annex 1 countries. Just like the Howard Government.

In a serious blunder, the draft Garnaut Report actually owned up to this.

> The fact that the emission reduction targets in absolute terms are much less stringent shows how the per capita approach *protects Australia's position* by allowing for population growth, a key factor in providing Australia with the least stringent 2020 reduction targets of any of the developed countries/regions modeled. [emphasis added]

We can be sure this has been carefully noted by officials around the world. It sounds a lot like the sort of self-serving sophistry that the Howard Government used to defend its position of protecting trade interests at all costs.

8. Australian special deal 2—Treatment of population growth. The model of linear convergence taking account of changing populations is responsible for Australia being allocated what appears to be a very lenient target. Population growth in this country, unlike most others, is largely a policy choice. If we decide we want the economic and social benefits of high rates of immigration, why should we be permitted to impose the costs of our decision (in the form of higher national greenhouse gas emissions) on the rest of the world? For any stabilisation target, any extra tonne of emissions Australia puts out because it wants the benefits of immigration has to come off someone else's budget. Tell that to India.

9. Australian special deal 3—Ignores our hot air. It appears that both Professor Garnaut and the Rudd Government believe that the slate can be wiped clean and the sins of Australia under the Howard Government will be forgotten by the rest of the world. In the spirit of reconciliation and

progress, that may be so, although it would be a sign of good faith for the new Government to declare that Australia is willing to do more than its fair share to compensate for our history of free riding. It should be remembered that the Australia clause, which allowed us to count post-1990 reductions in emissions from land clearing towards our Kyoto target, meant that our emissions from all sources other than land clearing will have risen by close to 30 per cent above 1990 levels in the 2008–12 commitment period.

Most of the decline in land clearing occurred before the Kyoto conference in 1997 and was therefore equivalent to the 'hot air' embodied in the Russian target. Russian hot air was due to the collapse of Soviet industry after the fall of the Berlin Wall while Australia's hot air was due to the collapse in land clearing after reaching peak levels in 1990. Yet after asking the rest of the world to wipe Australia's slate clean and allow us to retain the benefits of the Kyoto deal, Garnaut proposes that Russia be denied the benefits of the hot air included in its Kyoto target. This will not be well received.

In sum

Despite its admirable attempts to warn us of the implications of the science and the effort given to developing a fair model of burden sharing, the Garnaut Report's recommendations reflect an ignorance of the historical context of the debate and the perceptions of fairness that will shape its reception here and abroad. In short, Garnaut's subtle negotiating strategy has already foundered on its awful optics.

By so forthrightly and accurately acknowledging the true implications of the science in his earlier reports, Professor Garnaut took on a duty to alert the community and the Government to the dangers, and inform them that cutting emissions sharply is possible at very modest cost. After all, his own modeling indicates that if we pursued a 450 ppm target the cost to GNP would be trivial—instead of our real income doubling in 2040 we would have to wait until 2043.

This is the most important message of the report, but Garnaut has chosen not to emphasise it. Instead, he has decided that his job is to formulate a subtle, even tricky, global strategy for the Rudd Government to take to international forums. It should be no surprise that the gap he has now opened up between what the science demands and what he recommends has been met with dismay.

The Garnaut Review is being too clever by half: it is trying to preserve the Review's political relevance even though what it proposes involves terrible risks for us all. The bottom line is that the Garnaut Report provides the Rudd Government with the excuse it's been looking for to go soft while pretending otherwise, bids down the likely ambitions of developed and developing countries at the negotiations leading to Copenhagen, and erodes the chances of Australia playing a leadership role.

Mark Latham

Actions contradict polls

The Australian Financial Review, 16 October 2008

Nothing better demonstrates the illusory nature of opinion polls than the question of climate change. Last month, Newspoll claimed that a clear majority of Australians not only supported an emissions trading scheme (88 per cent) but were prepared to pay higher energy bills to make the scheme (ETS) work (58 per cent). These are interesting figures, especially when compared with the number of people who, in practice, have altered their lifestyles and lowered their living standards in the fight against greenhouse gases. The statistics for green electricity accounts, home energy conversions, green car purchases and food self-sufficiency show that no more than 10 per cent of Australians have tried to reduce their carbon footprint.

So what happened to the other 48 per cent in the Newspoll survey who said they were willing, as the saying goes, to put their money where their mouth is? They reflect a basic flaw in polling methodology. Unless people are familiar with a concept there is no point in asking them about it. Very few Australians understand the details of an ETS, so when telephoned by a polling company, the typical respondent is likely to fabricate their answer in two ways. First, they will try not to sound ignorant and second, they will tell the pollster what they think the pollster wants to hear. Given its dramatic portrayal in the media, opposing a solution to climate change is a bit like killing Lassie.

Most people like to appear generous and considerate when talking to others, even if their real view is that someone else should look after Lassie. This is the problem with the Newspoll nonsense. Talk is cheap. Greenhouse abatement costs money and unhappily, nine out of ten Australians are counting their pennies rather than their carbon units. While aware of the climate-change problem, they are yet to be jolted out of their carbon-dependent, middle-class lifestyles. The prevailing wisdom is that someone else will do something about it.

Even those in the vanguard of the public debate have found it difficult to turn their rhetoric into results. At the National Press Club last month, Ross Garnaut was asked about his carbon footprint and what he had done to reduce it. In response, he did not know how much carbon he used and could not point to any net decrease in his consumption. In Nashville, USA, the Oscar and Nobel prize-winning campaigner, Al Gore, lives in a house so vast it has eight bathrooms and energy requirements that are twenty times the American average. This is typical of the greenhouse debate; the elites implore the masses to cut their carbon consumption while failing to do so themselves. The free rider problem is not only between nations; it is between individuals. (For those wondering about my lifestyle, since 2005 I have reduced my carbon footprint by 43 per cent.)

Anyone who has experienced public life in Australia knows that the greatest barriers to reform are apathy and greed. Policy changes that threaten the household budget also threaten a government's survival. This is what makes the climate-change debate so surreal. The federal government has no intention of becoming an electoral kamikaze and the middle class has no intention of reducing its reliance on fossil fuels. Everything else is play acting.

The Environment Department's study of energy use in the Australian residential sector has forecast a '56 per cent increase in (household) energy consumption over the period 1990 to 2020', generating 'significant growth in greenhouse gas emissions'.

This trend is being fuelled by the standard fare of a consumerist society: bigger dwellings with fewer occupants; the proliferation of home entertainment appliances, and greater use of halogen lighting and whole-house heating systems.

Sometimes politicians are naive enough to believe their own propaganda. On climate change, however, the pollsters are guilty of self-delusion. Hugh Mackay, who has forged a public profile from interpreting the national mood, has argued that Australians are ready to embrace an 'imaginative, even drastic' approach to greenhouse abatement. This involves halving daily car usage through an odds-and-evens number plate system; banning people aged under twenty-six from driving, limiting air travel to special cases, and walking to the shops. Whoever Mackay includes in his polling, they cannot be residents of Australia's car-dependent suburbs. They would regard his agenda as laughable, as some kind of wacky eco-fascist prank. It's a long walk from Struggle Street to the shopping mall and an even longer walk home humping a flatscreen television on your back.

5
Political Legacies

Alan Ramsey

The inconvenient voice of politics
The Sydney Morning Herald, 9 April 2008

I knew John Button as one of the more significant Australian political figures of recent memory. Paul Keating says he'll always remember Button's 'penchant for devilment, for the zany and the unpredictable' and 'the fun in being around such a quixotic character'. Ten years ago, long after both men were gone from public life, Button remembered Keating very differently.

One thing Button remembered was the line in Keating's eighth successive budget speech as Bob Hawke's treasurer in 1990: 'This year inflation will fall further, the current account deficit will markedly improve, and employment will pick up'. All three would be delivered, Keating said, 'without the misery and despair of high unemployment and a savage recession'.

What happened?

Button would write in 1998:

> Unemployment had already risen 200,000 and was still going up. A lot of businesses were in trouble. Late in the year 'misery and despair' descended on the country like a yellow fog.
>
> Businessmen beat a path to my door [as the Hawke government's industry minister]. Tired of listening to complaints, I asked one senior businessman to talk to the prime minister or his treasurer. 'I have', he said. 'They're stone deaf.'

If accelerating climate change is now Al Gore's Inconvenient Truth, John Button during those Labor years was usually the Hawke Government's Inconvenient Voice. His candour infuriated his colleagues and delighted the journalists.

There were any number of examples.

Just before that 1990 budget, Keating's last as treasurer, a number of Treasury bureaucrats came 'in pairs, like the nuns of my childhood memory, watchful custodians of the official line', to brief Button in his office.

Button listened impatiently, and after they'd gone, he told his staff: 'We have fallen among f---wits'.

This is the bloke Keating now remembers for 'the fun being around such a quixotic character'.

Hawke never thought it much fun at the time.

Neither did Button. In his 1998 memoir, *As It Happened*, he recalled being 'very pissed off' by both Hawke and Keating throughout 1990 and how, after that 1990 budget, Keating had publicly attacked him following a television interview in which Button had 'doubted' that Australian living standards would rise 'in the next few years'. Although other ministers had made similar comments, Keating was 'pretty incoherent' about Button's remarks, even though he'd neither seen nor read what Button had actually said.

Hawke asked Button for a transcript and later called him to his office where, reading from the transcript, he quoted Button as having said: 'I believe that we're probably the most competent to handle difficult circumstances'. Recalled Button: 'Hawke raised his voice, put on his Mr Hyde demeanour, and read the sentence again, with added emphasis. "Probably", he said'.

'What the f--- to you mean by probably?'

An inconvenient voice.

I could write all day about Button and his influence during his ten years as a Hawke/Keating minister and government Senate leader and not do him justice. I thought him a lovely bloke and a great minister at a very difficult time in Australia's recent economic history, somebody who had the confidence of his ministerial constituency and the capacity and credibility to make people believers of the government's policies.

What he did well was tell the truth.

What he did even better was the way he crafted language in his quite sublime speech-making, almost always from his own notes, and as he would later craft the written word. He could write like no politician I have ever read.

And he was a friend. Thirteen years ago, on 8 April 1995, he flew from Melbourne to Sydney with Andrew Peacock to attend my wedding in the Botanic Gardens, two of only three ex-politicians there. It is a melancholy fact John Button died in the early hours of the thirteenth anniversary of that sunny Saturday afternoon.

His partner, Joan Grant, emailed at 8.10 a.m. yesterday:

> Dear friends, John died in his sleep. After the last few weeks I know it's what he wanted, and we are relieved he didn't have to go on with the misery any longer. I know you sorrow with us and loved his qualities of humanity and humour which affected so many people's lives so powerfully.
>
> Much love, Joan.

Geoff Gallop

A radical legacy

Griffith Review 19: Re-imagining Australia,
www.griffithreview.com

Like all great speeches, the Tenterfield Oration delivered on 24 October 1889—the most significant speech in Australian history—was a call to action, a call to the Australian people to achieve by peace what the Americans had achieved by war. The time had come, Sir Henry Parkes said, for 'an uprising in this fair land of a goodly fabric of free government' with 'all great national questions of magnitude affecting the welfare of the colonies' disposed of by 'a distinct executive and a distinct parliamentary power'.

Parkes was pointing to the need for a national system of government that embodied freedom. He was drawing upon the theories, insights and arguments of the British radical tradition—albeit modified by his experience of hard-edged parliamentary politics. This is the tradition of parliamentary and electoral reform, freedom of association and expression, national self-determination and social equality. From this tradition also emerged the argument for popular sovereignty, democracy and a republic. At a deeper level, the radicals recognised that good political systems weren't just important as a means to an end, but were ends in themselves. To put it in contemporary terms, they saw people as 'citizens' rather than 'consumers'.

Australian radicalism came from people like Parkes and John Dunmore Lang—two of the most important intellectual founding fathers, who laid the base on which men like Edmund Barton, Alfred Deakin and George Reid later built the nation.

When we think of founding fathers, we think of grey-haired, conservative old men who believe that the old ways are always best. Few Australians realise that our founding fathers were followers of, and sometimes proselytisers for, ideas that many of their contemporaries considered positively dangerous.

More than half a century before Federation, Parkes and Lang were calling for an end to transportation and the creation of a free society, federation, responsible parliamentary government with a bicameral legislature, equality of electoral districts and short, fixed parliamentary terms, universal manhood suffrage, a society without a privileged aristocracy or an impoverished working class, public education for all, and —at various times—an Australian republic.

This should sound familiar because, with the addition of votes for women, it is the Australia we gained in 1901 and live in today—enhanced, of course, by innovative social legislation and occasionally radical interpretations of the Constitution by the High Court.

It is important to remember that the time in which the radical social, political and constitutional demands were being formed—the 1840s and early 1850s—was a time of European revolution and political ferment in England.

Parkes, Lang and others got their ideas from egalitarian interpretations of the Bible, writings of the American revolutionaries, radical liberals like Jeremy Bentham and British radicals and Chartists—whose ideas conservatives considered seditious and revolutionary; indeed, support for them could lead to transportation.

There were many other important intellectual, social and economic influences on the establishment of Australian democracy, but the founding principles of our democracy were laid in a time of European revolution by men soaked in radical political ideas.

While sharing many constitutional principles, Lang and Parkes were chalk and cheese when it came to their visions of the future. Lang wanted a radical revolution; Parkes—at least in his later years—wanted radical reform to head off even more radical revolution. But the practical effect of their agitation was the same: the establishment of a liberal democracy in the former colony of New South Wales.

Ideas come and go. What seems radical at one time can seem conservative at another, and vice versa. This alerts us to the fact that radicalism is more than a set of ideas: it is a way of thinking that puts the thinker at a critical angle to society.

Many of the people who founded Australian democracy may have been self-taught, but they were good philosophers, unafraid to think in terms of first principles and ideals as they confronted the challenges of creating a nation in a time of change. We, by contrast, have allowed ourselves to become utilitarians and technocrats, dominated to the exclusion of almost all else by economics and accountancy.

These radical ideas and ways of thinking made the country from the 1850s to World War I the most advanced and envied democracy in the world. They gave us nationhood. Now it is true that they did not bequeath a republic in the form in which most now conceive it—with an Australian head of state.

But republicanism had other connotations in the nineteenth century. For many—including Mark McKenna, who discussed it in *The Traditions of Australian Republicanism*—the establishment of an independent democratic nation, free from tyranny and the control of an overbearing aristocracy, constituted a republic—'a republic in disguise'. The title Parkes first suggested for the nation—the *Commonwealth* of Australia—was an early modern translation of the Latin term *res publica*.

The significance of popular sovereignty isn't always fully appreciated. At the time of Federation, responsible government elected through universal suffrage was far from the norm. Universal manhood suffrage wasn't fully achieved in Britain until 1918 and unrestricted female suffrage was not granted until 1928.

In Germany, the government was responsible to the Kaiser until after World War I. Russia was an autocracy. While women were included in the franchise, original inhabitants were not, so the term 'universal' is highly qualified.

They also added the concept of the referendum. The federation itself had been created through a series of democratic acts drawn up by elected conventions and accepted by a popular referendum. One of the first great national controversies—conscription—was settled by two plebiscites. Try imagining today a national government putting such a contentious issue relating to matters of war, peace and foreign alliances to the people. It is almost inconceivable. Radicals had a significant influence over this remarkable achievement of nationhood, and many chose to work within the contours of the newly established system. This allowed them to achieve many important reforms which have never quite been accepted by conservatives and are still being fought over: conciliation and arbitration; a comprehensive opportunity and welfare state; and recognition of Aborigines, followed by land rights.

This was despite the serious reservations some radicals had about the limitations of the 1901 constitutional settlement. Many radicals had wanted full constitutional independence from Britain—which came later through the Balfour Declaration (1926), the Statute of Westminster (1931) and, much later, the *Australia Act (1986)*.

Those on the left opposed many of the liberal elements designed to prevent 'the tyranny of the majority'. Some resented the monarchical elements, which tied the system together and preserved the reserve powers of the Crown. Within the labour movement, a critique of the federal system itself and those elements that constrained the will of the majority emerged.

Radicalism stayed alive as a critique of the Constitution—and for some as a movement for an Australian republic with a strong and centralised national government. The concept of national development and full employment with social justice featured prominently in the thinking of Labor leaders John Curtin, Ben Chifley and 'Doc' Evatt. Their attitudes were also influenced by the economic impotence of state governments in the Depression and the need for national economic direction during and after World War II.

As far as state governments were concerned, there were many achievements, but radicals baulked at the lack of one vote one value, gerrymandered electoral boundaries and property franchises for second chambers. For those radicals keen to build a nation in a continent, the states were seen as barren ground. If change was to come, it would have to be led by the Commonwealth.

Add to this the growing belief in radical circles in the 1930s and beyond that the Constitution was being used opportunistically by reactionaries to block mandated reform. The dismissal of the Lang Labor government by New South Wales Governor Sir Philip Game in 1932 convinced many that the continued existence of the reserve powers of state and Commonwealth governors and governors-general pointed to the need for a republic. The obstructionism of state upper houses elected with a restrictive property franchise—such as the blocking of supply by the Victorian Legislative Council, which led to the defeat of the government of John Cain Senior in 1947—convinced radicals that upper houses themselves were the problem and electoral reform was needed.

In some states, it was Labor policy to abolish upper houses altogether. The blocking of attempts to control and nationalise banking in the late 1940s by the High Court and the Privy Council, using sometimes contentious legal reasoning, convinced others that judicial reform was also needed and that new constitutional ways had to be found to facilitate a new era of national development.

The greatest Australian radical of the twentieth century, Gough Whitlam, gave a modern flavour to his mix of democratic socialism and nationalism by adding many of the issues associated with the social and political movements of the 1960s. He took an activist view of the Commonwealth's constitutional and political position. Whitlam's radical constitutional innovation was to find new constitutional means to extend Commonwealth involvement in social and economic development—mainly through the use of tied grants to the states under section 96 of the Constitution and the creation of new bodies like Medibank and the Schools Commission to raise and disperse funds and lead national policy.

It was, however, the circumstances of his dismissal and defeat in 1975 that were most controversial. The combination of state and Senate obstruction and the exercise of reserve powers put the focus back on to the Constitution and what it meant for those seeking reform. It also raised a question mark about the Whitlam strategy and the assumptions behind it.

Ironically, while Whitlam's majoritarian and centralising version of radicalism was stealing the limelight, a new radicalism was being created—slowly and without fanfare—at the state level. Don Dunstan's governments in South Australia demonstrated what could be done by a state government. As the Labor Party's premier historian Ross McMullin wrote in *Light on the Hill* (Oxford University Press, 1991), 'after being renowned during the Playford era for its conservatism, South Australia became an enlightened pacesetter under Dunstan in many spheres, including electoral fairness, community welfare, consumer protection, planning and environment, education, equal opportunities, Aboriginal affairs, public administration and the arts'.

Dunstan was a pioneer, and similar changes followed in other states—mainly, though not wholly, from the efforts of modernising Labor administrations. In more recent times, this tradition has been developed further with innovations in democratic engagement and human rights protection coming from state Labor. These governments have proved that significant state-based progress could be made even under federal governments with more conservative priorities.

Perhaps more enduringly, through ambitious democratic experimentation the states set out to solve one of the problems the 1850s radicals and Federation hadn't been able to solve: the capacity of state institutions to frustrate radical social reforms. One by one, the state constitutional checks and balances were rid of their conservative biases: gerrymanders were negated; upper houses were given new proportional representation electoral systems; and anti-corruption commissions and monitoring agencies were set up to make state institutions more accountable.

The result is that it is much rarer these days to hear Labor complaints about the in-built conservative bias of the public service and the judiciary. The complaints are more likely to come from conservatives, who see radical elites. The result is that purposeful but practical reform has allowed Labor to dominate the states for the last decade despite one of the most right-wing federal governments the country has ever known.

Proportional representation and the rise of stronger third parties have reduced the likelihood that upper houses can frustrate radical reform. Despite the Coalition control of the Senate after 2004, it is still more likely to defend existing rights and generate pressure for more radical reform than the reverse.

In my view, the idea of a centralised national system as the necessary basis for radical change in Australia only made sense if there was electoral malapportionment and inbuilt conservative constitutional and institutional biases at the state level. Today radical progressives should embrace democratic checks and balances to further their agenda. This means a more positive embrace of the American elements of our Constitution, such as federalism and divided power.

While these radical constitutional reforms were transforming the states, other changes were occurring in Australian politics. One of the most remarkable features has been the left's embrace of market economics and economic rationalism, coupled with a more conservative and less populist political disposition. This was clearly demonstrated during the debate over the republic in the 1990s when the left opposed direct election of an Australian head of state. Australia's leading republicans couldn't contemplate sharing power with the people.

This opened Labor's ranks to arguments about choice in politics, diversity in society and innovation in public policy—all liberal values. It was an era of substantial revisionism in respect of the means and ends of power. Increasingly evidence-based public policy, rather than mere ideology, became the basis for thought and action.

At the same time, the right has become radical and regards the checks and balances created at Federation—the Senate, delineated state responsibilities, High Court balance—as impediments to the will of the people expressed through elections to the House of Representatives, and as standing in the way of radical right-wing reforming ambitions. Former Prime Minister John Howard explained his vision of 'aspirational nationalism' in his address to the Menzies Research Centre in April 2005: 'Fears of centralism rest on a complete misunderstanding of the government's thinking and reform direction. Where we seek a change in the federal–state balance, our goal is to expand individual choice, freedom and opportunity, not to expand the reach of central government'. And he told the Millennium Forum in August 2007:

> I am, first and last, an Australian nationalist. When I think about all this country is and everything it can become, I have little time for state parochialism . . . Sometimes [aspirational nationalism] will involve leaving things entirely to the states. Sometimes it will involve cooperative federalism. On other occasions it will require the Commonwealth *bypassing the states altogether* and dealing directly with local communities.

Howard was attempting to rewrite the constitution through political fiat. There was no need to read between the lines to get his vibe: that centralisation isn't just the most direct way to maximise the electoral benefit of pork barrelling but the best way to remove impediments to his version of national values.

The radicals' old dream of centralised national power has been taken over by the right in the interests of electoral pork barrelling, unchecked economic rationalism and populist cultural politics. Radicalism is as much a way of thinking as a program for government. One of the problems for Australian progressives is that they have been too locked into a centralising bureaucratic view, often unable to think in clear and decisive ways when it comes to non-economic issues. Progressive 'once radicals' have lost the intellectual ascendancy. We need to get it back by noting the space that now exists for a new and more liberal and participatory version of politics that supports social diversity and civil society.

Regaining the ascendancy won't be achieved through a lunge to the left, forgetting economics and responsible government and joining doomed crusades like the anti-globalisation movement. The answer lies in recapturing the radical democratic potential of federation and federalism.

Just as Henry Parkes and John Dunmore Lang faced huge challenges, we do so today. Their challenges were national development, national defence and interstate trade. Today, the challenges are environmental sustainability, development of human capital, and success in a globalised world economy without sacrificing equality. Addressing these issues gives progressives the opportunity to revive a sense of purpose and to reassert ourselves as a major intellectual and practical force for radical change. Pragmatism is a necessary and usually honourable reality of politics, but to regain the ascendancy, movements need more—they must have a sense of purpose and direction.

The dramatic decline in the Howard Government's popularity was not a rejection of strong leadership, but a rejection of arrogant, centralised power—a rejection of the trampling of state power, the overriding of checks and balances, and the abuse of the resources of the state. People want continuing economic reform, but not at the price of social progress and environmental irresponsibility. They don't want a swing to the left; they want balance.

Before you object that calling for balance is hardly radical, let me repeat—ideas that at one time seem conservative can at other times seem radical. In the mid-nineteenth century and at Federation, the idea of individual rights, popular sovereignty and a balanced federal constitution were radical democratic beliefs. They can be again today. We need a new radicalism that moves away from majoritarianism and centralism to one that emphasises the balance between individual rights and state and federal power.

To guarantee individual rights, progressives should push to enshrine a national charter of rights to constrain any government from slowly and unnecessarily chipping away at freedoms. We need a more sophisticated and proactive approach to the whole issue of rights protection that requires questions to be asked from the earliest to the last stages in the decision-making process. As Justice Michael Kirby said in the Annual Hawke Lecture in Adelaide in October 2007,

> In effect, [a charter of rights] provides a stimulus to the democratic process; it encourages us to think in terms respectful of the basic rights of one another. It promotes a culture of mutual respect of basic rights. But it leaves the last word to elected parliaments, whilst rendering them and their processes transparent and promoting vigorous debate on such matters.

Contemporary Australian society and our rapidly changing economy need a new commitment to federal–state co-operation. Instead of 'aspirational nationalism', we need 'co-operative federalism'. The proof of what can be achieved is already available. Over the last few years, Labor state governments led by Victoria, have worked together to create a new federal agenda that encompasses economic reform, human capital investment, infrastructure development, improving hospital, health, dental and aged care systems, and addressing sustainability. This agenda is designed to work without undermining the multiple centres of power required to promote innovation. Former Victorian premier Steve Bracks's *Third Wave of National Reform* blueprint, sent to the prime minister and other state premiers in August 2007 is a worthy successor to past initiatives and will succeed or fail depending on the level and depth of co-operation and cost-sharing.

To symbolise this new era of reform, we need a new movement to establish an Australian republic—one which demonstrates that reformers again trust the people by providing for a head of state to be directly elected, with clearly enumerated powers; one which views Australia not just as a republic, but as a pluralist, federal, progressive republic under popular sovereignty—a system that embodies the highest ideals of our liberal and democratic inheritance. Australia is incredibly fortunate and prosperous for most, but we didn't get there by taking the easy way out, relying on utilitarianism and pragmatism alone, or by focusing on economics and ignoring the insights of political philosophy into the relationship between citizenship, community-building and economic progress.

So my challenge is not to reject involvement in mainstream electoral politics but to recognise the radical reforming potentialities that still exist within our federal system of government. As reformers past and present have found there are new ways of bringing about quite radical change within the open boundaries set by the founding fathers, who took their political philosophy seriously.

Gerard Henderson

Liberals mustn't let Rudd dictate history of reform

The Sydney Morning Herald, 27 May 2008

The Labor Party and its supporters are very adept at writing their own history. Which is fair enough. It makes sense for all organisations, including political parties, to be interested in their pasts. The social democrats and leftists who back the ALP are also skilled at interpreting the history of their political opponents. This makes sense for Labor but poses a special challenge for those who back the Liberal Party.

So far the Opposition leader Brendan Nelson and his colleagues have experienced difficulty in defining where the Liberal-National Party Coalition stands following the defeat last November of the Howard Government. In the meantime, Labor is scoring some essentially uncontested points in establishing its own interpretation of its predecessor.

Last Wednesday in Melbourne, Kevin Rudd launched the new edition of *The Longest Decade*, written by the journalist George Megalogenis. The Prime Minister used the occasion to present his government's 'ambitious policy framework for reform for the future'. Rudd also compared the Howard Government unfavourably with the Labor administrations headed by Bob Hawke and Paul Keating between March 1983 and March 1996. He declared that Howard and his Treasurer Peter Costello presided over 'a wasted decade . . . of squandered opportunity'.

So the message is clear. According to Rudd in 2008, Howard was essentially a do-nothing, inert prime minister who failed to reform the Australian economy. But this was not his message in 2006 and 2007. Shortly before he became Labor leader, Rudd wrote an article in the November 2006 issue of *The Monthly* titled 'Howard's Brutopia'. He claimed that the conservative philosopher Michael Oakeshott (1901–90) 'starkly warned against a "brutopia"of unchecked market forces'. Rudd presented this genuinely conservative view in contrast to what he termed the free-market fundamentalism, economic neo-liberalism and unrestrained market capitalism advocated by those who supported the leading neo-liberal economist Friedrich Hayek (1899–1992).

I cannot find any reference to 'brutopia' in Oakeshott's writings. But Rudd's essential message was clear. He was depicting Howard as not a conservative but, rather, a radical advocate of free markets. In an article in *The Australian* on 18 December 2006, Howard responded that he was not a market fundamentalist. He added that the Coalition had presided over falling unemployment, rising real wages and a social safety net whereby 'the bottom 60 per cent of households are net beneficiaries from government benefits and services'. Rudd, who had become Labor leader in early December, stuck to his line. Writing in *The Australian* two days later, he again depicted Howard as a market fundamentalist who had 'gone too far' in implementing change. He stuck to this position throughout most of last year.

Well, Rudd's analysis in 2006 and 2007 may be accurate. Or his position today might be right. It's just that both positions cannot be correct. Howard and Costello cannot have been both Hayek-driven advocates of market fundamentalism and do-nothing types who squandered an opportunity to do anything—including, presumably, the things that mattered to those who wanted to establish a brutopia on Australian soil.

Like all prime ministers, Rudd is a busy man and he cannot devote the time to his speeches that he did in Opposition. Maybe his changed line of attack reflects his new speechwriting staff. The economist Andrew Charlton currently works in the prime minister's office. He is the author of the book *Ozonomics: Inside the Myth of Australia's Economic Superheroes*. Charlton's thesis was that Howard and Costello did little to reform the economy and that the real heroes of economic change Down Under were Hawke and Keating. Rudd launched *Ozonomics* last July.

These days *Ozonomics* does not present well. What would self-proclaimed economic conservatives like the prime minister and his Treasurer Wayne Swan say today about Charlton's claim in *Ozonomics* that 'the link between the budget balance and the level of interest rates is spurious'? Yet

Charlton's thesis, that virtually all the praise for economic reform in Australia over the past quarter of a century should go to Hawke and Keating, has carried over into Rudd's critique of the Coalition.

Rudd is point-scoring the way most popular, newly elected leaders do. The fact is that the Hawke, Keating and Howard governments all introduced significant economic change—which is why today, despite present difficulties, Australia has one of the strongest economies among the OECD nations. During his time as prime minister, Howard acknowledged the economic reform credentials of his Labor predecessors.

Neither Labor nor the Coalition engaged in market fundamentalism of a kind that would have been admired by a fan of Hayek. Both introduced substantial, but gradual, reform while maintaining a social safety net. The only possible exception is the Howard Government's WorkChoices legislation, which was widely depicted as too harsh. Yet it is unclear what Labor will do with the remnants of WorkChoices, which remains in place until 2010. Certainly Rudd and Julia Gillard have not dismantled the Coalition's industrial legacy at this stage. Judging by ACTU president Sharan Burrow's comments on *Meet the Press* on Sunday, there is concern within the trade union movement about whether Rudd will deliver on what many of his supporters regard as Labor's pre-election promises in this area.

In time, Rudd Labor will be tested as to whether it can successfully advance its reform agenda beyond the legacy of Hawke, Keating and Howard. Rudd's success could well turn on whether he can sustain the inflationary pressures which could result from the implementation of his climate change and industrial relations policies. In the meantime, the Liberal Party would be well advised to write its own histories and defend the legacies of Howard and Costello. Just as Rudd defends the legacies of Hawke and Keating.

Janet Albrechtsen

Romanticising Australian conservatism
Liberals and Power, November 2008

After the defeat of the Howard Government in November 2007, the relationship between the Australian people and conservatism resembles that of a long-successful marriage that has otherwise lost its zing. This is particularly the case with the Howard battlers, seduced by John Howard more than a decade ago to move from their otherwise Labor roots. That move signalled that Australians are naturally conservative.

However, taking these voters for granted after more than a decade in power, the Liberal Party rested on its laurels. The voters turned away at the hint of a suitor who resembled their previous democratic partner just enough to feel safe but who provided them with an emotional connection they began to crave. Re-establishing that connection is the core task of the Liberal Party as it tries to woo back the Howard battlers who deserted it last year.

Unfortunately, however, the defeat of the Howard Government drew two major responses. Both predictable, both wrong. While the Liberal Party has much to learn and much to change, the predictable prognoses have little or nothing to offer. The first school of criticism is found on the left, including the moderate wing of the Liberal Party. This theory holds that conservatism and its policies are dead. The left positively cooed that the wheel of history had turned and the march of progressivism, so rudely interrupted for more than eleven years, would resume.

It is a remarkable piece of wishful thinking. The centre of Australian politics is, and will remain, profoundly conservative. Kevin Rudd morphed into Mr Me-too, appropriating conservative policies but adding an additional, critical extra—the emotional dimension that voters craved. If you doubt the fundamentally Howard-like nature of Rudd's policies, you need only read David Marr's response to Rudd's victory speech on election night. The true left, epitomised by Marr, gagged when it realised that Rudd really did intend to follow John Howard's conservative policies.

The second school of thought is virtually the diametric opposite of the first. Led by Kevin Andrews and Concetta Ferrorianti-Wells, the 'true conservatives' came out swinging, suggesting that there was no basis for rethinking the agenda of the Liberal Party. This view is equally misguided. Blinkered by more than a decade of electoral success, some conservatives refused to see any messages in their defeat. Losing an election in a period of unprecedented prosperity is no mean feat. Many assumed it simply could not happen. Such shattering of political orthodoxy cannot happen if all is well.

All is not well within the Liberal Party. Liberals failed miserably in the area they have long claimed to be their greatest strength. Liberals (especially the conservative wing of the party) believe the core reason for their success is that they understand human nature better than the left. They deride the hopelessly romantic, utopian notions of progressive thought and instead design policies that work because they are founded on a more complete understanding of human nature. Recognising this, voters elected the Liberal Party again and again. And in the corners of voters' souls devoted to economic matters and national security, it was undoubtedly true that the Liberals understood their audience far better than their opponents—for a while.

But in an era of hyper-prosperity, voters' needs and desires have moved on. Kevin Rudd kept the sensible policies that played to the economy and national security, reassuring voters that he was no Gough Whitlam. And he added a killer ingredient. He coupled rationalism with emotion in his pitch to the Australian electorate. Like Barack Obama in the United States, Rudd and his team offered a new emotional connection to the electorate that the tired old Howard Government could not. Rudd successfully offered hope and change over experience and the status quo. Whether the US Democrat wins remains to be seen, but he has recognised the power of emotional appeal. In Australia, such an appeal could work in

2007 where it would have failed miserably in, say, 1975 or 1991, when the economy was front and centre of voters' minds.

Too many conservatives failed to see the cycle of politics turning. Right to the end, they derided the complacency of the electorate: how could a nation be so ungrateful? Well, it is time conservatives admit that was wrong; complacency is a natural human response to enjoying so much of something. And emotion is a critical part of being human. When the cycle moves, so must conservatism.

Liberals can either wait for an economic recession and the inevitable turn of the political cycle their way. Or they can do something. Doing something means Liberals must cater to a side of human nature they have long neglected. The Liberal Party has been so busy dominating the rational low ground, it abandoned the high moral ground, leaving the left to dominate that terrain. In prosperous times, when people look to more than the economy to satisfy their needs, when emotional arguments start to bite, the Liberal Party needs to claim that high moral ground. It does not mean rejecting core conservative beliefs. But it does mean recognising human nature. This is not necessarily an easy task.

In advocating a Liberal Party that understands the significance of emotion, the power of symbols and of language, while maintaining the traditional strength of conservative policy, I do not pretend I will always draw the line accurately. However, since in my view the Liberals require a synthesis of emotion and policy—a recognition that one cannot divorce policy from politics—the task must commence. If the Liberal Party recognises that man does not live by bread alone, especially at times when bread is in abundant supply, it is a large part of the way to future success. The detail may, of course, conceal the odd devil.

The death of conservatism?

Inevitably the defeat of the Howard Government led its critics to start gloating about the demise of conservatism. A new politics had been born, said the left. One that eschewed much of what the Howard Government stood for. Even moderates with leftist sensibilities succumbed to this pipe-dream, expecting newspapers, in particular my own, *The Australian*, to reflect and nurture the new landscape, chop down a few conservative voices and replace them with new voices from the left. Elections may allow the victors to rewrite history but that does not mean their draft will be an accurate one.

On the losing side, confidence wrecked, the Liberal Party began squabbling in the shadows. The moderates within the Liberal Party said, with an 'I told you so' tone, that the party needed to overhaul its policies, ditch much of what it stood for and pursue a more progressive agenda. The people had spoken, they said. Conservatism was on the nose with voters and if Liberals were to regain government, the party must swing smoothly to the left on a range of social issues.

The election result was, however, no win for the left. Neither did it confirm the position of the moderate faction of the Liberal Party, who often seem more at home in the Australian Labor Party. Those dancing on Howard's political grave have failed to notice that across the economic and cultural landscape, Howard proved that the centre of politics in Australia is inherently conservative. Only the more astute commentators from the left have recognised, and therefore bemoaned, that reality.

Most people will not articulate their beliefs as conservative. Indeed, many people may be loathe to call themselves conservative, such is the disdain that still lingers over this word. But look close enough and you find yourself wearing conservative values—and rather liking them—without even remembering how it happened. Subscribing to conservative values is not like wearing some hip T-shirt emblazoned with Che Guevara snapped up by young fashionistas traipsing down Sydney's Oxford Street. No, conservatism sneaks up on you.

Don't want to join a union or work as a full-time nine to five salary man?

Support welfare as a safety net, but not as a lifestyle?

Want to open your shop when it suits you?

Believe your choice to send your children to a non-government school ought to be supported, rather than ridiculed, by government?

Congratulations. You, like me, are members of the leave-me-be generation. And you're a conservative. Why? Because conservatism is founded on the principle that a society that allows people to make their own choices and live their own lives their way creates more happiness for more people than a society planned and run by a few, no matter how smart or well-intentioned those few are.

Howard recognised those tendencies in the Australian people. Yet, ironically he was also the master of his own defeat. His sheer dominance eventually dragged Labor to that conservative centre, making it a more competitive political force.

The moment Kevin Rudd was elected Labor leader, he filled every media sound bite declaring he was an 'economic conservative'. Indeed, Rudd adopted a 'me-too' stance on everything from immigration and border control to citizenship and national security. It was a case of more me-tooism on education with Rudd's pursuit of a back-to-basics agenda in subjects such as history, geography and English—subjects that had been distorted beyond recognition by the fads of education bureaucrats.

In the workplace, Labor finally worked out that a liberal philosophy had prevailed, one founded on the belief that individuals make better choices than the heavy hand of government or the clumsy collective mind-set of unions. Howard had overseen the transformation of the Australian workplace into an enterprise economy, where small business and individuals thrive and the attraction of collectivism and unions has declined. The fact that Labor now has a Minister for Small Business, Independent Contractors and the Service Economy is a recognition of that reality. And for all the rhetoric about abolishing WorkChoices, Labor's industrial relations policy recognises that transformation. Both before the election and after it, Rudd and Julia Gillard have publicly chastised the unions for imagining that unions are back in power. This careful positioning of Labor reveals the extent of Howard's conservative legacy.

Under Howard, other left-wing shibboleths were discarded. Unlimited welfare was replaced with a return to individual responsibility. Indigenous policies were premised on practical outcomes not symbolic gestures to the point where now, even Rudd, the leader of a centre-left party, talks more about practical reconciliation than symbolism. And his embrace of the Howard Government's 2007 intervention in the Northern Territory reveals broad community support to tackle endemic Indigenous child abuse with solutions the left would once not have countenanced.

The era of hardline conservatism is over

Important economic and cultural debates were fought and won by Howard and the Liberal Party in the period 1996–2007. Yet, to imagine that conservatism does not need to refashion itself after the 2007 electoral defeat is equally erroneous. Liberals cannot keep fighting the same old battles when the other side has, by and large, conceded defeat. That is why as leader Howard eventually turned from a successful cultural warrior to being an albatross around the neck of the Liberal Party.

Conservatives must recognise that the era of hardline conservatism is over—at least for now. But that was always going to happen. Conservatism has its cycles. Few remember that when Ronald Reagan left office, 57 per cent of Americans told pollsters that they wanted a change in direction. By contrast, only 47 per cent felt that way at the end of Bill Clinton's presidency.

That does not mean that Clinton was regarded as a better president. As John O'Sullivan, author of *The President, the Pope and the Prime Minister*, wrote in *The Australian*, when asked to 'rate presidents in terms of greatness, Americans in recent years have put [Reagan] just under (and sometimes above) Abraham Lincoln'. While Reagan's approval rating in office was a mediocre 53 per cent, since 1989 it has risen to 73 per cent. Those earlier poll results suggest that once the desire and momentum for change sets in, it is hard to stop. Margaret Thatcher and John Howard would encounter the same forces, mistakenly refusing to acknowledge that their time was up.

Thatcher fought the hard fights in the United Kingdom, only to be dumped as a relic of the past once the hard work had been largely done. As her loyal chancellor, Geoffrey Howe, would remark, Thatcher dragged Britain out of the 'last chance saloon', taking on the unions, the opponents of privatisation and the zealous supporters of welfare. Under her, the country embraced capitalism and free-market reforms that allowed Britain to prosper. She took the nation to war in the Falklands and won. She confronted Communism in the great twentieth-century battle of ideas and, together with Ronald Reagan, won. And yet, by 1990, an ungrateful nation had turned on her.

The Howard Government inherited a country that was in debt to the tune of $96 billion. Yet net Commonwealth debt today is zero. Real wages are up by 21.5 per cent; unemployment is at 33-year lows; and more than two million new jobs have been created. Taxes have been reduced every year since 2003. Inflation is half that under Labor. On national security, Howard was one of a handful of Western leaders to talk honestly about the threat to the West of Islamic fascism. He introduced tough anti-terrorism laws that horrified the chattering classes but resonated with mainstream Australia. The Labor Party realised this, and signed on to those laws. Howard became known, like the Iron Lady, as a conviction politician. Our own Man of Steel. Then the unthinkable happened. The Howard Government was tossed out and Howard went down in history as only the second Australian prime minister to lose his seat.

Both Thatcher and Howard were the dominant conservative conviction politicians of their time, challenging entrenched orthodoxies, unwavering in their belief in the power of capitalism and the individual. They challenged political correctness long before it was fashionable to do so. They rebuilt their conservative parties, winning election after election. And after eleven-and-a-half years in the top job both began to look like great leaders from the past, rather than inspiring leaders for the future.

Towards the end of their prime ministerships, both Thatcher and Howard preferred to fight on regardless, knowing that defeat was inevitable. The problem, reflected John Sergeant in his biography *Maggie*, was that: 'The Conservative agenda for the 1990s was beginning to look suspiciously like the Conservative agenda of the 1980s'. In other words, voters had moved on, eager for a new vision, but Thatcher was part of the past. The same happened in Australia in 2007.

There are analogies to be drawn from the United States also, as Republicans try to work out how to win back voters they have manifestly lost and will perhaps lose at the 2008 presidential election. In his new book *Comeback*, conservative commentator David Frum maps out a case for a revival of conservatism. Frum, a former speechwriter for George W. Bush, begins by explaining why the Republicans are losing. His message is that Republicans have been fighting old battles—based around free markets, smaller government and lower taxes—at a time when people have stopped listening. There was a time when warning against big government worked with voters. But as the left has moved to embrace those issues, the right needs to find new ground.

Much the same has happened in Australian. The Howard Government delivered massive tax cuts in the May 2007 budget, and promised another $31 billion if re-elected. There was no bounce from voters.

If the tax cuts drew a yawn from voters, the Howard Government's industrial relations policy caused them to positively wince. Howard appeared to be the ideological warrior on industrial relations at a time when the electorate had insufficient appetite for workplace reforms. The reforms were, quite simply, a bridge too far in times of prosperity. With employment at record highs, people were looking for something else and the Liberals failed to notice. Howard has always rejected the ideological tag, choosing to frame himself as the pragmatic conservative politician. But the perception was otherwise. And perceptions matter.

Conservatives lost the emotional argument in two critical areas

Industrial relations

On industrial relations, Labor and the unions ran a highly effective—and emotional—campaign to convince voters that the Howard Government's WorkChoices legislation was too extreme. It did not matter that individuals had no experience of being shafted by these laws. They were clearly worried that their children, their friends, their colleagues would be treated badly by employers who gained more power under the new laws.

The Howard Government failed to win the emotional argument. That failure led to the 2007 defeat—and it goes to the core of where conservatism needs to lift its game.

Conservatism is rooted in the reality of human nature. Conservatives have long prided themselves on the fact that conservative philosophy recognises the full gamut of human nature, from the mostly good to the sometimes bad and the occasionally ugly. Most people, when left to their own devices, behave appropriately and progress nicely without the need for government regulation. Regulation is required only to the extent necessary to provide safety nets for the vulnerable and to curb abuse. That is conservatism's core principle, and it underpinned the deregulation of the workforce by the

WorkChoices laws. Recognising how people behave and their innate desire for freedom, leads to better outcomes at an individual and societal level.

Yet those same policies (and others) were drafted and sold without taking account of another aspect of human nature. People are rational beings. But they are also emotional ones. The essential failure of the Howard Government was to frame and sell two policies—WorkChoices and climate change—without accommodating the emotional side of human nature.

In a time of continuing prosperity, the case was not made for WorkChoices. The Howard Government's argument that the further deregulation of the workplace would create further jobs, promising continued prosperity, was undermined by the effective fear campaign run by the union movement and the Labor Party. The perception was that the Howard Government lacked compassion for workers by shifting the balance of power towards employers and by setting safety nets too low. Policy cannot be divorced from politics. There is no need for the Liberal Party to walk away from a policy of workplace reform. But it must do so by confronting the politics of such reform. That requires the Liberal Party to reclaim language and concepts that the left have effectively appropriated.

The overwhelming argument against conservatives is that they somehow lack compassion. If I had a dollar for every time a critic levelled the accusation that I, as a conservative, lacked compassion, I could single-handedly drag a small African nation out of debt. Except that I would never do that because my conservatism prevents me from such unproductive handouts.

The left has, over the years, played to human emotions by claiming to be the party of 'social justice', 'compassion' and the clear implication is that the 'progressive left' is all about progress. It's a nonsense. Take welfare. For years, those who questioned welfare were regarded as mean-spirited. But let's admit that man is lazy. Allow people to live on welfare payments funded by others, and some will do so as long as they can. Conservatives recognise this human flaw. They seek to bring out the best in people by directing a person's self-interest in a way that helps people thrive, rather than merely survive. Require them to work if they can, encourage them to get better educated so they can get a better job, buy a home. Putting limits on welfare is, in the long run, a compassionate policy, one that allows people to progress.

The Liberal Party needs to reclaim words such as 'compassion' and 'progress' as its own—to make the case that its workplace policies are rooted in compassion and progress. That may require tinkering around the edges of the WorkChoices laws. But it does not require a rejection of the belief in workplace deregulation. It is a matter of how the party sells the message.

This brings us to the central message for the Liberal Party. Many conservatives failed to realise that in times of prosperity, voters begin to look for something else. Kevin Rudd tapped into that, presenting himself as safe on the economy with the added zing of connecting with the emotional needs of voters.

The parallels with the United States are worth revisiting. In his speech following the New Hampshire primaries in January 2008, Barack Obama delivered the archetypal post-prosperity election pitch. It will become known as the 'Yes, we can' speech where Obama chose inspiration over policy:

> For when we have faced down impossible odds, when we've been told we're not ready or that we shouldn't try or that we can't, generations of Americans have responded with a simple creed that sums up the spirit of a people: Yes, we can. Yes, we can. Yes, we can … Yes, we can, to opportunity and prosperity. Yes, we can heal this nation. Yes, we can repair this world. Yes, we can.

Rudd lacks Obama's rhetorical flushes, but he too sold a dream, where under the Labor Party things would change. There would be a government that addressed everything from quotidian household expenses (the rising cost of fuel to the price of groceries) to the bigger picture item of global warming. This was an overt pitch to the emotional side of people's nature.

The Labor Party will have no more chance of reducing the price of petrol or groceries or confronting global warming than the Coalition did. But the Labor Party pitched a perception, playing to voter's emotional concerns about these issues, promising to address these issues.

Climate change

Global warming was an issue central to the politics of the 2007 election. No other current issue is as drenched in emotion as climate change. The

Liberal Party stood steadfast to its policy of rejecting Kyoto. It was the rational argument. During the Kyoto period China and India will build 800 new coal-fired power plants. The combined CO_2 emissions from those plants alone will be five times the total reductions in CO_2 mandated by the Kyoto accord.

Sticking to such rational arguments, countries such as Australia refused to sign up to an inherently flawed protocol that covered thirty-five developed nations but not developing countries that account for 40 per cent of greenhouse gas emissions. Even more curious, between 2000 and 2004 Europe *increased* its emissions by 2.3 per cent compared to 1995–2000 levels. Emissions in the United States in 2000–04 were eight percentage points lower than during the 1995–2000 period.

But emotion played a critical part in the climate change debate. Just as those who, in the early days, advocated practical reconciliation for Indigenous communities were treated as mean-spirited heretics, those who rejected Kyoto as meaningless gesture politics were scoffed at as climate-change deniers who did not care about the environment. Whereas Howard was responsible for shifting the debate on Indigenous politics, he failed to do so on climate change. The Howard Government failed to craft an alternative message about the virtues of cautious, practical responses to climate change. The case for pragmatic conservatism needed to be carefully mapped out. But that did not happen.

Few Australians would have heard about the Howard Government's founding involvement in the Asia-Pacific Partnership on Clean Development and Climate (AP6). They would have had no idea that the Coalition was working towards closer engagement with non-Kyoto countries—those countries that account for half the world's emissions, energy use, gross domestic product and population.

At a time when the climate-change debate was hotting up, so to speak, there was an imperative to do two things: first, educate the community about the need to achieve real long-term reductions in greenhouse gas emissions beyond the Kyoto Protocol. Second, sign Kyoto and signal to voters that Australia took the issue of global warming seriously. Australia could have signed Kyoto without endorsing the religious zealotry of many of Kyoto's supporters. It could have signed as a pragmatic step, acknowledging its imperfections, but as part of a longer term post-Kyoto process that would reject symbolic gestures and utopian promises, instead embracing realistic, incremental steps based on empirical evidence.

Importantly, it could have signed Kyoto without damaging Australia's interests, because we had already met Kyoto targets. The Liberal Party did neither. Instead, it allowed itself to be perceived as the uncaring government that rejected Kyoto, choosing irresponsible inaction over action, effectively handing more credibility than they deserve to the advocates of Kyoto.

The Liberal Party could have committed itself to Kyoto and presented itself as the responsible leader on climate change without eschewing its conservative credentials. If conservatives truly understand human nature, then they must accept that emotion is an inherent part of how people respond to issues such as climate change. Naturally propelled by fear, people are attracted to those who promise a solution.

Where to from here?

In the most recent summer edition of *Policy* magazine published by the Centre for Independent Studies, Peter Saunders explains the great dilemma that capitalism has always confronted—no less so now when it appears to have prevailed. Critics such as the Australia Institute's Clive Hamilton peddle a Marxist view that capitalism has outlived its purpose—that it does not make people any happier and is bad for the soul. Don't ignore this as the rambling of a discontented leftist. As Saunders points out, 'substantial numbers of people don't just buy Clive's books; they also buy his arguments'.

The reason, as Saunders writes, is that

> capitalism lacks romantic appeal ... It does not set the pulse racing in the way that opposing ideologies like socialism, fascism, or environmentalism can. It does not stir the blood. It offers no grand vision for the future, for in an open market system the future is shaped not by the imposition of utopian blueprints, but by billions of individuals pursuing their own preferences ... whereas capitalism delivers but cannot inspire, socialism inspires despite never having delivered.

If capitalism appears soulless it is because, 'although it fills people's bellies, it struggles to engage their emotions'. That's the conundrum for conservatism also. It delivers the goods, but lacks inspiration about visions. I am not suggesting the Liberal Party should succumb to utopian blueprints in order to inspire. But it does need to reframe its message to take account of how human nature shifts as the economic cycle turns. At this juncture in the cycle, it means that the Liberal Party must learn to frame polices and pitch its messages in a way that tackles the full gamut of human responses, from the rational to the emotional.

On Indigenous affairs, John Howard managed to win the rational argument. Unlimited welfare has been replaced with individual responsibility. Individual rights, rather than collectivism, are now seen by many as the way out of misery for Indigenous people. But Howard lost the emotional argument. By refusing to apologise, he was continually on the defensive, allowing his critics to paint him as someone who lacked compassion. Howard could have and should have taken the initiative years ago, apologising on his terms and then moving on. As a matter of purely rational analysis, there are still many good reasons to worry about what an apology might mean. But saying sorry to Indigenous people is not a sell out of conservative principles. Instead it would be a pragmatic, Burkean change that reflected conservatism's core competencies. It would signal that the conservative side of politics recognised what drives people, that symbolism is important if only to then allow a more complete focus on the important job of delivering real outcomes to our most disadvantaged citizens.

A few years ago, addressing a group of students, I echoed the words of presidential candidate Barry Goldwater, in his 1960 book *The Conscience of a Conservative*. I suggested it was time to stop apologising for being a conservative. Goldwater said that too many Republicans apologised for being conservative by attaching labels to the 'c' word. Back then vice-president Richard Nixon said Republicans should be 'economic conservatives, but conservatives with a heart'. During his first term President Eisenhower said that he was 'a conservative when it comes to economic problems but liberal when it comes to human problems'. Other Republican leaders announced they were 'progressive conservatives'. George W Bush came to power in 2000, promising to be a 'compassionate conservative'. In the United Kingdom, David Cameron has been tapping into the newfangled happiness industry, where academics dwell over how happy we really are and concoct happiness indices. The Tory party is now apparently made up of 'happy conservatives'.

More than forty years after Goldwater explained why conservatism was nothing to be embarrassed about, I essentially agreed with him. I argued that with the results of failed progressive policies pouring in, and the results of conservative policies now emerging, it was time to be proud to be a conservative. No adjectives needed. Perhaps that was too rational a response.

At a time when conservatism is looking too ideological, it pays to remember that Australians, a pragmatic people, apparently do not much care for what looks like an ideological agenda. We may need to leave it up to the spin doctors and advertising gurus to dream up the right adjective to attach to conservatism. But the more important task is to pitch a message to voters that tackles the full gamut of human responses, from the rational to the emotional. When the Liberals start doing that, they will be on track to winning back voters who deserted them on 24 November 2007.

This piece was first published in Liberals and Power: The Road Ahead, *edited by Peter van Onselen, Melbourne University Publishing.*

Mark Latham

Now there's nothing left
The Australian Financial Review, 27 November 2008

One hundred and twenty-five years ago, as Friedrich Engels reached the last line of his speech at the graveside of Karl Marx in the Highgate Cemetery, London, he declared, with withering hubris, that 'Marx's name will endure through the ages, and so also will his work'.

Marxism, in fact, lasted little more than a century. In the context of the latest financial meltdown, it has left behind a political vacuum. For the first time, capitalism is in crisis and left-wing economics has been unable to advocate an alternative system of production, distribution and exchange.

Even if the global marketplace is to collapse irrevocably, there is nothing left to take its place; not Marxism, not socialism, not any of the leftisms propagated since the rise of the Industrial Revolution. If not the end of history, it appears to be the end of economic ideology. Margaret Thatcher must be happy. There is no alternative. If political leaders have a choice in the circumstances, it is very much Hobson's choice: capitalism or chaos.

These are demoralising times for the left. Normally it would be rejoicing at the turmoil in global markets, but with its ideology as bankrupt as Lehman Brothers, its political prospects are dismal. The most its parliamentary representatives can achieve is to patch up a system that, in principle, they abhor. Given the time and emotional demands of public life, it is difficult to know why they bother.

This is the cruel irony facing ministers from the left, such as Julia Gillard, Lindsay Tanner, Jenny Macklin and Anthony Albanese. All began their time in politics as university radicals, tearaways determined to replace the crippling inequality of capitalism with a more compassionate and just economic system. Such was the glory of their idealism and, as it transpires, their naivety. Now they are part of a federal Labor Cabinet chartered with saving capitalism from itself; a cabinet certain to preside over rising rates of unemployment and poverty in Australia.

This is what the Australian Labor Party factional machine does to people. It is an endless series of deals and compromises, which, bit by bit, drains away the idealism of mind and soul.

Sadly, with the march of time and the contagious cynicism of modern politics, good people find themselves on the dark side of human nature, unable to recognise the beliefs that propelled them into politics in the first place. The lions of the left have become claqueurs for the corporate sector; handmaidens to a system they once despised.

The only senior Labor figure to have advanced a detailed agenda for an alternative economic system is Race Mathews, the former Victorian government minister and long-time doyen of the Australian Fabian Society. In Jobs of Our Own he outlines the success of the Mondragon experience, with its extensive network of consumer and worker co-operatives in the Basque country of Spain.

Under this system, labour hires and controls capital, rather than the reverse. It has the virtues of economic democracy through the egalitarian ownership of property. Just as importantly, Mondragon's co-operatives are part of a social democracy, as the citizens who own and run these entities learn the habits of self-government in their community.

Like most people in politics with something different to say, Mathews is viewed as somewhat eccentric. Only a handful of Labor MPs are aware of his work. Unfortunately, the Labor movement has little interest in mutu-alism—the possibility of social and economic co-operation outside the coercive power of the state.

As a political ideal, collectivism has struggled to get off first base in Australia. The nation's identity has been forged around notions of rugged individualism and the taming of the outback. Australians have never iden-tified closely with economic struggles in the workplace or social activism in the community. They remain sceptical about the role of government and the benefits of trade union militancy. Their preferred social unit is suburban family life. Their favoured economic activity is suburban mall shopping. Indeed, it is difficult to think of a country, other than the United States, in which the fundamentals for collectivism are as weak.

This is what makes the politics of the financial crisis so paltry. As capitalism experiences its greatest failure and vulnerability in seventy years, the left has nothing substantial to say. But even if it did, it would be rejected as absurd in the Australian context. Situation hopeless: the enduring fate of left-wing politics through the ages.

Waleed Aly

It's just a jump to the left

The Sydney Morning Herald, 31 May 2008

Political battles used to be ideological. Political parties differed not merely in degree, but in essence. They proceeded from often opposing traditions in political thought that were based on different assumptions about how society should be structured.

Perhaps the most axiomatic difference was the political battle between capital and labour. This can crudely be distilled as a question of priority. Should government place the interests of workers above those of business? Should entrepreneurs be freed from the interference of the state, so they can get on with generating profit? Such questions are entirely foundational because they imply a broader inquiry about the proper role of government. Put simply, how big should government be? To what extent does it have a responsibility to underwrite the welfare of its citizens? Are such matters better left to the survival instincts of individuals and the chaotic forces of the market to determine?

A small, business-friendly government would provide little welfare and few public services. It would privatise as many state-owned enterprises as possible in the belief that the private sector delivers more efficiently. Its pro-business orientation would make it reluctant to regulate employers heavily: it is unlikely to be fond of trade unions, or other institutions established for the protection of workers' rights, which constitute an unwelcome intrusion into the market.

It is the division over these issues that, as much as anything, has come to define left and right in our political discourse. In truth, the left-right divide is problematic and artificial. It is well and good to argue that the right believes that government should butt out of social and economic affairs, but that leaves us with anarchists, who believe in no government at all, yet are usually deemed left. Alternatively, we may cite Hitler, usually judged to be on the right, whose government was large to the point of being infamously authoritarian. Hitler was also a critic of capitalism, while the French revolutionaries—from whom the very concept of the left derives—advocated the free market.

So the battle between labour and capital, between the large state and the small state is far from perfect as a definitive left-right flashpoint. But it is probably the most useful because it has been so central in the politics of the last century. Indeed, the labour-capital ideological divide is encoded in our political terrain.

It is why party politics in Australia, New Zealand, Ireland, Britain and (less clearly) Israel is a contest between a labour party and a conservative party.

But it was the Cold War that distilled this almost pure ideological division: communism against capitalism; state-run economies against the free market; big government against small government; labour against capital. The entire world was so bifurcated. Every nation was deemed either an ally of the Soviet Union or the United States. At stake was sole superpower status, and the power to remake the world order along the victor's ideological lines. The labour-capital divide had reached an almost impossible urgency. Never had it been so alive, so intense, so potentially cataclysmic.

So when the Cold War officially ended in 1989, it was a momentous event in ideological politics. Like its Eastern European communist allies, the Soviet Union had descended into economic ruin, and was forced to concede to the United States. The whole episode was not really a war so much as an ideological argument. With the devastating collapse of communism, that argument had been won.

Enter the triumphant 'Washington Consensus' that governments should deregulate their economies, liberalise trade and privatise public services. The state would be small, and the rights of workers determined largely by a deregulated market. That is, capital would be prioritised over labour. State intervention was damned, and traditional state enterprises—health, communications and transport—were axiomatically to be privatised. As the Soviets had shown, government could be relied upon to deliver nothing. This idea that probably found its most celebrated expression in the declaration of Ronald Reagan: 'Government is not the solution to our problem. Government is the problem.' Thus did American-inspired capitalism flourish.

In the process, everything was to be commodified. The logic of the market seeped into all areas of life until the social dimension would all but disappear from our reckoning. In Britain, Margaret Thatcher, having emasculated the trade unions, expressed this famously by asserting that 'there is no such thing as society—only individuals'. We are not social beings. We are economic ones; consumers in a market.

So capital trumped labour and a political shift to the right was complete. The political centre of gravity had moved.

To be clear, this did not mean that conservative parties were guaranteed government, or that labour parties were excluded from power. Far from it. In Australia, Labor ruled for thirteen years, from the last stages of the Cold War into its aftermath. Rather it meant something even more profound: that parties previously on the left of the ideological divide reinvented themselves in line with the new ideological consensus on the right. Politics became a contest between shades of a broadly similar ideology.

The Hawke and Keating governments are a good example. By reducing tariffs and floating the dollar, they exposed Australia to the global economy. By abandoning central wage-fixing and moving to enterprise bargaining between employers and employees, they moved further away from the traditional leftist terrain of siding unremittingly with labour, against capital. Labour remained left of the Coalition, but it was no longer of the left. Such differences as remained were matters of degree, not essence.

A similar phenomenon was at work in Britain, where, after eighteen years of Opposition, the Labour Party repackaged itself under Tony Blair as New Labour. And new it was. Gone was the party of the working class, trade unions and government intervention. Blair's Labour was a pro-market party courting aspirational middle Britain. London became the preferred destination of the world's super-rich and multinational corporations, and Britain rode the unrestrained wave of a booming financial sector. Despite revelations that the wealthiest companies are hugely avoiding tax, New Labour has failed to close the legal loopholes that make this possible, probably for fear of being branded anti-business.

Such radical transformations were inevitable. After all, what did it mean to be a labour party in a world where the ideological debate had been resolved in favour of capital? This is why I believe Kevin Rudd when he reiterates his faith in the market, and brands himself a 'fiscal conservative'. He has little choice. Blair preached a post-ideological 'Third Way'. Rudd talks of transcending the left-right divide.

This is only possible when the fundamental ideological assumptions of the major parties are in common. And it is clear that the parties of the right have not altered theirs drastically, which leaves only one alternative: the shared political assumptions are their own.

That is what makes the current political moment so intriguing. It was momentous events in world politics—the end of the Cold War and the collapse of communism—that delivered the present right-leaning consensus. But look around us now. Global warming presents itself as the ultimate apocalyptic threat, while the global economy is in the midst of a credit crisis that, if the worst case is realised, would deliver unthinkable levels of unemployment and homelessness. It's an impressive doomsday scenario. Our jobs, our homes, our very planet are all precarious.

The common thread connecting these potential crises is that the more untamed operations of the market have been a major contributing factor in their creation. It is industrialised economies that carry disproportionate responsibility for the carbon emissions that drive climate change. The short-term goals of profit have thus far proved incompatible with the long-term challenges of the environment.

Similarly, the credit crisis is a product of the free market taken to its logical, deregulated extreme. The practice of offering big mortgages on a vast scale to poor people who could never repay is not only exploitative, it was once illegal in the United States. This changed under the Bush administration, opening the doors to the financial instability that has brought the global financial system to the brink of collapse. The determination of government not to intervene made this possible.

This is a starkly altered political terrain. Suddenly there is a different logic. If these crises play themselves out particularly savagely, it is clear which policy settings will be fashionable. Publics will scream for greater government intervention to protect consumers from the most exploitive bank practices, and to protect the environment from the most unsustainable habits of the market. That is an end to the orthodoxy of unfettered markets and small governments. In short, a collective jump to the left. Not a comprehensive rejection of the free market, but an understanding that politics has an economic role to play beyond merely allowing capital to do as it pleases.

Will this come to pass? Arguably, the process is already under way. In the United States, the most market-driven country, 43 per cent said they would prefer a large government that provided more services. That is still a minority, but it is the highest level of support for that proposition since 1991, when it was first asked in polling. Australians last year revolted against the Howard Government's WorkChoices reforms, indicating they prefer security in their labour conditions to hard-headed free-market ideology.

Then there is the credit crisis. Already, the British government has (reluctantly) taken over a failing bank, Northern Rock, in order to prevent Britons from sustaining huge losses. In the United States, the Federal Reserve was forced to rescue the giant investment bank Bear Stearns with a US$30 billion loan. It is an unsavoury scene, really: enormous companies that have thrived in a deregulated environment, turning to public institutions to be saved when their recklessness catches up with them. Even so, the public tolerates such interventions because they recognise the suffering they prevent.

State intervention is back.

Meanwhile, conservative politicians are striking some odd poses. In the United States, the Republican presidential candidate John McCain is talking like a Democrat, embarking on a national 'poverty tour' and spruiking his plans to make health care cheaper. In doing so, he is deliberately distancing himself from George Bush, who won power by moving to the right. McCain seeks to do the same by shifting left. In Britain, the Opposition leader, David Cameron, is attempting to woo the trade union movement. He has appointed a personal trade union envoy, and confirmed he would happily address the Trades Union Congress if invited.

The Conservatives recently dominated local elections across Britain. Exit polls suggested a desire to punish the Labour Government for an attempted tax reform that would have hit low earners hardest. Suddenly, Cameron is presenting himself as a champion of the poor, protecting them from higher taxes. It is an odd sight.

Of course, none of this yet amounts to an established leftward movement in the political centre of gravity, and whether or not such a shift will complete itself depends on what happens next. If, as some are cautiously whispering, the worst of the credit crisis is over, any disturbance to politics will be minimised. But on the gloomiest predictions, we are staring at the worst economic period since the Depression. If enough people lose their homes, if enough people's share portfolios lose their value, if enough people lose their jobs, and if global warming manages to impose itself vividly and urgently on our imaginations, a political shift simply must follow. The age of American ideological consensus will have passed. Perhaps the age of Sweden will be to come.

Mungo MacCallum

We are witnessing the last days of the Nationals
Crikey, 28 July 2008

I think it was in 1970 that I first predicted the demise of the National Party, then the Australian Country Party (ACP).

The 1969 federal election had reduced its parliamentary numbers, and demography, I pontificated, was moving inexorably against it. Australians were deserting the bush for the cities in ever-increasing numbers, and the trend could not be reversed.

While the ACP remained part of a ruling Coalition, it could maintain the gerrymander by which rural electorates need to have a far smaller number of voters than their city counterparts, and continue subsidising this declining constituency to the extent that even in those far off days every adult resident of the bush received the equivalent of nearly $20 000 a year in taxpayer support.

But the 1969 election had shown that the Coalition was on its last legs; a cloud no bigger than Gough Whitlam was looming across the political landscape and the capacity of the Country Party to deliver the spoils of victory appeared certain to come to an end the next time the voters went to the polls.

Moreover, the said EG Whitlam had already shown an unexpected ability to win over the notoriously conservative rural electorate. In a ground-breaking by-election he had won the Queensland heartland seat of Capricornia for Labor, and had repeated the feat in Dawson in the general election.

Obviously in the early days of Federation a party to represent the special interests of the outback made sense and it could not be denied that the Country Party, under the formidable leadership of such men as Sir Earle Page, Sir Arthur Fadden and Sir John McEwen had been an important force in Australian politics, at times vital in keeping the mainstream conservative party—Liberals, Nationals, United Australia, now Liberals again—in power. But now its support was eroding on all sides, and its days were clearly numbered.

Well, they were, and they still are, even if the number is now approaching 14 000.

It is true that the party isn't what it was in 1970. Its parliamentary strength has declined, and it has changed its name to the Nationals, although the only perceptible benefit is that its youth branch can now line up with the Young Libs and the Young Labs without embarrassment. 'I'm a Young Nat' sounds much better than the previous version.

But the rural rump remains the great survivor of Australian politics, and like Mark Twain, can declare triumphantly that reports of its imminent demise have been greatly exaggerated. Still, here comes another one: the weekend merger with the Liberals in Queensland is the real, honest to goodness, fair dinkum beginning of the end.

The first thing to note about the National Party of Australia is that its name, like that of its fellow coalitionists the Liberal Party, is a lie. The Nationals are not, and never have been, national. And these days they are restricted to the eastern mainland. Whatever tenuous grasp they held in Western Australia and South Australia has long since been slipped away, they were never a presence in Tasmania and in the Northern Territory the conservatives have always been united in a single Country Liberal Party.

Only in Queensland, New South Wales and Victoria do the Nationals exist as a separate entity, and even here they have sometimes appeared confused about their identity. In Victoria, for instance, they actually spent some time in coalition with Labor. In New South Wales they have been in and out of coalition with the Libs, but in Queensland they have often treated the Libs as just as much an enemy as Labor.

Queensland, however, has always been their real power base, the only place where they have ever held government in their own right or even as senior partner, albeit with the aid of a truly ferocious gerrymander. And even after Labor governments have imposed a form of democracy on the state the Nationals remain a far more powerful force than the Libs, so from a National point of view a merger makes a certain amount of sense.

Anywhere else, a merger would constitute something close to a Liberal takeover, with the Nats simply absorbed into their more widespread partner. Even the prospect leads serious Nats to threaten the formation of a new Country Party to look after the sectional interests which are still, theoretically at least, their raison d'etre. The Queensland Nats figured they were strong enough to call the tune, although some of the more conspiratorial Libs under the leadership of disgraced former minister Santo Santoro are already plotting to subvert the newly formed Liberal National Party to their own purposes.

They may or may not succeed, but whatever happens one thing is clear: the old Queensland National Party is dead, and this has serious and potentially fatal implications for the remnants of the party in its other footholds. For the moment, Queensland's federal members will retain their identities, the Libs as Libs and the Nats as Nats. But what happens after future elections? Are the newly elected NLP members Nats or Libs? If it becomes their choice, they would be mad not to go with the strength. The pressure for a merger at the federal level, if only to tidy up such anomalies, can only increase.

Similarly the Queensland precedent can hardly be ignored in New South Wales and especially Victoria, where one federal member, Julian McGauran, saw no difficulty in deserting the Nats for the Libs less than two years ago. Where McGauran has gone, others will be tempted to follow. The Queensland Nats have scrambled the eggs and in the long term there is no real alternative for their colleagues but to join the omelet.

It must be galling to the feds and their leader Warren Truss, who are still celebrating a big win in the Gippsland by-election and anticipating more of the same in Lyne. But the long-awaited reckoning is finally upon them. They are in their last days, and this time we're not talking about 14 000 of them.

6
How Divided Are We?

Brendan Gleeson

Waking from the dream
Griffith Review 20: Cities on the Edge,
www.griffithreview.com

> Fire in the heavens, and fire along the hills,
> And fire made solid in the flinty stone,
> thick-mass'd or scatter'd pebble, fire that fills
> the breathless hour that lives in fire alone . . .

Christopher Brennan, *Poems 1913*

It's been a bad couple of decades for dreamers. So many collective dreams
shattered into ugly shards. The devastation was democratic. Almost every
political and social constituency suffered the agonies of disillusion. The
mass dream of home ownership has been broken apart by property markets left wild and directionless by policy neglect. The Baby Boomer surge
in housing wealth is a feast of the elders, leaving the following generations
to the wolves of insecurity and penury. The neo-liberal dream of the bound-
less economy ('Go for Growth') is drowning in frightful waves of ecological feedback and, even worse, popular doubt. In Australia, the rise of
neo-liberalism and the collapse of the previously settled order moved Paul
Kelly to declare the 'end of certainty' in 1992. Not exactly the end of history, but not far off. The compact that had restrained class conflict in the
twentieth century was a system that emphasised political certainty over
ambiguity and contest, at the cost of flexibility. The deliberate dismantling
of this by successive federal governments from the 1970s unleashed market
forces on previously shielded areas in the public sector and domestic life.
Market settings were the new 'fundamentals' upon which economic and
social endeavour was to be based.

But that was then and this is now. Decades after its rise to ascendancy, neo-liberalism is revealing its inadequacy. The relentlessly rationalising and simplifying logic of the market is increasingly at odds with the great plural-ity of values and lifestyles that replaced social conformism: the drive to *laissez faire* fundamentals has passed cultural change, going in the other direction. Economists and political simplifiers sense growing irrelevance in public conversations enriched and complicated by social change. They have less to say about the new social concerns: collapsing eco-systems and envi-ronmental degradation; cultural enrichment and tension; new wealth and work-life balance; religious decline and spiritual yearning; probity in poli-tics; morality in public life; the cult of pleasure; the epidemic of sadness, and so forth.

None of this can be dismissed as peripheral or less important than the bottom line. The age of the individual is being quietly supplanted by a re-emerging collectivism.

If dreams project our hopes (and fears), does this fracturing endanger hope? If so, who can carry on? As our feudal forebears knew, 'without hope our hearts would break', but Australians have not put much faith in hope since nineteenth-century settlers considered it 'vanity'. Perhaps they were right, and the audacity of hope that has inspired Barack Obama's campaign is just rhetorical delusion. As Kafka observed in another era of fallen dreams: 'Oh yes, there is hope infinite hope. But not for us'.

I suspect that what we witness and feel as a collective turmoil of dis-illusion is the reawakening of arguments thought resolved, not the whole-sale annihilation of dreams. It may be the age-old struggle between individual and collective ambitions, between us and Nature. It is sharpened by the constant intrusion of new 'realities'—climate change, water short-ages, petrol price inflation, overcrowding, unaffordable housing to name a few—but remains nonetheless a long-run contest of some surprisingly old propositions.

Homes for (war) heroes, later homes for all, but now new shortages and stresses have produced the growth in Australia of homelessness and a growing inter-generational divide in housing chances. Not everyone thought the dream of mass home ownership was sensible, but for years it worked for many people, with a large dollop of public investment in the infrastruc-ture and regulations that made it possible. An old debate is re-emerging. In

1983, Jim Kemeny described the relentless pursuit of home ownership as *The Great Australian Nightmare,* an ideological delusion that locked us into house price inflation and limited real housing choice. Kemeny might have had a point, and he wasn't the first to make it. In many countries, there has long been deep scepticism about the value and the practicality of universal home ownership. Some dreamed of mass social housing, with money diverted away from the real estate and home finance industries into social projects. The new calls for a revival of social housing for the increasing numbers of Australians unable to mount the mortgage treadmill draw on this tradition. They do so in new ways, recognising that some of the national wealth diverted into the private realm during the boom will have to be lured back to social housing through tax incentives that guarantee returns to investors in new public and community stock.

An economy of growth and endless expanding abundance eventually reaches its limits, and now the entire material system is threatened with natural default. An old contest is re-emerging between 'Promethean' and 'bounded' views of Nature. In 1883, Frederick Engels warned: 'Let us not, however, flatter ourselves overmuch on account of our human victories over Nature. For each such victory Nature takes its revenge on us'. Climate change, you'd have to say, is a pretty spectacular form of revenge. The old criticism of economic growth which neo-liberals declared heresy seems to have the angels on its side.

So it's not the end of history, the death notice for thought signed by the 'neo-cons', but the rude intrusion of unruly Nature into contests that seemed to be closing off. Just as one dream seems to have vanquished its competitors, and history seems poised to hang up its hat, these new intrusions reinstate a contest of ideas. Both Labor and the Coalition appear shocked and awed by the calamities pressing down on dreams of peace and security: global terrorism, climate change, housing affordability, water shortages and sclerotic cities. As Steve Dovers from the Australian National University put it recently, after two centuries we still seem to be struggling to settle Australia. We haven't resolved the first vexing questions presented to us by a unique continent—the original owners, the fragile land, the scarce resources, the capricious climate, remoteness and the insecurities this generates. These first challenges to the settlement project just keep coming back, some of them in ever more frightening forms.

Inevitably, some dreams fall away. Not even rude Nature can reawaken them: a bunyip aristocracy for Australia; a green interior watered by dammed and redirected rivers; a nation of hardy bush folk rejecting the ruinous urbanism of the old world. The noisy nineteenth-century argument between the city and the bush gave way in the twentieth century to a quieter kind of compromise—a continued fascination with the bush myth in cinema and literature and a long sleepy disavowal of our deeply urban nature.

Australians are in two minds today. Many of us celebrate the economic boom that has generated new levels of prosperity, and pushed unemployment and want to the margins of consciousness. And yet growing numbers of Australians are increasingly disturbed by two comets that seem to be streaking across and spoiling the bright skies of prosperity—climate change and oil scarcity. One fiery trail reports a climate cooked and despoiled by human greed. The other marks the disappearing trail of a vital resource, the energy that propelled us to greatness, and yet ultimately became our downfall. Both entwine menacingly above us: one glowering with rising strength, the other fading and failing away.

The heavens aroused and inflamed are an awful force. Their anger shakes the groundwork of everyday life: the jobs, the holidays, the hobbies that fill our days. The very earth upon which we stand seems to be moving under our feet; things—solid things—around us seem to be swaying. The wonderful climate—the envy of the world—seems to be turning on us. *Terra Australis* is becoming Terror Australis, a blast furnace of drought, heat and capricious tempests. The nation is gripped by concern about scarcity. Not of good domestic help, Chilean wine or smart European ovens. It's water, the fundamental means of existence, that we are running out of. In April 2007, then Prime Minister John Howard intoned gravely that the nation's food bowl, the Murray–Darling Basin, might soon fail. There was talk of the need to import food. Even in cities, traditionally immune to drought, years of prolonged water shortage showed in the greying, lifeless gardens of suburbia, where there lurked a quiet, deepening gloom about the deaths of things once cherished and nurtured.

Meanwhile oil, the lifeblood of our economy and everyday lives, seems to be slipping away. It's harder, more expensive, to keep a grip on lifestyles based on cheap petrol and unrestrained mobility. 'Pain at the pump' is another little unfolding agony in everyday life. Daily we hear more about 'peak oil': a looming moment when the world's oil reserves will start to decline. The idea has been about for a while, but has been dismissed by governments and industry as the baseless rantings of survivalists, doomsayers and eccentric dons. Not so anymore. Both the Australian Senate and the United States Auditor-General have recently warned that the peak is real and imminent. No matter when it occurs, explosive global demand and geopolitical instability mean that the golden age of oil abundance is behind us. Chevron admits that 'the age of easy oil is over'. In January 2008, Shell chief executive Jeroen van der Veer predicted a global fuel crisis in just seven years.

Since the first fire in a cave, access to energy has defined human existence. We learnt to be pretty careful conservers of the stocks we had. But Promethean modernity put an end to that quaint practice: more fossil fuels could always be found, and technology could transform them. Peak oil is shattering the perpetual motion dream of the carbon economy. For most of us, the oil default is sudden, unexpected and deeply inconvenient. The busy free-ranging lives celebrated—indeed mandated—by neo-liberalism are threatened. Aspiration is turning to desperation. In early 2007, a survey of more than five thousand Australian families identified rising petrol prices as the main source of financial concern.

Sometimes passing through and surviving one (modest) crisis engenders not a sharpened wariness but its opposite, a heightened sense of invulnerability. So it seems with the 1970s oil shocks, which by the 1990s had passed comfortably into memories, adding evidence to the theory that market societies were indeed the 'end of history', our highest and most invulnerable social form. This explains why the unexpected return of oil scarcity seems so deeply unsettling, cracking open a cemented faith in our invincibility. All the more unnerving is the mounting evidence that coal, our other great—if these days unseen—energy source, is fuelling climate change. Most of us are guiltily aware that Australia is a global 'filthy man', stoking the global carbon economy with cheap, dirty coal. Dashed inconvenient that exporting it doesn't distance us from the problem, or ultimately from blame.

These shocks and shifts are disturbing, with rising electrical force, the political climate of Australia. And now, somehow, politics—that unpredictable hand of change—has passed the microphone to the climate change warriors, and the news is grim. Not surprising, then, is evidence of a deeper sense of unease in the social consciousness; the substrate of politics. A new social sensibility is evident, rising awareness of our exposure to sudden, even wild, changes in the basic forces that industrial capitalism had considered vanquished, pacified and shackled to the wheel of progress.

This is where the two minds situation kicks in, problematically for most of us. It is why our heads hurt. We are intimately aware of, and buoyed along by, the economic wave that has carried most (but not all) of us to material prosperity: the jobs, the toys and the travel opportunities. We know at the personal scale how to manipulate our own role in the larger miracle economy for personal gain. But most of us have no immediate connection to the big forces at play in environmental change, and thus little sense of how to comprehend and intervene in these processes. The consequences of the environmental and resource crises are manifesting in our daily lives: rocketing petrol bills, dead lawns, tedious water restrictions, and heat—damned unseasonable, wearing heat. But the same sense of autonomy and power that many of us feel at work isn't available in these increasingly pressing circumstances. The feeling of frustrated disconnection, of impotency in the face of threat, seems to well and grow.

In this most urban of nations, it is not surprising that cities, and our urban way of life, have been the subject of increasingly critical commentary. For the past few decades, environmental criticism of urban growth patterns has formed the nucleus of a small but growing public debate about the cities. This criticism has correctly implicated cities in the sustainability crisis. It's all very well to wring our hands about the scarifying effects of mining and farming, but it is cities with their voracious consumption habits that create the need for resource extraction in the first place. And yes, it's in cities where the world—and especially Australia—must confront and account for the problem of environmental bankruptcy.

When the Howard Government in 1990 extracted a sweet deal from the Kyoto Treaty that it did not sign, by having reductions in land clearing included in the calculations of net carbon emissions, the states were left with the political dirty work of reining it in. Farmers were unhappy. They had some cause for complaint with the cities and the 'growth machine economy' that drives them these days. As the Climate Institute pointed out in 2006:

> Australia's farmers have been responsible for virtually the entire share of the nation's greenhouse reductions . . . Over the same period, emissions from energy and transport have and continue to skyrocket. For example, total energy sector emissions are projected to be 45 per cent above 1990 levels by 2010.

Let's not pretend that this scenario sanctifies the farming sector, much of which continues to ignore or defy the sustainability threat, but it's clear that the urban economic system has been left largely off the hook of climate change response. 'Urban greens' are regularly criticised for pushing the sustainability burden on to farmers. And yet the sustainability critique of cities in Australia has gained traction in certain policy domains—such as urban planning—and exerts an increasing influence on public debates. A number of critical 'truths' have been established, notably—and to date most powerfully—the proposition that Australia's traditionally 'sprawling' model of urban development must be supplanted by a new approach based upon compaction and higher density living.

There are problems with the politics and debates that have driven this urban criticism. First, it hasn't produced much effective change to the deeply unsustainable nature of the Australian urban system. Second, it has been informed by a ludicrously elitist view of the Australian urban experience that has constructed suburbs and suburbanisation as the root of the sustainability crisis. This view, strongly entrenched in green, and increasingly mainstream, urban criticism flies in the face of mounting scientific evidence which points to the consumptive neo-liberal lifestyle not the nature of one's dwelling as the root of our environmental woes.

The image of mindless suburban consumption is misleading. New Australian research supported by the Australian Conservation Foundation shows that rich, inner-urban areas consume more of Nature than does suburbia. There is plenty of evidence that suburban Australians are much less sanguine about their lifestyles and increasingly worried about how their homes and neighbourhoods will cope with water shortages, congestion and wild weather. The remarkable fall in Brisbane's per capita water consumption in recent years is a largely unheralded achievement of suburban households.

The green (sub)urban critique is also a polarising view that has marginalised the majority of Australians, who live in suburbs, from urban environmental discussion. As the Australian urban scholar Aidan Davison observes, suburban Australia has been relatively immune to, and uncaring about, the elitist critique, not even willing to upbraid its lovechild for its betrayal—remember, environmentalism was originally a suburban movement. Of more concern is the increasing policy reach of the anti-suburban agenda, and its implications for equity and sustainability. If the suburbs are unfairly held to be responsible for climate change and resource scarcity, a great injustice is possible. Suburbia may be 'punished' for its environmental 'misbehaviour' and denied the public investment that it desperately needs to meet the new vulnerability threats, especially rising oil prices. This is a deeply unfair prospect—letting the inner cities off the hook, when arguably they contribute the lion's share of urban environmental stress, and denying suburbs the investment they need, especially in public transport, after decades of major public spending on inner city infrastructure.

There are other, more technical, problems with the green urban critique that need to be acknowledged. First, even if packing everyone in closer together through urban consolidation significantly reduces energy consumption (and it probably doesn't), the time scales involved are well beyond those needed to address climate change. The scientific consensus is that we must radically reduce greenhouse emissions within the next decade. Cities are hard to reshape. The 'built environment' is a heavy, fixed thing that is slow and expensive to change. The 'fire in the heavens' won't be doused in time by the decades it would take to push (yes, push) most urban Australians into higher density living. More urgent responses are needed, including—most inconveniently—an immediate reduction in energy use by those already in high-density environments.

The idea that Australia is in two minds about the economic party and its uninvited guests is really a suburban conception. Most of us live in suburbs, in cities, towns or sea- and tree-change areas, and it's here that pollsters are registering the sudden seismic shift in sentiment that redefined politics in 2007, the upsurge of concern (and anger) about climate change. From this perspective, our urban environmental debates and responses seem appallingly inadequate. By blaming and marginalising the suburbs, they worsen the inability of many Australians to connect the environmental crisis with their everyday lives. It's in the nature of things that people tend to dismiss criticisms that seem both unsympathetic to and ignorant about the basic life choices they have exercised. The anti-suburban critique produces not lengthening queues for confessionals but a widening disconnection between the suburban consciousness and organised environmental debate and action. This impoverishes both sides of the urban equation and explains much of the malaise of urban politics in Australia today. Mark Latham had it (half) right when he spoke of a political culture rent by divisions between inner city 'insiders' and suburban 'outsiders'. His initial mistake—a position recanted in his infamous diaries—was to pour scorn on the insiders and beatify the suburban outsiders.

This is the rub. The entire urban body is implicated in the sustainability crisis; all elements are part of the problem, if not equally to blame. The misguided and self-defeating anti-suburbanism, which characterises much of the environmental critique, is mirrored in the equally harebrained arguments of certain self-appointed defenders of suburbia. Suburbia may not be the consumptive bogey imagined by green critique, but it is nonetheless deeply implicated in the sustainability crisis that our cities have helped to engender. And, as with 'inner city living', the idea and the reality of suburbia represent a moving historical feast. Contemporary suburban lifestyles are vastly less sustainable than their predecessors. There is a truth to the 'McMansion' critique, although the revulsion from sections of the green design fraternity seems motivated more by aesthetic complaint than environmental criticism. The compelling view is that, while suburbs may not be the authors of doom, they are not immune from environmental (and social) critique. The suburbs—like everywhere—have to change if we are to meet and defeat the crisis and become resilient.

The suburbs aren't dormitories, but increasingly rich employment, retail and recreation worlds. So the response to environmental threat must change complex suburban lifestyles, and the diverse environments in which they occur, to reduce their environmental and resource claims on non-urban Australia. The idea of a much more 'environmentally contained' suburbia seems obvious. The environmental renovation must occur both in our established (especially ageing) suburbs and in any new areas we develop.

There are new reasons why we cannot continue with suburbanisation as we have in the past. Most of our extensive metropolitan regions no longer have the 'green fields' that previously hosted suburban development. The city edges are pushing out now into 'brown field' lands, well beyond the coast and its well-watered temperate climes. New suburban development in these peri-urban areas will be difficult, expensive, and in many areas simply not worth it. The edges are now pushing up against urban water catchments and regions that provide critical 'environmental services' to city populations (recreation, scenic amenity, biodiversity and so on). The suburban model may not be the author of our troubles, but it is nonetheless running out of steam in most of our metropolitan regions. And while there's still some—indeed considerable—land banked and appropriate for future suburban expansion, there is a clear environmental case for breaking with the recent mega-home development model. Providing sustainable and secure shelter for all should be the ideal. There was a long time when suburban expansion was the best means to do this for the many, if not all. This is simply no longer the case. There remains limited potential for further suburban growth around our major cities, but it must be done differently, with sustainability and security overriding objects.

The fire in the heavens looms over us all. We urbanites ignited it and have stoked its flames for nearly two centuries. It is the cities, therefore—and yes, the world's rich 'developed' cities—which bear principal responsibility for the conflagration that threatens. Australia is a nation of cities that bears a special duty to address climate change and the related problem of depleted resources—especially oil and water. The cities need to swiftly and massively reduce their ecological footprints and remove their heels from the throat of Nature. This does not mean consuming the same amount, just more cleverly and more efficiently, as some experts claim. The time has run out for technological fixes and market adjustments that will somehow preserve the growth machine economy. The best science tells us that we have very few years in which to make radical adjustments to our ecological demands if we are to prevent the worst possible effects of climate change and resource depletion. The great urban commentator Hugh Stretton likens the sustainability crisis to a time of war. Here the only path to salvation lies in a swift, centrally co-ordinated response to a massive threat, including resource rationing and the outlawing of some forms of consumption. Cities will have to be rationed and learn in time to ration themselves.

The wealthiest urbanites carry a heavy obligation that they seem as yet unwilling to acknowledge, let alone act upon, to massively reduce material consumption. Some of them reside in the middle and outer suburbs, but many do not. Our urban environmental debates have obscured the fact that it is the brute and wholesale consumption of goods and services, not just petrol, gas or electricity, which has denuded and inflamed Nature. In this sense, cities have been the stages for an epic consumption carnival, where the richly costumed burghers have played the biggest part in the drama that followed. And there have, of course, been many 'spectres at the feast'—the losers in the great global economic game.

None of this is as simple as it sounds because those with the highest consumption also have the most to lose. Power is inevitably at play in situations where a whole social form—a city—is threatened collectively by its own behaviour, but especially by the actions of some. This is why strong, centrally coordinated action is required to ensure both that urban consumption is rapidly reined in, and that this occurs in the fairest and most efficient way possible.

It is time to move beyond the 'urban good, suburban bad' (or vice versa) polarity that has created a wounding, enervating gulf in Australia's urban debates. It is an abyss of miscomprehension and conflict that has consumed our energy and prevented reaching a much-needed consensus on how to meet the sustainability threat. The main alternative argument offered here is that sketched above: that the doorway to sustainability is closing rapidly and the only valid pathway through it, in the time we have left, involves a radical and immediate cut in resource use across the urban spectrum, but most especially by high-consumption groups. If households consume less, especially wasteful and harmful commodities, then industry and business will have to adjust, hopefully putting more effort into the production of durable, high-quality goods and services.

As Hugh Stretton points out, the 'wartime' character of the times we are entering necessitates strong emphasis on the values of social solidarity and fairness. In short, we'll have to pull together to get through this. It's the old story: if parts of the herd make a break for themselves, we'll all be picked off—including the bolters. This requires a clear sense of common purpose, and transparent fairness in the allocation of burdens and tasks that will arise in the struggle to win through the sustainability threat. Our urban debates to date have not been founded in a realistic or fair appreciation of who and what is contributing most to environmental overload. The suburban blame game is the biggest instance of this failing.

But what of social solidarity: the sense of common purpose and resolve that we'll need? This, of course, won't occur unless we develop the equitable view of the problem that I'm urging and create a new dream. The 'urban–suburban' polarity is a pointless obstacle and needs to be replaced by a cohesive view of urban environmental responsibility. But beyond this we'll require social structures that nurture and maintain social solidarity. We already possess this in the public realm, the civic community that transcends divisions based on class, gender, ethnicity and the like. Sadly, we've let this vital life-force of democracy sink to a low ebb, especially in our cities where most of these movements first found support, at the very time when it will be most needed to ensure that the sustainability threat is addressed on democratic not autocratic terms.

There are voices of despair, or at least resignation, which claim that the fight is over before it begins in earnest. Global warming cannot be contained, finite resources cannot be substituted—the smoking ruin scenario is inevitable, they say. That spirit denies the hope that is essential to the best of the human condition. It assumes that those who set fire to the heavens cannot undo their handiwork and rebuild a relationship with Nature on respectful, sustainable terms. On the contrary, as with all great human problems, the answer lies in changing human behaviour, not relying on the feverous search for technological fixes (including urban compaction). This simple premise is for many—especially the captains of the neo-liberal growth machine—inconvenient and unlovely. We have to consume less—much less—and very quickly, if we are to avoid the immolation that threatens. The cities might be the source of the problem, but they're also where its solution is to be found.

Australia's new social pluralism has been most obvious in the cities, but is seeping steadily into rural and regional Australia, as struggling communities open their hearts and homes to refugees, greenies and sea- and tree-changers. The cities, where most of us have long lived, were expanded and transformed by post-war immigration and gave birth to social movements including environmentalism. They were also home to the debris of neo-liberal economics—a reserve army of redundant labour cashiered on the disability support pension, homeless people living in absolute poverty and mouldering worlds of exclusion in peri-urban backblocks and ageing middle-ring suburbs.

Much was made of Howard's age as a cause of his defeat. I'm not convinced. Yes, he looked like Captain Mainwaring in the Mersey Hospital rescue and Janette, as Mungo caddishly points out, does remind one of Hyacinth from *Keeping Up Appearances*. But I don't think age was central. It was surely how out of touch, to use that clichéd but necessary term, Howard's agenda was to a pluralised society increasingly united by concern about climate change.

The debate about market globalisation is reopening, and with it the debates about the cities which lie at its heart. The prophets promised a world economy of growth and endless expanding abundance, provided we stuck ruthlessly to the market fundamentals. And world leaders have hardly disappointed them in recent decades; the 'Washington consensus' was the starting point of national politics in countless nations. Growth rates were ramped up, restrictions and doubts swept aside, fields and forests opened to plunder.

Now the entire material system seems threatened with natural default. An old contest is on display. In the red corner are those certain that human ingenuity will prevail over all natural obstacles; in the green corner, those convinced we must proceed with doubt and care. German sociologist Ulrich Beck reminds us that the move from magical to modern thought was based on two guiding values: reason and doubt. *In dubito ergo sum*, to complete Descartes. Beck describes how the rise of Prometheanism in early industrial capitalism corrupted the Enlightenment project, producing 'excessive rationalisation' in society and politics. We know it today in the fragile dreams that yearn for hope but which deny its vital twin, doubt. The great migration of humanity from rural to urban settings that was once regarded as the harbinger of development and democracy is increasingly coupled with global ecological collapse. From the destruction of habitats for urban development to the insatiable need for materials for urban living and the shattered connection between production and consumption, the shift to cities is happening without restraint. It is certainly not being managed in the interests of an increasingly intemperate Nature. In less than a century, we have become an urban species, *Homo urbanis*. From Nature's perspective, *Homo diabolos* might be more apposite. More than half of humanity now lives in large urban settings. In Australia, just about everyone does.

This has happened very quickly: a century ago, only 250 million people, 15 per cent of the world's (much smaller) population, lived in cities. This dimension of modernisation is hard to explain as 'development'. More than one billion people now live in miserable, informal settings, massive squatter camps and *barrios* ringing developing cities, ageing, worsening and intractable to improvement. By the middle of this century, two-thirds of the world's population will live in cities; nineteen of these cities will have more than 20 million inhabitants. The prominent US urban scholar Mike Davis, the author of *Planet of Slums* (Verso, 2007), argues that much contemporary urban growth is taking us 'back to Dickens'. Architects and aesthetes fear that the global economy is producing a world of suburbs. Davis shows that slums are proliferating much more quickly and with far more hideous consequences. Many of these festering settlements will be the first lines of defence, or defeat, as global warming makes sea levels rise. The prospect of Nature in control of a game of slum clearance is too horrible to contemplate. But we must.

Closer to home, the remarkable growth of south-east Queensland exemplifies the storm of urbanisation that is remaking us as an urban species. Older residents recall the now-discarded saying that Brisbane was Australia's largest country town. It was the biggest town in a state long dominated by a sturdy and populous rural sector. From the 1960s, the Gold Coast started to look at least superficially urban, with its towers, glitz and Oz schlock, but no one thought it much more than an urban illusion, a stage set for tourism. Despite its brash boosterism, the Bjelke-Petersen Government was never going to usher the state out of its long twilight of sepia-tinged conservatism and murky sleaze. The corruption racket was called 'the joke'—probably a fair metaphor for the whole Porpoise Spit-style politics that held the state back for so long.

The ending of the joke coincided with—perhaps even unleashed—the boom in the state's south-east corner which has grown furiously for the past two decades—between 55 000 and 80 000 people each year since 1986. South-east Queensland is now a wonderfully complex regional hybrid, linking Brisbane with the cities of Ipswich, Logan, and the Gold and Sunshine Coasts. Current population growth, largely from interstate, runs at nearly a thousand new arrivals a week. By 2026 there could be as many as four-and-a-half million residents in the region, which may overtake Melbourne as the nation's second largest metropolis. But ending the joke, and the lifting of the gloom, exposed underlying problems that threatened to make the growth unmanageable, including institutional and development cultures resistant to sound urban planning; prolonged inaction on resource pressures, especially water; and decrepit infrastructure. That the growth surge has not ended in outright chaos testifies to the success of reformers in dealing with these traditional political infirmities, especially the antipathy for planning and the preference for white shoe development.

But the region went to the brink of default: its water supply has nearly run out in the last few years, while the prospect of transport gridlock was probably delayed, at least for a while, by the introduction of a highly effective integrated ticketing in its public transport system. Many threats remain: housing stress, road congestion, air pollution and rising greenhouse emissions. In the face of continuing growth, they look very worrying. But there is improved resilience in the south-east Queensland governance system, nourished by a new belief in planning at the local and state levels and by a new maturity and commitment to the sustainability ideal in much of its development industry. Further development of these new strengths will need to occur if the region is to retain its liveability and improve its sustainability.

The housing affordability squeeze that preoccupies public discussion in south-east Queensland these days is symptomatic of a growing failure of our cities to adequately house their inhabitants. Once celebrated as our greatest strength, our housing system looks a little deranged these days. Freewheeling growth has generated an affordability crisis in Australian cities, locking out the young and exposing many borrowers to potentially catastrophic debt. We've lost our cherished status as the nation with the highest levels of home ownership to places we thought were laggards: Britain and Ireland. In the post-war decades, the home ownership level peaked at around 70 per cent, but has been declining in recent years. First home owners have left or been forced from the market in droves. An increasingly mobile, consumption-driven Gen Y, or at least parts of it, can't see the point of a mortgage. Hugh Mackay reports that, among young adults, there is 'genuine confusion about whether homeownership is a good investment or not'.

Now about one-third of Australian households own their homes and a further third are buying. More than three million households will be paying rent within a decade—a significant proportion of the nation, which will no longer be able to proudly describe itself as a home-owning democracy. The rapidly growing rental community inhabits an increasingly costly and stressed market; a growing number of people live in ill-suited, poor-quality and/or overly expensive housing. At the same time, average dwelling sizes in the home-owner sector and, interestingly, in the upper end of the rental market have been rising rapidly. The average floor area of new houses has grown by over 40 per cent in the past two decades.

While homes for the wealthy continue to bulge outwards, many Australians have been pushed out of housing altogether. There's disagreement on exactly how many homeless people there are in Australia now, but all of the numbers are shocking. In 2006 the Commonwealth's Supported Accommodation Assistance Program (SAAP) services supported over 160 000 people, many of them children. About 14 000 people sleep rough each night, and rising mortgage default in suburbia is adding to that number. In south-east Queensland, there have been several reports of groups of homeless people, including families, camping in parks and showgrounds. In January 2008, *The Australian* reported overflowing urban hostels and shelters. In Newcastle, homeless people were living in 'wretched circumstances', forced to camp in backyards and parks.

The national housing 'system'—if it can be called that—is misallocating housing resources at an increasingly dysfunctional scale. We're heading in the direction of 'feast or famine' without much apparent will to change course. Perhaps this is because the ideal of universal private home ownership has lost its enchantment as markets fail to deliver. The national homelessness inquiry and the new funding promised by the Rudd Government in 2008 may signal hope. It's the opportunity to widen the lens and rethink how we house ourselves as a nation. Achieving housing security, not ownership, for all should be our guiding premise. The market will never deliver universal ownership, and if we remain mesmerised by this ideal we will condemn in any period significant numbers of Australians to insecure and inappropriate housing or to outright homelessness. The public housing sector needs revitalisation, but we also need to generate new mainstream housing options that will provide pleasant and secure accommodation for those not able or willing to take the long mortgage road. Communal shared housing, for example, might better suit the fluid lifestyles of the young and provide better security and affordability than private tenancy. This broader rethink is invited as we deal with the scandalous homelessness emergency.

Another old argument continues. Elites have long squabbled about the imperfections of the working class and what ought to be done about their flaws. As the middle classes expanded and the wealthy lost their early monopoly on suburbia and conspicuous consumption, elite criticism extended to petty bourgeois tastes. The war on the poor had its nasty phases. The British *Poor Law* of 1834 and its forensic coding of the 'deserving' and 'undeserving' poor come to mind. Later in the same century, economic liberals devised a penal form of philanthropy, 'scientific charity', to break the bad habits of the lower orders. Think work for the dole on bread and water, and throw in a slapping for shirkers. Their real argument was with the soft-headed liberals who thought charity was a Christian duty, not a tool of class discipline.

I spent many months of my doctoral studies in the Victorian State Library's La Trobe Collection reading the forty-one minute books that recorded the work of the Melbourne Ladies' Benevolent Society in the second half of the nineteenth century. The well-intentioned ladies of the society 'visited' poor working-class families in the first suburbs of Melbourne—Fitzroy, Carlton, Collingwood—dispensing advice and subsistence rations. I read and transcribed innumerable entries in the minutes, looking for evidence about the daily life of poor disabled people. One entry struck me for its colour and unintended humour. After months of getting to know the 'ladies' and their indispositions, I felt I could almost hear the 'tut-tuts' which must have attended the following alarming account: 'Miss Kernot reported that on visiting [X] she found bread and butter on the table, the baby screaming, and the mother reading a penny dreadful'. Not dirt poor, but badly behaved—bumptiously so. As colonial social history shows, the first suburban proletariat in the Australian colonies constantly distressed elites and officialdom with their nonchalant intemperance. The Victorian holy trinity—thrift, temperance and obedience—had little appeal to the 'lower orders', who were fond of sport, gambling, boozing and generally having a good time.

Fear of the 'penny dreadful' tastes of ordinary folks seems to fuel angst today about another suburban working-class tribe, the 'Aspirationals' and their attachment to reality TV and the emblematic 'McMansion'. Legions of the well off and well trained have decried its awfulness. Historian Mark Peel writes:

> It's interesting that an American word—McMansions—coined to describe the sprawling palaces of the super rich, has, in this country, been turned against ordinary four-bedroom houses. It's also interesting that most newspaper photos of new estates use a telephoto lens that presses the houses up against each other, emphasising their bulk and closeness.

It is largely about behaviour and dress sense. But note also the existence of a contrary position in a shouting match about Aspirationals. This supposedly anti-elitist view sanctifies them as a sturdy modern peasantry whose instincts, unblemished by intellect or art, are beyond reproach. To demonise or beatify: both perspectives are calculating views of working-class people. Both perceive them as pieces in a culture war, not real people with prosaic strengths and weaknesses. Their support by the early Mark Latham—continued in the online Australian journal, *The New City* (www.thenewcity.info)—blithely overlooked the financial entrapments and social pitfalls that face working-class improvers in the neo-liberal economy. These include the risks of penury and exclusion as debts mount and suburban Aspirationals are left adrift in areas with little fallback to quality public services, particularly public transport. It also neglected how the Howard Government's clever targeting of subsidies to those living in these suburbs outflanked even pragmatic Laborism. Latham later shifted from his 'Mark-1' enthusiasm to a much more critical view of working-class ambition in the new economy.

Back in 2002, Mark-1 and I debated this at an Evatt Foundation breakfast. The small group of hardy souls who attended saw us circling each other, never really attacking. I think we liked each other too much for that. I certainly regarded him as one of the few Australian politicians courageous enough to try to place urban issues on the public agenda despite chronic official indifference (of which more soon). For this alone, we need him back in public life.

At the breakfast, we agreed the suburbs were central to the Australian experience. But we diverged on the social virtues of new suburban forms, especially the master-planned estate. At the time, we both lived with our families in such estates in south-western Sydney. Our experiences nudged us to different conclusions about the bootstrapping ambitions of our neighbours. Mark-1's image of working-class improvers heroically providing for themselves and their offspring on a suburban frontier was not one I shared. It seemed to me that much of the largesse they were enjoying—proximity to new motorways and regional parks, new 'affordable' private schools—was publicly subsidised or provided, although this was rendered invisible in the marketing and the public debate. To my mind, there was a danger that 'Aspirational fervour' was creating an image of a class fragment that didn't really exist. They were no more independent of the state than the rest of us, and quite inclined to take what they could get from the communal tin (ditto the developers who expected the infrastructure subsidies and happily took the windfall gains).

Opposition to public largesse defined Latham's politics. He stepped bravely on to the tracks in an attempt to halt the federal gravy train (the only public transport used by politicians). Yet in the debate about suburbia I felt that he overlooked the huge federal subsidies propping up the new fringe estates: private education, child-care and health were subsidised, and the choice to use them was regarded as evidence of moral virtue. Developers may pay one-off state levies, but the federal subsidy flow continued and grew as Howard's middle-class welfare embraced those who aspired to upward mobility but needed, even if they did not want to acknowledge, a hand up. The institutions of respectable middle-class life were extended to many new outer suburban communities. In 2004, Prime Minister Howard crowed:

> Under this government about three non-government schools which charge on average less than $2000 in fees have been established ... you are talking here about schools for the battlers who want a bit of choice ... I have been to many of them and they are on the outskirts of the cities of this country.

As the confessional introductory essay to Latham's *Diaries* (MUP, 2006) reveals, 'Mark-2' came to regret his uncritical enthusiasm for his neighbours, who he came to see as self-absorbed and materialistic. The feeling was mutual: they were not inclined to vote for him. The subsection entitled 'The Sick Society' is intensely revealing of personal ideological disappointment. A true believer in the improving power of reformed capitalism finds the system up to its old tricks again. Latham finds himself regretting 'the commercialisation of public services and the grotesque expansion of market forces into social relationships'. (He had been an advocate of Public–Private Partnerships.) Furthermore, 'questions of status and self-esteem are now determined by the accumulation of material goods, not the maintenance of mateship . . . The politics of "me", the individual, replaces the politics of "we", the community'. The ladder of opportunity took the Aspirationals to Harvey Norman, not enlightenment. McMansion land is now an artefact of 'the sorry state of advanced capitalism: the ruling culture encourages people to reach for four wheel drives, double storey homes, reality television and gossip magazines to find meaning and satisfaction in their lives'. He reinstates a word the neo-libs wished banished: capitalism. Now it's simply another 'ism' that disappoints:

> I wanted working people to enjoy a better standard of living, but had assumed as they climbed the economic ladder, they would still care about the community in which they lived . . . especially the poor and disadvantaged. This was my misjudgement . . . they . . . left their old, working-class neighbourhoods behind and embraced the new values of consumerism.

Another old argument re-enters: the progressive 'embourgoisment' of the working classes and the loss of social solidarity—leading to, among other things, 'angst towards the disadvantaged'.

The plurality of contemporary suburban life deserves stronger recognition in public culture. Suburbia is a much more complex landscape than it was. This was richly explained in Mark Peel's account of life in outer suburban Melbourne, 'The inside story of life on the outer', published in *The Age* in 2007. It should be compulsory reading for those who would still dismiss suburbia (usually from afar) as monocultural or anachronistic. As a gay couple, Peel and his partner failed to find the prejudice of which friends had warned them. 'In our experience, people weren't unwelcome because of an identity or culture, but if and when they proved angry, vexatious and careless neighbours.' His neighbours included 'Koreans, Filipinos, Greeks, Indians, English, Dutch, Samoans and New Zealanders . . . mixing as neighbours, partners and friends'.

Some diversity is not to be celebrated, though. The growing socio-economic polarities within our cities represent an unwelcome trend. Analysing deprivation in the eight capital cities using 2006 census data, Griffith University's Scott Baum exposes what he terms the 'suburban scars' that mark decades of economic restructuring. More than 10 per cent were considered highly deprived 'poverty traps' where multiple disadvantages— poor neighbours, poor services, dispiriting environs, isolation—combined to lock inhabitants into long-term poverty. At the other end of the deprivation scale, Baum finds a wealthy mirror image: just over 10 per cent of suburbs containing high concentrations of wealth in established older areas of affluence and in the newer bastions of gentrified privilege in the inner cities. Within suburbia, the same polarities were revealed. Gated republics celebrating order, similarity and privilege are juxtaposed with the dystopian sinkholes studded with tattoo parlours, payday lenders, sex shops, takeaways and two-dollar bargain bins. The suburban love affair continues but in much more complex ways, and masks pockets of disenchantment and entrapment.

Urban scholars in Australia have long had to endure an odd and debilitating cultural schizophrenia that has robbed the field of recognition and confidence. The running joke is that we hold meetings in public phone booths. The same has gone for the urban professions, especially the long invisible profession of urban planning. Griffith University's Lesley Johnson relates the experience of George Clarke, a leading Sydney post-war planner, who in 1959 was asked by a member of the New South Wales parliament, 'urban . . . what's that word mean?' We must assume that eventually he got it. After much lethargy, the states eventually rolled out plans and policies that helped to prevent the worst forms of North American sprawl, notwithstanding many—often monumental—failures of will along the way.

State and municipal corruption was—indeed, it remains—an endemic threat to the integrity of land development processes, as Geoffrey Atherden's *Grass Roots* whimsically reminded us.

The recent corruption inquiry in Wollongong showed that in real life it was much more venal and frequently bizarre. The tawdry Illawarra tale had it all: money changing hands secretly; a planner sleeping with developers; harassment and intimidation; underworld heavies and dodgy politicians. Many richly coloured identities seemed straight out of *The Sopranos*. All of this conjured by the urban development game. Amazingly, none of them seemed to think they'd be caught. *The Sydney Morning Herald* used just three words to summarise the affair: 'Dirty, sexy, money'. When I think of coastal development in Australia, I'm mindful of proverbial wisdom, '*quos Deus vult perdere prius dementat*' (whom God wishes to destroy he first makes mad). So much of our coastal municipal politics is 'organised madness'.

In contrast to urbanised countries in Europe, Australian city governance and policy structures are relatively under-developed. Yet transport, housing affordability and community renewal increasingly preoccupy political agendas. The urban refuseniks have, however, dominated in national politics. The moment of national maturity marked by the Whitlam Government's urban and regional development program in the early 1970s starkly contrasts with the decades of efforts to prevent the development of any national urban policy agenda. Prime Minister John Howard refused to acknowledge, let alone adopt, an urban agenda, despite friendly urging from business lobbies, including the Property Council and the Urban Development Institute. The development industry opposed dismantling the Hawke/Keating governments' Better Cities program, itself a shadow of the Whitlam urban agenda. The perception that Howard ran a business-friendly government has interesting flaws—property and urban development have always required a regulatory framework.

The long reign of national political refusal contrasts with the quiet enthusiasm of Australians for urban life. Australians have from earliest times embraced cities and suburbs. The English journalist REN Twopenny wrote *Town Life in Australia* in 1883, and reported that 'the Australian townsman' had 'inherited so thoroughly' the English love of suburban living. Overseas observers report our urban passion, but Australians have relentlessly refused to discuss, let alone celebrate, our urban love affair in public culture. Anti-urbanism is a heart murmur with which the nation was born. Geographer Clive Forster quotes the New South Wales Government Statistician, TA Coghlan, who in 1897 lamented 'the abnormal aggregation of the population into their capital cities', viewing this as 'a most unfortunate element in the progress of the colonies'. He was doubtless motivated by a fear that Australia would reproduce the toxic cities of Victorian industrialism. We didn't. There were problems with slums and disease, but they were nothing like the urban pestilence left behind in Europe. The opening of suburban opportunity to the masses in the early twentieth century helps to explain the good health and high living standards enjoyed by Australians. In 1905, the influential American city planning advocate Frederick Howe wrote: 'The great cities of Australia are spread out into the suburbs in a splendid way. For miles about are broad roads with small houses, gardens, and an opportunity for touch with the freer, sweeter life which the country offers'.

The denial of our innate urbanism, and the pleasure and productivity that we have derived from our cities, is a national trait worth abandoning. This collective daydream means that we risk neglecting problems until they become too intrusive and threatening to ignore, and by then difficult, expensive or impossible to repair. Our cities and suburbs have harboured a set of social and ecological stresses that are approaching critical levels. The 'Human Settlements' section of the *2006 State of the Environment Report* makes grim reading. Between 1998 and 2004, Australian energy use per capita grew by 4 per cent at a time when we should be making radical cuts to individual greenhouse emissions. There's no sign of improvement: 'Primary energy consumption is forecast to increase by 48 per cent . . . by the year 2019 . . . It is significantly above the expected rate of population increase, and it is driven by the continued growth in per capita consumption and economic growth'. The mass urban embrace of air conditioning, as well as raising overall electricity consumption, is shifting peak demand to summer, driving the expansion of water-guzzling power generation systems.

The mounting water deficits are well known: less nationally understood is just how close south-east Queensland has come to outright default in recent years. Politicians looked genuinely scared as they announced evertougher restrictions on water use. The rains returned in early 2008, but climate change reminds us that urban water crisis is now a permanent spectre facing our cities. The other big urban pressure cooker is the stampede on to our long-neglected public transport systems as petrol prices surge. Every city has registered large jumps in the number of people trying to use public transport. This has mildly tempered the malign neglect of public transport in some cities. In Brisbane, municipal politics now centres on which political party can build new buses quickly enough to meet surging demand for services—though the spending remains dwarfed by the vast sums being thrown at new road tunnels and bridges. By contrast, in Sydney they're still dumping half-hearted plans to build new rail lines.

If not stopped, the long slide to a more divided society will surely end in tears. We cannot allow further social polarisation without expecting some serious communal trouble. Still, some fairies continue to make joyful song at the bottom of the garden, bless them. Sea-change and tree-change inspire rousing songs of liberation, celebrating the mass release of the citizenry from urban confinement. This is an intoxicating but deeply misleading vision of Australia as it enters the third millennium.

There is no mass urban entrapment. Australia's long marriage to city living continues. None of the deeper paradoxes of suburban life register in the contemporary argy bargy about Aspirationals and McMansions. These new urban arguments making their way into the public domain, as caricatured as they are, may yet signal the breaking down of urban silence in popular culture. I sense that public interest in, and discussion of, urban affairs have never been stronger. After prolonged neglect, the various media are increasingly willing to put urban issues on centre stage. Key metro papers have dedicated urban affairs reporters. *The Sydney Morning Herald* and Brisbane's *Courier-Mail* have campaigned for stronger metropolitan planning and governance, drawing and generating considerable public interest.

During the 1990s, the *Herald* increased its interest in urban issues, and campaigned with rising vigour for improved planning and management of Sydney. It was rightly critical of the Carr Government, targeting its failures to invest in public transport and develop a sound metropolitan plan for Sydney, as well as various policy fiascos, including the nationally notorious Cross-City Tunnel.

Anne Davies's excoriating 2006 *Herald* essay, 'The great Carr crash' summarised the troubled urban legacy of Carr's decade-long rule. In a later interview with pre-political Maxine McKew, Carr brushed the criticism aside as 'barking mad', bragging of a sixty-one billion dollar investment in capital works. And what of Sydney's crumbling and occasionally lethal public transport system? The resort to public–private partnerships and user tolls for roads? The crumbling public realm of western Sydney? The Olympics were a bright exception to a record of malign urban neglect. They showcased what was possible with strong planning and quality public infrastructure. Pretty much everything worked, was on time and stayed in place. Everyone noted the contrast with the shambolic free-enterprise Atlanta games in 1996. For some reason, the same government that staged them failed to apply the lessons of this brilliantly successful experiment to its mainstream urban management responsibilities.

New South Wales had talented planning professionals, including at the highest levels, but let them languish without much interest or support. Many drifted away from the public service or were moved on. In his last days, Carr finally got work underway to prepare a metropolitan plan for Sydney, a much-lamented hole in the state's urban policy fabric. For a time, it looked as if the state might finally show some policy resolve and move to tighten the governance of Sydney at least. A good plan for Sydney emerged, but so did new hostility to planning in the Cabinet. By March 2008, the *Herald* reported a survey which found that 'One in five Sydneysiders are so sick of traffic and the high cost of living they are considering moving to another city'.

Many look to the new Rudd Government with hope. It went into the 2007 election without a comprehensive urban agenda. But there have been encouraging early signals that it recognises the importance of an urban response to the environmental and social threats facing Australia. The prime minister's 2020 summit identified ten key topics for discussion and cities made the list—just.

One thing that must be urged on the new government is urban resolve. A merely advisory or voluntary urban approach will not effect the deep changes needed to our cities to make them sustainable and secure. The job cannot be left to the states: they lack the resources and the powers needed to transform and make safe the national settlement system. And several are too mired in deeply impious planning systems to lend honest help to the cause of policy strengthening. A lesson to learn from the states' struggles to confront urban problems in the last decade is that resolute action is almost always welcomed by the public and accepted by industry. 'Institutional shocks' seem the only way of cutting through accumulated confusion and inertia. The occasionally inspired New South Wales government rapidly transformed the state's residential building sector via its 2004 BASIX regulatory initiative, which overnight managed to kill off some of the most wasteful new home products. Initially apprehensive, the industry adjusted and moved on. Similarly, green improvements to the national building code are forcing universal changes to construction practices, but not quickly enough. The Queensland government's dramatic intervention in south-east Queensland's growth through its highly directive 2005 blueprint plan was welcomed by the public and by the development industry. In February 2008, SBS *Insight* in a program on 'City Limits', featured an AV Jennings executive urging the federal government to introduce tougher sustainability standards in the development sector to clarify the regulatory framework so that developers could get on with their business. The only explanation for continued lack of resolve on urban issues must be the entrenched grip of neo-liberalism on the major political parties and the bureaucracy. The public and major sections of industry do not share this view.

In 2007, my centre at Griffith, the Urban Research Program, participated in an 'Our Future, Your Say' campaign led by the *Courier-Mail,* and also involving Channel Nine Brisbane and The Brisbane Institute. The series repeated a 2003 campaign by the *Courier-Mail* that helped stimulate public support for a new approach to managing growth in traditionally freewheeling south-east Queensland. A series of well-attended public forums complemented the newspaper's ongoing coverage of urban issues during the middle and latter months of 2007. The forums drew influential speakers, including Peter Garrett, Malcolm Turnbull, Brisbane Lord Mayor Campbell Newman, Queensland Transport Minister Paul Lucas and Anna Bligh. The planning and infrastructure improvements of recent years received re-endorsement, but the government was urged to rethink its unblushing zeal for growth and to intensify its efforts to deal with congestion and over-development. A marvellously vivid, intensely thoughtful youth forum urged closer attention to the needs of the generations which will inherit the south-east Queensland estate from the baby boomers.

Bligh's leadership succession confirmed and extended Queensland's new enthusiasm for urban policy. The new premier announced that tackling urban congestion would be a key priority for her government, and established a state urban land development agency. The Deputy Premier, Paul Lucas, was given the planning and infrastructure portfolio, underlining its strong cabinet status. The national planning community now looks to south-east Queensland and Perth for inspiration. From Sydney, planner Pat Fensham remarks: 'New South Wales planners can only dream of the situation in Queensland . . .' This was not the way Sydney spoke about any aspect of Queensland when I was a Brisbane schoolboy in the late 1970s.

The growth paradox is likely to be the biggest challenge facing south-east Queensland planning. It takes two quite vexing dimensions. The big spend underway on infrastructure is trying to address perilous deficits, especially in water and transport. Much of it, especially the massive new tunnels, tollways and bridges, will worsen greenhouse emissions. But should we let the place grind to a halt or dry up? How can we turn around the super-tankers of car dependency and resource profligacy? The second paradox is political. There is rising pressure from longer-term residents for a growth cap. But how do you put up the 'full' sign in a democracy like Australia? These questions will surely vex the next rethink of the regional plan, due soon.

The City of Sydney has exercised urban leadership where the state of New South Wales arguably has not. In 2007 it began a process to articulate a new strategic vision, 'Sustainable Sydney 2030', that included eagerly attended public forums and talks. Everyone, it seemed, wanted to discuss the future of their city in a context of widely shared anxiety about declining liveability and sustainability. It was interesting to see how wide the interest in urban futures has now become. In my experience, public planning forums in the past were largely perfunctory, sometimes disagreeable, gatherings of specialist professionals and residents seeking wider theatres for local grievances. The Sydney forums couldn't have been more different. One event I attended included Cate Blanchett, who spoke about the need for Sydney to avoid the type of wholesale sanitising development that drives artists away. Yet the evidence is showing that Sydney is falling behind the rest of Australia as people in artistic and cultural jobs abandon the state. Civic discussion of urban issues has flourished in Melbourne, thanks at least in part to the long advocacy of one of Australia's most influential urbanists, Paul Mees. A series of public Future Melbourne forums drew large numbers in 2006 and 2007. *The Age* continues regularly to make space for critical discussion of urban issues. A recent example was a splendidly disconcerting essay on 'Monstrous Melbourne' by RMIT academic Paul James that questioned the environmental plausibility of the city's much honked 'liveability' claims. I'm less aware of the state of public discussion of urban issues in the other major cities. It's worth noting, however, the strong support that Perth residents have shown for their state government's urban initiatives in rail network improvement, metropolitan planning, urban renewal and innovative urban design. The recent Perth 'Network City' plan emerged from a strikingly honest attempt to engage public opinion. The South Australian Thinkers in Residence program has brought influential urban scholars to Australia. Closer to my own patch, in 2006 the Gold Coast City Council became the first Australian government of any kind to fund a chair in urban policy and planning with a mission to generate public interest in and awareness of urban policy issues. So what? Perhaps you have to be an urban academic or professional to appreciate the extent of this cultural shift. Such public attention to urban issues was completely unimaginable just a decade ago. In this part of the world, *Homo urbanis* may be waking from its Arcadian dream. Paul James comments on our new urban self-awareness: 'The strange thing about this pronouncement is that it shocks us. Like climate change, it is part of a process that has been happening for decades. It is as if we have been woken after a generation of sleepwalking'. Sleepwalking—a nice metaphor for our long dozy urban denial now ended by ecological and social tremors.

Beyond the media, and the formal realms of civic debate, I sense rising public interest in the state of our cities and neighbourhoods. It may reflect a growing sense that we cannot continue to take our urban home worlds for granted. The world's largest national assemblage of landlords now looks nervously to the state of the urban property markets, and critically to the urban institutions that govern them. The urban denizens of the world's driest continent now comprehend, in the face of prolonged drought and climate change, their tenuous dependence on vulnerable water systems. And the space allocated in popular culture for suburban recognition and exploration seems to be opening out into a much more authentic and lively scope. It wasn't my cup of tea, but *Neighbours* was an important cultural circuit breaker. It simply ignored the very idea that one could be critical of suburban life.

We now have an appreciable tradition of film and television that has explored the suburban experience in a variety of ways, and with contrasting emotions, ranging from empathy and interest to horror. The mass appeal of films like *The Castle* can only be fully explained by their sympathy with our suburban experience, with all its prosaic miseries and joys. Still most suburban citizens conduct lives that are 'too uneventful' to be recorded in other social conversations, such as media commentary and often, regrettably, scholarly analysis. And yet it is within the domains of the 'ordinary', the Fountain Lakes of our metropolitan regions that the future of our cities is being shaped.

A big shift is underway in these urban life-worlds that is of far more consequence to the future of our cities, and therefore the nation, than the sandrush currently afflicting the coast. The first three decades after World War II were marked by convulsive growth in cities, but also by a remarkable degree of social stability rooted in an absence of major class faultlines. There was almost none of the precipitous block-by-block social division that blights American cities. Class differences were there, but they were painted in broad brushstrokes across the Australian urban landscape. There were separate regions inhabited by the rich, by workers, and a broad middle class—but also many areas where mixing occurred. I recall from my child-hood in the far North Shore of Sydney in the early 1970s suburbs that were socially mixed to the point of bedlam. This was the Pittwater region, including places like Mona Vale, Bayview, Church Point, Newport, Avalon and, at its tip, Palm Beach, all gloriously arrayed around the far northern beaches and Broken Bay. Today it's a millionaires' paradise, visited by Hollywood stars and favoured by the local elites, and the *Sydney Morning Herald* reports 'Peter Weir prefers the familiarity of Palm Beach to the glitz of Hollywood'. He 'is just like any other well-to-do local'. Not that there is any other type of local.

When I lived there in the 1970s, it was rather different, home to a strange mixture of oddsters, inheritors, artists, ferals, improvers, losers, the crassly bourgeois and the very bloody comfortable. Pittwater High, my school for a time, exposed me to a near-complete spectrum of Australian life, an amazingly eclectic mix of social types that seemed to cohabit. Only farmers and miners were missing. I regard the experience as a gift to my socialisation. You heard the occasional bad word about 'Westies' coming to 'our' beaches ('surfboards bolted to roof racks . . . haw, haw'), but they were a species my friends and I knew nothing about. I wasn't even sure where they came from. As I recall, their usual detractors were the scraggy kids of local battlers who wagged school and hung around beaches and milk bars all day. Today, the Pittwater region is transformed by decades of volcanic pressure in property markets and socio-economic change. Most of the oddsters and battlers have left, some cashed up on inflated property values, replaced by increasingly homogenous bastions of conspicuous wealth and good taste.

Places like Pittwater in the decades after World War II were machines for social integration. I've no doubt they contributed to our lethargic but real commitment to tolerance. In these contexts, unless you were a committed hermit you not only saw 'other' people, you were bound to share your everyday life with them, in schools, shops, sporting teams, at church, in parks, at beaches. I was centre halfback for the Pittwater Tigers, a motley crew of Aussie Rules outsiders who took it up to the nobs from French's Forest, and other better provided for teams. We were usually whipped, but battled on, relishing our hard-bitten, loser-but-watch-out mindset. A cog in the machine for mixing.

As the Archbishop of Canterbury, Dr Rowan Williams, put it recently, social intolerance is largely a failure of imagination; it thrives when we are unable to imagine our contrary communities. I remember Pittwater as a place that greatly stimulated my imagination: poor kids who taught me bushcraft, how to sail a boat (or plank) and how to build a bike from old parts; wealthy family friends who showed that money was no barrier to a life defined by generosity and simplicity, and with none of the anxious desire to impress and control that seems so great a part of contemporary affluence; the middle-class people, like my parents, who had chanced upon this wonderland by luck or inheritance, and lived humbly and very happily with their good fortune. Only now, at my age, and in a very different and changing Australia, do I realise how good and instructive these times were for me.

Things began to change rapidly from the 1970s, which saw the shift towards more restless and divided class landscapes in our cities. In places like Pittwater, prolonged class cleansing has generated new communities where wealth is openly celebrated, not to say demanded. My own 'wind-shield survey' of Pittwater a few years ago amazed me. How could such a lazy and messy place become so self-consciously pure and tidy in twenty years? Science confirms the assessment. Urban scholarship shows us that our cities are now much more socio-economically divided. And we see it, sense it, in the rise of gated communities, the growth of a private security apparatus, the occasional eruption of communal unrest, even riots (Macquarie Fields, Redfern, Cronulla, Palm Island). More of us are reconceiving home as a secure lifestyle package. More of us are falling backwards into poverty sinkholes. It's all a bit unsettling. The spectres at the feast may not dampen wealthy appetites, but they add apprehension to taste.

The principal solvent for previously settled bonds of social position and regional landscape has been the program of structural adjustment that has been carried with bipartisan fervour across the political horizon for nearly three decades by successive national governments. For many, the social price of the miracle economy has been high. The rising economic tide didn't lift all boats and left many castaways behind. Thought banished by growth, 'absolute' poverty returned to our cities as small congregations of ageing winos were joined by homeless legions: lost youths, mentally ill and broken families. About half of them are under twenty-four, most have mental health issues. These Australians never had it so bad. It is yet another old problem reinstating itself on the public agenda.

The new Prime Minister Kevin Rudd identified soaring homelessness and social exclusion among the legacies of his predecessor as he assumed office. But the threat of penury is much broader than this. Many were left high and dry by Howard, including Aspirationals: cheered into unsustainable debt, lured by private consumption subsidies that the state cannot continue to maintain, and enticed or driven into risky new working conditions. Rudd must be aware of the electoral lift he received from the mortgage-stressed outer suburbs of our major cities, especially Sydney. Throughout 2007, the shadows of negative equity and mortgage default were lengthening in Howard's most prized electoral trophies. Jackie Kelly saw it coming and fled the field (even if she forgot to tell hubby to do the same). Can Labor free itself from the bilateral consensus on property boosterism? Will Rudd abandon the boom-burb politics that cheered the Aspirationals over the debt cliff? How long will the ludicrous and unsustainable subsidies to private health and education be maintained?

Not that the states should escape censure. They've had in their hands many tools and resources that could have been used to stem the tide of social stress. What did they fail to do? Humane gambling policies, better funded social and public housing, public transport improvements in poor areas, property and betterment levies to tax windfall gains and fund social improvements, investment in urban public realms, doors sealed to the snake oil merchants of public–private partnerships.

In many quarters, it remains heresy to speak of ill or threat. An ideological hallmark of neo-liberalism was to quickly and roughly declaim any critic of social conditions as 'negative', 'miserable' or just 'not focused on the positives'. It's a head plate that many social scientists have been ordered to wear and was especially effective in cowing the universities, and the entire endeavour of social science. Scholars reporting the increasingly obvious trend towards social polarisation got the 'negative hand wringers' tag, or were charged with political conspiracy—as were climate scientists during Howard's aggressive reign of scepticism.

My book *Australian Heartlands* (Allen & Unwin, 2006) aroused the happy police. It argued that all was not well in suburban Australia, and I predicted that the Aspirationals would be left high and dry as the 'miracle economy' receded and the debt dunes swept over them. A *Courier-Mail* reviewer dismissed the book as 'gloomy and dysfunctional' and suggested that I 'get out a bit more'. The weekend supplement in the same issue ran a cover feature on homelessness. It was emblazoned 'Welcome to the Smart State, where 26,000 people are homeless; where any low-to-middle income family is three, maybe four, bad turns from the gutter'. It was a stunning and disturbing story from a gifted young reporter, Trent Dalton, recalling the Victorian slum journalism of London's Henry Mayhew and Melbourne's incomparable John Stanley James, pseudonym 'The Vagabond'. I read Dalton's account of his journey among the urban homeless with mixed feelings, exhilarated by its insights into our wholesale vulnerability to personal collapse, disheartened by the palpable sense that this was Victorian London, Melbourne, whatever . . . on historical replay.

Many of the insights, and much of the animus in *Australian Heartlands* were drawn from years sitting in trains criss-crossing Sydney, observing the increasingly fragmented social geography outside—the sinkholes, the gated cantons, the cheap consolidation, the aching neglect of the public domain. I shared my journeys with vomiting smackheads, prowling dealers, the howling mentally ill, the out of it and the scared. I travelled without valuables, and looked straight ahead. Like many of the residents of western Sydney, I relied on a public transport system that could charitably be described as utterly miserable. Nothing ran on time, everything was begrudged, apart from the inexplicable tolerance of the frontline staff. They'd been thrown to the wolves but remained mostly brave and gracious.

As I type these words, years later, anger flares as I recall one awful year when I was a complete captive of this shambolic train system. We were a one-car family and there was—in theory—a train service connecting my home and workplace so I was determined to use it. The journey linked my workplace at the Urban Frontiers Program in Macarthur, on Sydney's south-western edge, and our flat in Parramatta, a shabby, noise box knocked up during the 1990s. It was around the time of the Olympics in 2000. Transport for the Games worked wonderfully; good organisation helped by lots of residents leaving town or not driving. Meanwhile, the rest of us made do with rail and bus systems that got worse, not better. In the months after the flame and the tourists left town, I realised with increasing despair that the well-oiled machinery of the Games was for show, not intended for normal domestic service.

It's all coming back, the countless episodes of delayed or cancelled trains. The worst times were the winter return journeys when the darkness added chilled austerity to the whole tedious, confusing experience. As the time to leave work approached, the dread would build as I thought about what lay ahead: windswept East German-like platforms; the garbled who-the-fuck-knows announcements; the interminable waiting for a train that should have come; skulking hoods in the dark; the fearful station staff holed up in their prefab bunkers; the wafting smell of piss and vomit; the few sad others, usually migrants, braving this mindless trauma. Fellow travellers avoided eye contact, though sometimes I'd catch a fleeting stare. They were clearly wondering what the honky was doing here. Meanwhile, my thought balloon: 'Will I get home tonight? Will I see my son before he goes to sleep?'

The point is not my year of urban frustration, or its continuing occasional emotional reverberations. It's that most of those lost souls who joined me on those Kafkaesque misadventures are probably still there, condemned to ride the ghost trains of western Sydney, too poor to have a car. I escaped a landscape of urban neglect, which included our miserably built flat near the seedy centre of Parramatta. (I'm glad to hear that local leadership has helped to renew its public realm in recent years.) We traded the leaky cubby house for a home in a new estate near my Macarthur campus, right in the heart of Aspirational country. It was an interesting transition, from a place where no one spoke to you to a place where neighbours took a keen, occasionally intrusive, interest in what you did, how you kept yourself. There was a vaguely present sense of norms assumed and policed. I related this to a newspaper journalist interviewing me after the publication of *Australian Heartlands*. Incredulity was the response: not here in Australia—that *Truman Show* stuff only happens in America. Against my wishes, she sent a photographer to the estate we'd lived in for some images. A few days later, she emailed that when the photographer got out of his car and took photos, local residents rang the police. She wondered whether I'd had a point.

There was another, related Americanisation underway in the region's social geography. This was the emergence of poor places of which people—even the working class—were fearful, and which they wanted to avoid. The new suburban order was partly motivated and defined by a desire to get away from public housing estates and their residents. Some years later, an executive with a major master-planning developer remarked to me that a successful renewal of the area's public housing estates would clearly harm his business. With the demise of Latham, and now Howard, we don't much hear about Aspirationalism anymore. At the peak of the rhetoric, it was championed as a policy triumph, a new route up the ladder of opportunity, blazed by economic reform. Gabrielle Gwyther's doctoral study helped us to understand that it was also a cultural frame created by massive and unforgivable governance failure, the undermining of public housing that began in the 1970s and that remains a policy pestilence to this day.

My boss at the time, the urban geographer Bill Randolph, and I would drive through public housing estates. In some, you knew you had to keep the wheels rolling. Don't stop; not a good idea. It felt like my student days in Los Angeles. I had returned from the United States in the early 1990s to what I thought was the primordial peace of suburban Australia. It was the shattering of my own dream of an Australia that would forever avoid the pit of urban division. We were still a long way from what I experienced in Los Angeles and, on later visits, Detroit. But had a tipping point been reached in the suburbs? Once the decline to a segregated, fearful world had begun, how could it possibly be arrested, let alone reversed? The sorry record of the long fight back against desegregation in US cities isn't very encouraging.

There are a few pattern books we can look to in describing the history of human affairs, including political economy, or the eternal struggles between the winners, the won-over and the losers. My idea of dreaming and rousing works with this pattern especially, the rude rousing sometimes catalysing a major shift in political economic direction and in the distribution of power. The Great Depression aroused mass anger in Western nations and forced a new dispensation on the capitalist political order that we knew as the Welfare State. The ecological collapse now threatening the global economic system may force another political economic realignment and redistribution of power. Many scenarios are possible, some of them ghastly—including the eco-apocalypses imagined in Cormac McCarthy's novel *The Road* or the 2006 film *Children of Men*. Eco-autocracies may emerge in times of breakdown and chaos. Let's hope not. There's still time for a democratic transition to sustainability and security, but it's running out. From outer space, the denial and inaction of the Howard years must have looked like lunacy.

So where does this bring us now? I think the West is experiencing a moment of rude rousing from many dreams. In Australia, it's as if the whole dormitory has woken simultaneously, angry Nature shattering the windows with sudden force. What happened to the warm narcosis of the miracle economy? How did the dream of freedom morph into a schlockbuster about global warming and oil vulnerability? Who brought this horror upon us? As consensus strengthens on the threat posed by global warming, the tendency to blame and punish also strengthens, as John Howard found out. For some time, a swathe of the urban commentariat in Australia has been blaming the people who punished Howard's inaction on climate change. They have a seductively neat answer to the question of culpability: suburbia. Suburbia is the consumptive beast whose appetite has ruined us all.

A widely shared, if not unanimous, assumption in scholarly and policy circles is that suburbs are at once the source and the worst reflection of the sustainability crisis. The view has resonated with increasing strength in some domains of popular culture—and perhaps more strongly in elite cultural circuits. The geographer Clive Forster recalls comment from a national radio documentary in the early 1990s:

> Australian cities have reached a mid life crisis. Two hundred years after European invasion and the beginnings of urban development in this country, we are looking down at the sprawling belly of our cities and exclaiming, 'Oh my God, how did that happen?' We are full of regret for our gluttonous consumption of space and now we are questioning the ideology on which our lifestyle has been based.

Imported US totems, such as 'sprawl', 'smart growth' and 'new urbanism', have signed the landscape of Australian urban scholarship and debate.

Although sprawl is defined as unplanned low-density urban development, the term has tended to blanket the suburban form, well planned or otherwise. Sprawl's totemic power is signified by the deathly potency granted it in scholarship and commentary, especially in the United States. Joel Hirschhorn's 2005 book reports that *Sprawl Kills* (Sterling & Ross) and annihilates comprehensively by also stealing 'your time, health and money'. Australian architectural critic Elizabeth Farrelly provides forensic detail: 'the traffic jams and the water shortages, the poisonous air and the childhood asthma, the obesity, the neuroses, the depression'. Most Australians in suburbia remain unaware of, or untroubled by, the sprawl bogey.

The continuing stand-off between a mainstream of intellectual critique and a mainstream of everyday life is concerning. The critical position on suburbia assumed by much urban commentary has poor scientific foundations. At best, the suburban critique may reflect a serious over-estimation of the influence of urban form on sustainability. In particular, the faith of many analyses in residential density as a simple lever that can be used to manipulate urban sustainability appears to be misplaced. New Australian scientific analysis points to the consumptive lifestyle, not the nature of one's dwelling, as the root of environmental woes. The 2007 urban consumption analyses produced for the Australian Conservation Foundation by the Centre for Integrated Sustainability Analysis at the University of Sydney turn conventional eco-criticism of suburbia on its head. The *Main Findings* report concludes:

> despite the lower environmental impacts associated with less car use, inner city households outstrip the rest of Australia in every other category of consumption. Even in the area of housing, the opportunities for relatively efficient, compact living appear to be overwhelmed by the energy and water demands of modern urban living, such as air conditioning, spa baths, down-lighting and luxury electronics and appliances, as well as by a higher proportion of individuals living alone or in small households. In each state and territory, the centre of the capital city is the area with the highest environmental impacts, followed by the inner suburban areas.

The point is that total household energy consumption, and therefore greenhouse emissions, are made of both direct and indirect components.

The former is the energy used to maintain everyday lives—petrol, gas and electricity—and the latter is the energy embodied in goods and services consumed by households. While most, if not all, of the focus of urban commentary and policy is on direct energy use, in reality, 'direct household and person use accounts for only 30 per cent of our total greenhouse gas pollution, 23 per cent of our total water use, and just 10 per cent of our total eco-footprint'.

So the energy use most influenced by the size of our house and its location only accounts for a small share of greenhouse emissions. Free-ranging consumption of goods and services produced well outside our life-worlds are causing the problem. Shoving everyone into high-rises won't solve it. In fact, if every Australian household switched to renewable energy and stopped driving their cars tomorrow, total household emissions would decline by only about 18 per cent. It is our consumption appetites that are the real problem, and the biggest guts are not in suburbs.

The 'suburban gothic' tale has produced its equally melodramatic counter-narrative, The Great Australian Dream Swindle. This tale of planning noir bemoans a stolen generation of home ownership dreams. A cinema-scoped fable of hopeful newlyweds in wagons turned back from suburban frontiers by unfeeling black-robed bureaucrats. The black robes have halted the natural order of suburban things by slowing the tide of brick veneer. Those who weave the tale—the Great Australian Dreamers—wish to safeguard the long slumber of suburban conventional wisdom. Here, social intelligence is reduced to the pragmatic axiom: what has (appeared) to work, will always work, and therefore must be always right. Not the attitude, I suggest, of a society that will survive the threat of ecological collapse.

Neither set of protagonists, Goths or Dreamers, comprehends the sustainability threats facing urban, including suburban, Australia. Global warming and oil vulnerability can't be ignored, and neither can they be solved through simple manipulations of urban form like densification. I think both debating positions are hopelessly utopian and, if I may, contrived: one reducing Nature to a one-way street where physical form determines human behaviour; the other dismissing Nature as a frontier land for infinite exploitation. Both testify to the power of arguments based on distorted views of Nature to lead us astray and to produce, in the face of threat, collective dreaming and inaction.

It may appear that I'm down on collective dreams entirely. I'm not, only the ones that imagine us liberated from, or in simple command of, Nature and therefore history. When in power, these dreams tend to produce the kind of collective narcolepsy from which Mackay thinks we are waking now. I've no objections to social dreams that avoid this error ('lights on hills', etc.), and much enthusiasm for those who imagine humanity restored to Nature, as with Martin Luther King's vision of a species freed from the absurdity of racism.

An underlying proposition in this essay is that supernatural dreams may exercise great power to shape, even control, collective consciousness and purpose for a time, but inevitably are swept aside by Nature itself. The imaginings that stand the test of time are, logically, those that do not refuse history or Nature—ideas like human solidarity, natural dependency, the possibility of failure and the frailty of endeavour. Both left and right marched in the twentieth century away from Nature, each succumbing to Prometheanism and a hubris that claimed the power to stop history. I believe it's why both imaginations now are shattering in the face of a Nature that will no longer be scorned.

My alternative imagining of the urban takes Nature as a starting and ending point for human experience, including urban life—not something from which we can free ourselves or attain mastery over. Nature can't be exploited beyond or protected behind an urban growth boundary; it shapes (not determines) and makes possible the entire urban experience, including life in the gilded towers of apartment land. The ACF analysis reminds us just how potent a natural force our inner cities are, and of their natural dependency. It signposts a way through the debating polarities that together have been blocking movement to a naturalised, historically fluid conception of the suburbs. This sees them as shifting landscapes of social and environmental possibilities; neither dystopias nor utopias, but fluid human life worlds whose physical qualities inform but do not determine their sustainability. The view declines the lure of historicism: the fixing of suburbia in time as a landscape with a preset natural disposition that cannot be changed.

One simple way to falsify this view, if you live in suburbia, is to talk to an elderly neighbour who has lived in their home for a long time.

Discussions like this reveal to me an historical suburbia that was immensely more sustainable than the model we have now, based much more on modest consumption, mutual help and local provision. And these suburban places were vastly less consumptive than the inner cities of today. The historical scholarship of Patrick Mullins and Patrick Troy recalls a suburban form that could provide for much of its own needs.

Climate change and energy insecurity are real and present threats to the stability and sustainability of human society. The imminence, scale and speed of both threats appear to overwhelm the principal mitigation strategies on offer. Through the months of writing this essay, I've witnessed the scientific consensus consistently pegging back the horizon for action to prevent grave climate harm. It now seems that we have ten years or less to make massive cuts to carbon emissions to avoid ecological default. Jim Hansen, director of NASA's Goddard Institute for Space Studies and senior Bush Administration climate modeller, writes: 'We have to stabilise emissions of carbon dioxide within a decade . . . [or] many things could become unstoppable . . . we cannot wait for new technologies like capturing emissions from burning coal. We have to act with what we have'.

Technological fixes and market adjustments both have vulnerabilities and timeframes that appear to make them unviable. Some schemes—notably the switch to renewal energy—are nonetheless necessary to long-term security and sustainability. Others fail on both these counts—especially the deathly lures of nuclear energy and bio-fuels. The project of urban consolidation—at least that premised on its ability to cut energy consumption—is another dead end. The ACF work exposes both the false hope of physical determinism and the culpability of elite consumption. Even if its conclusions were flawed (other scientific evidence backs this up), there's another reason why compaction isn't a means of escape from climate peril: there's simply no time. Urban environments are a highly fixed form of capital, and they take a surprisingly long time to reconfigure in the scale imagined by some consolidationists—usually generations. None of this is a message that deeply pleases me. As an urban scholar, I'd love to think that simple improvement to city planning and design could stave off the environmental crisis. It can't. The only feasible strategy to meet the threat appears to be a massive and sudden decrease in consumption and a rationing of key resources, especially water, oil and energy. British environmental commentator George Monbiot agrees, recently offering that the looming world recession may in fact be the pathway out of peril if it forces down consumption in rich economies.

We face a time of threat akin to global war: the peril is grave but not insurmountable. And yet the West's energies and resources have been poured into the fight against a much more spectral threat: terrorism. Sir John Houghton, former head of the British Meteorological Bureau and senior member of the Intergovernmental Panel on Climate Change, observes that climate change kills more people than terrorism and poses at least as great a threat to human security as 'chemical, nuclear or biological weapons, or indeed international terrorism'.

In 1970, Hugh Stretton, Australia's first great urbanist, wrote and self-published an urban bestseller, *Ideas for Australian Cities*. The book disdained the anti-suburbanism of elites and offered a much more intelligent assessment of suburbia's strengths, weaknesses and possibilities. His most recent book, *Australia Fair* (UNSW Press, 2005), addresses the environmental menace and concludes, as I do, that some form of resource rationing will be forced upon us. Reflecting on the great rationing exercises that saw us through World War II and its reconstruction phase, Stretton believes that their success can be repeated:

> But it is likely to depend, now as then, on three achievements which look unlikely as this is written. We must believe the dangers are real and deadly. We must hope to survive them by radical action, self-restraint and sacrifice. And we must attract the necessary solidarity by a serious reduction of our inequalities.

Restraint, sacrifice, solidarity: these are words that would shatter the dream of neo-liberal Prometheanism. Generating large consumption cuts is surely the province of the nation-state. By electing the Rudd Government, Australians authorised a serious project. So the task of reining in consumption is now theoretically possible. The Garnaut Climate Change Review will outline the prospects in 2008. We may be entering a more sophisticated phase of Prometheanism, hinged on the belief that resource use can be decoupled from economic expansion. I very much doubt it, but at least we have the prospect of a national climate response based on a serious reckoning of the threat.

The terrible scales of natural disruption facing the cities contrast starkly with the fragile institutional systems and meagre resources dedicated to urban resilience. In one sense, planning is the urban Maginot Line, its capacities already sidelined by the global environmental menace. The ACF analysis indicates the moderate influence that urban form—the main object of planning effort—has on energy use and greenhouse emissions. Urban form, however, has a much more potent bearing on household use of, and dependency on, the direct forms of energy—notably oil—that are likely soon to be in scarce supply.

In the fight against global warming, I see planning's prime contribution as urban adaptation in search of climate-resilient cities. This means the creation of urban environments that will withstand the vagaries of a harmed climate and rising resource shortages. Good planning and design can reduce the vulnerability of cities to shortages in key resources—notably water, coal and oil. An immediate and wholesale improvement to public transport in the suburbs is the first planning improvement we should make in our quest for climate resilience. Other insights and possibilities will emerge as we free ourselves from a suburban debate polarised between censure and celebration.

When we reinstate history to urban discussion, we recover the alternative suburban futures discarded by both the Goths and the Dreamers. Outright proscription and simple prescription give way to consideration of new possibilities based on old insights—in this case, perhaps, a suburbia that recovers the values of modesty, solidarity and locality but in new ways. At present, as Patrick Troy, eminent Australian urbanist, points out, the cult of suburban censure is blocking thought on alternative possibilities for suburbia, including the prospect that it may be the landscape best suited to safe adaptation in a warming climate. Its space and greenery offer immediate resources for on-site collection and disposal of water, generation of energy and production of food. Suburbia's adaptive potential has been understated or ignored by commentary and policy. Others are pointing this out to us—renowned international ecologist Herbert Giardet recently told the International Solar Cities Congress in Adelaide: 'The suburb is perfect for low-energy . . . Low density is good for wind and solar power because there's more space to generate locally'.

Suburban scorn weakens more than our ability to think of a way out of the looming crisis. It threatens solidarity by demonising the social mainstream. Aidan Davison argues that anti-suburbanism engenders disenchantment and withdrawal by the (sub)urban civil society that originally gave birth to environmentalism. The wall of hostility raised by suburban critique is hindering the generation of a societal response to global warming and oil depletion. It fails Stretton's tests by unfairly apportioning blame and by undermining the conditions for solidarity.

The suburbs will be the main theatres in the defensive war against global warming, and need to be engaged and treated fairly in the debates and actions that will address climate change and energy insecurity. The first great task of urban adaptation must be a green suburban renovation.

A critical view is invited of the urban environments created by what Clive Hamilton has termed the 'growth fetish' economy of recent neo-liberalism. These landscapes include the walled estates of civic refusal that pepper our cities, the more environmentally egregious mega-homes, and the vertical sprawl produced by wild, market-driven consolidation. The narcissism of communal gating can't be allowed to continue if we are to rebuild the solidarity needed to confront the stresses ahead. Equally, we must restore material capacity and civic confidence in our suburban exclusion zones.

Maintaining equity, and therefore solidarity, will be critical to the success of mitigation and adaptation strategies. Urban science and policy should ponder how equity is to be maintained in the face of threat, disturbance and displacement. As Steve Biddulph put it recently, 'we co-operate or die'. Yet co-operation will not thrive without a fair distribution of burden and effort. It is, as Mark Peel states, time to 'talk of shared sacrifices led by those with most to give'. The ACF consumption maps show us where they live.

A prescient letter to the editor in the *Courier-Mail* in late 2007 captured the essence of the problem. The letter laments the role of elites in climate debates, including the 'knowledgeable' and the 'rich and famous', observing their continued ability to 'fly their private, corporate or government-funded jets' while the 'numerous' rest 'are warned that if the worst does materialise it will be our fault if we do not immediately turn off our air conditioners, use smaller cars, burn less fuel and save all the rainwater we can muster'. Moreover, 'no rationing is mentioned to bring equitable sharing of the load. So the haves can still outspend the have-nots'.

I doubt the author had read the ACF's report, which is still yet to resonate popularly. But I think the letter's sentiment anticipates a divisive politics that may well emerge when the broader community begins to comprehend that it is the gilded coin, not the dreadful penny, that most bankrupts our climate. While a small part of me cheers the justice of the claim, the outbreak of suburban complaint mostly fills me with dread. We cannot afford yet another obstacle to the task of preparing for what lies ahead. There is an immediate need to promote, and if necessary prescribe, a culture of moderation among elites. This will include restraints on the most conspicuously damaging forms of consumption, including air travel and the import of bulky and weighty luxuries.

The latest human Promethean dream may be shattering, but its political and moral legacies will not easily be overcome. Most of our leadership cannot think outside the narrow frame of neo-liberalism. The universities have lost, or had removed, much of their capacity to craft alternative thinking. We are in a situation of serious ethical and intellectual deprivation at a time of peril. It's been a long time since we had faith in the kind of concerted public endeavour that will be needed to bring us to safety. The values of social justice and social solidarity seem quaintly archaic, while the concepts of restraint and modesty seem barmy. These values and ambitions will have to be restored to public life and to institutional purpose if we wish to find a common passage through the coming storm. To begin this restoration, we must rouse ourselves from the Promethean dream and reawaken our most basic human obligations—to each other, to those to come, and to the ecology that will nurture—or at least endure—us all. Without these commitments, society might survive but democracy may not. At worst, Nature may simply decide to go on without us. In an age of ambiguity, we can be sure of one thing: *Homo urbanis* will meet its destiny in the city.

Don Watson

The moral equivalent of Anzac
The Monthly, May 2008

Broadcasting from the MCG on Anzac Day a few years back, as the din that always follows the minute's silence and reveille died away, a football commentator remarked with great reverence upon the sacrifices made to defend 'our lifestyle'. Greater love hath no man than this, that he would lay down his lifestyle for his friends.

In a world as virtual as it is real, where choice seems almost infinite and valued above all things and gratification is never more than a few keystrokes away, the words 'life' and 'lifestyle' have become all but interchangeable. Lifestyle is life accented with dreams, aspirations and entitlements, life with multitudes of choices, life going forward—*enhanced* life. A minute's searching on the web reveals the extent of it: there are lifestyle condoms, lifestyle butchers, lifestyle shops, lifestyle properties and even lifestyle funerals. There is a lifestyle television channel, a Lifestyle Navy and an Army lifestyle. The food and drink, clothing, health, sex, security and shelter that all previous generations considered the necessities of life are today necessities of life*style*.

In countries like our own it seems possible that, relative to lifestyle, life has less meaning than it used to. Life is for people accustomed to scarcity, risk and struggle—for losers, if you like; lifestyle is for those who live in apparent perennial abundance and are determined to have a slice of it.

In the midst of lifestyle we are, nonetheless, still in death. We love our fallen with unbending devotion. Bookshops devote whole stands to new books on Australians in the Great War and others since. Thousands of young Australians gather every year at Gallipoli to observe the Anzac rituals with the solemnity of an age much more dutiful than their own. While some trek to the Dardenelles, thousands more attend Anzac Day services at home. Our leaders, who have never fired a shot or had one fired at them, fashion platitudes to suit the task of tying sacrifice and slaughter to a pre-scriptive set of contemporary Australian values. 'We are fighting now for the same values the Anzacs fought for in 1915', John Howard said at the funeral of the last Gallipoli veteran, in 2002. These values he named as 'courage, valour, mateship, decency . . . a willingness as a nation to do the right thing, whatever the cost'.

He may as well have emptied his old sock drawer on the cenotaph—but war always did encourage vapouring in non-combatants. To be sure, every good Australian soldier holds with courage, valour, mateship, decency and doing the right thing. But, had they been asked, good Turkish and German soldiers would have held with them too. Sitting in his trench in Belgium, Corporal Hitler would have held with them, along with all the good British, French, Russian and American soldiers fighting on our side. If the meaning of Anzac is to be found in these values, our legend has hardly an original feather to fly with.

In truth, the soldiers went to the Great War much as soldiers always have: for all manner of reasons, personal as well as patriotic. And, as always, as much as they fought *for* something, they fought *against* what they took the other to be. They were *for* Australia and the British race and the British Empire, and they were *against* Germany and the German race and German imperial ambitions. As Bill Gammage found in his classic study of their letters, *The Broken Years*, 'By 1914 most young Australians had thoroughly learnt an adherence to war, race, and glory . . .' They knew where their duty lay because they had been taught it, and they looked for-ward to getting the can-opener into the Turk and the Hun.

Forty years or so ago, Australians' relationship with Anzac was less assured. Whatever spirit had possessed the old soldiers on the battlefields of Gallipoli, Belgium and France, on Anzac Days it seemed to consist in roughly equal measure of sad reflection and even sadder jingoism; of men haunted by the experience of war and men bent on crushing any deviation from the nation's xenophobic norms. Anzac was a great day in the nation's life. It was also the day when tensions in the nation's (male) psyche bared themselves a little, and it was this that attracted the playwrights.

Now the original Anzacs are dead and the survivors of World War II are all in a mellower stage of life, this ambivalence has faded. The old soldiers have reached from the grave and regained their grip on the country. Schoolchildren learn flag-flying and 'positive' Australian history. They are told what the modern military is told when it departs for foreign wars: that the values of the Anzacs are the eternal values of Australia (and its alliances), that we fight in Iraq and elsewhere against terror for these values and that to deviate from them is to be less than Australian.

Yet if we take seriously the many soldiers who have written memorably on war, values seem to have nothing to do with it. The seminal French historian Marc Bloch knew a lot about war and not only because he had made intensive studies of it. He led a platoon on the Western Front in World War I; aged 53, he fought against the invading Germans in 1940; and until his capture, torture and execution by the Gestapo in 1944, he was a leader of the French Resistance. It is recorded that his last words were '*Vive la France!*' Yet in his memoir of the Great War, he wrote: 'I believe that few soldiers, except the most noble or intelligent, think of their country while conducting themselves bravely; they are much more often guided by a sense of personal honour, which is very strong when it is reinforced by the group'.

Bloch having been a short French-Jewish intellectual, the Australian World War I historian and Anzac auteur C. E. W. Bean might have thought of him much as he thought of the German-Jewish general Sir John Monash—which is to say, not much. But Bloch knew at least as much about war—and patriotism—as Bean, and Bean could have no argument with his conclusion. For in describing what makes his beloved *poilu*, the common man, an uncommonly brave soldier and a member of a brave battalion, and how one depends upon the other, Bloch may as well be describing Bean's Anzacs. It was for the honour of their battalions that those brave Australian (and other) soldiers often said they fought; it was to their battalions that they felt the deepest loyalty; and it was in the battalion, 'our father and our mother of unforgettable years', that the legend took shape.

In his memoirs, the Civil War General and American President Ulysses S. Grant wrote in a vein similar to Bloch's. Grant did not believe the nation should celebrate the anniversaries of victory or mourn those of defeat. War was too complex a business, the behaviour of men too ambivalent and contradictory, and the reporting too unreliable to be reduced to anything that could be semaphored with a flag or a cliché. 'Truthful history' was the best tribute a nation could pay: history that did 'full credit to the courage, endurance and soldierly ability of the American citizen, no matter what section of the country he hailed from, or in what ranks he fought'.

Grant's memoirs contain brilliant descriptions of battlefield strategy and, unlike Bean's, sudden, graphic accounts of men's heads and limbs being suddenly torn from their bodies. But in Grant you won't find any values beyond military values, unless you take his condemnation of those who whipped up the frenzy for war as a condemnation of their values. He fought in one war, the Mexican-American, for a cause he despised; and in another, the Civil War, against a cause he thought 'one of the worst for which a people ever fought'. But Grant was the least sanctimonious of memoirists. He did not dwell on causes, good or bad, but on what the situation required. As much he admired his own, he admired the Mexican and Rebel soldiers for the qualities that are admirable in *all* soldiers: for how well they fought, how well they faced death, what moral heights they rose to. From Homer on, all good writing about war shares this admiration and wonder: it is the outlook that allowed the expatriate Australian Frederic Manning to write in one of the very best novels to come out of World War I, *Her Privates We*, that the slaughter was 'magnificent'—as a 'moral effort'.

There are many good reasons to be wary of military legends, especially those that have escaped the exploits from which they descend. They can be used, for instance, to propel a country into futile and destructive wars. They can do a lot to keep a population stupid, or encourage them to live in the belief that they possess unique values which are not in fact unique and which they do not in fact possess. They can create a collective consciousness bound by falsehood and even fantasy: such that new generations lose touch with the fact that people from other countries fought just as bravely and with equal effect and paid an equal price; or come to think, as John Howard appeared to, that the legend and truthful history are the same thing. In fact, any truthful history of the Anzacs would contain countless examples of men who went to war for reasons more mundane or self-interested than patriotic, along with ample evidence that they were notorious for killing prisoners and wounded enemy soldiers, for 'ratting' the enemy and for 'souveniring' from the enemy dead. As Gammage says—and Grandad's letters slyly reveal—'many of them' killed 'brutally, savagely and unnecessarily'. Great warriors frequently do.

No one would want the country to forget the wars or fail to honour those who died in them. No historian can think it possible that a war in which 60 000 of the 330 000 volunteers died and whose effects still wash down through families and communities *could* be forgotten, or begrudge Les Carlyon the hordes of readers his epic books attract. No one can read them and no one can stand on those battlefields and regret the fact of Anzac Day.

The feelings are no doubt sincere. The ceremonies continue to be moving, the rituals as rich in meaning as they were at the beginning. But what is being remembered on this day of remembrance? Anzac Day began as a day for the soldiers who returned to remember those who did not. This was a principle in keeping with what countless soldiers have written down the years: that only those who have been in battle can know what it is like, that the experience of war demands things of a human being that no other experience does and creates one who is different in certain ways. It creates bonds of a certain kind.

It is inevitable and no bad thing, necessarily, that Anzac Day has been taken up by people who don't have the soldiers' experience. But the day's been second-guessed. The more politicians and media commentators talk of the values of Anzac Day, traduce it for convenient contemporary instruction and daub themselves with the soldiers' moral courage, the more like a kitsch religion it becomes.

If we want to keep the pathos free of politics, the bravery unconfused with acts performed in a swimming pool or on a football field, the sacrifice *kept* sacred and not submerged in the narcissistic puddle of modern lifestyle, we need to take the Anzacs not for idealised images of ourselves, but for what they were. Which is to say, soldiers: colonial soldiers, educated to believe in the cause of the British Empire and trained to do their duty at any cost. They were not some pre-conscious version of us, and if they fought on behalf of our modern lifestyle or our national identity, it was only incidental. Study them and they will disappoint our vanity. Search for the heart of Anzac and we might not recognise it.

The American philosopher William James was a man of peace: not a pacifist but an opponent of the militarists who around the turn of the last century were as hyperactive in America as they were in Europe. By 1906 he had decided that the only way to win the argument with the warmongers was to 'enter more deeply' into their point of view. We should begin, he said, by conceding the military virtues: discipline, duty, honour, 'intrepidity', 'contempt of softness, surrender of private interest, obedience to command'. 'All the qualities of a man acquire dignity when he knows that the service of the collectivity that owns him needs him.' This much of the militarists' point of view the anti-militarists should allow—and then they should propose, instead of war, its 'moral equivalent'.

This moral equivalent, in James's scheme, would be 'a conscription of the whole youthful population, to form for a certain number of years a part of the army enlisted against *Nature*'. The rich no less than the poor would be sent to the mines, factories, fields, the fishing fleets; to build roads and tunnels and skyscrapers; to wash clothes and dishes and windows. Thus 'the injustice would tend to be evened out, and numerous other goods to the commonwealth would follow'. Youth—gilded and ungilded—would 'get the childishness knocked out of them', without having life knocked out of them as well. They would be made better citizens, society would prosper—and militarists would no longer be able to say that only war can bring out the best in humanity. It was a fair point then and an even fairer one now, when American administrations fight their wars with poor conscripts and private armies while the middle classes get on with their lifestyles.

We might think about it too. If we must see the Anzacs as our saviours, the wellspring of our identity and soul, let us enter into a more honest relationship with them. We may as well turn Amish as try to lead the lives they led; nor can we go to any kind of war resembling the one they fought. But we could recreate the civilian militias in which, after 1910, they had been obliged to serve—everyone from the age of twelve to twenty-six. With a few modifications, we could do it again. Women and non-'British' residents must not be left out this time, and fifty is the new thirty, after all. So let's say every Australian between the ages of eighteen and forty-eight could be, for a time equal to the average tour in World War I, a civilian Anzac.

Let those who are suited to soldiering learn how to do it. Let those who are not engage in the moral equivalent, submitting to military rigour not in a war *against* Nature as James recommended, but *for* it. Let battalions of citizen soldiers answer the bugle calls of climate change and environmental degradation. They can fight erosion, salt and evaporation. Let rabbits, cane toads, water buffalo, mynah birds, carp and pigs be their enemy: arm them against every feral animal, and let them deal with the corpses. Send them to fight against blackberries and willows on the banks of the streams, the forests and gullies. Give them tanks, solar panels and recycling devices to install. Let them plant trees. By all these works they will be drawn closer to the land from which in legend the Anzacs came, the apotheosis of the bushman and the pioneer.

Formed into battalions and platoons, they can supplement the ranks of firefighters and other emergency services; they can be the coastguard; they can supply essential human care to the aged, the infirm, the lonely, addicted and homeless. In remote Indigenous communities they can meet the chronic need for well-motivated administrators, builders, plumbers, mechanics, health workers and horticulturalists, replace criminally neglectful bureaucrats and parasitic contractors, and teach such basic skills to the inhabitants. Let the citizen militias do it; and in doing so learn from Indigenous Australians some of their knowledge of the place. They can volunteer for their service abroad, especially among the underdeveloped countries of our region, and do wonders for the dispossessed and our country's reputation.

The deeds of such a citizen militia might transform environments and bring hope to despairing communities. But if the Anzac myth holds good, the more radical effect will be on the people serving. They will pick up skills, gain experience of discipline, lose weight, and learn something of duty and what it means to sacrifice; the chances are that few of them will face death and have to give up their lives, but they will *all* have to give up their lifestyles.

For at least two years every maturing Australian will be separated from the supports or dysfunction of family and enter into a situation where the fortunes of birth, and privileges of wealth and school, will count for nothing. Children will be liberated from the ambitions their parents have for them, and parents from their needful children. They will be cut off from shopping. All other lifestyle addictions, including career resumés, will be abandoned. Every draftee will be obliged to trade at least a portion of his or her narcissistic self-possession for the interests of the group and the common moral effort. And all the while they will be coming to more nearly know what they mean when they say 'Lest We Forget'.

Legends are never like the people who believe them, of course, or for that matter the people who made them. But a people truly devoted to a legend will be willing to prove the truth of it in experience. We could put the proposition to the vote: 'Are you in favour of the government, in the spirit of Anzac and its values, having the power to compel all men and women between the ages of eighteen and forty-eight to sacrifice their lifestyles and serve the Commonwealth for a period of not less than two years?'

It's an outrageous idea, of course, and no one should take it seriously. The cost alone is unthinkable. Then again, we might get a better return than we got on 60 000 dead from a population of four million. (That's not counting the wounded, those who died young and those who were traumatised for the rest of their lives, with consequences passed on to their children.) And weird though it is to think in these times that the country needs regimenting, it might not be as weird as taking into the twenty-first century a legend of warrior mates with which the society has about as much in common as Kevin Rudd has with Dad Rudd and Dr Nelson with the vice-admiral of that name.

Clive Hamilton

Art or porn is not the question
Crikey, 26 May 2008

For decades in post-war Israel performances of works by Richard Wagner were banned. The associations between Nazi Germany and Wagner's music were too strong in the minds of most Israelis.

The argument was not about the quality of Wagner's music but the political meaning of it. I make this observation in the context of the furore over Bill Henson's photographic exhibition, which includes pictures of a naked 13-year-old girl, to remind us that art, like sport, cannot be separated from politics.

All art engages with culture, at least good art does. Henson has been praised by critics and supporters for challenging our sensibilities and pushing the boundaries of social acceptability. So why is Henson, by all accounts a garrulous man, refusing to defend his work?

Artists and the artistic community cannot push the boundaries of social acceptance and then, when they get a reaction, step back declaring 'I'm just an artist' or 'Art is sacrosanct and should be above the fray', especially when the reaction is the one they wanted, if in smaller doses.

There are at least three ways of looking at Henson's latest images. The first is to see them as artistic representations designed to elicit certain feelings and ideas concerned with themes like the vulnerability of youth, the transformation of children into adults, and the contrast between teenage angst and the pointlessness of life.

Something along these lines is Henson's primary purpose and, it's fair to assume, is the type of experience anticipated by most of those who would have visited the Roslyn Oxley9 Gallery to see Henson's work.

The second way of looking at the pictures is through the eyes of ped-erasts and perhaps the much larger number of men who have normal sexual lives but cannot help finding these sorts of images disturbingly erotic.

In most of the public comment on the controversy these are the only two ways of understanding Henson's photographs—they are either art or pornography. Within this conventional frame, they are art in my opinion. Despite her nakedness, the girl is not posed or presented in a sexualised way; if they are consumed in a pornographic way it is not the artist's intention.

Although not expert in the law, I would be very surprised if a court convicted anyone for taking or displaying these pictures. However, decid-ing that the photographs are not pornographic does not end the ethical argument. Despite the predictable positions taken by moral campaigners and civil libertarians, the situation is more complicated, which brings me to the third way of seeing Henson's pictures.

Over the last decade or so advertisers and the wider culture have increasingly eroticised children. They have been over-loaded with adult sexual material and have had attributed to them forms of adult sexual behaviour, including being dressed, posed and made up as if they were sexually active, taught that having crushes and sexual feelings is normal and even that engaging in various sexual practices at their age is fine. Children as young as eight and nine are now routinely treated in this way.

This has been a recent phenomenon—previously it was only teenagers of around sixteen or more who were presented this way—yet it has occurred slowly enough for most Australians to be inured to it or to accept that that is just how the world is. After all, when even respectable retailers like David Jones eroticise 10 and 12-year-old girls in their advertisements, it is easy to dismiss any objections we may have as peculiar to ourselves.

The eroticisation of childhood means that we have been conditioned to see children differently, as having adult sexual characteristics, urges and desires. How else can we explain why we seem to accept mothers going shopping with 12-year-old daughters dressed like prostitutes? Why are we blasé about pre-teens watching video clips showing simulated intercourse? And why do we allow girls magazines widely read by pre-teens to advise that anal sex is a 'personal choice'?

Why have we done nothing about these and a hundred other manifestations of child sexualisation?

In such a cultural environment, the naked body of a child, particularly a girl of 12 showing the first signs of sexual development, can no longer be viewed 'innocently', and cannot but be seen by everyone, other than hermits, in a sexual context.

If Henson did not know this then he should have, and so should the gallery owner and the girl's parents. Putting the images on the internet was unforgivable, for in doing so they relinquished all control over how the images are seen and consumed.

It is fair to ask whether Henson was entirely innocent of the sexual context in which his pictures would be viewed. Even among his fans, there seems to be a widespread feeling that his earlier images of intoxicated youths engaged in sex in dingy settings are 'creepy' and exploitative.

Yet it is now clear that over the last two years, the Australian public has woken from its apathy and has become restive over the exploitation of children by the marketers and purveyors of popular culture. We should not be surprised that this disquiet has boiled over in response to the Henson exhibition.

I suspect that the extraordinary levels of anxiety over paedophilia in recent years have represented, at least in part, an over-compensation by society for its complicity in permitting children to be sexualised.

Now that anger is being directed at the real targets, Henson's latest work might be collateral damage or it might be more deeply implicated.

Chris Masters

Moonlight reflections

Griffith Review 21: Hidden Queensland,
www.griffithreview.com

Revisiting 'The Moonlight State' required distance. The effort involved in investigating systemic police corruption in Queensland for *Four Corners* back in 1987 nearly finished me. It was all hard labour, relentless and depressing, month after month, well into the night. Drug dealers and prostitutes don't keep office hours. They are not the most enlightening folk, and their stories are rarely uplifting.

When the program was broadcast in May 1987, I had come to a personal view that if this was what it took to do substantial journalism then the job was not worth it. At the time, if I could have stepped back, I might have seen the better view. Entrenched corruption had been revealed. Police Commissioner Sir Terence Lewis was later jailed; the long reign of the Bjelke-Petersen Government which had sustained him soon ended; and Queensland was allowed to begin the process of recovery.

Formal credit for breaking the story went to the *Courier-Mail*, with Phil Dickie winning the Gold Walkley Award. For me, there were thirteen more years down the sewer defending the ABC's report. I came to think of that period as my death by a thousand courts.

During the subsequent defamation decade, there was no choice but to find the energy for the ordeal. The stakes were higher than the reputation of the program. The fight was about defending investigative journalism. The years reeled by. The ABC won. A retrial was ordered and the ABC won again. And by the time the century had turned, I was over my curiosity about the secret life of Queensland.

I could at last look away—and did so eagerly, but for an occasional nervous rearward glance, as if to check whether an angry posse of police and lawyers was still on my tail.

Some questions remained unanswered. Not the least was why the program worked when other similar reports had not. I could see some reasons, but clearly forces external to our own work were also important. Premier Joh's twenty-year grip on power had slipped, allowing ambition and insurrection to swell in the National Party. Commissioner Lewis was also losing control, as his Rum Corps system of grafting became more visible to national police agencies.

The *Four Corners* inquiry had focused more on police corruption than politics. An inquiry commissioned by Sir Joh's deputy, Bill Gunn, and undertaken by the formidable Tony Fitzgerald, later made the link to political corruption that helped sink Gunn's own party. Some ministers were jailed for minor offences such as the misuse of expenses. Joh's senior ally, the so-called Minister for Everything Russell Hinze, was found to have received around four million dollars in bribes. He died before he could be tried. Sir Joh was also investigated for corruption, but charged with perjury.

The case against the former premier was famously abandoned in 1991 when a jury split—with one of two dissenters a member of the Young Nationals. The lack of resolution left open one of the biggest questions: was Sir Joh Bjelke-Petersen a crook? Queenslanders remained divided on the great divider. Ask and they will tell you. Joh was a villain; Joh was a martyr.

When he died in 2005, the bitterness and the questions were not laid to rest. The ailing old man had been seen being pushed around in a wheelchair by the state's Labor Premier, Peter Beattie, who further offended the party memory by granting Joh a state funeral. A new question had surfaced about Joh's personal wealth. The former multi-millionaire proved to be dead broke. Beattie had rejected a claim of $338 million to compensate for losses blamed on the Fitzgerald Inquiry, but he did agree to payment of a small annual postage allowance. When the family called asking for the cheque, Beattie knew they needed the money.

The cost of Joh's legal representation, some of it unpaid, did not seem to fully explain the loss of that presumed fortune. And the frail state of the family's finances made it clear that there was no access to seams of hidden treasure.

When I returned to Queensland, the subject of Joh and his govern-ment came up time and again. The Fitzgerald Inquiry had profoundly dem-onstrated a mess of crookedness. But over and over, I heard the proposition that Joh was the best leader of the best government Queensland had ever seen—and not just from taxi drivers. Former National Party ministers would say of Hinze: 'But he was a good minister', as if the corruption could easily be reconciled.

This was the most troubling question. Why did it not seem to matter? Is there, deep within the soul of this nation of prisoners and prison guards, a secret belief that corruption works, and is part of who we are?

More time passed, and someone told me the twentieth anniversary of Joh's near 20-year term as premier was coming up. So I took a breath and asked my executive producer at *Four Corners,* Sue Spencer, whether this might be a good time to examine these questions. Soon, body and soul, I was back in the moonlight state.

Tracking the political circumstances that had ended Joh's reign was the easiest part. Politicians have a good feel for the weight of history. They are often a big part of it. We approached Joh's former colleagues and, although sometimes prickly at first, most agreed to talk. In the main they were positive and defensive—*history had been unfair to their leader.* But the passage of time also produced the odd flush of candour.

Their account took me behind the bumblebee persona to a clever political operator who in twenty years doubled the party's vote. A notori-ous gerrymander had helped, but did not account for this extraordinary political achievement. Joh's political guile had given him hero status within the conservative right and grudging respect among Labor opponents, state and federal.

In his early period in particular, Joh presided over strong economic growth, which transformed Queensland from its Cinderella status. He had relied on clever advice from the likes of Treasury boss Sir Leo Hielscher, but had made an undeniable contribution. As Hielscher put it: 'He was outstanding in his appreciation of what the objective was [but] he didn't know very much about how to get there'.

Bjelke-Petersen was ahead of his time in image management, appearing at least to be engaged with his public, particularly those outside Queensland's populous south-east corner. He was one of the first to employ advisers, such as ABC reporter Allen Callaghan, who knew how to set the media agenda. 'Feeding the chooks', as Joh described it, became a routine and enduring practice.

And Joh played his own part well. As Callaghan told me, all that mangling of the dictionary did not make him a bad communicator. Up close, people—even enemies—had their animosity blunted by disarming charm. Joh would remember your name and, as old mate Bill Roberts recalled, would 'take the teapot around'.

There were weaknesses. The other side of the legendary bush battler upbringing—sweating from dusk to dawn; bunking down for fifteen years in a cow bail—meant he not just eschewed the scholarly, but allowed himself an anti-intellectual vanity. Joh was not one for reading. He would champion 'commonsense' ideas that were anything but. Milan Brych, who promised a cure for cancer, was one of a band of conmen and heartbreakers to get through Joh's door.

As he became more successful, it became that much more difficult to tell him he was wrong. A key adviser, Ken Crooke, explained that Joh did not want naysayers around him. He preferred positive people who could find a way get things done. It may have been his embedded Christian convictions that generated a moral certainty which at times proved delusional.

Joh's colleagues saw him as a stickler for propriety. The premier would insist on travel being strictly for government business. But he loved flying so much that he didn't seem to be able to help himself. Joh would wangle a place on the government aircraft to head off to negotiate a coal contract when all around him knew there was no need for him to be there. Up the front with his pilot, Beryl Young, there was peace and calm—perhaps at times disturbed by the anguished muttering of ministers and public servants down the back.

Another indulgence was playing god. When he stepped down from the plane at a country airstrip, Joh would walk into the embrace of an adoring court. Think of a Country Party version of a deplaning Rolling Stone. Liberal Treasurer Sir Llew Edwards, one of many to have mixed views on Joh, would see the fans press forward, pushing for a small hospital to be built in their town. Edwards said Joh would typically turn and tell him: 'You look after these good people, Llew'. When Edwards later did the sums and discovered it would be cheaper to buy them a bus than duplicate a service that was one town away, Joh would be less pleased.

Before his death, another Liberal Treasurer, Sir Thomas Hiley, shared with me another revealing tale. Driving through Country Party heartland, he remembered Joh asking the driver to stop as they passed a farmer selling watermelons. Joh sent the driver to pick up a melon. He soon returned, explaining that the farmer wanted a shilling. They drove on without the melon. Hiley wasn't the only one to tell me Joh had a curious sense of the privilege of office.

And when it came to retaining office, Joh respected few—if any—boundaries. Towards the end of his long run, checks and balances that might have been applied by the National Party machine began to fall away. Joh began to war with party chairman Sir Robert Sparkes, preferring the advice of carpet-baggers such as 'Top Level' Ted Lyons. Bjelke-Petersen and Lyons set up an up an account, Kaldeal, with a view to funding candidates and a political direction of their choosing. A donation from a Singapore businessman, Robert Sng, led to the humiliating ordeal of a public trial.

When Sng arrived in Joh's office in 1986, his credentials amounted to not much more than the $300 000 he was prepared to donate—money hurriedly borrowed from a backyard lender in Sydney. Sng would later end up in a Philippines prison. He could not claim the credibility of rival tenderers for a riverfront hotel development.

Sir Joh Bjelke-Petersen's later account of this transaction to the Fitzgerald Inquiry resulted in first a saga of an ultimately abandoned perjury trial, and second a saga of a Criminal Justice Commission inquiry which found the jury had been manipulated by background players in Joh's legal team.

The long and sorry episode deepened rather than healed old wounds, A telling account of the divide is the story of the Crooke brothers, Ken and

Gary. The former, a Bjelke-Petersen senior adviser and close family friend, saw nothing but honesty in Joh, and in the end an old man 'being charged with having a bad memory'.

Gary Crooke, senior counsel with the Fitzgerald Inquiry, remains pained by the way people excused Joh's 'moral lapses' because of his 'contribution to public works'.

The Sng matter, though unresolved, is revealing all the same. Fitzgerald investigator Inspector John Huey told me that, although he saw the payment as corrupt, he found no evidence of Joh using any of the money for personal gain. Huey's problem was that rival tenderers might not be given the same consideration.

In his last decade as premier, Joh had come to see himself as an über chief executive officer, presiding over the business of Queensland. His high profile made him a good fundraiser, but this backdoor bargaining was not good governance and not even good politics. By the 1980s, there were too many cronies. It was only a matter of time before those who missed out turned on the party. Fellow ministers were also becoming suspicious about the way business was done.

In 1985, Joh had given his blessing to a doubtful project with dubious backing: a proposed 107-storey skyscraper next to Brisbane's Central Railway. Though never constructed, 'the world's tallest building' as it was proclaimed continues to cast a long shadow. The government agreed to pre-purchase office space. Joh had overridden existing advice, pushing the project so hard that at least one minister came to the view there must have been the promise of a bribe. There was unaccustomed opposition in Cabinet. Health Minister Mike Ahern saw defiance of the premier's will on this project as the catalyst for Joh's sacking of ministers. This set up the circumstances that led to Ahern's successful November 1987 challenge for the leadership.

It had been an amazing year, and an amazing fall from grace. The November 1986 election was a massive victory for Joh: his party won an extra eight seats. The Nationals were ruling alone, with Joh having let slip the steadying hand of the Liberals in the previous election.

Bjelke-Petersen, still answering his own phone unchecked, turned more to the advice of Ted Lyons and the extreme right of his support base.

And this was where the mad tilt for Canberra began. One National Party insider told me he remembered well the first time he heard about a meeting of plotters to make Joh prime minister because it was D-Day—6 June 1986.

Mike Gore, a white-shoe developer who had been helped by Joh, organised the meeting. He said he had a lot of money and a lot of backing from enthusiasts such as Lang Hancock, Kerry Packer and other entrepreneurs inclined to view government and process as little more than a nuisance. The plan remained secret for the rest of the year. The collaborators did not want Queensland voters to know that the man they would re-elect was not intending to stick around

Joh's Industry and Technology Minister, Peter McKechnie, had seen it coming. He remembered Joh coming into Cabinet, complaining that there was no effective opposition to the Hawke Labor Government and asking them to come up with a challenger to Liberal leader John Howard. When no names came forward, Joh declared: 'I'll have to do it myself'.

McKechnie is not alone in believing another plotter was his Cabinet colleague Russ Hinze. McKechnie thought the second part of the plan was to have Hinze replace Bjelke-Petersen as premier. At this stage, the Queensland National Party had a very effective backroom team, which was trapped into supporting a campaign that party leader Robert Sparkes knew was ridiculous.

The end came almost a year to the day after it began. The Joh for PM backers had neither the money nor organisation to rearrange the federal Coalition. This was finally made apparent at a private meeting at John Howard's Sydney home in June 1987. Howard, who saw Joh as a wrecker of conservative politics, let fly at Bjelke-Petersen's team while Joh sat on the plane chatting to Beryl. One who was there told me the campaign was dead from that moment.

Not that I would want to push the metaphor, but when Joh returned to Brisbane it might have felt like Berlin 1945: the Russians approaching in one direction and the Americans in another. By now, the Fitzgerald Inquiry was underway.

Deputy Premier Bill Gunn had commissioned it in Joh's absence. Ambition may have been a motive as questions were mounting about Joh's acuity, integrity and electoral appeal. But Gunn also wanted to settle ongoing concern about racketeering in the vice industry, which had again surfaced. Gunn was dissatisfied with Lewis's dissembling. Among the older hands, suspicion had lingered since his controversial appointment back in 1976. At that time, outgoing Police Commissioner Ray Whitrod made his belief public that Terry Lewis was a crook.

Even so, Terry and Joh quickly became a pair, the commissioner attending to the premier's bidding and squirming a place in the inner circle. This annoyed police ministers who, responding to whispers and allegations, found Lewis going behind their backs and straight to the premier.

In the preceding decade, the local media—the *Courier-Mail,* the *Brisbane Sun* and the ABC—had regularly sounded warnings, which were routinely managed by the premier's media unit to limit the damage control. Police whistleblowers would be subjected to Bjelke-Petersen's biblical wrath, the premier often cruelly casting out the non-believers. The premier with the appeal of a kindly uncle had a vicious streak, which served to silence dissent and elevate his standing as a strong leader.

The quid pro quo for Terry Lewis was that he was able to proceed with some of the grubby tricks he had learned as a sergeant standing over prostitutes and petty criminals. As he rose through police and social ranks to become Sir Terence, he failed to surrender what many police considered an informal tax on the underworld.

A close mate of Lewis who made no secret of his weakness for money, retired Licensing Branch sergeant Jack Herbert, was recruited to act as a go-between, collecting payments from franchised brothel keepers and the like and distributing them to select police, in on what they called The Joke.

It was an unsustainable arrangement. Most criminal bargaining is disorganised and lantana like. Conversely, there was architecture to The Joke, which when the time came made it more visible and easier to disentangle.

There was also sophistry to the private justification that it was benign, that once the criminals were 'green-lighted' for running brothels and illegal gambling, they ensnared the police into protecting them for more serious crimes such as drug-trafficking. Another problem was that it was all so undemocratic. Griping developed in the ranks closer to the streets, where they could not fail to notice the gold disappearing upwards.

Years on, I would have a memorable encounter with Jack Herbert, who admitted that he had allowed himself to believe they were untouchable. As he pointed out, Lewis was in a position to sack troublesome police ministers. And they had a former cop turned politician, Don 'Shady' Lane, who could warn of what was being discussed in Cabinet. They also had other well-placed cockatoos in strategic positions, such as the Bureau of Criminal Intelligence (BCI) —which, as it happened, was where it went wrong.

My first knowledge of systemic corruption in Queensland surfaced in 1986 in Canberra. A friend in the Australian Bureau of Criminal Intelligence told me of a Queensland BCI officer being offered a bribe by a superior to suppress information on one of the protected syndicates headed by Gerry Bellino.

I spoke to the officer, Jim Slade, who 'off the record' confirmed the story. Other contacts within the National Crime Authority and the Australian Federal Police built a bigger picture of joint operations in Queensland frequently collapsing. One NCA officer, working on the Gold Coast, told me of his exasperation listening in to criminals and realising they had obviously been prewarned.

Later I would learn that NCA chairman Donald Stewart was having the same problems at a higher level. When he sought a reference from the Queensland government for a local operation, there was obstruction that sharpened suspicion.

Then, in March 1987, Jack Herbert's wife Peggy noticed a film crew outside their Bowen Hills home, and the jokers started to panic. The acquisitive Herbert had made a silly mistake, buying the house fifteen months earlier from Gerry Bellino and his partner Vic Conte. Greed had overwhelmed caution. Herbert took possession of the property at a knock-down rate in part-compensation for bribes owed. The Jordan Terrace house was important evidence which linked police to the underworld.

Lewis and his cronies were already unnerved by *Four Corners'* inquiries. Queensland undercover police had been assigned to watch us. But a friendly force also intervened in the form of Australian Federal Police officers, also watching and supplying me with helpful warnings. Lewis told Herbert to shut down contact lest they be filmed. Herbert said they all became jumpy, seeing *Four Corners* crews everywhere.

When 'The Moonlight State' went to air on 11 May 1987, I knew we had strong evidence, but I was less aware of those other elements in the air—the instability of the Bjelke-Petersen regime and the high pressure system moving in on the crooked police—that would increase the volatility of the report.

I was not the only one to fail to see what was coming. When Joh's close ally Russ Hinze watched the program, press secretary Russell Grenning said he was delighted. Hinze disliked Lewis enough to enjoy seeing him squirm. There had been occasion when, because of Lewis, he had been forced to squirm. As police minister in the early 1980s, at a press conference Russell Hinze had famously denied the existence of brothels and casinos operating within plain sight of reporters. Russell Grenning told me the denial had been qualified with carefully chosen words: 'My commissioner assures me . . .' Looking through the film archive, I found he was right. With ample cunning of his own, Hinze, of course, knew better.

So did Bill Gunn when he became police minister, another of a range of reasons why he avoided the conventional three-step of allegation, denial and cover-up. Coverage in the national media meant the embarrassment could not so readily be contained. There had been blushing, too, among the party faithful who had railed against condom-vending machines on the campus of the University of Queensland, but saw much worse on the ABC.

When casting for names to run the inquiry, Justice Minister Neville Harper recommended a quiet, intelligent Brisbane judge who had not specialised in criminal work, Tony Fitzgerald. If there was a belief that Fitzgerald was not street-smart enough to outwit the cops, it would not have been shared by National Party counsel Ian Callinan QC, who is also said to have pushed for Fitzgerald.

Another factor that ended up making a difference was the energy and commitment applied by some members of the Brisbane legal community. There had been disquiet ever since the National Hotel Inquiry of the early 1960s investigated a similar pattern of complaints and let the constabulary off the hook. Since then, there had been exasperation at the barely ingenuous serial verballing and smarting at the proposition that the cops might again outsmart the lawyers.

Joh Bjelke-Petersen opposed Gunn's inquiry; the bush-bred premier warned his colleagues that when you lift an old piece of tin you are likely to find a dead cat or an angry snake. As they began to find much worse, there was some wobbling among the Nationals.

This was dealt with somewhat dramatically by Joh's successor, Mike Ahern, one of only a handful of ministers with a degree. When Ahern heard of plans to dump Fitzgerald's recommendations, he delivered a public guarantee that they be implemented 'lock stock and barrel'. Unforgiven by some as a traitor to his party, he remains for others a hero to Queensland.

Whether or to what degree Bjelke-Petersen was in on The Joke remains contentious. While I heard from at least one well-placed source that, in the parlance, Joh was 'getting a bag' from the cops, I came to see this as unlikely. While Bjelke-Petersen had been worse than negligent in his stewardship of the police, no evidence emerged to directly connect him to the corruption. Jack Herbert, who accepted an indemnity from the Fitzgerald Inquiry on the proviso he told all the truth, knew of no link to Joh.

One reason the suspicion lingered among investigators and a few of Joh's colleagues was that they knew at this time, through the 1980s, that he had money troubles. Keen to help his son John start his own farm, Joh borrowed $1.5 million. Seeking further working capital and taking the advice of his mate Edward Lyons, Joh refinanced the debt, borrowing $3 million in Swiss francs. Like many others caught at the time, he then watched interest rates escalate to a point where he had trouble meeting the payments.

When Bjelke-Petersen entered parliament forty years earlier, he was considered a wealthy man. But the money had not stuck. Joh's contracting work was his main source of income. Without him, the business waned. And as an entrepreneur he had less success, losing money on aerial agriculture and oil exploration.

The worst mistake was rejecting his parliamentary superannuation entitlement, a decision he came to regret. He did so early in his career—some say for ideological reasons, others because he did not properly understand it and figured he could better manage his money. But money management was not his forte, as his wife and bookkeeper Lady Florence explained: 'I don't know whether he always actually thought of the money part of the thing. He just knew what he wanted to do . . . we wanted to establish John up there and give him the opportunity.'

When Sir Joh is accused of corruption, the finger points mostly at 'Ten Mile'. The European Asian Bank had granted him the loan, seeing that assisting the premier would open avenues in Queensland, and 'if refused negatively affect business in the state'.

Public money was spent upgrading roads and infrastructure to the property. The industrialist Sir Leslie Thiess helped out. A defamation jury found in 1992 that Thiess had bribed Bjelke-Petersen 'on a large scale and on many occasions'. A maintenance yard manager for Thiess told Channel Nine that his boss had authorised repairs of a bulldozer for the premier, and after Bjelke-Petersen noticed a vice in the yard, instructed it be sent to him.

In 1986, an out of court defamation settlement of $400 000 from Alan Bond was used to pay interest on the loan. The Australian Broadcasting Tribunal later found Bjelke-Petersen had placed the then Channel Nine owner in a position of 'commercial blackmail'. Aware of all this, Fitzgerald investigators looked hard. According to son John, they even searched the rafters of the 'Ten Mile' homestead. It is easy to see why they might have expected to find secret stashes of loot and perhaps a stray Swiss bank account.

The portrait of Joh revealed as the evidence emerged has remained difficult to process, particularly for Joh haters. Bjelke-Petersen was more a scammer than a hard grafter like Hinze. He saw no breach in using his office to help his family and picking up a bit of farm equipment along the way. Conflict of interest was never a concept well understood by him. His behaviour could be considered worse than that of ministers such as Geoff Muntz, Leisha Harvey and Brian Austin, who were gaoled for abusing the privilege of office. An independent prosecutor decided against charging Joh with corruption and retrying him on the perjury charge.

By then Joh was eighty, and it hardly seemed worth it. It is also worth mentioning that the various advantages sought had done the family finances no good. So, on the questions of personal corruption, Joh was not as bad as his enemies claim and neither was he the saint seen by his friends.

As far as political corruption goes, though, he was as crooked as they come.

For me, the most telling corruption is one of character. It is one of history's favourite tales. As Joh came to achieve absolute power, he gave in to the seduction of the plane, the hotel suites and the royal treatment. His improving appetite for these indulgences kept successors at bay and ultimately helped stunt the Coalition. Joh was like one of those huge Queensland fig trees, under which nothing grows.

Over time, vanity opened wider the door on poor judgement. Privately as well as publicly, he turned out to be no great economic manager. When he left office at the end of 1987, on a range of economic indicators Queensland was not performing well. Another indulgence had been to politicise the hated bureaucracy, which ironically had helped build his reputation as a progressive leader.

Here is his biggest failure. While loyalists still push the proposition that the greatness in Joh was his leadership, the evidence reveals the opposite. In the end he was being led—by a sometimes tawdry bunch. Joh was, and is, the 'battered image of our weakness', his brethren using this image to turn their frailties into strength.

The Joh era delivered other unexpected outcomes. He not only brought his own party close to destruction, but helped reinvent the enemy. Through the rubble of the Bjelke-Petersen era emerged a populist Labor prime minister.

Wayne Goss is proud of having selected an unknown, Kevin Rudd, as his chief of staff when in opposition in 1988. Rudd is still known to insiders as 'Dr Death' for allegedly visiting even greater violence upon the public sector when he became director general of the Cabinet Office. Hard decisions were made. The way government worked changed. The formula developed through the reform era—of planning and building ideas, developing and costing policy ahead of implementation—would be exported to the nation when Kevin Rudd became prime minister in 2007.

A common criticism of process overtaking progress fails to recognise just how far process had broken down in the Joh era. A failure of process sunk him in the end. Integrity of government is not just a moral issue: there are practical consequences. If the system is crook, that system fails to work.

Wayne Goss rebuilt the system, restoring integrity and more. I have not seen a city so dramatically changed in twenty years as Brisbane. With traffic jams and all, it is now much more than a big country town.

The critics take a similar line on the cops. I hear from time to time that things are supposed to be as bad as ever. But when my colleagues and I search for the evidence, there—somewhat frustratingly—is little to find. It may be, as some think, that in this new era of open government the evidence, curiously, is easier to hide. It may be true that the smarties have found sneakier ways to disguise misbehaviour.

What I know is that a couple of spivs from Fortitude Valley no longer control the Queensland police. Homosexuals aren't routinely bashed. Honest police are much less likely to be punished for resisting corruption. And a dishonest police commissioner was sent to gaol—a terrific start. Skills acquired by Fitzgerald investigators were exported to other reform bodies. An important generational change in policing, still in a painful cycle, grew across to Western Australia and south to New South Wales.

Queensland is still getting over the anger and bitterness of one generation's subjection to long-neglected reform. When change is that dramatic, a different social and economic order too swiftly emerges. Good gets done, but good people also get hurt. Take the story of the Crooke brothers, both talented and decent. Gary has been favoured by the new era. He runs the Queensland Integrity Commission and, as one of the exporters of Fitzgerald skill-sets, formerly assisted the Wood inquiry into police corruption in New South Wales and chaired the National Crime Authority. Ken, who was a powerful figure in the Bjelke-Petersen administration, watched the era vanish.

All through Queensland, there are similar examples of people on both sides wrong-footed as the world was reshaped around them. It is sad to hear that Tony Fitzgerald does not go to reunions and that Peter Beattie is still hated for breaking bread with Bjelke-Petersen.

But Queenslanders, and others like me, are getting over it.

Brian Toohey

Our very own police state

The Australian Financial Review, 10 October 2008

When Robert Menzies was Coalition prime minister at the height of the Cold War, he ensured that the Australian Security Intelligence Organisation (ASIO) was the only body legally entitled to obtain a warrant to tap telephones. ASIO undoubtedly misused these and other powers. But there were two saving graces. One was that it only tapped a few dozen phones a year. The other was that it was confined to collecting and analysing information labelled 'intelligence'. Unlike today, naming an ASIO employee was not a criminal offence. Nor did ASIO have executive powers that the Hope royal commission warned in the mid 1970s would move it closer to being like a secret police force.

Today, ASIO not only has police powers, the police and many other government agencies possess ASIO's previously exclusive power to tap phones and gather security intelligence. The newcomers have shouldered ASIO aside in the rush to tap. Contrary to the popular impression that phone taps are common in the United States, an analysis by Labor backbencher Daryl Melham shows that an Australian phone is twenty times more likely to be legally tapped than an American one. A total of 3280 phone intercepts were authorised in 2006–2007. Seven applications were rejected or withdrawn before approval. The official breakdown of the figures shows that only thirty-three taps were related to terrorism. Although ASIO no longer reveals how many phones it taps, it's understood to be less than 10 per cent of the total. Even so, the figure is more than during the Whitlam/Fraser years when an annual average of eighty-five taps occurred between 1974 and 1983.

Since 1 August, New South Wales police have had the power to spray unidentified isotopes on people they wish to track. No warrant is required for the first five days. Although the police claim the isotope is harmless, they refuse to identify it, regardless of the concerns of those who are allergic to various chemicals. The right allowed to the police in New South Wales to deploy isotope sprays, to surreptitiously access computer hard drives and to install hidden cameras and listening devices, has already been granted in some other states and is likely to spread to the remainder. But this is only another, little noticed, step in a series of changes that give Australian governments the legal power to do many things which would be illegal if done in the private sector, including bribery, breaking and entering premises, hacking into computers, and intercepting phone calls, faxes and emails.

Labor premiers are no keener than their Coalition opponents to rein in the power of executive government. Earlier this year, the South Australian Premier, Mike Rann, introduced a new law drawing on the provisions of anti-terrorism legislation to declare bikie gangs illegal organisations. It is now a criminal offence to 'associate' with members of these groups. The law is so sweeping that members of a Christian motorcycle group in South Australia complain that they risk being jailed for mixing with other bikies in an effort to gain converts.

Rann is not reluctant to brand people as terrorists. On 15 August, he described farmers who had allegedly diverted water from the Paroo River in Queensland as having committed 'an act of terrorism against the nation'. Even if such anti-social behaviour had occurred, it would seem to stop well short of the standard definition of terrorism as an act of 'politically motivated violence'.

Other states have used special legislative provisions, originally confined to terrorism, to prevent the activities of executive government being subjected to judicial or other review. A law introduced by the New South Wales Labor government stopped the actions of 'protected persons' associated with the Catholic World Youth Day Authority from being 'challenged, reviewed, quashed or called into question before any court of law or administrative review body'.

This wording is taken directly from the New South Wales Terrorism (Police Powers) Act of 2001, which was introduced by the then Labor

Premier Bob Carr. Despite a long a history of police corruption and miscon-
duct in New South Wales, the act essentially removes all constraints on the
police after they declare, of their own volition, that a terrorist emergency
exists.

At the federal level, Prime Minister John Howard used the understandable public revulsion at terrorist atrocities to change the law in ways
that go far beyond any reasonable effort to counter terrorism. The Australian
Federal Police (AFP), for example, can now enter premises without a warrant and demand the production of any document it claims might have
some connection to major crime, regardless of whether it has anything to do
with terrorism. It is an offence, punishable by a 2-year jail sentence, for
anyone to reveal that the AFP has ordered them to hand over such documents, including material supplied by whistleblowers to the media.

Under Howard, the courts were increasingly precluded from reviewing executive decisions, particularly those affecting asylum seekers. This
extended more unchecked power to public servants just as distressing examples of administrative blunders proliferated. The changes occurred against
a backdrop in which centuries-old legal protections inherited from Britain
have been eroded with little community backlash. Traditional conservatives
warned in vain about the inherent dangers of removing effective checks and
balances on executive power as many of the protections embedded in
English law, including the principles embodied in the Magna Carta in 1215,
were jettisoned with bipartisan support after 11 September 2001.

In this context, a University of New South Wales law professor,
George Williams, notes that Menzies was 'steeped' in English legal traditions of protecting individual liberty against the intrusions of the state.
Despite departures such as the attempt to ban the Communist Party in
1950, Williams sees Menzies as reflecting those traditions to a much greater
extent than Howard did half a century later.

Although judicial overview remains limited, Labor's Immigration
Minister Chris Evans, backed by Kevin Rudd, has improved the treatment
of asylum seekers. There are few other signs, however, that Rudd intends
to restore the balance between the individual and the state so it is more in
keeping with the values that both major political parties supported for
most of the post-war era. During that era, most Australians were brought
up to believe that they had inherited a justice system in which *habeas*

corpus always applied; the onus of proof was on the prosecution not the defendant; everyone was entitled to the presumption of innocence and the right to silence; the accused was allowed to see the evidence relied on by the Crown and so on. All of these rights have been truncated to some extent by the action of governments in the past decade.

Although some commentators and political leaders insist that Islamic terrorism constitutes a threat to the continued existence of Western democratic nations, others object that there is clearly no prospect that al Qaeda and its associates will take over and run non-Islamic countries. This is in clear contrast to Germany and Japan, whose aggression in the 1930s and 1940s triggered a world war in which around seventy million people died. During the Cold War, a full-scale nuclear exchange could have left 300 million people dead and entire societies crippled.

From this perspective, terrorists murder innocent people (or attempt to do so) on a much smaller scale than occurs with state-on-state violence in a major war. Murder and conspiracy to murder have long been comprehensively covered by the criminal law without severely eroding the legal rights of the accused. Many aspects of the forty-four pieces of anti-terrorism legislation introduced since 2001 strip away these rights—even for those accused of far more minor offences than murder, or in some cases, not accused on anything at all.

A former High Court judge, Michael McHugh, has cautioned against overreacting. In a paper published in the *Australian Bar Review* in 2007, McHugh noted that terrorist groups during the last century included pre-World War I anarchists, the Stern Gang's fight for an Israeli state in the early 1940s, the Mau Mau uprising against British rule in Kenya, the revolutionary Red Brigades in Italy in the 1970s and 1980s, Spain's Basque separatist group (ETA) and the Irish Republican Army. These groups caused undoubted fear. Apart from the Stern Gang's success, the others lost or have largely faded away. McHugh said that the upshot was that the Anglo-Australian-American world had survived 'without changing the fundamental values that have been the hallmarks of its legal systems'. But McHugh said he was worried about the constitutionality and scope of some of the recent changes to the Australian legal system in response to al Qaeda.

At the height of the Cold War in 1952, the then attorney-general in the Menzies Cabinet, John Spicer, ran into stiff opposition from within the prime minister's department when he tried to expand offences relating to espionage and official secrets. A senior official, Alan McKnight, wrote to Menzies with an uncompromising bluntness. Among wide-ranging changes, Spicer wanted to impose the death penalty for spying; seven years' jail for anyone who took meteorological observations prejudicial to national defence; and the introduction of the official registration of anyone who received mail on behalf of others.

McKnight wrote: 'After studying the bill, one feels that every deed is an offence and whether prosecution will follow, or not, is simply a matter of official discretion'. He said an airline passenger who tried to take a photo of Sydney Harbour Bridge but accidentally photographed a nearby oil storage facility would commit a *prima facie* offence, attracting the death penalty. The onus would be on the accused to prove that no crime had occurred. McKnight also noted that more than 220 000 public servants would have the right to search, without warrant, anyone suspected of breaching any aspect of the proposed new law.

The Menzies Cabinet threw the draft bill out in its entirety. A later Attorney-General, Garfield Barwick, managed to toughen the anti-subversion laws in 1961, but not before agreeing to extensive amendments. The Whitlam, Fraser and Hawke governments mostly held the line against a serious slide towards a national security state, although police and various crime commissions gained extra powers during this period. The Keating Government was less restrained, introducing draft bills to suppress publication of foreign affairs, defence and intelligence material that could allegedly harm relations with other countries, regardless of whether such an outcome may sometimes be justified. The bills lapsed following the election of the Howard Government in 1996 (only for tougher variants to be introduced after 11 September 2001).

No sensible person suggests that individual liberty enjoyed a golden era in Australia before 2001. While ASIO's formal powers were restricted in the 1950s and 1960s, the agency operated with few constraints—apart from those imposed with an extraordinary degree of incompetence, as revealed in the royal commission conducted in the mid 1970s by the then New South Wales Supreme Court judge, Robert Hope. When the National Archives released declassified versions of Hope's reports in May 2008, they revealed ASIO to have been a highly dysfunctional organisation.

Speaking at the official release of the reports in May, the royal commission's secretary George Brownbill said ASIO's files 'disclosed numerous cases where gossip and tittle-tattle about people and their so-called "Communist sympathies" was recounted to certain figures in the Menzies government and then revealed in some cases under parliamentary privilege'.

Today, ASIO is much more circumspect. It is less clear that the same can be said for the AFP, which provided information to the then Immigration Minister, Kevin Andrews, who used it to make a damaging allegation about the former Gold Coast doctor Mohamed Haneef after terrorism-related charges against him collapsed in 2007 due to a lack of evidence.

Against this backdrop, Brownbill said: 'One of people's great fears, and rightly, is of "secret police". We found the state police special branches were, if that is possible, worse than their ASIO counterparts in their disregard of due process, careful intelligence gathering and assessment, and their lack of accountability'.

Brownbill reminded his audience that ASIO was never intended to be more than 'an intelligence collection and assessment agency. If the law was broken, then it was a matter for the law enforcement authorities'. He said that Hope believed that the lawful functions of the police and intelligence agencies must remain separate. 'Unhappily', Brownbill said, 'this fundamental principle has been muddied in recent changes to the law. In my view, that has been a source of difficulty for both ASIO and the Federal Police'.

Prompted in part by Hope's findings, the police special branches were disbanded in the 1970s. In the wake of September 11 most have been resurrected under different names. Apart from looking for terrorists, these new units have revived the old special branch role of gathering intelligence on anyone who might be a potential demonstrator. Bob Carr went further than the Howard Government wanted when he gave a terrorism reference to the New South Wales state crime commission and announced that the then head of ASIO, Dennis Richardson, would join its board. Richardson refused. But Carr still assigned 100 investigators to undertake special anti-terrorism work for a commission that possesses more draconian powers than ASIO, but is not subject to the oversight applied to the latter by a parliamentary intelligence committee and an inspector-general.

The alacrity with which the state police moved into the growth area involving 'politically motivated violence' has been more than matched at the federal end, where the law enforcement and intelligence agencies have received massive budget increases—in ASIO's case, over 500 per cent since 2001–2002. The AFP has expanded into ASIO's previously exclusive preserve of gathering security intelligence. Despite the move into this sensitive territory, the AFP does not face the same oversight arrangements as ASIO.

Critics such as an ex-head of the former National Crime Authority, John Broome, argue that the AFP has become unduly preoccupied with terrorism. Since September 2001, the number of serious crimes referred by the AFP to the Director of Public Prosecutions has fallen to half the previous level.

For its part, ASIO has intruded on traditional police functions after a new law was introduced in 2002 to give it special questioning powers. Under this law, people who are not suspected of any crime can be detained at ASIO's request for seven days and questioned by its officers who act as anonymous agents of the state. An innocent person who refuses to answer questions, or reveals that they were detained, let alone what they were asked, can be jailed for five years. So can journalists who report alleged miscarriages of justice under this system.

In privately held conversations, former ASIO officers have expressed strong fears that these changes risk moving closer to the creation of a secret police force. They say no one should be able to detain people, or compel them to answer questions, unless they are made accountable by having to reveal real names.

Most people would be happy to provide information about possible terrorist activities if they were convinced that no miscarriage of justice would ensue. Such confidence was eroded by a decision from US President George Bush to authorise the Central Intelligence Agency (CIA) to assassinate suspected terrorists without trial and to kidnap and transport others for torture in brutal authoritarian states—the latter process is euphemistically described as 'rendition'.

To its credit, ASIO has only made sparing use of its special questioning powers. This could change under future directors general. Sometimes the information sought by ASIO under its special questioning powers may relate to overseas suspects wanted by the CIA or even more unscrupulous counter-parties.

Intelligence information can easily be wrong, including material that ASIO supplies to overseas agencies without recourse to its special questioning powers. This is one reason police are not allowed to assassinate people suspected of committing an offence on the basis of criminal intelligence. Even if the intelligence is correct, extra-judicial execution and torture remains illegal.

A Sydney University law professor, Ben Saul, says that Australian governments can be regarded as having a legal duty to try to prevent their citizens from being transferred for torture to other countries. But there appears to have been an almost casual indifference at the highest levels of government to the rendition of Sydney man Mamdouh Habib. Habib was detained by US agents in Pakistan in 2001 and interviewed in the presence of officials from the Foreign Affairs Department, the AFP and ASIO. The CIA then rendered Habib to Egypt where he was tortured over several months before being transferred to the US military jail at Guantanamo Bay and released without charge in January 2005.

The head of ASIO, Paul O'Sullivan, told a Senate committee in June this year that a US official had asked his predecessor Dennis Richardson in October 2001 for Australia's views on the proposed transfer of Habib to Egypt. Despite the closeness of the alliance, the United States ignored any Australian opposition. Perhaps this is unsurprising, as Australian objections seem to have been confined to what O'Sullivan described as an 'oral pull-aside' of an unspecified American official by Richardson. Apparently, no ministerial representations were made to try to prevent the United States rendering Habib for torture—in violation of an international law endorsed by the Australian parliament.

Despite Richardson's unequivocal statement to the Senate committee in 2005 that ASIO 'definitely' knew by February 2002 that Habib was in Egypt, the then Attorney-General Phillip Ruddock said as recently as 13 August 2008, that his understanding was that Richardson 'formed a view of where he [Habib] might be ... simply on the basis of supposition'. The then Foreign Minister, Alexander Downer said on 9 September that he had 'no idea' whether the Americans had taken Habib to Egypt, although 'somebody did'.

The ministerial response to Habib's treatment is in marked contrast to the Canadian response after one of its nationals, Maher Arar, was kidnapped in New York in 2002 and rendered by the CIA to Syria where he was savagely tortured. A thorough official inquiry produced a 12-volume report which found that Arar was an innocent man who had suffered partly because of the behaviour of Canadian authorities. The conservative Canadian Prime Minister Stephen Harper subsequently apologised formally to Arar and offered C$10.5 million in compensation. Apparently in Australia the Rudd Government has no intention of commissioning a single volume on Habib's case.

ASIO was directly involved in the kidnapping of University of New South Wales medical student Izhar ul-Haque, who had briefly attended a Pakistani training camp. At the time, the camp was not run by a declared terrorist organisation. On returning to Australia in 2003, ul-Haque told officials at Sydney airport what he had done. Neither ASIO nor the AFP showed any further interest until almost twelve months later when they asked ul-Haque to become an informer against other Muslims in Sydney. He declined, saying he wanted to concentrate on his studies, and was subsequently charged with terrorism offences.

The case collapsed after New South Wales Supreme Court judge Michael Adams found that—prior to the charges being laid—two ASIO officers had 'committed criminal offences of false imprisonment and kidnapping'. Adams said ASIO's conduct constituted 'an unlawful interference with personal liberty ... by agents of the state'. Although ASIO comes under the Attorney-General's portfolio, the unusual reaction of then departmental head Robert Cornall was to ask the New South Wales Judicial Commission to discipline the judge for not being fair to the agency. The commission found no grounds to do so.

The importance of an independent judiciary and a sceptical media was highlighted even more forcefully by the AFP's protracted pursuit of Mohamed Haneef. In July 2007, AFP commissioner Mick Keelty approved charges against Haneef of the 'reckless' provision of material support for a terrorist group by giving a mobile phone SIM card, containing unused credit, to a second cousin when he left the United Kingdom for a job in Australia. In fact, the cousin was not a terrorist, as the British police established several days before the AFP charged Haneef.

Shortly after the case began, the Director of Public Prosecutions (DPP) recommended that the charges be dropped because of a lack of evidence. It was not until more than twelve months (and $8.2 million) later that the AFP admitted that Haneef was no longer a suspect. Yet ASIO's head Paul O'Sullivan said that his agency had given written advice to the Howard Government, before Haneef was charged that, there were no grounds for believing he was involved in terrorism. In these circumstances, a strong argument exists that, far from combating terrorism, the AFP's behaviour towards Haneef risked radicalising Islamic youth—the outcome for which fundamentalist clerics are usually criticised. Yet the government expressed its full confidence in Keelty in early September, as did shadow ministers.

Few observers believe it is possible to prevent every conceivable terrorist act, any more than it is possible to fully eradicate all premeditated violent crime. But there is widespread agreement that intelligence agencies and the police should try to stop terrorists harming others. The debate focuses on the extent to which existing laws needed to be extended after 11 September 2001. Not all contributors to the debate are easily typecast. Dennis Richardson, while ASIO head, told a parliamentary committee in 2005 that no further powers were needed. Yet the parliament subsequently expanded the anti-terrorism laws.

Petro Georgiou, a Liberal backbencher who now holds Menzies' former seat of Kooyong, introduced a bill in March to establish an independent reviewer of the terrorism laws on a permanent basis. Georgiou said: 'The challenge of protecting security without undermining fundamental rights requires constant vigilance'. His proposal had earlier received the unanimous bipartisan support of the parliamentary joint committee on intelligence and security. Last week federal Attorney-General Robert McClelland indicated he was considering asking the Inspector-General of Intelligence and Security, Ian Carnell, to review the operations of the legislation. Carnell supports the idea but says this would create a conflict with his present duties.

Regardless of the eventual outcome of the debate over the terrorism laws, there has been little discussion of the way their influence has pervaded other state and federal legislation as outlined above. Particularly when confronted by strong public emotions, opposition parties usually support new constraints on individual freedom and further restrictions on the checks and balances provided by the courts. Menzies, while not himself immune, warned against seeking short-term political gain in response to public pressure. In a collection of speeches published in 1958, he said, 'Public opinion in a reasonably educated community will, I believe, in the long run, tend to be sound and just; but day-to-day is quite capable of being not only wrong, but so extravagant as to be unjust and oppressive'.

Police in recent years have not only been granted expanded powers unrelated to terrorism, they have dusted off old laws not used in recent memory. In May this year, New South Wales police raided a Sydney art gallery and removed nude portraits from a Bill Henson exhibition. The police considered laying charges on obscenity grounds, but the DPP advised against doing so. Meanwhile, the AFP visited the National Gallery in Canberra and removed some of Henson's works (later returned).

Police also have become much more active than in earlier decades in attempting to discover the source of 'leaks' involving information that politicians and public servants don't want aired in public. In April, around sixteen state police raided the *Sunday Times*'s offices in Perth following the publication of information about a $16 million advertising campaign designed to assist the then state Labor government in an election campaign expected later in the year. All exits from the building were blocked and staff had their bags searched.

In July, the AFP investigated the phone records of the Nine network's Laurie Oakes after leaks about the government's FuelWatch program.

In September, seven AFP members searched the home of a *Canberra Times* journalist Philip Dorling and seized papers, computers containing personal family data and a mobile phone, following a leak about which countries were of interest to the Defence Intelligence organisation.

A spokesman for a coalition of media groups, Greg Baxter, said the raid on Dorling's home raised serious questions about the commitment to free speech. He said, 'There is no evidence that national security or public safety was at risk or that this information could lead to a serious crime and therefore there are simply no legitimate grounds for the police raid'.

In late September the AFP raided the Gold Coast home of a person suspected of leaking information for a newspaper article about the Australian Communications and Media Authority.

Despite the implications for free speech, the Rudd Government has not taken any steps to repeal the Howard Government's resurrection of the previously defunct crime of sedition. Under Rudd, a 7-year jail sentence can still be imposed on anyone who 'brings the sovereign into hatred or contempt' or 'urges disaffection' against the Constitution, the government or the parliament. If the prime minister wished to abolish this antiquated crime, he should have the support of the Opposition leader, Malcolm Turnbull. While a backbencher, Turnbull strongly opposed Howard's revival of sedition as a crime, arguing that it conferred an undue degree of power on the state.

7
Weathering the Storm

Peter Hartcher

Central banker who goosed us all
The Sydney Morning Herald, 28 November 2008

Kevin Rudd is quite wrong in his labelling of the cause of the global financial crisis. And Malcolm Turnbull is quite wrong in his core prescription of what to do about it.

Rudd has grown attached to his description of the crisis as a result of 'extreme capitalism'. That's akin to saying the Titanic sank because of 'extreme sailing'. The US economy and financial markets collapsed not because of the doctrine of capitalism, any more than the Titanic sank because of the practice of international shipping. The cause of the calamity was bad policy, just as the cause of the Titanic's fate was bad navigating.

At core, the made-in-America disaster is a simple matter. There were two parts to it.

First, US house prices were pumped up to unsustainable levels—a bubble—with prices so high they were bound to pop. In itself, this is not an unusual event. Booms and busts in asset prices, whether real estate or shares, are pretty common.

So common that in the post-war era rich countries have suffered a sharemarket bust every thirteen years on average, and a real estate bust every twenty years on average, according to a study of nineteen countries by the International Monetary Fund.

In four centuries of financial capitalism, this is a persistent problem— a rising market tends to move beyond all reason into hysterical excess. A bubble forms. It inevitably bursts. No news there. But on this occasion, the US housing bubble was bigger and uglier than your typical bubble.

Many of the world's central banks had been trying to keep bubbles under control. They were learning from two big lessons. One was Japan's implosion in 1989, when sharemarket and real estate bubbles burst simultaneously, leading to a decade of stagnation.

The other was America's 2000 sharemarket crash, the so-called Tech Wreck, when a bubble in technology share prices popped. This led to the US recession of 2001.

Can central banks really exercise any control over bubbles in asset prices? Yes. The Reserve Bank of Australia successfully dampened the Australian real estate bubble in 2002–03, using a combination of rhetoric and higher interest rates.

But in America, the country's top central banker, Alan Greenspan, drew a different lesson.

It was best summed up in this exchange with a sympathetic US senator in July 2001. As the American economy headed into recession, with 2.3 million jobs lost and US$7.8 trillion in wealth destroyed, the senator said to Greenspan during a congressional hearing: 'If this is the bust, the boom was sure as hell worth it. You agree with that, right?' Greenspan calmly offered: 'Certainly'.

While other countries' central banks tried to avoid creating bubbles, the Fed set about creating a new one. Greenspan wanted to get the US economy out of its 2001 recession as quickly as possible. And he wanted to keep it growing until his looming mandatory retirement date of January 2006.

He goosed the US economy far too hard. He cut the official US interest rate to a ludicrous low of just 1 per cent—below the inflation rate—and held it there for a full year to mid-2004. In effect, Greenspan was subsidising US banks to borrow money. Money gushed into housing prices and the bubble burgeoned into an obscenely large mutation. Greenspan knew it would lead to a bust, but on the next guy's watch.

This was the core error. It was not 'extreme capitalism'. It was bad policy.

The second part was the failure of prudential regulation; particularly, failing to regulate the so-called subprime mortgage market and its derivatives.

This part of the story has received most of the publicity. But it only magnified the effects of the inevitable collapse. The housing market was always going to bust. And this was always going to lead to another US recession. I am not being wise in hindsight. I made this forecast in my 2005 book, *Bubble Man: Alan Greenspan and the Missing 7 Trillion Dollars*.

But the irresponsible behaviour in the financial markets amplified the size of the crash, and turned an American recession into a global one.

Whose job was it to police the US financial institutions and markets? Again, it was Alan Greenspan's Federal Reserve. Although his prudential responsibility was to regulate the banks and the markets, he had a conflict of interest.

He was already feeding cheap money into the economy to generate maximum speed. The last thing he wanted was to curb this by regulating the way money was being handed around. So he didn't.

In Australia, this task of policing the banks and the financial markets is given to the separate Australian Prudential Regulation Authority for exactly this reason. The US is now considering adopting the same structure.

Why does it matter what Rudd calls it? Because from the diagnosis comes the cure. The fault was not capitalism, extreme or lame. It was bad policy.

As for Malcolm Turnbull, he has made some sensible suggestions on how the government should respond to the crisis, but the one he made this week is not one of them. Turnbull claims the government must not allow a budget deficit. Already, Rudd has used half the projected budget surplus for this fiscal year as a package to stimulate growth.

On Wednesday Rudd sensibly started to prepare the country for the possibility the surplus may evaporate entirely. This is exactly as it should be.

Budget policy should lean in the opposite direction to the prevailing economic conditions. When the economy is growing well, the government should set aside its windfall revenues as surpluses. When the economy is shrinking, the government should go into deficit to stimulate growth. That is the way sensible budget policy works.

Turnbull knows this well. To pretend it is some sort of irresponsibility of Rudd's is itself an act of irresponsibility. It marks the descent of Turnbull to economic stuntsmanship, no better than his predecessor, Brendan Nelson.

George Megalogenis

Out of their depths

The Australian, 22 November 2008

Capitalism has two ways of making money that lasts. It can find new consumers or, with the help of technology and snazzy marketing, persuade existing customers to buy pretty much the same thing again and again.

The moment the West knew it could beat communism was when it learnt to trust its workforce with a living wage. This transformed the proletariat that Karl Marx thought was ripe for revolution from units of production into discretionary spenders.

Life's necessities—food, clothing, shelter, transport and a sprawling music collection—are meant to be purchased in perpetuity. The richer societies become, the more money is poured into the middle item on this list: bricks 'n' mortar. If you don't trade up, you can always renovate. If you don't fancy builders disrupting your existence, you can always buy new things for the house.

The harder part for capitalism has been translating on to the world stage its most valuable long-run insight that growth is driven by ordinary folk, not rich people chasing ever-increasing paper profits.

The first two waves of globalisation identified by the World Bank occurred in 1870–1914 and 1950–80.

They were flawed operations because the West viewed other nations as it once had its own citizens, as playthings to be exploited.

Treasury secretary Ken Henry made this point a little more diplomatically in a speech to the first economic outlook conference hosted by *The Australian* and the Melbourne Institute in 2002.

'Interestingly, the first two surges of globalisation did not produce any general catch-up by the population of developing countries on the steadily improving living standards in western Europe and the New World', he said.

It is only during phase three, since 1980, that the West has got the hang of appreciating developing nations as consumers in their own right, rather than mere colonies or branch offices. Excuse the theoretical introduction, but some context is necessary to see what might happen next.

It has been a little too tempting to view the recession underway in the West as the end of capitalism as we know it. A brand of capitalism is surely dead. But the notion that governments and regulators need to reassert themselves in the marketplace is not new. We have been here before.

The bigger question is whether the experience of boom and then bust alters the way people relate to one another: as shoppers, wage slaves, employers, enterprises, governments and nations.

Will this crisis generate the insights needed to build a more viable version of the 1950s and 1960s, a period that combined a happy mix of thrift, job security and rapidly increasing living standards?

Or will the globe's collective top end of town condemn us to a lost decade or two in the Japanese sense, marked by rolling recessions, interest rates near zero and no sensible person prepared to take a risk?

The share markets here and abroad have collapsed to the levels of five years ago or longer, as if all that headline growth in the new millennium was not real but a book entry mirage. But something real did happen over the past five years in particular. China and India were welcomed as paid-up members of capitalism. And Russia and Brazil became significant players in their own rights.

The *Economist* magazine reported last week that these societies are beginning to consume like the United States.

'As recently as 2005, America bought 10 million more cars than the total of the BRICs: Brazil, Russia, India and China', the magazine says. 'This year, sales of cars in the BRICs should overtake those in America.'

This statistic tells two stories in one: the extent of the slump in the United States and the West's increasing reliance on the developing world to support the whole show.

What is clear is that capitalism will need to find a fresh driver of growth to ensure the next recovery is worthwhile. This is easier said than done because in the West, at least, there is a sense that the public has suddenly discovered the concept of hanging on to what they've got.

Not every recession changes the nature of capitalism, because the business cycle usually takes care of itself. The economy spends a year or so in the dumps before consumers can resume the grand task of updating their material possessions.

A series of crises, or one almighty crash, are required to shift policy orthodoxy.

It was the combination of recessions in the mid 1970s, early 1980s and again in the early 1990s that elevated the theory of deregulation into an operating principle for most governments.

Today's advisers and politicians are, in effect, the children of that consensus. Many are too young to recall the relative stability of the 1950s and 1960s that they are now seeking to re-create, in which banks play the role of public utilities, businesses crave the loyalty of staff and customers alike, and households don't need to borrow like crazy to make a simple trip to the shopping mall.

Deregulation's second generation faces a challenge that may be beyond their corporate memory. They need to shed the excess baggage of no-rules capitalism and figure out how much intervention is required to give the economy its next sustained wind. The risk is the advisers assume too much control from here on because while they trust markets in theory, they don't trust the people who play them.

Meanwhile, the politicians face the pincer of the electoral cycle.

Whenever re-regulation is on the agenda, the business lobbies, led by the car-makers, revert to type and demand even more taxpayer support. No one said capitalism was free of hypocrisy.

Now the good news. Last weekend's G20 summit in Washington offered a surprising moment of self-realisation. The world leaders discussed intervention, of course, but they also mentioned the unfinished business of deregulation: trade liberalisation.

White House incumbent George W. Bush may have few friends left. But he spoke some serious sense after the meeting was over.

'Leaders at this summit agreed [to] reject protectionism and to refrain from erecting new trade barriers', the president said. 'Temptation in times of economic stress will be to say, "Oh, trade isn't worth it, let's just throw up protective barriers." And yet that attitude was rejected, thankfully.'

The global financial crisis—a term only a merchant banker or jargon-loving bureaucrat could have coined—is, touch wood, not likely to lead to a third world war. It may not even see a return to protection because the BRICs are too tempting to turn one's back on.

Assume the best case scenario, that the West understands the need to wind back, not revive protection. That still leaves the riddle of what will drive the next decade or more of growth within domestic markets such as ours.

US president-elect Barack Obama is banking on climate change to make his argument for him. 'My presidency will mark a new chapter in America's leadership on climate change that will strengthen our security and create millions of new jobs', he told a conference convened by California's Republican Governor Arnold Schwarzenegger this week.

Like Kevin Rudd, Obama has yet to say exactly how emissions trading will work. However, if you take a longer view, switching a nation to new energy sources is a form of reconstruction, but without a world war to prompt it.

Laura Tingle

The treasurer who looked into the void
The Australian Financial Review, 18 October 2008

Just over a week ago, Wayne Swan was sitting in the sumptuous office of an international banker in New York looking out over Central Park. World stockmarkets were in free fall and even cool heads were agitated.

The messages he was getting in the decimated financial centre were bad enough and the Australian treasurer was not to know that even worse would come when he reached Washington. Still, it took a personal anecdote to bring home to Swan the extent of the deterioration in the world's financial system—and the economic outlook. The head of a large bank whom Swan had met many times previously recounted a story about an old university friend, now a significant figure in American IT who phoned him from time to time for a bit of financial advice. Swan recounts the story.

'This (IT) bloke said to the financial services guy, "Look I've really got to come round and see you, find out what's going on."'

'So the (IT) guy comes round and starts telling him that he needs to access all of his money. He's got to get out of the country and he's going to go and live in a cave in Brazil.'

According to Swan, the banker 'previously seemed to be a relatively sensible, sane, sort of no-nonsense guy'.

Yet the banker then looks at Swan and says: 'You know what? I thought at the time, shit maybe he's right. It's the beginning of the end of the world'.

Swan's point in telling the story is to try to capture the extraordinary movement in sentiment which greeted him in New York and Washington last week in contrast to his previous visits. It was this turbulent mood which can be credited for driving the Australian government's extraordinary interventions of the past week when it moved both to guarantee bank deposits here and to announce an unprecedented fiscal stimulus for an economy that, at this point, is still growing at the relatively robust rate of 2.7 per cent.

While Australians have watched the local sharemarket heaving downwards, there has been a sense that Australian banks are somehow isolated from the catastrophes gripping the United States and Europe. Thus the perceptions here of what is happening seemed curiously out of step with the urgent pre-emptive measures suddenly imposed by a now anxious government. Australian banks have no great exposures to bad debts. Their vulnerability is apparently only in accessing wholesale funds. Since the start of the year, there have been two distinct periods when those funds have, for all intents and purposes, dried up for weeks at a time.

One consolation has been that the flight to safety from the sharemarket over the course of 2008 has helped boost the banks' access to domestic deposits. They were also able to lock in significant licks of term funding while the markets were functioning better earlier in the year.

But what happens if the various bank bail-out schemes announced around the world over the past week do not succeed in stabilising markets and start to free up lending again, no one knows.

Swan travelled from New York to Washington for IMF meetings, then an emergency meeting of G20 finance ministers, only to get an even grimmer assessment from his counterparts in governments around the world. These men and women were talking to him from the standpoint of governments that had, in some cases, made several attempts at propping up their financial systems or economies, only to see their efforts undermined by their lack of coordination.

Their advice to Swan was simple: 'Act early and act really swiftly'. This was the advice of 'various senior economists and just about all of the leaders I saw', he says. 'They were all sitting there saying, "look, what we have been doing so far hasn't been quick enough and hasn't been working. It just has to be bigger".'

You don't get any of that here—this message that the outlook is so risky that you shouldn't take the risk of not doing anything you can, that the damage of under-estimating is bigger than the risk of over-estimating ... When you've got the chief economist of the IMF saying just pull every lever that you can ...

It's not that there has been any lack of appreciation of the seriousness of challenges facing the financial system. It's just that the worries were not understood by the public at large.

Swan reveals that back in January, February and March,

> it was bad here in the sense it was bad amongst key people in financial markets. They were deeply pessimistic. None of that was public. It stabilised after (the forced sale of US investment broker) Bear Stearns for a while.
>
> But it was the experience of the Prime Minister and I during that period—and when we were both overseas for meetings in March—that left us very much of the view that we ought to be taking the position we took at our budget. Now a lot of people at the time of the budget were questioning the strategy, were critical we didn't cut hard enough —for which we made no apology because we actually thought the downside risk was greater.

In fact, Rudd and Swan had talked to Treasury Secretary Ken Henry in February outside the context of budget preparations—about exactly what the government would need to do if things went seriously nasty in the financial markets.

These early discussions explain why there is an unexpected buoyancy in Canberra at the moment. Senior ministers and bureaucrats are exhausted by the work that has gone into framing a response to the crisis but have been given great confidence by the fact that they had contingency plans, and are living on the adrenalin of knowing that they are now in the box seat of steering the country through an historic crisis.

'It's one of those times that makes political life worthwhile', Swan says, 'because you actually might be able to make a difference.'

Along with the extraordinary unknowns of what now happens in global markets and to the real economy is the equally unfathomable issue of how governments deal with the new power they have assumed. They have taken previously unthinkable decisions to partially or fully nationalise their banks, and the fate of much of the capitalist world could be seen to rest on what happens in China—the last of the great centralised economies.

There is the angst in business about government proposals to try to curb a perceived culture of excessive risk taking with a regulatory regime which will punish institutions that reward such behaviour with big salary packages.

'People want a bit more accountability', Swan says. 'There's a very good reason why banks, you know, always had good regulation and we just found out what happens when they don't.' His argument is that what is needed isn't 'necessarily more regulation, it's got to be smarter regulation. Of course there's going to be a bit more responsibility'.

Swan downplays the prospects of governments rising as a much bigger, long-term force in the world markets. 'I don't think anyone is envisioning that they want to remain [as bank shareholders] for a long time', he says.

> I think the whole objective at the moment is to normalise and then hopefully get back some of the money they spent and maybe make a profit as things normalise and get out. What's more important is actually getting the regulatory framework right for all this, which is the medium-term objective that we've been following through all those [international] meetings.
>
> So there's a longer-term reform agenda which has got to go on and we've been progressing, which has in a sense been swamped by dealing with the immediate stabilisation but which can't be allowed to lapse. We've got to find the cause of the fire, not only deal with the fire.

This past week's $10.4 billion package is designed to give confidence a shot in the arm immediately, help keep it propped up over Christmas when the things with longer lead times, such as infrastructure spending, might be able to kick in, along with the budget automatic stabilisers, the impact of interest rate decisions already taken by the Reserve Bank and to come, and the stimulatory effects of a lower Australian dollar.

'It's about getting ahead of where we are and not reacting after it happens', Swan says. 'It's actually about putting the fire out before it starts.'

What we do know is there's been a sharp impact on confidence in households, business, and markets. So you've got to deal with it. There's three rounds of policy. There's monetary policy which the Reserve moved on. There's fiscal policy which we just moved on and there are those broader interventions in the financial system to stabilise it which we've moved on.

'Housing', he says, is 'a market that needs some strengthening—obviously or we wouldn't do it'.

We are putting out a package to boost and strengthen demand in the economy. And this is a very important part of the economy that needs a boost now. It's a temporary measure. It's not going on past June 30 next year. We've done it because we think it needs to be done now and we also think it's a more immediate way of doing things than simply waiting for the full impact of monetary policy to flow through.

The other thing that's sobering is that the IMF revised down its growth forecast for emerging economies [for which read China], but what was more sobering to me [about discussions with other finance ministers at the IMF] was just the way in which a number of them were talking about the impact of this on their real economy as well.

Meanwhile, the government must still bed down its staggeringly large guarantees for the financial system. And this plan for the moment remains more of a headache than saving the economy.

There has been an ominous silence on the detail of how the scheme would work—particularly for banks' wholesale funding—how it would be priced, how it would be accounted for. For example, the government doesn't really know how exactly it would represent potentially enormous contingent liabilities in the budget, let alone work out how to price the guarantee facility.

Realistically, it is probably the case that they were hoping it is a guarantee that no bank will ever have to use. But the banks have already been talking to the government, wanting to know the price of the guarantee.

As the week ended, there seemed to be a stand-off, with the government saying on the one hand, 'tell us what you are proposing to do in any specific transaction and we'll tell you what it will cost you' and the banks saying, 'tell us how much it will cost and we'll tell you what we'll do'.

The whole scheme may need to be quietly—or even loudly—revamped significantly before it actually sees the light of day. But the government probably doesn't care too much at this stage.

This week, the Australian government was able to hit local markets and consumers with a double whammy of confidence-boosting measures that were launched more successfully than those attempted overseas. On Friday, it was attempting to reassure business about what it was doing to try to keep the economy ticking over, even if it couldn't provide the reassurance of firm numbers.

Throughout the year, Rudd and particularly Swan have been working hard with the business and financial communities to build up relationships of trust. What started as a process to build Labor's economic credentials has become more a partnership of getting the economy through difficult times.

Swan's ultimate ambition is to make sure no one in Australia wants to go off to live in a cave in Brazil.

Mark Latham

Building a house of cards

The Australian Financial Review, 30 October 2008

No good ever comes from government intervention in the housing market. This is the lesson economic historians should record from the meltdown in global markets. Forget Kevin Rudd's populist claptrap about extreme capitalism. The root cause of the crisis is extreme politics.

Internationally, governments have fostered the myth of universal home ownership, offering large subsidies for families that put themselves into mortgage debt beyond their means. Politics 101 tells election candidates to promise material gains beyond the capacity of governments to deliver.

The most enticing pledge of all is property; the puissant lure of your own patch of land. In the modern economy, with its large and globally integrated capital markets, this has generated huge increases in household debt and the securitisation of mortgages into new financial products. In effect, the creation of a debt pyramid with the political promise of home ownership at its base.

In the flurry of analysis about the financial crisis, the scale of public subsidies for property development has been ignored. In the United States, prospective home owners enjoy tax deductibility on their mortgages, exemptions from capital gains tax and imputed rent, and special incentives for low-income households. Each new president and Congress, in pursuit of re-election, has created additional sweeteners, reaching further down the income scale with the false hope of home ownership. Americans have led the way with the collapse of their sub-prime lending market and debt pyramid. Other nations are following.

In Australia, subsidies and tax expenditures for the property sector exceed $70 billion a year. This places the federal government's $10 billion fiscal stimulus package in perspective. It is a small proportion of the money politicians devote each year to the promise of property ownership. As in the United States, these incentives have distorted the market in favour of housing investment and encouraged an unsustainable base of household debt.

The impact of an international recession on Australia will be severe as risk takers in the small business and housing sectors find themselves under-employed and over-leveraged.

Yet the political cycle rolls on regardless. Having seen the US mortgage market implode, how has the Australian government responded? By doubling and tripling its new home owner grants, encouraging greater debt even though real incomes are likely to fall. Having witnessed the decline of the US securities market due to mortgage delinquency, what special measure has our government adopted? Eight billion dollars of public expenditure to secure privately minted mortgages in the second-tier lending market.

The public debate about the crisis has followed a predictable pattern, with both sides trying to fit events into their ideological view of the world. Right-wingers say the problem has been too much financial regulation while the left claims there has not been enough. But this argument overlooks a greater truth. Pyramids do not fall apart from the top. They collapse from the bottom. While it has become fashionable to demonise the financial markets, they have been doing only what capitalist economies expect them to do. Dogs bark, financial institutions buy and sell money.

The focus on the upper reaches of the system ignores the issues that have become problematic for the global economy. From a historical perspective, the deflation of a financial bubble is not new. Nor is its contagion effects, although globalisation has deepened the interdependence of markets.

The need for greater market transparency is not new either—this is a work in perpetuity for regulators as financial products continue to evolve. The novel aspect of the crisis is its origins in the household sector.

In the past, economies have experienced booms and busts according to the balance sheets of corporations, known as the business cycle. The US sub-prime collapse is evidence of a new phenomenon: the household cycle.

Advanced capitalism has made finance available to consumers on a mass scale. Higher social expectations about material goods have led to highly leveraged household balance sheets, in turn creating a new source of economic volatility. While governments are accustomed to regulating corporations, they have no such experience with household budgets. Indeed, it is the antithesis of their electoral strategies, whereby they offer additional handouts to 'assist working families under financial pressure'. The uncertainty of the household cycle, with its exaggerated periods of boom and bust, is here to stay.

Prime Minister Kevin Rudd

Realism and true grit will get us through this
Address to National Press Club, Canberra, 15 October 2008

Last year in my formal reply to the last budget of the Howard Government I referred to a great remark from a great American President, John F. Kennedy. Speaking at a time of unprecedented American prosperity, Kennedy said: 'The time to fix the roof is when the sun is still shining'.

And I said back then that the sun was shining on Australia. Back then, because of an unprecedented global economic boom, the sun had been shining on Australia for the better part of a decade.

But all that began to change, a little more than three months later, with the beginning of what we now have come to call the global financial crisis. What began as a patch of bad weather in America has now become a cyclone that threatens to engulf the world.

It has smashed its way across the globe. It has swept aside financial institutions that had survived a combination of world wars and great depressions across the centuries. And it has even threatened the finances of nations themselves, with one nation-state declaring itself to be officially bankrupt.

These are testing times. But my message to the nation today is that while these winds of ill fortune have battered institutions and shattered confidence across the world, the Australian financial system remains strong.

As we contemplate the impact of this financial crisis on real economies, real people and real lives, it must also galvanise us to act in the future so that we never allow greed and lax regulation to put us in this position again. I addressed this matter in my recent speech to the United Nations General Assembly. One of the points in that speech related to executive remuneration. At that time, I said that financial institutions needed to have clear incentives to promote responsible behaviour, rather than unrestrained greed. I spoke of the need for the Basel II rules on capital adequacy to pick up this concept, specifically that regulators should set higher capital requirements for financial firms with executive remuneration packages that reward short-term returns or excessive risk-taking.

At the meeting of the Group of 20 industrialised nations next month, Australia will be arguing that the G20 engage with the Financial Stability Forum, to agree to a clear timetable for implementing this and other actions needed to protect financial stability in the future. We will be urging the G20 to commission an action agenda in collaboration with the International Monetary Fun, the Financial Stability Forum and the Basel Committee on Banking Supervision on the best means of implementing this initiative, preferably by the end of this calendar year.

Consistent with this, the Australian government will be working with the relevant Australian regulators to design a template that could be adopted by the international authorities—a template that links capital adequacy requirements to executive remuneration in a way that acts against excessive risk-taking in our financial institutions.

The Australian government and the Australian Prudential Regulation Authority will also examine what domestic policy actions would be appropriate in pursuit of this objective.

There are times in our personal lives which are of such moment that we are forced to rethink all the plans we had for our future happiness and prosperity. The same can be said of the lives of nations. The events of recent days have seen the wealth of families, companies and even sovereign states, stripped back to a degree and at a rate unprecedented in our lifetime.

Stock exchanges around the globe have responded emotionally rather than rationally to the economic crisis brought on by the collapse of the sub-prime mortgage market. The champions of extreme capitalism have been found to have feet of clay.

For the first time, our people are reading about—and my government is participating in—decisions to inject trillions of dollars back into an international financial community frozen by fear. Fear of the unknown.

To put it simply—when markets fail, governments must act. We know that from history. As a government and as a nation we must respond to the twin evils at the root of this malaise: greed and fear. Fear is the first demon we must see off. Dealing with the greed that has caused the fear will come after that.

Seventy-five years ago, the world was in the grip of a much deeper and more immobilising crisis than the one we are confronting today. US President Franklin Delano Roosevelt personally directed his government's response to that most calamitous of all collapses. One of his rules in dealing with the challenges of his time was to refrain from what he called issuing proclamations of overenthusiastic assurance. He correctly saw that we cannot ballyhoo ourselves back to prosperity.

I believe that we too must level with the Australian people about the size and seriousness of the threat to our national prosperity brought on by the evaporation of capital, realistic about the threats, but equally realistic about the strengths.

Anyone who grew up on the land, knows that you can't control the weather. Sunshine every day and rainy nights, that's what you dream of. But life's not like that. There are good years, and there are hard years. And you don't choose the order in which they come. But the hard years teach you to never give up. You learn resilience. You learn courage. You learn to plough on. That's what we as Australians must do, in the hard times that lie ahead. This is as much about our spirit as it is about the concrete decisions of policy we take.

We are not a people who panic. As Australians we take the good and the bad in our stride. We go forward. And we intend to join with other nations to rebuild the architecture of the global economy, so this global financial crisis is not repeated in the future. This will be tough. But I have absolute confidence that the nation will make it through together.

This speech can be found online at www.pm.gov.au/media/interview/2008/ interview_0554.cfm, and was published in The Australian Financial Review *on 16 October 2008.*

Bernard Keane

Big bang reform v. Rudd, Mr 5 per cent
Crikey, 2 October 2008

There's something faintly pathetic about the prime minister sitting down with the mugs who make up our state premiers today to debate the minutiae of consumer credit laws, hazardous materials and registering business names. The contrast between that and the conflagration engulfing financial markets makes the whole Council of Australian Governments (COAG) process look like an exercise in unreality.

Appearances are deceiving, however. The boring work of getting the Australian federation to work in as effective and business-friendly a manner as possible is a key reform, and the prime minister's determination to cajole, beg and bribe the states into harmonising their regulatory frameworks across a range of areas is laudable.

Economic reform in Australia doesn't tend to get noticed unless it comes with a capital R—the floating of the dollar, the end of protectionism, a new industrial relations regime, a GST. The smaller stuff, the 5 per cent stuff, is mainly of interest to businesses. That's why *The Australian Financial Review* devotes plenty of space to today's COAG meeting.

Same with the local government summit announced the week before last. That looked bizarre at the time—the world financial system in meltdown, and Rudd is talking about inviting mayors to Canberra?

But it wasn't actually a bad idea at all; given their importance to Australian businesses and to the country's economic and social infrastructure, anything that improves the performance of local governments (not taking bribes from developers springs to mind) will have significant flow-on benefits.

This is the nature of the Rudd Government. It's a 5 per cent government, the reform program of which is focussed on the unglamorous world of regulatory harmonisation, better consumer information and greater efficiency of administration, one that knows that a single set of OH&S regulations or less local government red tape won't change the world but will reduce business costs, or that better-informed consumers will get markets and service providers working more efficiently.

Such reforms yield significant long-term benefits because they mount up across the economy, year in and year out. We don't notice it because we've become used to big bang reform, led by a Keating or (to a much lesser extent) a Costello telling us it's critical to Australia's future.

Public-private partnerships are also on the COAG agenda today. The goal is to try to establish consistent guidelines for partnerships to minimise costs for businesses. But the biggest issue about public-private partnerships won't be dealt with—the problem of how to manage risk. Barring some sort of miracle recovery in the financial sector, this problem is going to have major repercussions for Australia's economic growth for decades to come.

John Quiggin wrote a series of articles for *Crikey* last year on the role of risk management across societies, suggesting that risk might be one of the central ideas of the early twenty-first century. He didn't focus specifically on financial risk, but the financial crisis has proved him right, although perhaps in a more dramatic fashion than he anticipated. The crisis arose from a grievous misjudgement about risk, a conviction that 'risk management' could amount to 'risk elimination' if it was spread thinly enough and hidden well enough.

As it turned out, that only spread the damage further.

So now we're in a risk-averse financial world, so risk-averse that no one wants to lend anyone anything.

Leveraging taxpayers' funds for infrastructure projects will now be far harder. Public-private partnerships are supposed to maximise the capacity of governments with limited funds to get major projects built now rather than years hence, but they've been plagued by an incapacity of both governments and infrastructure providers to get the risk balance right.

Usually, the likes of Mac Bank have played bureaucrats for suckers, leaving government stuck with all the downside while they reap monopoly rents. Occasionally, though, it's been the private sector left with an under-performing asset like the cross-city tunnel in Sydney.

Getting the balance right is now even harder because the cost of money has gone up and the appetite for risk among lenders has vanished. COAG fiddling with PPP guidelines is all fine as far as it goes, but the central problem of apportioning risk remains, and can only be solved by state governments getting smarter when developing projects, so each individual infrastructure proposal can be risk-assessed on its merits. This will be a key role for Infrastructure Australia when it assesses major projects for funding.

If the credit crunch continues for any length of time, however, there'll be no resolving the risk problem. Governments will simply have to take more responsibility for infrastructure, which will mean borrowing more—provided their credit ratings remain intact—spending less and raising taxes. There may not be too much of a surplus to dip into from next financial year.

The most equitable and economically efficient means of accessing more funding for infrastructure is by making its users pay for it. Despite the growth of tollways, most of our road system remains free to motorists and road transport companies. Our water infrastructure is loaded with cross-subsidies and relies on rationing, not pricing, to curb demand. And our health infrastructure has virtually no price signals at all. Tougher fiscal times might encourage tougher decisions about how we fund our infrastructure.

And now that the economic growth of the last decade looks like slowing significantly, the Howard years look more like a wasted opportunity than ever. Imagine if some of that money used for electoral bribes and handouts had been directed towards urban infrastructure—particularly public transport. Or even funnelled into superannuation, providing Australia with a greater buffer against the credit crisis. We'll be paying for Howard and Costello's profligacy for years to come.

Dennis Shanahan

Living up to its promise
The Australian, 22 November 2008

During the last sitting week of parliament, affable Defence Minister Joel Fitzgibbon took advantage of a lull in proceedings to hand Kevin Rudd a quickly scribbled note. Even from a distance it was clear it was a plea for a chat with the prime minister, and Rudd immediately concurred, motioning Fitzgibbon, not a close friend but a crucial numbers man during his leadership bid, to sit in the vacant chair beside him. It was a friendly, open-handed wave with the air of an avuncular counsellor offering a sympathetic ear.

Fitzgibbon's mood was intense. He immediately began to discuss his problem, and Rudd listened in a relaxed manner as the minister's right index finger sketched lines and subsets on the leather-topped table.

Oblivious to his colleagues and the counting of a parliamentary division, Fitzgibbon earnestly conferred with his leader. After less than eight minutes, he looked a little relieved but still less than happy for a normally ebullient man who has Rudd's confidence and support.

Two days later, Fitzgibbon was chairing a secluded meeting of his defence chiefs to sort out concerns over the production of the government's national security review and the defence white paper, which are aimed at updating and reassessing Australia's intelligence and defence capacities and needs but which have been dogged by delays.

At the heart of that parliamentary vignette was all that is good and bad about the style, habits, attitudes and character of Rudd, elected prime minister a year ago on 24 November. Rudd is riding high in the opinion polls, battling the global financial crisis, still the centre of attention and still well ahead of his third Liberal opponent in just two years. As perhaps the least-prepared prime minister that Australia has had for decades, he has had a good first year of delivering promises, including the early high point of the apology to the Stolen Generations. He also has avoided ministerial scandals, big mistakes and instability.

But that Fitzgibbon had to approach Rudd in full public gaze, including the assembled Opposition, is evidence that Rudd is central to the administration, politics and control of the Labor government, and that has its drawbacks.

There is still a concentration on Kevinism, understandably given his success and personal satisfaction rating of 65 per cent in the latest Newspoll survey, only a smidgeon away from his record 71 per cent rating in April. Yet the centralising of Rudd's role shows his reluctance to delegate or trust others, and leads to internal managerial shortcomings.

But that Fitzgibbon was able to go away and address problems confronting Australia's national security strategy is evidence of Rudd being in calm control when he does make a decision and consults his colleagues.

Apart from the new government still essentially being about Rudd, his popularity and authority, the encounter with his frustrated and isolated defence minister occurred in large part for several fundamental reasons. The first is the understandable delay in a long-term Opposition coming to grips with being in government and its early tendency to use state political techniques that are heavily reliant on appearances and news cycles. Rudd's tight inner circle is aware of this challenge and is consciously moving towards a program that looks ahead and concentrates on a couple of big issues at a time.

There is a realisation that Labor's lack of a narrative to explain and link its decisions overall for the public, which threatened to leave the government ill-defined, requires concentration to address and not an over-enthusiastic, scattergun approach with too many themes. Of course, the advent of the global financial crisis has meant Rudd, Treasurer Wayne Swan and Finance Minister Lindsay Tanner, along with the rest of the government, are being defined by their reaction to a huge external threat. It has been part of an extremely steep learning curve for a new government.

It is here, within the operations of government, that Rudd's leadership characteristics and style are crucial for a positive outcome in a slowing world economy.

Certainly Rudd doesn't blindly hold the view that his government can't be a oncer, especially if unemployment rises and there is little money in the budget to spend to meet high expectations.

Some of the defining characteristics of Rudd as a prime minister and leader are: deep but narrow enthusiasms and interests; interference in areas that interest him; trusting only a handful of people, whom he tends to overload; tardiness in developing wide cabinet consultation; an obsessive determination to get on top of issues; his willingness to consult trusted public servants (and defence chiefs) directly and often but otherwise talking with too few people; a commitment to meeting promises; and the all-consuming challenge of the global financial crisis. All of these characteristics, difficulties or quirks are showing signs of being addressed by '24/7 Kevin' in his typically hands-on and micro-managing manner.

There have been delays in dealing with submissions to cabinet and its National Security Committee; there are delays in communicating the decisions to ministers and departments; and there are continuing stories of prime ministerial calls to people late at night, in the early hours of the morning and soon after dawn, as the man in the Lodge seems to shut down only between 2 a.m. and 6 a.m.

As he says, in time-honoured Strine, he's 'flat out like a lizard drinking'.

There are also suggestions that requests for information that 'the PM needs to know' are often not destined to form part of a submission or action as assumed but merely self-tutoring, where Rudd wants to get on top of an unfamiliar area. As he becomes more confident, the requests ease off. Conversely, he can endlessly interfere where he feels confident, and constant, last-minute demands for changes to submissions and speeches can delay decisions and create backlogs.

Rudd believes the first twelve months have been good for a Labor Party that was so long in Opposition and is faced with the greatest financial and economic crisis since the Depression.

'It's been tough and demanding, with two realities: legitimate expectations of the government newly elected replacing a government of nearly a decade and, secondly, being confronted almost immediately with the impact of the worst financial crisis since the first half of last century', Rudd told the Inquirer in an interview before leaving for the Asia-Pacific Economic Co-operation summit in Peru this weekend.

'I think people get that', he says, but adds that the real test for his government is how it handles the crisis.

'I think what [the voters] want to know is, are you working your butt off in handling it? Are you being fair dinkum about the challenge and are you being practical about the response?'

After a $10.4 billion economic stimulus package, guarantees for bank deposits, a string of interest rate cuts, $6 billion support for the car industry and $300 million for local councils, Rudd is confident voters will give the government credit.

'I think most people will conclude we are working diligently', he says, but he has concerns about the ongoing impact of the global credit crisis on Australia's budget bottom line and his government's ability to keep up reforms and stay on top of the economy.

Rudd is no easy subscriber to the view that Labor can't be a oncer government and, like every government elected since World War II, will get at least two terms. It is a theory that has a dangerous air of complacency and arrogance, and one that Rudd rejects outright.

When asked if he can assume a win at the next election, due in 2010, his adamant reply is: 'Absolutely not. It's never been my view: I'm not built that way and I don't think that way', he says, and tough economic times only make him more convinced of the difficulty of winning any election.

While there is a recognition the government will have to continue to develop reforms in education, industrial relations, tax and welfare, his two almost all-consuming subjects now are the financial crisis and the carbon pollution reduction scheme.

Rudd has daily briefings with the treasurer, and with Treasury Secretary Ken Henry whenever possible, which can last a couple of hours as they get across the detail of the latest financial developments.

These are regularly followed by a two or three-hour meeting about climate change or hours of National Security Committee meetings.

Despite Swan's nervous start as treasurer, and previously being at political loggerheads with Rudd when he was trying to knock off Kim

Beazley as Labor leader, the two old Queensland mates have re-established a close relationship.

Rudd is pleased with Swan's work ethic and the hours he puts in, and those close to the prime minister say the two have become 'joined at the hip'. The man who accused Rudd of undermining Beazley now has his 'unswerving support'.

Others in the government say the blokey Brisbane bond is working again and the relationship is close after two decades together in 'the political and economic trenches'. 'They are the two hardest working people in the government and everyone else tries to keep up', one insider says.

It is certainly a hallmark of Rudd's behaviour that once he trusts someone he tends to want to trust them with everything. Swan and Henry have been given huge burdens on tax reform, welfare reform, handling the financial crisis response and crunching the numbers on an emissions trading scheme. As a result, Treasury is feeling the pressure and Henry has become a political target, accused of lending his credibility to an inexperienced government.

The same is true of Julia Gillard, who fulfils the job of deputy prime minister—which includes a lot of time as acting prime minister directing Cabinet and parliament—and holds the portfolios of education and workplace relations.

Although the plan may be to ease the industrial relations burden from Gillard once Labor's legislation is in place, it is only her natural abilities and organisational flair that keep her from being swamped.

Water and Climate Change Minister Penny Wong—'the Wongster', as Rudd affectionately calls her—also is shouldering a heavy burden as she runs the government's projects to replenish and revive the Murray–Darling basin while developing a carbon pollution reduction scheme with a tight 2010 deadline.

Politically, Rudd has done extremely well with Labor's election promises and the great symbols of ratifying the Kyoto Protocol on climate change and directing the parliamentary apology to the Stolen Generations.

Yet the inexperience of a government preparing its first budget left Rudd politically mugged by pensioners. It was a hurtful shock to the government to discover pensioners turning on it when they felt they had been short-changed. John Howard always made a great deal publicly of pensioner funds in the budget so that their political impact was much greater than their dollar contribution. It was a political mistake that left Labor feeling a bit betrayed, but it's not a mistake that will be repeated.

That's the positive side of Rudd's unquenchable thirst for information, his tireless need to be in control and his interference from on high: he's taking nothing for granted and is adjusting his political strategy to stay in government.

Michelle Grattan

Eye of the storm
The Age, 15 November 2008

When the history of Kevin Rudd's Government is written, its first year's iconic image will be of the prime minister, sleeves rolled up, flanked by key advisers, grappling on Saturday, 11 October, with the local fallout of the financial crisis abroad.

That was the weekend when the government moved from being on the sidelines to crafting extensive direct action—notably the guarantee of bank deposits and borrowings and its fiscal stimulus package—as the crisis started to seriously bear down on Australia.

The dramatic shift of the tectonic plates of the international financial system, transforming the world's and Australia's economic landscapes, has become the overwhelming dynamic as the government prepares to celebrate its first anniversary.

Treasury's advice in the transition 'Red Book' it gave the government after the 24 November election has proved more prophetic than the bureaucrats could have dreamed.

'You have been elected at a pivotal economic juncture', Treasury told its new masters. 'You have inherited an economy that is experiencing its longest period of uninterrupted growth since Federation, but which faces a number of short and medium-term challenges that are becoming increasingly acute. The economic policy directions struck in the coming 12 months will be critical.'

Despite its dramatic rhetoric, Treasury late last year was still sanguine about growth, projecting 3.5 per cent in its budget update for 2008–09. Its main worry was inflation. A year later, Treasury has scaled back to 2 per cent growth for 2008–09 (the Reserve Bank is more pessimistic), and the debate is about whether Australia can avoid recession. A $22 billion May budget surplus has shrunk to an expected $5.4 billion. The speculation is that before long the budget will go into deficit.

Former Prime Minister Bob Hawke notes about Rudd: 'No (previous) prime minister has ever faced the double whammy of a world financial crisis of significant proportions plus the economic challenge of climate change'.

The crisis has been taking several hours of Rudd's time daily. He is now in Washington for the G20 meeting. Treasurer Wayne Swan (also in Washington) is often exhausted. Policy has had to be made on the run, and if necessary adjusted later. Most of the government's future plans are up for review.

It's not all bad for Rudd, however. As one ministerial staffer says: 'The financial crisis has been the circuit breaker to allow him to step up to the plate and show leadership'. One Labor man says that without it, the talk would still be of Labor needing a narrative.

Events have hastened the end of that everything-is-possible optimism characterising new administrations. But the government has kept its head and its discipline; it has lost no minister to scandal or maladministration.

Rudd, with 71 per cent approval, is still smiled on by the public. *The Age*/Nielsen pollster John Stirton points out this isn't unusual. Nielsen data shows 'the last six Australian prime ministers have maintained or increased their popularity with voters in their first year'; Rudd is on the high end of the scale (second to Hawke).

Four (Rudd, John Howard, Hawke and Malcolm Fraser) were in a winning position one year into the job. Paul Keating and Gough Whitlam were struggling, although both went on to win the subsequent election.

Though history and current polling is in his favour, Rudd's majority of only 16 makes the 2010 election within reach for the Opposition, which rapidly replaced Brendan Nelson with Malcolm Turnbull, injecting both unpredictability and vitality into the Coalition's attack.

As in previous administrations, this government is very much shaped by the style of its leader. Rudd—a former bureaucrat—is a stickler for process, which prompted the droll observation that his government 'hit the ground reviewing'. That commitment to process involves many meetings and much paper, and care that decisions are properly recorded so there is no confusion later.

Rudd's colleagues see him as super-human in his relentless work habit. They regard their leader with respect rather than warmth. A backbencher says: 'He's a very clinical person. He reminds me of someone performing serious surgery in a way where there's no passion or emotion'.

Rudd, however, sweats over important speeches. He so fiddled with his United Nations General Assembly address that the final draft was run off twenty minutes before delivery. When he gave a big business speech on 10 October, he abandoned the draft and wrote it virtually from scratch. (Later that night at Kirribilli, he had the infamously leaked George Bush phone call about the G20.)

But he can also enjoy a touch of humour. At drinks to thank public servants for their work on the economic security package, Rudd gave Treasury secretary Ken Henry a present. Henry opened it to find a copy of John Maynard Keynes's *General Theory*—particularly appropriate, given the Keynesian nature of the package.

Ministers find Rudd approachable and say he runs Cabinet well, but there is criticism that the decision-making process can be too confined to the Rudd circle. A kitchen cabinet (formally the Strategic Priorities and Budget Committee) of Rudd, Deputy Prime Minister Julia Gillard, Swan and Finance Minister Lindsay Tanner in effect makes most of the key economic decisions.

By temperament, experience and sense of history, this government is much better equipped to handle the international economic buffeting than was the Scullin Government when it was hit by the 1929 Depression, or the Whitlam Government coping with the 1970s oil shock. Still, it remains hostage to outside events. And to forces within the system, too. So far, the new Senate has proved an irritant for the government but not a serious block; however, the big tests are still ahead, especially when it presents its climate change legislation.

Rudd arrived in office with nearly as many promises as Whitlam did, and equal determination to implement them. His first budget resembled an overstuffed Christmas stocking, crowned with the tax cuts. Rudd's insistence on delivering on his word, which he thought important in building trust, has been a hallmark of this first year. Now that future policies are under tougher scrutiny, his meticulousness is political credit in the bank.

For the longer term, Rudd pledged more co-operative federalism (already looking pie in the sky) and a comprehensive infrastructure program (for which funds are likely to be tighter than expected). He announced after the 2020 summit an overhaul of the tax system, preceded by a major inquiry.

Rudd's penchant for reviews, while not unreasonable, puts a hobble on rapid reform; equally, these ensure the government will be hit with many ideas in the 2010 election countdown and when money will be scarce.

A third of the way through the term, Rudd cannot point to such dramatic economic reform as the Hawke Government—which quickly floated the dollar—could boast at a comparable point. On the other hand, there is less opportunity for mammoth structural change these days.

In general, the government has handled the economy deftly although there have been glitches. The most serious was the initial failure to put a cap on the bank deposit guarantee. This exacerbated the flow of money out of mortgage funds, leading to more of them freezing investors' dollars.

One minister observes: 'You can't be as sure-footed as people would like when no one is sure what the proper footing is'.

Australian National University professor of economics Bob Gregory, a one-time Reserve Bank board member, says there is no doubt the government has done well in economic management. But he points to some flaws 'around the edges'. Apart from the problem over the banking guarantee, he was surprised the government 'flipped and flopped' about pension increases.

Then there is the rhetorical trap in which the government finds itself. To justify its economic measures, Gregory says, it has to warn of disasters around the corner when the numbers are still showing growth, and people—apart from those with investments—are not yet feeling the full consequences of the financial crisis.

Despite official projections of a continuing surplus, Gregory predicts the government will be looking at a deficit some time in its second year, which he says will put the spotlight on Employment Minister Gillard (as jobless numbers go up) and Tanner (with the need for spending priorities to be reordered).

More than the Whitlam or even Hawke governments (the Accord with the union movement notwithstanding), the Rudd Government was helped to office, in practical terms, by the unions, which provided huge funds and manpower in marginal seats to fight WorkChoices.

Yet the unions find themselves, while not actually in the cold, certainly not on the Rudd A-list. One union leader says: 'In the area of industrial relations we are treated equally as the employers are treated—that is not a good thing, because in the end it's our party'.

The union movement thinks the coming industrial relations legislation rolling back WorkChoices does not go far enough. Some union sources sheet part of the blame back to their own leadership, for not being tough enough in pre-election negotiations. The government is delivering exactly what it foreshadowed.

Bill Ludwig, boss of the Australian Workers' Union (whose son Joe is a minister) reflects the ambivalence in the movement. 'Any Labor government is a darn sight better than a conservative government. I think it will be a good government in the long haul', he says. But it was a 'bit conservative' in its pre-election promises—such as the undertaking to keep the very powerful Australian Building and Construction Commission until 2010. (The ABCC is one of the few issues causing a rumble in the quiescent Caucus, but the stirring has been successfully contained.)

Ludwig also says the government is being too slow in winding back WorkChoices. Rudd has both thrown off Labor tradition and embraced it. He is more distant from the unions than Hawke (unsurprisingly) and Keating. But in his commitment to a sweeping and activist government policy on infrastructure, there is much of the old-style Labor approach. And he is distinctly interventionist in his industry policy, shown in the multi-billion-dollar car plan and his frequent refrain that he doesn't want to live in a country that doesn't make things.

Two of the government's early defining gestures were the ratification of the Kyoto Protocol on greenhouse gas emissions and the apology to the Stolen Generations. In each case, the initial euphoria has been followed by controversy over detail as policy moves beyond symbolism into practical details.

The emissions trading scheme, which the government still says it plans to start in 2010, despite the economic crisis, will have a modest beginning, which will disappoint the more radical advocates. John Connor, head of the Climate Institute, says the real judgement about the first year cannot be made until December, when the government puts out its white paper, with medium-term targets, and 'we see the colour of their mustard'.

'It's been a solid and credible consultation process', Connor says. 'I was very impressed with the way they communicated the Treasury model-ling—showing that significant reductions of emissions are affordable and achievable.'

While respecting the need for symbolism, a test the Howard Government failed, the Rudd Government has been as pragmatic as its predecessor on Indigenous affairs, continuing the Northern Territory inter-vention and declining to make some of the changes critics wanted.

There is a spectrum of opinion about its performance. Pat Dodson said sharply in his recent Sydney Peace Prize lecture: 'Much that the Closing the Gap policy is about is laudable but it is not compensation to the indi-viduals who suffered under the child-removal policies aimed at ridding Australia of its Indigenous peoples'.

Warren Mundine (a former Labor Party president but with an inde-pendent voice on Aboriginal affairs) believes the government is 'heading in the right direction'; a pragmatic approach is the only way to improve Indigenous society over the next decade, he says.

Rudd has combined the predictable with the unexpected. No one should have been surprised that he appointed the nation's first female gov-ernor-general (Queenslander Quentin Bryce). More out-of-the-blue was that former Deputy Prime Minister Tim Fischer was given the plum post of Australia's first full-time ambassador to the Vatican. The new Chief Justice of the High Court, Robert French, was a good choice—but Rudd is said to have actually preferred a Queenslander (there were getting to be too many from the prime minister's home state among government appointments). Like Howard before him, Rudd keeps a careful hand on the patronage.

Unlike Howard, he has been sparing with the axe. Departmental sec-retaries known to be sympathetic to the former government survived. Inherited political appointees, such as United Nations ambassador Robert Hill and ambassador to Rome Amanda Vanstone, were not recalled.

Rudd's stricture to the public servants—in essence, don't complain about hard work and long hours—might have annoyed some, but he has operated closely with, and relied upon, the senior bureaucrats in the financial crisis.

In no area has Rudd shown his style and ambition more than in foreign policy. He has not let the domestic demands of the first year limit an extensive travel schedule, including an 18-day around-the-world trip in March–April. His plans for middle-power diplomacy are grand, including eyeing a Security Council seat for Australia and floating the idea of an Asia-Pacific Community.

He has used the global financial crisis to help him pursue his desire for international influence. He devoted much of his speech at the United Nations to outlining a plan for how the world should handle future financial arrangements and he urged the international community to work through the G20 in planning for the future. This weekend he gets to take his place at that table.

8
Hope and Strife

Craig Sherborne

Coup-coup land: Life under Fiji's interim government

The Monthly, October 2008

In coup-coup land people live in cages.

'How come the people live in cages, Babba?'

'They're not cages!' Babba scoffs.

But Babba is wrong. They are cages: houses wrapped in wire grills that are sturdier-looking than the shanty homes they protect. Wire covers backyards, too, like a kennel-run for the kids, to keep menace at bay. Fences crowned with barbed wire. Padlocks as big as grapefruit. And this is a nice palm-jungle rural road, where girls wait in neatly ironed grey uniforms for the school bus to Nadi. Sure, young Fijian men amble along the dusty roads, shirts tied around their heads, carrying machetes. But they don't look that threatening. The machetes are for coconut splitting. They are poor, they are bored—healthily muscled, though, and with a wide grin to offer the Fijian g'day: *Bula*.

Even the funeral parlours here are caged, as if there's profitable trade in pawning corpses. In shop windows, houses are advertised for lease as having a 'good compound, fully fenced all over and with full security system'. And security guards. Fiji has more security guards than you can poke a nightstick at. In Lautoka, in the main island's north-west, the Chilli Tree cafe, a quiet Formica place to get quiche and a cuppa, has a security guard sitting on a stool at the door. He opens the door for you, sits back down and stares as if roaming hoards are about to raid the pasta mix.

Babba is a 40-year-old horseman who rents out his raggedy nags to backpackers for beach rides. 'No, my friend', he says. 'They are not cages. They are good protection.'

'From what?'

'Crime. There's crime everywhere in the world.'

'Must be a crime spree to need that sort of protection.'

He shakes his head, dismissing such a notion. 'Steel wire, I think, is cheaper in Fiji than anywhere else.'

The caged houses and businesses are, Babba says, mostly Indian occupied. 'That is a very complex matter here in Fiji—between native Fijians and Indians. Our last coup was a coup to help the Indians, that's what they said.'

There have been four coups in Fiji since 1987, though the first and second blended into one, as they were only four months apart. All are considered 'bloodless', but that's not quite true. In the 2000 coup, four soldiers were killed. For twenty-one years the place has lurched from democracy to dictatorship, to quasi-democracy, to belligerent—if bumbling—dictatorship. The last coup, the one Babba speaks of, took place in 2006 and is touted by the current dictatorship (which refers to itself as an interim government) as 'the coup to end all coups'. The one that will prevent people couping up to do it all again.

Babba is having a good coup. 'I like this last coup. It is helping rural people. It is helping Indians. I say that as an Indian myself. It's good for my business, because before it happened there was talk that tourists were going to be charged for using the beaches. That would have driven me out of work.'

Ronnie, a Nadi odd-jobber, boasts of running a small, part-time pimping operation—'Nice Fijian girl $100 the night, or $20 the hour'—likes the coup, too. 'The military don't bother people who don't bother them. They stick to themselves. Look around you. Do you see soldiers anywhere?'

Tourists in All-Blacks T-shirts or Collingwood caps come out of Nadi airport and lead their Pepsi-sucking sulky brood straight to the resorts—to the buffets and cocktails, the golf carts, the air-conditioning and internet access. To the servile greetings of the staff with hibiscus behind their ears: the *Bula* offered so often, as if there's a quota of pleasantness to get through, that it starts to grate. *Bula*-shit.

Sitting in resort mini-vans, visored by their Bollé sunglasses, the tourists wouldn't know there was a coup. Nor, perhaps, would they care—

they're not this brother's keeper. For them, a coup is a footy team recruiting a star player. Off through sun-glaring, coconut-bunched holiday Fiji they go. They want the ocean's blue carpet with creamy tassels, not politics and poverty. They see the place is shabby, rusty. They see roadsides of stinking litter that council men rake into heaps and set alight until the charred bases of plastic bottles and tin cans are all that remain. But en route to their resorts the sun-fun seekers need only take a 'bracing glimpse at the poor', to quote Auberon Waugh about one of his brief, loathed excursions outside of England. They can think: Well, things can't be that bad here—we got $1.30 for an Australian dollar at the currency exchange, and Christ knows we're paying $1000 for four nights, food and drink not included.

Some might have read a report on how New Zealand's Prime Minister, Helen Clark, compares Fiji to Zimbabwe. How the New Zealand Pacific Business Council wishes she wouldn't make such 'exaggerated claims': it could affect New Zealand's $450-million-a-year export trade in the region. How the Fijian Attorney-General, Aiyaz Sayed-Khaiyum, rejects the Zimbabwe tag as 'preposterous'.

One or two might be a spirited fossicker for truth and go in search of Zimbabwe-like 11 million per cent inflation. In Zimbabwe, a loaf of bread costs $1.6 trillion—albeit Zimbabwe dollars, which have the commercial value of dandruff. In Fiji, a loaf is FJ$2–5, depending on quality. Not that bread is a staple of the Fijian diet: cassava root (a kind of bland parsnip) is the preferred substitute. At Terry Walk, in downtown Suva, navel oranges sell for FJ$4.30 a kilogram, and apples for $5.70. They are Australian oranges, New Zealand apples. Can't they grown their own oranges in this perfect weather, these lush-green unused valleys?

Fiji does have one thing in common with Zimbabwe: a bill of rights, one of those feel-good flourishes of legal puff that any wily dictator discards like a dud scratchy. According to reports from non-government organisations, Fiji's military is responsible for two hundred human-rights abuses, as well as constitutional and legal breaches, since the 2006 coup. There are accusations of torture and humiliation, intimidation, civilians being stripped naked and forced to fondle each other. The military has said that the abusers were often not soldiers, but bandits impersonating soldiers.

To direct foul language at a member of the military is considered a crime in Fiji. If you write a letter to the editor of one of the country's three daily newspapers, you might well be taken into custody if your missive is deemed anti-military. There have been blogger reports of deaths in custody, though no substantiated figures are available. The military even has the power to interfere in citizens' private lives, to mediate in marital and property disputes. Fiji's media reports this, and routinely journalists are 'detained for questioning' for their stories, though the process is more bully-boy bluff than anything.

Serafina Silaitoga, a reporter for News Limited's *Fiji Times*, was questioned by police recently because of a story she'd written about the imminent resignation of the Finance Minister, Mahendra Chaudhry. Coup leader Commodore Voreqe (Frank) Bainimarama, the interim prime minister, phoned-in the interrogation order from the Beijing Olympics, where he was watching his country's six competing athletes. Silaitoga refused to give a statement, her paper's lawyer protested against her treatment, and authorities dropped the matter.

Two Australian media executives—Russell Hunter, from the *Fiji Sun*, and Evan Hannah, from the *Fiji Times*—were deported for offending the regime. The official line was that they had breached their work permits. According to the *Fiji Times*' editor-in-chief, Netani Rika:

> Evan and I were warned that certain people in the government were not happy with us reporting in a manner they were not comfortable with. I was told that if we failed to comply with instructions, then what had recently happened to Russell Hunter would happen to Evan. If they just came out and told us not to be anti-government there would be a public outcry. So they sit on the verge of it, come up with terms such as 'be pro-Fiji' in the same way that the Singaporean media is pro-Singapore.

Even published wisecracks about government buildings needing a lick of paint can lead to interrogation. 'That's how bad it has got. They say, "We want to come and take your reporter and get a statement" over something so minor which they think makes them look bad. The '87 coup was a bit like this. But this is the worst the media has ever been harassed.'

Not that harassment works. Editorials still criticise; letters regularly accuse government ministers of corruption and cronyism. Commentators effuse moral outrage. Sitiveni Rabuka, the leader of the first coup, is a popular *Fiji Times* columnist. In his 12 August instalment, he compared Bainimarama's political agenda to the bombing of Hiroshima in 1945. 'Ours [social reform] can still result in the annihilation of a race', he wrote. A photo of a razed Hiroshima was published with the article.

But Fiji is not World War II, where millions perished. Bainimarama may be a dictator, but he's dictator-lite. Rika's justification for the piece is routine journo-speak about 'public interest': that Rabuka's opinions are his own, not Rika's or the paper's; and that such an article, however shocking, helps air people's concerns.

When you fill out Fiji's arrival card, you know you've come to a country with paranoid rulers. Understandably, the authorities demand a visitor not 'behave in a manner prejudicial to peace or good order'. But in coup-land the masters have added this Audensque couplet insisting visitors not,

> engage in any religious vocation
> except with the approval of the Department of Immigration

The current regime and the churches, especially the Methodist Church, don't get along. Methodism is the religion of Indigenous Fijians. There are around 300 000 Methodists here: more than two-thirds of the population. At the church's August conference in the capital, Suva, military officials appeared on television vowing to 'monitor' conference speakers. 'Any attempt to turn their conference into a political assembly of any matter, the police will have to take action', a spokesman said. Church leaders ignored the threat, and no action was taken. The Methodist General Secretary, Reverend Waqairatu, declared the interim government illegal and demanded that Bainimarama keep his promise to hold elections in March 2009, a promise that Bainimarama has backed away from.

Critics of the church accuse it of having more concern for Indigenous Fijians losing their political clout under Bainimarama than for democracy. For this is an unusual postcolonial country: here the Indigenous people are the oppressors of another race. They are in the majority; they are in charge. And they have the Indians to push around.

Indigenous people own 80 per cent of Fiji's land; 12 per cent is state-owned; the balance is freehold. Those percentages can't change without constitutional reform. Indians are forced to lease land from the Fijians, but leasing is limited. Indians complain that the tenancy laws are racist, bad for business, agriculture and the wider economy; Fijians complain that the rent they receive from Indians is set pitifully low. The Indians want more land so they can farm, and longer lease terms of fifty years, instead of the current thirty. They don't ask to be allowed to own that land.

Sashi Kiran, the founder of FRIEND, a support and training service for Lautoka's rural poor, disabled, ex-prisoners and street kids, says that ownership and tenancy are at the heart of Fiji's strife. 'Land and religion, even in rich countries—these are hot issues. With Fijians it's the land. They are spiritually connected to it. In the 2000 coup, many Indians were evicted from the land.' Some believe that the coup occurred because many leases were due for renewal nationwide and Fijian nationalists wanted the contracts scrapped.

From 1874 until independence, in 1970, Fiji was a British colony for sugar-cane plantations. In 1879, indentured labourers were shipped in from India and contracted for five-year stints in the sweltering fields, most of which were run by the Australian firm Colonial Sugar Refining. Indians were bashed and whipped, and unfairly paid. Future generations were allowed to lease farmland from native Fijians for their own sugar enterprises, but the relationship between Indians and Fijians was fraught. Fijians viewed the Indians as money-grubbing invaders, out to take over the country.

The Indians passively accepted their fate. But by 1970 they outnumbered Indigenous Fijians and began agitating for more rights, especially the right to more leasehold land. The post-independence constitution allowed Indians equal rights—sort of. They were given, under Fiji's ethnic-based electoral system, the same number of seats as Fijians in the House of Representatives, though an Indigenous aristocracy, the Great Council of Chiefs, had veto rights in the upper house. And for a while the new Fiji progressed promisingly: racial tension eased, and the economy was buoyant. As Rajendra Prasad noted in his 2004 book *Tears in Paradise*, a history of Indo-Fijian culture, Fiji was 'receiving applause and accolades from the international community for its success in achieving independence without bitterness or violence'.

But the racism hadn't gone away; it was merely hiding—and privately embittering a new band of Fijian nationalists. They resented Indian power-sharing and commercial enterprise, and feared a common electoral roll would replace the race-based roll and weaken Indigenous people's political power. They persuaded the chiefs that Indians should be banned from being prime minister or governor-general.

The racially mixed Fiji Labour Party, under the leadership of Prime Minister Dr Timoci Bavadra, himself an Indigenous Fijian, began a campaign to scrap this policy. But the nationalist movement had gathered too much momentum to be stopped, and its supporters were taking to the streets to protest power-sharing. That's when the first coup happened, in May 1987.

Sitiveni Rabuka, the third-ranked officer in the Indigenous-dominated Fijian military, held government members captive for a week. He established an interim administration, which, amazingly, ousted government members agreed to join. Rabuka's more radical supporters feared a counter-coup and insisted on another coup of their own, four months later. This second uprising was more radical and involved taking control of the judiciary, sacking the governor-general and declaring Fiji a republic. Indians were attacked and their businesses and temples burnt.

In 1990, the regime drew up a new constitution that enshrined Indigenous political dominance and ensured that Rabuka could never be tried for treason for his coup. He eventually became prime minister. But coup-culture ravaged the economy, and Fiji's business and professional classes had fled the country. (Following the first coup, more than 120 000 people—mostly Indians, the skilled farmers and experienced merchants—had emigrated. Economists estimate that more than half of Fiji's skilled sector has gone since then.) Nationalists believed that Fiji would return to a village-based, traditional way of life; but Rabuka realised such as attitude would create squalor, and that the Indians' business know-how was vital to Fiji's survival.

Rabuka decided he'd allow Indians to be a little more equal. 'He made a U-turn, abandoning racism and taking the road of multiracialism, to the astonishment of most', Prasad wrote. The Constitution was revamped: a generation of Indian politicians could now advance to senior positions, not least Mahendra Chaudhry, who became prime minister in 1999.

Yet Rabuka was reviled by many Indigenous Fijians for stewarding this new Fiji. He was voted from office. Extremists took to street-protesting again, bullying Indians who stood in their way; Indian houses were burned down, businesses torched, shops looted. Indians themselves were rarely attacked, Sashi Kiran recalls:

> Fijians could intimidate Indians, but not actually bring themselves to hit them. Much of the racism is whipped up from those at the top, in Suva, but out in the communities the races have to live side-by-side, and do so very peacefully. At coup-time you do see people separate on buses. Then they get back together and say sorry to each other. Even though the heart may be hurting.

In May 2000, a group of radicals united under the leadership of George Speight, a half-competent opportunist from Suva's shady business circles. He launched coup number three, invading parliament, declaring the Chaudhry government defunct and holding the cabinet hostage for fifty-six days. But unlike Rabuka, Speight didn't have widespread support among Fijians. The army wasn't enthusiastic, wasn't inspired to seize power as it had been under the charismatic Rabuka, who was one of their own.

Old class resentments within Indigenous ranks, between the easterners and westerners of the islands, caused the chiefs to bicker. Realising his coup was collapsing, Speight released the hostages and tried to cut a deal with authorities. He was arrested and sentenced to life in prison. Indigenous nationalism didn't fail with him, though. In 2001, it triumphed at the polls, when Laisenia Qarase was elected prime minister. By this time, many Indians thought their situation hopeless.

Then came the 2006 coup. A coup not like the three before it. This coup wasn't anti-Indian. Yes, Bainimarama was a Fijian military man, but he claimed his was a kind of anti-coup. A social justice coup. A coup for democracy, one that would be good and decent, that would end the oppression of Indians, introduce economic modernisation and eliminate the country's coup-culture.

Naturally, this was attractive to Indians. Mahendra Chaudhry's political career was revived: he was appointed finance minister. Not long before his resignation, in August, he boasted in the *Fiji Business Magazine* that the post-coup economy was on the mend, with exports for the first five months of 2008 up one-quarter on the same period for 2006, and debt falling. But the magazine challenged the accuracy of his figures, claiming that the economy was shrinking in the usual post-coup fashion. The Australian clothing companies Rip Curl and Billabong have been frightened off, for example; their factories in Fiji had been turning out 300 000 units a year.

A 2003 study by the economist Dr Wadan Narsey calculated that the poverty line for people in rural Fiji was about FJ$125 a week. But, according to Joseph Veramu, the director of the University of the South Pacific's Lautoka campus, 'People are getting paid $1 or $1.20 an hour to be security guards. And that's considered a princely sum'.

Sashi Kiran agrees. She says that most Indians would struggle to earn more than FJ$50 a week.

> Outsiders come to Fiji and don't consider people desperately poor. People are not skeletons here. That's because they are making a subsistence living from fishing or growing a few vegetables. One breadwinner may feed five or six people, and there is no access to medical services. Diseases such as diabetes are not managed. We are told the medicine sits in warehouses in Suva, but is doesn't get out. Actual government power largely remains in Suva, regardless of what political party we are talking about. People only come out to the rural areas to get votes.

She and FRIEND want to create commercial networks for small farmers to supply produce to resort chains and supermarkets. 'Eighty per cent of food in the hotels and resorts is imported—that could be grown here.' The current leasehold restrictions cruel that plan.

In Suva, I talk with Mannawe, who's just back from working in Iraq as a security guard. He's keen to go there again. It beats driving taxis for a pittance. 'The danger is second to the money', he says. 'We are brave, we

Fijian men. If I could earn $30000 and be there for just a handful of months, I'd be a rich man—for a Fijian.'

Fijian men like this sort of work, Joseph Veramu says.

> We have 5000 Fijians in the British army, and that's a great way to make money to send home. Our soldiers are seen as a bit like the Ghurkhas. The Fijian mentality looks up to military officers, and some-how that makes a coup seem normal to people. For Fijian people, being a warrior is their life. It's part of being a machismo male.

The symbolic centrepiece of Bainimarama's agenda is a People's Charter, part of a program for 'productive and social purposes'. A new electoral system will abolish the last vestiges of racial voting and introduce propor-tional representation in five new electorates covering all Fiji's islands. 'We want to vote for a seat as you do in Australia', Veramu says. 'The interim government views racial voting as divisive. It thinks it is causing coups.' But he dislikes the charter. 'This needs to be delivered through a democratic process, not simply imposed upon the people.' And he doubts racial inte-gration will occur, charter or no charter. 'People will still stick to their own races. School is where we must deal with that. Hindi and Muslim schools should have more Fijian children in them.'

Reverend Akuila Yabaki, the CEO of the Citizens' Constitutional Forum, a pro-multicultural, pro-democracy advocacy group, is anti-coup but supports Bainimarama's charter, especially the relaxing of land-lease laws. 'Land is a rich resource but ethno-politics rules everything in this country', he says. 'Thousands of Indians have been evicted from the land over the years.'

This is the dilemma for social-justice activists: they might hate the coup, but they love the principles behind it. 'We actually felt that, yes, the coup was for social justice. It was bizarre', says Peni Moore, a feminist and anti-violence campaigner of European descent. 'In the lead-up, there was a host of bills to be passed in parliament that we opposed. One was a so-called reconciliation bill, part of which would give the chiefs immunity for their involvement in the 2000 coup. That to me was very wrong.' Moore also takes the Bainimarama regime's side in its treatment of the

Fijian media: 'From the start of the 1987 coup, our media has supported racism. Bainimarama is a liberal. They hate him for that.'

For his part, the *Fiji Times*' Netani Rika doubts that the reforms will work. 'The concept of one Fiji, unity, setting aside people's differences, is very noble. But no document or legislation is going to make all Fijians, regardless of ethnicity, come together. People must want to. If you demand it of us, then those who sit on the fence are just going to say no', he says. 'We still send our students to school which are segregated. No charter will change that. There are racial vilification laws in Fiji, but no one takes any notice of them.'

In the lead-up to the recent Pacific Islands Forum, in Niue, Fiji was threatened with suspension from proceedings if the 2009 elections were to be delayed. Bainimarama argued that they would have to wait until the electoral system was reformed. It might take an extra year, he said. That was just an excuse for breaking his promise, Helen Clark replied. New Zealand imposed travel restrictions on Fijians and refused Bainimarama access to forum-related meetings on its soil. He responded by refusing to go to Niue.

Peni Moore is angry at the New Zealand and Australian governments for 'trying to disrupt the charter and electoral-reform process when they should be supporting it as a human-rights initiative'. And Reverend Yabaki is similarly frustrated by the two neighbours' hardline stance: 'They're much harder on this coup than they were on the other coups. You don't see people fighting in the streets here'.

Fijians don't speak of Bainimarama as a madman, a megalomaniacal Mugabe-type. Moore describes him as a socially awkward military man, used to giving orders and having them obeyed. 'I say to him: Frank, you've got to be patient. You've got to listen to other people's views. That's how you get good ideas. That's how you get goodwill.' Even Netani Rika refers to Bainimarama, almost affectionately, as Frank. But Rika believes the only way to end coup-culture is to get rid of the army, and that's unlikely to happen. 'As long as we have an army we will always have trouble.' Coup five, coup six, seven . . .

Guy Rundle

I hope, I hope, I hope: Election eve in DC
Crikey, 4 November 2008

Cab from Union Station, that great barrel-vaulted hall, the first of many suggestions of Rome you get in this most European of cities. Sharing the ride with a young couple from Germany—because there's no cabs, there's no hotel rooms—who are barely aware of the election. Not because they're not interested in it, but because they simply assume that Obama will win.

The possibility of a McCain upset—something I think is a lesser, but real, possibility, around a 20 per cent chance—does not occur to them. 'But how could anyone take McCain seriously?' Frauka says. 'Ja ja', says Horst. OK his name's not Horst and he says 'yeah yeah' but he's totally her bespectacled biatch. The white cabbie keeps his counsel. 'How would it be possible?'

It would be easy to throw back at these two harmless Germans—and that's a phrase no one who lived in most of the twentieth century would recognise—the old *Not the Nine O'Clock News* joke that the country became 'the first in Europe to start two land wars and then win the Eurovision song contest with a song about peace'.

But these are space-travellers from post-historical Europe, a place which whatever its vicissitudes, things get done, things get co-ordinated, stuff is thrashed out rationally. They have no idea what they are hitting, Frauka and not-Horst, that their travel is not in space but in time, to some place that is an amalgam of the nineteenth and twentieth and—god-helpus in its voting system the eighteenth—centuries, a place of struggle between class, between race, an undeclared, multidimensional war that cuts up the air.

Fall trees everywhere; along the train line from Philadelphia, along DC's broad avenues, trees bursting into flame, orange, red and yellow. Fall, the season of tragedy. On Friday night everyone was out for Halloween, neighbourhoods alight with pumpkin lanterns, lights in houses, kids and parents in costumes—trad ghosts and goblins and 7-year-old Sarah Palins, hair-bun, redjacket and fake specs—and you're reminded again of a double feeling.

One is the old mix of resentment and fascination, what Wim Wenders hit when he said 'the Americans have colonised our subconscious', that wow, here you are, in a Pennsylvania suburb watching Halloween feeling, how many movies did you see in rumpus rooms, old VHSs rented from the local milkbar/video store, which had a Halloween scene in it, horrors or comedies?

Here it is, the actual thing, the real, so preceded by its simulacra that it is more fascinating to you, than it is to Americans themselves. Americans just live in America, this rather mundane place of malls and ticky-tacky foreclosed houses, crappy jobs in Dilbertesque offices or chain restaurants. You—i.e. me, but also you—on the other hand, lived in Moorabbin, in Punchbowl, in Caboolture, in Glenelg, in Cottesloe, in (insert Tasmanian locale here)—and an almost identical American existence gained a gloss that its own participants do not feel.

More than anything you envy, as a citizen of one new world society immersed in another, how much ceremony they have, how much ritual, how much American life is still beyond profanation, is the sacred. Halloween, the State of the Union, Thanksgiving, Homecoming, Prom Night and Graduation, fraternities, parades, etc. etc.

When soldiers walk through airport arrival gates, people applaud. You didn't have to approve of the consent to understand as an Australian that something else is going on, something you are not only excluded from, but are defined against, the idea of 'fuss' and 'being a wanker'.

Despite the best and worst efforts of various parties, we resist any serious attempt at real celebration of nationhood. Australia Day doesn't exist, and ANZAC Day is a bizarre spectacle—in Turkey it's just a stop on the Contiki tour, in Australia it's some weird ghoul festival where people pretend to be their great grandparents by wearing their medals—and that's it. There ain't nothing else, but the beach.

My own vice is to be a serial nationalist. I loved Britain because I was half-English, but I loved Finland too, and Sweden, after about three months there, their strangeness, their pagan undercurrent, the sense that however civilised they were, the edge of the forest was close, and beyond that, all bets were off.

So it's not difficult to fall in love with America either, because for most of us, it was always there. If you grew up anytime post 1960s, you grew up on *Scooby Doo* and *Spiderman*, on *Mad* magazine and Pez sweets, on *Grease* and roller-disco, et cetera and et cetera.

I remember going to what I am told was the second McDonalds opened in Australia, in Elsternwick in the mid 1970s. Had one ever tasted anything like this before, the cheeseburger that melted on the tongue? It did so because it was 60 per cent sugar, and fell apart on the first hit of saliva, but, hey, it felt like the host, like the body of Christ. It was a sacrament, the incarnation of all those things you'd seen on the recently coloured television screen.

So America is always waiting for you. Soon as you get here, the feeling is unheimlich, uncanny. You are more at home than you were at home, you have pretty much stepped into the television screen and found it real, but that homeliness feels . . . unhomely. It was meant to keep its distance, to be forever out of reach, and here it is.

But even more strangely, America does not know America. This is a country built on the audacity of revolution, of radical and bitter conflict, of the idea that there is a necessary violence to social relations, which cannot be avoided. That violence is often directed against the weaker—native Americans, blacks, trade unionists, the Vietnamese—but America is made and reconstructed when violence or forcefulness is taken up by the weak, when the abstract sentiments of the founding documents are put into play.

Empire came so quickly to America—with the Louisiana purchase in 1803, an act which was, incidentally, flagrantly unconstitutional—that its revolutionary nature was buried almost immediately. Yet it was founded not by the second stage revolution of Jefferson and John Adams and others, but by the initial uprisings and agitation in Boston in the 1760s, directed largely by Samuel Adams, a man whom most Americans will know only as the name on a popular—and disgustingly sweet—brand of beer.

Adams fomented the American revolution in the 1760s. He made it in fact—he joined a whole series of local grievances of contradictory groups, from importers to inland farmers, to sailors—to a common theme of a general revolution, a thing which none of them had hitherto considered. He schemed, he lied, he cheated, he rabble-roused to persuade reasonable people, who wanted a normal life, to an unreasonable and violent conclusion. His world historical importance is that he was the first professional revolutionary—he had only one goal, which was the creation of revolution. Nothing more, nothing less, nothing else.

A devout Christian, he led mobs trying to lynch British soldiers. When the first shots were fired on Lexington green, a confrontation he had largely provoked, he was in hiding, with John Hancock, because the British had a death penalty on his head. He would later organise the sacking of Hancock, a lifelong comrade and friend, because he thought there was a better candidate for leader of the revolutionary army, a bloke named Washington, whose selection he ensured by sleazy politicking in Philadelphia taverns during the constitutional conventions.

Finally he wrote the articles of Confederation, the document of union that preceded the Constitution. The Confederation articles were unworkable, but they were a far more radical and democratic idea of what a nation could be—that it would be a confederation of united states—of people governing themselves, with a president of minimal powers sorting out differences between them.

Sam Adams's articles of Confederation were a post nation-state form, before the nation-state even got going. They were designed to frustrate any drive to empire, making it impossible for the president to be a de facto emperor. Almost immediately it became clear that if America were to be a trading nation—not what either Sam Adams or even Jefferson particularly wanted—treaties would need to be signed (with the Ottoman empire initially) and a president would need to have both commercial and military powers, and well, here we frikkin are.

Of all the founding fathers, Sam Adams is forgotten. Every twenty years someone writes a biography of him, trying to restore his place, but it fades away, before the second-tier revolutionaries, Jefferson, Washington and that utter charlatan Benjamin Franklin. Of course he is. A revolutionary order, if it wishes to become an empire, must forget its foundation as a series of radical gestures. The weird thing about America is that its founding base is a non-base: those words in the Declaration of Independence:

> When in the Course of human events, it becomes necessary for one people to dissolve the political bands which have connected them with another, and to assume among the powers of the earth, the separate and equal station to which the Laws of Nature and of Nature's God entitle them ...

The nub is in the question of legitimacy. How do you determine when it is necessary to dissolve bonds? The deep import of the D of I is anarchistic—it puts the bias of right towards the revolutionaries, the breaker-uppers. If you're going to keep a country together you need to bury that impulse really deep, have it forgotten.

But you can't ever bury it completely. The more you try to squash it, the more it returns as the repressed. The repression is obvious, it is two million in prison, it is 'American exceptionalism' it is 'we never surrender' it is etc. etc. Its opposite is more elusive.

It returns in dreams of chaos, in Tarantino films, in neighbourhoods the cops won't go, yes in Halloween, or in John Brown and Harpers Ferry, and Bill Ayres and Bernadine Dohrn, and people who come to the conclusion that such great evil is being done in their name that they must risk the death of innocents to stand in its path.

Yes of course the right are right. Barack Obama, though almost certainly a centrist now, was formed in the crucible of the left—of radical leftist circles in Hawaii, Occidental college in California, of the Harlem and Chicago lefts. Of course he is a transformational person utterly unlike that worthless c-cklicking twunt Tiny Blair (remember him?).

There is no need to doubt his own record from his autobiography, that he worked through black liberation, Marxism, the New Party etc. etc., and ultimately came to a conclusion that corresponds to Anthony Giddens's idea of the radical centre, that things could be done in the heart of it all.

So if for all that he wins, yes, I think this will be a transformation of America, its self, its role in the world, a situation that will be productive. A situation far beyond the greasy trading of political advantage.

For all the hundreds of people, the thousands I have met in America, I hope he wins, for their improved access to healthcare, even those who opposed it as socialism. Their capacity for self-delusion is total. When you tell them of (Oz) medicare, they cannot believe it—twenty bucks for a GP visit, free blood tests . . . they think of its signs and wonders . . .

Had there been a Republican Congress I would have urged a McCain victory, because that would have got us to a third world war quicker, and that can only be to the good, in revolutionary terms. But a split Congress—White House admin . . . there's no good in it . . .

I think a unified presidency and Congress, of Democratic nature, would be the last gasp of the idea that Western capitalism can restore itself which of course it can't, but would allow a space for other things to develop. America has ceased to be interesting. China, India, that's interesting. America has ascended to its final status, which is as subject matter for a Hopper picture.

I hope I hope I hope that a sufficient number of people have been summoned to the future by Obama's concrete proposals and general approach to vote for a future. But who knows?

And in the final hours, Obama's white grandma died. I vaguely recall that Mungo got into trouble for saying in 1974 that the best thing Bob Menzies could do would be to die for his party and give them a state funeral, and come on, you'd have to think it's possible that McCain even now is in Arizona with his hands around his 96-year-old mother's neck . . .

But God it's hard not to be moved. There's a 110-year-old woman in Texas, whose father was a slave, a SLAVE, and she's voting this week. Come on . . . blow wind and crack thou cheeks and let a coupla tears go for that . . . she is part of the same historical moment, but there is so much more than that . . . we are the dreams our parents had, their dreams of dreams, the sense of possibility projected into the future . . .who knows who 'Toot', Obama's grandmother, was?

She was a white Kansan woman who accepted her crazy hippy daughter's mixed-race child and raised him through his adolescence. Forget all judgements for a moment. She stepped up, she gave him something, now on display. If the Obama campaign means anything, if its victory means anything, it is that we do not live by our fears but by our hopes, our sense of what is possible, of the best in any national etc. tradition we find ourselves in.

And should it fail . . . well godhelpus . . . but we go on we can't go on we go on . . .

The cab pulls up. Remind yourself that you live in an empire, not a dream, the sugar-white dome of the Capitol in the window. The old Marxist in me wants conflict, dissatisfaction and chaos, but the man who has one life on earth, rapidly draining away, can only say I hope that Americans tap into their radical past, the ghost of Sam Adams, their political unconscious, and rip it up, and f-ck the empire, and go Obama, and I am now going to a bar to drink to Toot, and her daughter, Obama's mother ('getting up at 4 a.m. to learn English ain't a holiday for me either Buster'), who never saw this come to pass, but whose dreams were folded into realities at every moment . . .

Ya es da dia.

Noel Pearson

Man with his work cut out
The Australian, 8 November 2008

In ordinary times, just the election of the first African American president of the United States would be greatness and history enough. But these are not normal times. No one can know in advance whether the hour and the man are met in the person of Barack Hussein Obama.

Great expectations centre on what Obama will mean for race in America's future.

African American intellectual Shelby Steele was wrong about Obama's capacity to manage the politics of race in his path to the presidency. But he was right that racism is not the insuperable barrier the victim leadership among blacks and liberal whites have for too long made it out to be. While Steele's political analysis was faulty, his analysis of the psychology of race remains true.

Steele speaks of two masking strategies undertaken by blacks in the United States to make their way as a minority in a world controlled by the white majority: challenging and bargaining. Challengers are people such as Jesse Jackson, who challenge discrimination and racialism in the majority. Prior to the achievement of civil rights, challengers had a long and rich pedigree stretching back from Martin Luther King back to WEB DuBois and anti-slavery campaigner Frederick Douglas.

Steele does not completely decry challenging: in the era of segregation and prior to civil rights, it was indeed imperative. Steele's thesis is, however, that in the post-civil rights period challenging became the predominant method of a new victim leadership that challenged white America, and extracted (Steele's word is extorted) concessions on the basis of their guilt, for the past and for continuing prejudice.

White guilt became a source of social leverage for too many black leaders.

Obama, like a pantheon of successful African Americans from Sidney Poitier to Oprah Winfrey, makes a bargain with white America: 'I won't hold your history of racism against you if you don't use my race against me'. The bargainer also has a long lineage in American history, exemplified by Booker T Washington. In the era of segregation the bargainer's popular characterisation was the derogatory Uncle Tom. In the post-civil rights era, bargaining became respectable.

Is there any alternative to this terrible binary for black Americans? Or black Australians for that matter?

Put aside millennial hopes that Obama will achieve a post-racial America or some other form of race transcendence. Rather, Obama can achieve an apex within Steele's dialectical paradigm: a position where blacks and whites take responsibility for race. For both the emphases of responsibility will be different. For whites to take responsibility, they must not dismiss racialism as a real social evil, and they must understand that past discrimination left a legacy. For blacks to take responsibility, they must wake up to the fact that racism does not present the kind of barriers to full citizenship that it once represented and that it is not a catch-all explanation for all of their problems. And critically, problems of race—however real they may be—must not justify a psychology and politics of victimhood.

The leader that achieves this apex of responsibility concerning race will be one who both challenges and bargains. Obama has used both during the course of his campaign. While he was predominantly the bargainer, there were also indications of his inclination to challenge. Obama will achieve great things for racial politics if he fashions a post-victimhood challenge for whites and blacks (we can and will all live up to our creed) and a post-victimhood bargain (blacks can take a fair place in America without needing white guilt).

Beyond the question of race, there are three domestic policy agendas that confront the United States in this time of crisis, to which Obama must forge solutions: the problem of the American underclasses; the problem of the American working poor; and the need for a national gain-sharing deal between those who take the upside and those who wear the downside of globalisation.

There is already precedent that the first challenge is amenable to solutions, and much progress has already been made. A decade after the welfare reforms introduced by Bill Clinton in 1996 and those prescriptions falling under the policy rubric of the 'new paternalism'—mandating personal responsibility and matching it with new opportunity—the way forward is clear for the new president-elect. He must redouble these efforts. He must break through on the kind of education reforms that were intended but not achieved by Bush's No Child Left Behind policy. If he is to succeed, he must find solutions to the greatest barrier facing education reform: the teachers' unions which represent the strongest power base within his Democratic Party. Like Paul Keating and Bill Kelty faced with economic reform in Australia, Obama must enjoin his closest allies to the cause of reform.

Of course it will be the extent to which Obama is determined to tackle the problems of the underclass that will largely determine whether the election of a black president will have meant anything substantial for African-Americans.

Australians can scarcely relate to the dimensions of the second challenge: the working poor. Most Australians, while used to the problem of poverty suffered by those who do not work, would be horrified at how so many millions of people can work hard and take responsibility, and yet remain poor.

The impact of economic change on the lot of the working classes in the United States, and the hollowing-out of the lower middle classes, is a challenge to which Obama has devoted much promise of hope and change. During the long period of boom, no real solutions emerged for the many Americans cobbling together a living from multiple jobs, working long hours in conditions that Australians can scarcely imagine. Now in the time of economic crisis, Obama has held out the expectation he will fix the woes of working America. The problem of the working poor is a structural phenomenon of globalisation in developed countries.

The third challenge suggests a solution to the first two. The winners from globalisation must make a deal with the losers. One half of the nation can't just take the upside and the other half the downside. The argument that free-market economics and globalisation is about growing the cake for everyone's benefit can be accepted by all members of the nation. But it is not only the size of the cake that has grown, but also the allocation of the share of the cake, which has changed incredibly in favour of the advantaged.

Former Clinton administration Labour Secretary Robert Reich recently pointed out that the top 1 per cent of Americans took home 20 per cent of the country's total national income. In 1980 the top 1 per cent took 8 per cent.

If the United States is to continue to pursue prosperity through globalisation, then the national economy must be reformed so that gain-sharing is the central policy principle.

Plainly the danger is that Obama and the Democrats will retreat from globalisation. The opportunities of globalisation are not the problem: they are part of the solution. The challenge for Obama is how to ensure all American citizens share the costs and benefits.

The global financial crisis makes it impossible for the advantaged classes who have enjoyed such enormous benefits from globalisation to continue to insist on their right to privatise the upside and socialise the downside. Viewed like this, the economic crisis facing the president-elect presents him with an opportunity to revitalise and reform America in ways that would otherwise have been impossible.

Contributors

Phillip Adams is a veteran of Australian punditry, film and radio, and is among our most widely published columnists. His career began in 1954 in Melbourne's *The Guardian* and *The Bulletin*. Long associations with *The Australian* and *The Age* followed, with detours to *The Sydney Morning Herald*, *The Advertiser*, the *Courier-Mail*, *Nation Review*, *The National Times* and *The London Times*. Described by Robert Manne as 'perhaps the most remarkable broadcaster in the history of this country', he has presented *Late Night Live* for more than twenty years and currently contributes a weekly column to *The Australian.*

Janet Albrechtsen writes a weekly column for *The Australian*. A former lawyer with a doctorate in law, she has also written for the *Wall Street Journal*, *The Australian Financial Review*, *The Sydney Morning Herald*, *The Age* and other publications. She is a member of the board of the Australian Broadcasting Corporation.

Waleed Aly is a lecturer in politics at Monash University where he also works within the Global Terrorism Research Centre. His political and social commentary has appeared in *The Guardian*, *The Australian*, *The Sydney Morning Herald* and *The Age*, as well as in regular segments on ABC TV and radio. His first book, *People Like Us*, was published in 2007.

Shaun Carney is Associate Editor and National Political Columnist with *The Age*. A graduate of Monash University, he is the author of two books, *Australia In Accord*, which examined the labour market changes of the 1980s, and a biography, *Peter Costello: The New Liberal*. In 2003, he received a commendation from the Walkley Award judges for his column-writing.

Michael Costello is the Chief Executive Officer of ActewAGL. He is currently Chairman of Ecowise Environmental Pty Limited and of the National Stock Exchange Limited. Costello was previously the secretary of the Department of Foreign Affairs and Trade and the Department of Industrial Relations. He was chief of staff to the Hon Kim Beazley AC, a former Labor Opposition leader, and to the Hon Bill

Hayden AC when he was the Minister for Foreign Affairs. Costello was also deputy managing director of the Australian Stock Exchange.

Annabel Crabb is a political columnist and sketchwriter for *The Sydney Morning Herald*. She is a former political correspondent for *The Age* and *The Advertiser*, and spent several years in London as correspondent for *The Sunday Age* and the *Sun Herald*. She is the author of *Losing It: The Inside Story of Labor in Opposition*, and is soon to publish a *Quarterly Essay* on Liberal leader Malcolm Turnbull. She is a regular panellist on ABC TV's *Insiders*, and a radio commentator on Sydney's 2UE and ABC 702, as well as ABC 891 Adelaide. Annabel lives in Sydney.

Michael Duffy is a journalist with *The Sydney Morning Herald*, and co-presents *Counterpoint* on Radio National. He has written biographies of John Macarthur, Tony Abbott and Mark Latham.

Tom Dusevic is Associate Editor and National Affairs Correspondent of the *The Australian Financial Review*. Based in Sydney, he writes about people, politics, economics and social issues. Dusevic has also worked as an editor and reporter at *The Australian*, *Good Weekend* and *Time*. He has won a Walkley Award for Commentary and the Citi Journalism Award for Business Writing.

Tim Flannery is an internationally acclaimed scientist, explorer and conservationist. His books include the landmark works *The Future Eaters* and *The Weather Makers*, which has been translated into twenty-five languages. In 2007 he was honoured as Australian of the Year. He is a founding member of the Wentworth Group of Concerned Scientists, a director of the Australian Wildlife Conservancy, and the National Geographic Society's representative in Australasia. In 2007 he co-founded and was appointed Chair of the Copenhagen Climate Council, a coalition of community, business and political leaders who have come together to confront climate change.

Raimond Gaita is Foundation Professor of Philosophy at Australian Catholic University, Professor of Moral Philosophy at King's College, University of London, and a fellow of the Australian Academy of the Humanities. His books include *Good and Evil: An Absolute Conception*, *Romulus, My Father* (made into an award-winning film of the same name), *A Common Humanity: Thinking About Love and Truth and Justice*, *The Philosopher's Dog*, *Why The War was Wrong* (as editor and contributor) and *Breach of Trust: Truth, Morality and Politics* (*Quarterly Essay 16*).

Geoff Gallop studied at the University of Western Australia and at Oxford and Murdoch universities after attending school in Geraldton. From 1986 to 2006 he was a member of the Western Australian Legislative Assembly. Gallop was a minister in the Lawrence Labor Government from 1990 to 1993, the leader of the Opposition from 1996 to 2001 and the premier of Western Australia from 2001 to 2006. After retiring from politics he was appointed Professor and Director of the Graduate School of Government, the University of Sydney, a position he still holds. In 2008 he was made a Companion of the Order of Australia.

Brendan Gleeson is Director of the Urban Research Program at Griffith University and a leading commentator on urban Australia. He is co-author (with Nicholas Low) of *Justice, Society and Nature: An Exploration of Political Ecology*. In 2006 Gleeson's *Australian Heartlands: Making Space for Hope in the Suburbs* won the inaugural John Iremonger Award for Writing on Public Issues. Most recently he has been appointed as a member of the Urban Land Development Authority and as a fellow of the Academy of Social Sciences. Brendan currently lives in the Brisbane suburbs with his partner and their two children.

Michelle Grattan is currently Political Editor of *The Age*. She has covered federal politics since the 1970s. She edited *Australian Prime Ministers* and wrote *Back on the Wool Track*.

Nicholas Gruen is trained in history, statistics, education, law and economics. He has worked as a teacher at universities and schools, a cartoonist, a consultant, a policy adviser to two federal ministers and an associate commissioner with the Productivity Commission. Since 2000 he has been CEO of Lateral Economics, an economic consultancy, and Peaches, a finance company. He has also been appointed by federal and state governments to several boards and inquiries. He is Chairman of *On Line Opinion*, is a substantial contributor to Australia's thriving blog scene on Club Troppo and has a regular column in *The Australian Financial Review*.

Clive Hamilton is the author of several books including most recently *The Freedom Paradox*. He is Professor of Public Ethics at the Centre for Applied Philosophy and Public Ethics, Charles Sturt University. He is based in Canberra.

Peter Hartcher is the Political Editor and International Editor of *The Sydney Morning Herald* and a visiting fellow at the Lowy Institute for International Policy. His last book was a critical assessment of the US economy. *Bubble Man: Alan Greenspan and the Missing Seven Trillion Dollars* was published in 2005 and predicted the collapse of the US housing market and a recession. His 2009 book is *To The Bitter End: The Dramatic Story Behind the Fall of John Howard and the Rise of Kevin Rudd*. Before taking his current position at the *SMH* in 2003, Hartcher wrote for *The Australian Financial Review* for a decade, as its Washington correspondent, Asia-Pacific editor and Tokyo correspondent. He is a Gold Walkley Award winner.

Gerard Henderson is Executive Director of The Sydney Institute. He writes each Tuesday for *The Sydney Morning Herald* and *The West Australian*, comments regularly on radio and appears on ABC TV's *Insiders* and Sky News' *Agenda*. He is also a published author. He was appointed by the Keating Government to the board of the Australia Foundation for Culture and the Humanities and by the Howard Government to the Foreign Affairs Council. He was invited to participate in the 2020 summit held in April 2008.

Jennifer Hewett is the National Affairs Correspondent for *The Australian*, joining the paper in April 2007. She has written about federal politics for more than twenty years. She previously worked for *The Australian Financial Review* and *The Sydney*

Morning Herald in Canberra, Sydney, New York and Washington. She specialises in politics, economics and business writing.

John Hewson has had virtually four careers: as an academic and economist; businessman; political advisor and politician; and media commentator and columnist. He has worked for the Treasury, the Reserve Bank of Australia and the International Monetary Fund. In business he is best known as a founder of Macquarie Bank, Chairman of ABN AMRO Australia and as Chairman/Director of a host of public and private companies and charities. He worked as an adviser in the Fraser Government, and was the federal Opposition leader. He has also written regularly for *BRW* and *The Australian Financial Review*, and comments regularly on radio and television.

Christine Jackman began her career as a journalist with the *Courier-Mail* in Brisbane in 1993, where she first began writing about politics, including the rise of Pauline Hanson and One Nation. She has worked as a foreign correspondent in New York, where she covered Bill Clinton's impeachment and the 2000 presidential election, in the Canberra press gallery and as *The Australian*'s social issues writer. She is now a senior writer for *The Weekend Australian Magazine*. Her first book, *Inside Kevin07*, was published in 2008.

Bernard Keane studied history at the University of Sydney and in 1993 moved to Canberra to join the Australian Public Service. Since then, he has been a public servant, speechwriter and blogger. In February 2008 he joined *Crikey* as its Canberra correspondent and works in the parliamentary press gallery.

Paul Kelly is Editor-at-Large of *The Australian* and a commentator on ABC TV's *Insiders*. He was previously Editor-in-Chief of *The Australian*. He has covered Australian governments from Gough Whitlam to Kevin Rudd and has written six books on politics and history including *The End of Certainty* and *The Hawke Ascendancy*. He holds a Doctor of Letters from the University of Melbourne and was a 2002 fellow at the Kennedy School of Government at Harvard University. He is a Walkley Award winner and was Graham Perkin Journalist of the Year in 1990.

Marcia Langton is Professor of Australian Indigenous Studies in the School of Population Health at the University of Melbourne. She is co-editor of two published collections on agreements with Indigenous people: *Honour Among Nations* and *Settling with Indigenous People*. Her doctorate is a study of the Aboriginal land tenure system of eastern Cape York Peninsula. She is co-editor of *First Australians: An Illustrated History*, the companion book to the epic SBS TV series.

Mark Latham was a member of Parliament from 1994 to 2005 and the federal Opposition leader from December 2003 to January 2005. His candid and compelling account of his parliamentary career, *The Latham Diaries*, was published in 2005. Latham's previous books are *Reviving Labor's Agenda: A Program for Local Reform*; *Civilising Global Capital: New Thinking for Australian Labor*; *What Did You Learn Today?: Creating An Education Revolution*; *The Enabling State:*

Putting People Before Democracy; and *From the Suburbs: Building a Nation from our Neighbourhoods.*

Mungo MacCallum has been a political commentator for more than forty years. He worked in the Canberra press gallery from 1969 to 1988 and before, during and since has contributed to every major Australian outlet in press, radio and television. He has published eight books, the most recent being *Poll Dancing: The Story of the 2007 Election.*

Robert Manne is Professor of Politics at La Trobe University and Chair of the Editorial Board of *The Monthly*. He is the author of *The Petrov Affair*, *In Denial: The Stolen Generations and the Right* and *Left, Right, Left*. Most recently, he has edited *Dear Mr Rudd: Ideas for a Better Australia* and WEH Stanner's *The Dreaming and Other Essays.*

Chris Masters worked at ABC TV's *Four Corners* between 1983 and 2008. He is the program's longest-serving reporter. Among his reports are 'French Connections', which won a Gold Walkley Award, 'The Big League' and 'The Moonlight State', which triggered royal commissions in NSW and Queensland. Masters has written three books, *Inside Story*, *Not for Publication* and *Jonestown*. The latter won three awards, one of them a further Walkley, his fifth. He received a Public Service Medal in 1999 and was awarded an Honorary Doctorate in Communication from RMIT University in 2005.

George Megalogenis is a senior writer for *The Australian* newspaper based in Melbourne. He spent eleven years in the Canberra press gallery between 1988 and 1999, is the author of *Faultlines* and *The Longest Decade* and a regular panellist on ABC TV's *Insiders* and Triple R FM's *Breakfasters.*

Noel Pearson was born in 1965 and raised in Hope Vale, a mission station where survivors of the European invasion rebuilt a vibrant Aboriginal community. In Hope Vale he learnt Guugu Yimithirr and Kuku Yalanji. After completing a history and law degree, Pearson worked for recognition of native title: in the 1990s he became a national figure during the drafting of the Native Title Act and in connection with the Wik native title case. Since 1999, Pearson has been developing policies to combat passive welfare and substance abuse in Indigenous communities, and formulated a critique of the High Court's native title judgements after Mabo and Wik. He is currently director of the Cape York Institute.

Alan Ramsey worked in the Canberra press gallery for forty-three years for various publications including *The Australian*, *The National Times* and *Time*. For the last twenty-two years until he retired in December 2008 he was national political columnist for **The Sydney Morning Herald**. He was a pallbearer at John Button's funeral.

Nicolas Rothwell is *The Australian* newspaper's chief northern correspondent, and has written extensively on the issues canvassed in the article in this volume. His recent essays are collected in *Another Country*. A further volume of northern essays will be published next year.

Kevin Rudd was sworn in as the twenty-sixth Prime Minister of Australia on 3 December 2007. Prior to entering Parliament in 1998, Rudd worked as a diplomat, as a senior official in the Queensland government, and as a consultant helping Australian firms to establish and build their business links in China and in Taiwan. Rudd has written extensively on Chinese politics, Chinese foreign policy, Australia–Asia relations and globalisation.

Guy Rundle is currently the foreign correspondent for *Crikey* online daily. He was co-editor of *Arena Magazine* between 1992 and 2006, is a frequent contributor to a wide range of Australian publications, and the writer of a number of hit stage shows with the satirist Max Gillies.

Imre Salusinszky is NSW Political Reporter and a columnist with *The Australian*. He began his journalistic career with *The Age* in the late 1970s, reporting from the Old Parliament House in Canberra, but subsequently took a 25-year detour into university teaching and research in English literature. In 2006 he was appointed Chair of the Literature Board of the Australia Council for the Arts.

Dennis Shanahan is the Political Editor of *The Australian* based in the Canberra press gallery. He has worked for metropolitan daily newspapers for thirty-seven years, starting as a copy boy at *The Daily Mirror* in Sydney. He did his cadetship on *The Sydney Morning Herald* and later studied at the University of NSW before gaining a master's degree in journalism at Columbia University, New York. He has been *The Australian's* Political Editor and Canberra Bureau Chief for the past twenty years covering the Hawke, Keating, Howard and Rudd governments. He is married to Angela and has nine children.

Paul Sheehan is a columnist and editorial writer for *The Sydney Morning Herald*. His work has been collected previously in *The Best American Essays*, *The Best Australian Essays* and *The Best Australian Political Writing*. He is the author of three books, all bestsellers: *Girls Like You*, *Among the Barbarians* and *The Electronic Whorehouse*.

Craig Sherborne is the author of *Hoi Polloi* (2005), short listed for the Victorian and Queensland premiers prizes, and its acclaimed sequel *Muck* (2007), winner of the 2008 Queensland Premier's Prize for non-fiction. He has published three books of poetry, including *Necessary Evil* in 2006. His journalism and essays have appeared in most of Australia's leading intellectual publications. He is a regular contributor to *The Monthly*.

Margaret Simons is an award-winning freelance journalist and the author of seven books and numerous essays and articles. She is also a part-time lecturer at Swinburne University of Technology. She blogs on journalism and the media at *The Content Makers*. Her most recent work includes *The Content Makers: Understanding the Future of the Australian Media* and *Faith, Money and Power: What the Religious Revival Means for Politics*.

Lenore Taylor started reporting federal politics in the Old Parliament House in 1988 as a young reporter for *The Canberra Times*. Apart from a three-year stint as the

London-based European correspondent for *The Australian Financial Review*, she has observed the goings-on in Canberra with enduring fascination ever since, for both the *AFR* and *The Australian*, where she is currently National Correspondent. She writes news, analysis and a column in *The Weekend Australian*. She is a regular political commentator on radio and television, including on ABC TV's *Insiders*. In 2007 she won the prestigious Paul Lyneham Award for Press Gallery Journalism.

Laura Tingle has reported politics from the Canberra press gallery for twenty years for *The Australian*, *The Age*, *The Sydney Morning Herald* and *The Australian Financial Review*. Before this, she covered financial markets for the *AFR* and economics for *The Australian*. Her 1994 book *Chasing the Future* documented how the recession of the early 1990s changed Australia's political and economic debate. She is currently Political Editor of *The Australian Financial Review*, and has won both a Walkley Award for Journalism and the Paul Lyneham Award for Excellence in Press Gallery Journalism.

Brian Toohey is a Sydney-based journalist who is a regular contributor to *The Australian Financial Review*. He also writes for other outlets and appears as a commentator on radio and television covering economic, defence and general political issues. Toohey has been *The Australian Financial Review*'s chief political correspondent and later Washington correspondent. He also edited the former *National Times*. Apart from journalism, Toohey is the author or co-author of four books. These include *Tumbling Dice: The Making of Modern Economic Policy* and *Oyster: The Story of the Australian Secret Intelligence Service*.

Paul Toohey is *The Australian*'s Darwin correspondent. He is a two-time Walkley Award-winning journalist. His publications include *God's Little Acre*, *Rocky Goes West* and *Last Drinks: The Impact of the Northern Territory Intervention* (*Quarterly Essay 30*).

Don Watson's *Recollections of a Bleeding Heart: A Portrait of Paul Keating PM* won *The Age* Book of the Year and Non-Fiction Prizes, the *Courier-Mail* Book of the Year and the National Biography Award. His *Quarterly Essay*, *Rabbit Syndrome: Australia and America*, won the Alfred Deakin Essay Prize. *Death Sentence*, Watson's bestselling book about the decay of public language, won the Australian Booksellers Association Book of the Year. *American Journeys* is his most recent book, and has won *The Age* Non-Fiction and Book of the Year Awards 2008. It also won the inaugural Indie Award for Non-Fiction and the Walkley Award for Non-Fiction.